VASILI KLYUCHEVSKY

★

THE RISE
OF THE ROMANOVS

translated and edited by

LILIANA ARCHIBALD

assisted by Mark Scholl

BARNES
&NOBLE
BOOKS
NEW YORK

This edition published by Barnes & Noble, Inc.,
by arrangement with St. Martin's Press.

1993 Barnes & Noble Books

ISBN 1-56619-325-7

Printed and bound in the United States of America

M 9 8 7 6 5 4 3 2 1

CONTENTS

FOREWORD

VASILI KLYUCHEVSKY delivered his lectures, which were subsequently published, at the University of Moscow. The third volume of his *History of Russia* was first published in 1908. The edition of 1937, itself a reprint of the first edition, was the one used for the present translation. This third volume, which I have entitled *The Rise of the Romanovs*, is concerned with seventeenth-century Russia, and deals with the social, political, economic and religious changes which took place during the Time of Troubles and the reigns of the first Romanovs.

Klyuchevsky believed that it was peasant indebtedness that was primarily responsible for the establishment of serfdom. His systematic analysis, therefore, of the agrarian system in general, and the condition of the peasant in particular is vital to any clear understanding of seventeenth-century Russian history.

Anatole Mazour asserts that Klyuchevsky's approach to any past event was 'never that of the cold logician-scientist with lancet poised to probe, but rather that of the keen, sympathetically intuitive psychologist; yet never did his rich and fertile imagination betray the scientific accuracy of his observations or his judgement. Therefore his generalisations are usually sound, his characters emerge from the distant past clothed in flesh and blood, and the whole process of historical development becomes a vivid, integrated panorama. His striking accomplishment is in harmonisation within himself of the qualities of an erudite historian, a sociologist, an artist and a teacher.'[1]

[1] Anatole G. Mazour, *Modern Russian Historiography* (D. Van Nostrand Inc., 1958) p. 117.

This translation has been undertaken with the hope that Klyuchevsky's accomplishments may be shared by those who have no knowledge of Russian. It is for this reason that references have been made only to publications in western European languages.

Hopefully too, students of Russian history, who know Russian, may be persuaded that certain aspects of the seventeenth century deserve closer study. Disproportionate attention has been given to recent periods in Russian history, with the result that in text-books, for instance, the seventeenth century has been dealt with only cursorily. Our understanding of Russian law, its administration and its procedures is abysmal. Even the *Ulozhenie* of 1649, which remained the basic legal code of Russia until 1833, has not received the attention it deserves. More remarkable, however, is the absence, outside some periodical literature, of any modern treatment of Russian institutions such as the Boyar Duma or the Zemsky Sobor. If, therefore, this translation stimulates curiosity, and persuades some scholars that a venture into the pre-Petrine era would be useful, it will have achieved its primary objective.

There are the usual difficulties in translating from Russian into English: Russian words often look clumsy in English print. I have adopted a system of transliteration which, I hope, will not offend the English reader, and have, as far as possible, avoided phonetic signs. Certain words defy translation: nothing can be done with *obrok*, *gubnoe starosta*, *kanstler*, etc., and in these cases the nearest English equivalent has been put into brackets after it, or, where no reasonable equivalent can be found, the Russian word has been left in the text, and an explanation has been given in a footnote or in the Glossary.

Finally, I should like to thank my friends for their comments, assistance and encouragement.

LILIANA ARCHIBALD

Yugorsky Shai
Pechora
Eniseisk
R U S S I A
1598
Tobolsk
Stockholm
Pskov
Moscow
Kazan
Smolensk
Kiev
Astrakhan
Bosphorus
Constantinople

S W E D E N
Stockholm
Gulf of Finland
BALTIC SEA
LIVONIA
Riga
Pskov
LITHUANIA
W. Drina
Kovno
Braslov
Polotsk
Vilna
Poznan
Podliashie
Grodno
Vistula
WHITE
Wittenberg
Bug
Warsaw
P O L A N D
Lublin
Cracow
VOLYNI
Berestechko
GALICIA
Lvov
Zborov
Chudno
Danube
Kozlov
PODOLIA
MOLDAVIA
Dniester
Zagreb
WALLACHIA
Danube

TO SWEDEN 1617
PEACE OF STOLBOVO
Pskov
Moscow
Smolensk
TO POLAND
1618
TREATY OF
DULINO
Kiev
Azov

Chapter One

★

THE ONLY remaining period in Russian history fully accessible
to historical research opens at the beginning of the seventeenth
century and closes with the accession of Alexander II in 1855.
The election to the throne in 1613 of the new dynasty's first Tsar
serves as a convenient point of departure. The turbulent era of the
Pretenders was the link interposed between the old dynasty,[1]
which became extinct in 1598, and the new, Romanov dynasty[2]
which was profoundly affected by this era.

The two hundred and forty-two years from 1613 to 1855 have
an interest independent of the long time span. It is possible
throughout these years to observe the persistent recurrence of
important influences, mostly destructive, which were never
eradicated, and which remained part of the fundamental fabric
of life in Russia until the end of the nineteenth century. Moreover,
these two hundred and forty-two years represent more than just
another period in Russian history: *they span the whole of modern
Russian history*. The ideas and attitudes which were evolved
throughout these years were familiar to, and influenced the social
awareness of, nineteenth-century Russians. A study of these two
and a half centuries confirmed the nineteenth-century Russian
in his belief that, in so far as they were characteristics derived from

[1] Klyuchevsky refers to the dynasty founded by Rurik as 'the old dynasty'
throughout this book.

[2] The origin of the Romanovs is unclear; complications occur because
during the early Muscovite period changing names was common practice.
The earliest reference to what was to become the Romanov dynasty can be
found in a Chronicle dated 1346. See Anatole G. Mazour, *Rise and Fall of the
Romanovs* (Anvil, 1960) pp. 1–2.

the past, he was scrutinising his own personality and values. His curiosity was stimulated, and there was a danger that he would be carried away by his own enthusiasm; and that over-identification with his own native historical and social development might result in a lack of objectivity.

What were the salient features of the sixteenth century? Until the end of the sixteenth century there had been a correlation between the political situation of the country and the geographical distribution of its population. Muscovy was the creation of those Russians concentrated in the very middle of the eastern European plain, at the confluence of its water systems on the upper Volga. These people were known as Great Russians, whose political unification took place under Ivan Kalita.[1] The Grand Duke of Muscovy ruled over a united Great Russia with the help of Muscovite boyars who emerged from the old Muscovite nobility, the previously independent Princes and their boyars. The state became increasingly dependent on the *tiaglo*:[2] a system of taxation which allocated special compulsory obligations due to the state among different classes of society.[3] However, as a result of this system of taxation, the peasants, hitherto the backbone of the country's economy, and still legally free, had already entered into debtor–creditor relationships with the landowners who were threatening them with legalised bondage.

During the second decade of the seventeenth century new factors emerged which had not been present during the first decade: a new dynasty ascended the throne of Muscovy, and it was seeking to expand its territorial influence. Hitherto Muscovy

[1] Ivan I (1331–40). He was known as Kalita, or Money Bag, and was the first ruler of Muscovy to call himself 'Grand Duke (or Grand Prince) of Moscow and all Russia'. For a history of the rise to supremacy of the Prince and Princi-pality of Moscow see John Fennell, *The Emergence of Moscow 1304–1359* (Secker & Warburg, 1968) and in particular pp. 111–96.

[2] For a discussion of the changing significance through time of this ex-pression see Michael Confino, *Domaines et Seigneurs en Russie* (Institut d'Études Slaves de l'Université de Paris, Paris, 1963) pp. 107–13.

[3] This particular definition of *tiaglo* remained valid until the seventeenth century. The word came into use during the era of the Mongol hegemony. See Jerome Blum, *Lord and Peasant in Russia* (Princeton U.P., 1961) pp. 104–5.

had consisted of territories settled by the Great Russians. During the second decade Muscovy expanded far beyond its original borders, gradually embracing the whole Russian plain to include Little Russia,[1] White Russia[2] and finally New Russia,[3] a new Russian territory which had been opened up by the colonisation of the southern Steppes. Whereas previously Muscovy had stretched from the White and the Baltic Seas to the Black and the Caspian Seas, to the Urals and along the Caucasian mountain ranges, now it extended far beyond the Caucasian mountains to the south, and the Urals and the Caspian Sea to the east.[4]

Simultaneously, important changes were taking place in the structure of society. Contemporaneous with the new dynasty there arose a new ruling class. The ancient boyar families were dying out: they were few and in economic decline. This, in and of itself, removed all existing political restraints on the power of the sovereign. In their place arose a new upper class, the *dvoryanstvo*,[5] who emerged from the metropolitan and provincial

[1] By Little Russia was meant the Left-Bank Ukraine.

[2] White Russia or Belorussia was also known as West Russia. See N. P. Vakar, 'The name "White Russia" ', *American Slavic and East European Review*, VIII (Oct 1949) 201–13.

[3] By New Russia was meant the open Black Sea steppes. See B. H. Sumner, *Survey of Russian History* (Duckworth, 1944) pp. 45–6. By the middle of the fifteenth century the differentiation of the three present-day East Slavic languages – Russian (Great Russian), Ukrainian (Little Russian), and White Russian – took place. See George Vernadsky, *Russia at the Dawn of the Modern Age* (Yale U.P., 1959) p. 2.

[4] Ivan IV (1533–85) inherited a realm of about 900,000 square miles. By the time Michael Romanov mounted the throne in 1613 it had grown to approximately 3·3 million square miles, and when Peter the Great began his reign in 1682 the State covered 5·6 million square miles. See Blum, *Lord and Peasant in Russia*, p. 120.

[5] The Code of Laws of the Russian Empire, vol. IX, part I, paragraph 15 defined the nobility as follows:

The appellation of nobility is the result of the qualities and virtues of men who having been foremost in the past, distinguished themselves by their services and turning their very services into merit, acquired for their descendants the distinction of noble birth; are treated as noble all those who either descend from noble ancestors or having received the title from the Monarch in recognition of their deserts.

service classes: a heterogeneous mass amongst whom were also to be found some boyars. Previously the political structure of the state had been based upon an allocation of responsibilities between different classes; now the classes themselves were being compartmentalised.

In time, and especially under Peter the Great, the number and complexity of state obligations increased and affected all social classes. The exactions levied and strains imposed at all economic levels effectively eliminated the freedom of the peasants.[1] Free landowning peasants became enserfed and were subjected to yet greater burdens; while the condition of serfdom itself created obligations unique to it.

The labouring classes lost their political rights, but they no longer, as previously, worked only in agriculture. True, the economy was still primarily agricultural, but mining, manufacturing and handicrafts were becoming increasingly more important;[2] .moreover, an attempt was being made to exploit the country's hitherto untouched natural resources.

The following are the most important features which appear in the period under review: a new dynasty, new and enlarged territorial boundaries, a new class structure with a new ruling class at its head, and new economic developments. The connection between these features may not be apparent immediately, yet two parallel trends can be discerned. First, up to the middle of the nineteenth century territorial expansion grew in inverse proportion to the degree of freedom enjoyed by the people; and second, as the labouring classes became more efficient, so their political rights were eroded. In other words, the more efficient

[1] The process by which peasants came to be legally enserfed by the middle of the seventeenth century has been clearly described in R. E. F. Smith, *The Enserfment of Russian Peasantry* (Cambridge U.P., 1968) pp. 1–27.

[2] It is important to put this statement into its proper perspective. From 1576 to 1673 for instance, only four paper mills were built, and that while in the sixteenth century the extraction of metals was fairly common, the first high furnace was built in Tula only in 1628. Russia's first wool cloth factory was established in Moscow as late as 1684. See Bertrand Gille, *Histoire économique et sociale de la Russie du moyen âge au XXᵉ siècle* (Paris, 1949) pp. 63–9; and Roger Portal, *L'Oural au XVIIIᵉ siècle* (Paris, 1950) pp. 9–22.

labour became the less freedom did it enjoy. This relationship between the national economy and the social structure is at variance with the commonly held view that slave labour is inefficient in comparison with free labour, and that a vigorous labouring class is unlikely to develop if the legal system is weighted against it. This economic inconsistency exacerbated political relations. A comparison between the outlook of nations and the lives of individuals presupposes that national power is a function of vigorous internal activity by peoples and individuals, which only emerges when there exists a sense of political freedom.

The influence exerted by Russian territorial expansion upon the relationship between state and society shows that this assumption is incorrect. In fact the obverse was true: territorial expansion and greater power resulted in a persistent contraction of individual liberties. The policies pursued by the state imposed such strains on society that it was unable to respond; the acquisition of new territories through wars increased the powers of the state, but had an inhibiting effect on the activities of the people. The external successes of this new Russia are reminiscent of a bird, whose wings are useless as it is buffeted about and carried along by a whirlwind.

To the two contradictions discussed above a third must be added. Mention has been made of the absorption of the Muscovite boyars by the nobility (*dvoryanstvo*). The abolition of *mestnichestvo*[1] in 1682 speeded this process and created a single class who were liable for state service. The old aristocracy of boyars had previously been the ruling class; the abolition of a system of precedence was a tentative step towards democratic government, and it was followed by others. Under Peter the Great the old aristocracy of boyars was engulfed by men from all levels of society. Furthermore this included foreigners, 'white' untaxed, and 'black' taxed people, as well as serfs who had earned promotion through long service.

---

[1] *Mestnichestvo* was a peculiar system of precedence which existed in Muscovy towards the end of the fifteenth century. It developed because the Moscow boyars were trying to protect their status against the influx of formerly appanaged Princes and their retainers. See Marc Raeff, *Origins of the Russian Intelligentsia* (Harcourt, Brace & World Inc., New York, 1966) pp. 19–21; and Blum, *Lord and Peasant in Russia*, pp. 137–8.

The Table of Ranks of 1722 opened the doors of government service to all levels of society which led into the 'better, older nobility'. It was not unreasonable, therefore, to suppose that this social shuffling in the ruling class would lead to a democratic levelling of society as a whole. However, although the ruling class owed less to heredity, its political powers were increasing. The ennobled men of service received individual and social privileges which the old aristocracy of boyars had not enjoyed. Estates hitherto held in service tenure[1] became personal property of the nobles and the peasants became their serfs. Under Peter III the nobility was freed from the obligation of compulsory service;[2] under Catherine II the nobility acquired a new corporate organisation with powers of self-government, the right to play a part in local administration and justice, and 'to petition and complain' to the Crown.[3] Under Nicholas I this privilege was extended to allow the assemblies of the nobility the right to petition the Crown concerning the needs of all the other social classes in their districts.[4]

The increase in these privileges led to an extension in the political power of the nobility. Already in the seventeenth

[1] By an estate held in service tenure I mean a *pomestie* estate; by an heritable estate I mean a *votchina* estate. Lands held on conditional service tenure began to be granted on an extensive scale by Ivan III, and under Ivan IV this form of tenure was even further extended. See James Mavor, *An Economic History of Russia*, 2nd ed. (Dent, 1925) I 34–41 and 107–8; Michael Florinsky, *Russia* (Macmillan, New York, 1953) I 102 and 176–7; Raeff, *Origins of the Russian Intelligentsia*, pp. 15–16; and Blum, *Lord and Peasant in Russia*, pp. 170–1 and 174–81.

[2] Peter III announced to the Senate on 17 January 1762 his intention to free the nobility from this obligation of compulsory service; on 18 February 1762 he issued a manifesto which put the service of the nobility on a voluntary basis, and gave them the right, except in time of war, to resign from the army and civil administration. See Florinsky, *Russia*, I 497–8; and Paul Dukes, *Catherine the Great and the Russian Nobility* (Cambridge U.P., 1967) pp. 38–46.

[3] A brief exposition of administrative reforms under Catherine can be found in Florinsky, *Russia*, I, 569–75; for a detailed discussion see Dukes, *Catherine the Great and the Russian Nobility*; also Raeff, *Origins of the Russian Intelligentsia*, pp. 111–21.

[4] For details of the Statute of 6 December 1831 which deals with this and other privileges see Florinsky, *Russia*, II 774–5.

century the government had begun to govern society through the nobility, while in the eighteenth century the nobility tried to rule society through the government.[1] Although the nobility appealed to political principles in its attempt to govern, it failed; and in the nineteenth century the nobility became synonymous with officialdom which served as a prolific nursery. Indeed, towards the middle of the nineteenth century Russia was governed neither by an aristocracy nor by a democracy, but by a bureaucracy. This bureaucracy was an appendage to society, devoid of social meaning, a faceless mass of people united only by their common interest in status seeking.

In this way, tentative moves towards a more democratic system of government produced greater social inequality and fragmentation. Furthermore, this social inequality resulted in the alienation of the ruling classes from the rest of society. It is said that education draws people together, and acts as a social leveller. In Russia, however, this did not happen. Increasing contacts with western Europe brought new ideas, customs, knowledge and culture into Russia; but these influenced only the upper classes, and adversely affected the masses who suffered from cautious, partial and ineffectual reforms. Education became the monopoly of the ruling classes: the ignorant, ordinary person could not benefit from an education for fear that he might endanger the state. Towards the end of the seventeenth century those responsible for establishing an academy in Moscow, which was the first institute of higher learning in Russia, found it possible without exception to admit 'people of all ranks, background and dignity'. One hundred and fifty years later, in the reign of Nicholas I, a secret commission was set up under the chairmanship of Count Kochubey[2] to consider necessary reforms.

[1] In 1730, on the death of Peter III, the Supreme Privy Council proposed that Anne should be obliged upon her accession to agree to a series of constitutional 'Articles' based upon those forced upon the Swedish monarchy in 1720. See *The European Nobility in the Eighteenth Century*, ed. A. Goodwin (Black, 1953) pp. 178–80.

[2] Count Victor Kochubey (1768–1834) was titular head of the department of foreign affairs during the early years of the reign of Alexander I. He was also

Following the suicide of a household serf who had studied painting, the commission categorically stated that only harm would come from allowing serfs to be admitted to 'institutions where they become accustomed to a certain way of life, a way of thinking, and ideas which are above their station'.[1]

The contradictions inherent in the three processes mentioned above, were similarly present in every important event from 1613 to 1855. It would be wrong to think of these contradictions as anomalies, as something outside the rules of historical behaviour. It is more useful to think of them as historical antinomies, exceptions to the normal laws of historical behaviour, the consequences of unique, indigenous circumstances. Nevertheless, after a period of adjustment there was a reversion to a more normal historical pattern. The analogy here is with a human being suffering from a nervous complaint, who functions organically in a normal way, and only manifests those abnormal characteristics appropriate to his condition.

These antinomies can be explained by an investigation into the relationship between the requirements of state and the people's ability to satisfy them. When a European country faced new and difficult problems it relied on its own people for solutions, a reliance which was generally justified. The reason for this was the normal regular life of the people, who were free to work and think as they wished, and who were consequently able to come to their country's assistance without undue strain. These circumstances had been deliberately created by a state which could provide for an increase in taxation, and rely upon the skills of

---

one of Alexander's liberal friends and served on the 'non-official committee' which was charged with producing a constitution for Russia. However the committee failed to produce a constitutional charter. A brief outline of the proceedings and recommendations of the committee of 6 December 1826 under the chairmanship of Count Victor Kochubey can be found in Florinsky, *Russia*, II 765–7.

[1] For a similar attitude consider Count Lambert, a leader of the right-wing group in the Committee of Education of 1826. 'Children of different social origins', said Lambert, 'should not be educated together.' See N. Hans, *The Russian Tradition in Education* (Routledge & Kegan Paul, 1963) pp. 25–8.

able, conscientious and well trained servants. The important point to notice is that in such countries educational activities depended on imperceptible and subtle, albeit harmonious, efforts of individuals and independent, unofficial groups, who were often able to anticipate the needs of the state.

In Russia, however, the opposite happened. When Tsar Michael ascended the throne of a shattered country, he turned to the country for help through the medium of the *Zemsky Sobor*. He found that its representatives were devoted and obedient subjects, but they were neither capable collaborators nor able to pay substantial taxes. As a result, the government was forced to consider other solutions. The merchants of Moscow suggested that use might be made of foreigners who could show poor Russians how to develop crafts and trades which would enable them to earn a living. This solution was adopted time and again, as a result of which the state became enmeshed in a network of difficulties, which had not been foreseen. The government tried to find assistance from its own people, but was unsuccessful, and had therefore, somewhat reluctantly, to turn to Western Europe where it observed an ancient, complex society which had available the necessary skills and ideas. Craftsmen and teachers were hurriedly brought to Russia to introduce their skills; factories were built in haste, and pupils were driven to the newly established schools. But the state was impatient and could not wait for these compulsory students to learn their letters: fresh sacrifices were demanded that sapped the nation's vitality, and further restricted the liberty of the people. The demands of state, instead of strengthening society, exhausted it. Enlightenment for revenue-earning purposes produced no lasting benefit, and feverish educational attempts caused both boredom and an aversion to learning that was equalled only by the rising generation's detestation of compulsory military service. State education began to look like a government edict, in the sense that the state found a steady stream of young men to be educated according to a specific curriculum. An expensive Corps of Cadets was created for the nobility; engineering schools, educational establishments, grammar schools, an Academy of Arts were all founded for the children of the nobility and wealthy merchants. In such noble hothouses tropical plants were grown, but for two centuries not one agricultural school was founded nor were there any educational establishments for the people. For four or five generations the new, Europeanised Russia, was a country of guards' barracks, government offices and noblemen's estates. The noblemen filled the barracks and supplied the offices with lightly distilled products from inbred institutions and exotic boarding schools full of ignoramuses; in exchange the country got retired brigadiers in uniform. This process of extracting state servants from society led to a purely utilitarian approach to learning. From the upper classes, and increasingly from the nobility, was created a new caste of state officials, divorced from the rest of society by rank, privilege, prejudice, and even more by its abuse of power.

Territorial expansion exhausted the country; it increased the power of the state but did not raise the standard of living. New, democratic elements were taken into the structure of government, but this merely intensified social inequality. The development of new industries enriched the Treasury and individual entrepreneurs, but not the labouring classes, who became politically emasculated. All these mistakes had a common source: the unnatural relationship between the country's internal development and its foreign policy. The national capacity to solve the problems which accompanied Russia's accelerated territorial expansion was further diminished; and mentally the people could not keep up with the government's economic activities. The state thrived, but the people decayed.

The influence exerted by external affairs on internal developments was nowhere so powerful as in Russia, and no other period demonstrates this so clearly as the one to be surveyed.

It is necessary, first of all, to review the important problems inherent in the foreign policy of Muscovy in the fifteenth and sixteenth centuries, their origin, and their connection with an even earlier period. At that time, pressure from external enemies somehow forced a kind of unity on multi-racial and scattered populations, from whom emerged the Russian people. In the next period, Tatar and Lithuanian invasions divided the country into Great Russia and Little Russia, and subsequently each had a different history. In the forest region of the upper Volga the Great Russians preserved, and even increased, their strength while patiently struggling against an austere nature and foreign enemies. These circumstances led to the creation of a relatively stable, military state.

There followed the unification of Great Russia, and the state's determination to re-establish the political and national unity of all Russian lands.

The main preoccupation of the old Muscovite ruling dynasty was how to achieve unification. The efforts and progress made, as well as the adoption of a rigorous and oppressive political system which resulted from this ambition, have already been mentioned. Following upon the territorial losses incurred during the Time of Troubles, the continuous external conflicts in the seventeenth century became extremely burdensome; and society suffered accordingly. Those who had retained their freedom of labour and movement, who had worked smallholdings, were now, due to the cost of the wars with Poland and Sweden, and in the interests of Treasury and state service, combined into large groupings, while a substantial part of the rural population fell into bondage.

Under Peter the Great the state exerted even stronger pressure on all classes, who were more heavily burdened even than in the seventeenth century with specific state obligations. The *kholopstvo* as an independent class of bondsmen and the 'free peoples', both hitherto untrammelled by state obligations, were now subjected to taxation and military service. Thus, a vague concept of a *general obligation*, crept into legislation, and while it was not all-embracing, it certainly affected most classes; moreover, it promised in time radically to alter the social structure. Concurrent with these developments there occurred a change in foreign policy. Hitherto, Russian wars in the West had been defensive in character, where the main objective had been to regain territories recently lost, or those considered traditionally belonging to Russia. But after Poltava[1] wars were waged for reasons of offence, aimed at

[1] i.e. after 1709. See V. Klyuchevsky, *Peter the Great*, trans. Liliana Archibald (Macmillan, 1958) pp. 70–3.

consolidating the gains made in eastern Europe by Peter the Great; or, as Russian diplomats expressed it so elegantly, at maintaining the European equilibrium. This complete change of policy resulted in greater expenses than ever before, which could never have supported a European posture had Peter not dramatically increased Russia's productive resources.

After Peter a new element was added to existing political considerations. His weak male and female successors were forced to look for support from society, and in particular from the nobility, to maintain the stability of the throne. In return for this support legislation increasingly began to mention *special class privileges*, instead of, as under Peter, class obligations. The nobility emancipated itself, got rid of the heavy burden of compulsory service, and not only regained its old privileges but acquired new and extensive rights, which also benefited the more important merchants.[1] In this way the upper classes were endowed with privileges and advantages, while the lower classes suffered from deprivations and burdens. Had this state of affairs been patiently endured by the people, Russia would not have remained part of the comity of European nations.

However, by the middle of the eighteenth century violence was no longer directed by the masses against the government, the boyars, the governors, and departmental officials as during the seventeenth century. Instead, revolts were caused by social unrest and were aimed at the *serf-owners*. Even the Pugachev rebellion was raised under the banner of legality and was aimed at overthrowing the usurper Catherine and her accomplices, the nobility.[2] With the ground virtually trembling under their feet the ruling classes, on Catherine's initiative, began to consider how to achieve a more equal society, and how to mitigate the worst aspects of serfdom. The solution was postponed from reign to reign, while

[1] For a discussion of the practical implications of special class privileges, see *The European Nobility in the Eighteenth Century*, ed. A. Goodwin, pp. 180–9.

[2] See Blum, *Lord and Peasant in Russia*, pp. 313–14 and 555–6. Between 1764 and 1769 in the Province of Moscow alone thirty serf-owners, nine of them women, were killed by their peasants. For the best and most easily accessible description of this rising see Roger Portal, *Pugacev; une révolution manquée*, vol. I of *Études d'histoire moderne et contemporaine* (1947).

officials considered and reconsidered ideas, making half-hearted attempts at improvement, which made a mockery of their pretensions to power of which they were so proud. The problem was only resolved in the middle of the nineteenth century, particularly after Sebastopol had shown even the most barren of minds the necessity for an immediate solution.[1]

The following applies to the period under review: *as defensive wars imposed increasingly greater strains on the country, so specific state obligations of even greater complexity were imposed on different social classes. When wars of defence became wars of offence, the upper classes were released from specific state obligations, and granted special privileges, while the lower classes were inundated with obligations. Finally, as popular discontent with the iniquitous system grew, so the government began to think about a more equitable social system.* These points are important, and essential to a proper understanding of the period.

Emerging from the events mentioned above there can be discerned in Russian society an increasing political awareness. Towards the end of the sixteenth century Muscovy had equipped itself with all the usual appurtenances of a state: supreme power, legislation, central and regional administrations, a powerful and ever-increasing bureaucracy, a social structure which became increasingly fragmented, an army, and even some vague notions about national representation. There was, however, no national debt. An institution is only a structure; to be successful and effective, it must be endowed with men of vision and purpose, who in turn must be guided by acceptable standards and morals. Obviously, none of this happens suddenly, but is the result of a difficult, and often painful, evolution. Muscovite state institutions were in existence at the time of the extinction of the old dynasty; but were Russian officials ready to deal with national problems in the interests of the people?

A brief estimate of the political outlook of Russians of the Muscovy period will show whether they were capable of understanding even a simple system of government, and interpreting its aims. Basically there must exist *a Sovereign, a people, a legal*

[1] A reference to the Emancipation of the Serfs in 1861.

system, and *a concern for general welfare*. The Sovereign in Muscovy arrogated to himself exalted attributes in his titles and pronouncements, for which there was no political prerogative and which consisted of triumphant embellishments or diplomatic pretensions, such as 'Sovereign of all the Russias'. The ancient appanage system still pervaded ordinary life, and influenced ideas and attitudes; it provided sovereignty with a real historical basis, which consisted in the belief that the state of Muscovy was the Sovereign's *votchina*, his own personal, divisible, property. New political ideas, however, which appeared as circumstances changed, challenged this stubbornly held belief. The unification of Great Russia by Muscovy produced the concept of a national Russian state, which categorically challenged existing beliefs, and forced the ruler of all the Russias to think of himself not as the supreme Sovereign of the Russian nation but as its hereditary master, the territorial owner of the Russian land. Ivan III asserted that 'since the time of our ancestors the whole of the Russian land has been our patrimony'.[1] Political thinking could not keep pace either with accelerated territorial expansion or dynastic pretensions, and converted prejudices (which sprang from the appanages) into a series of political misunderstandings. Similarly, there arose other political misconceptions. One such was the concept of Sovereign authority, which was represented as a fusion between two incompatible functions: Tsar and territorial owner. Furthermore no identification existed between nation and state; indeed, the state was regarded not as a national unit ruled by a Sovereign, but as an estate, which included among its assets all classes of society who lived on land belonging to that estate. In this way public welfare, which should have been the state's main concern, was subordinated to dynastic interests of territorial owners; even the law sounded like an instruction emanating from an estate office, belonging to the Moscow Kremlin estate; it organised a working programme affecting in particular the provincial administration, as well as ensuring

[1] Ivan III did not limit his vision to Great Russia; he was claiming suzerainty over all lands occupied by Orthodox Russians. See Ian Grey, *Ivan III and the Unification of Russia* (English U.P., 1944) p. 19.

that the tenants duly fulfilled their obligations to the state.

Until the seventeenth century Muscovite legislation postulated no basic principle defining either the function and rights of the Sovereign, or the basic rights and duties of the citizens. There was lacking, therefore, any appreciation of what fundamentally constituted a state.

The structure of government was the result of a particular historical development which owed a great deal to the national desire for order, but which lacked sophistication. Yet even so, the intelligent use of existing institutions was beyond the political capacity of their administrators. Indeed, the main fascination of this particular period lies in exploring the process involving the sudden appearance of new ideas which were subsequently adopted generally, and which became fundamental to the political system. It is also necessary to explore the way these ideas transformed a primitive state structure into a sophisticated government system. At this stage apparent contradictions in the system become susceptible to historical explanations.

The points touched on above merit closer study; a number of problems will have to be solved; and attention will also have to be paid to the existence of particular features which existed at the time of the accession of the new dynasty to the throne of Muscovy.

However, prior to its accession, the state of Muscovy was severely jolted to its very foundations. This jolt was the first, severe check to the development of these new ideas which were lacking in government under the old, dying dynasty. The jolt occurred at the beginning of the seventeenth century, and is known as 'The Troubles', or, as Kotoshikhin[1] called them, 'The

[1] Gregory Kotoshikhin, a government official who was disillusioned with the state of Alexian Muscovy, wrote a critique, *O Rossii v tsartstvovanie Aleksiia Mikhailovicha* [Russia in the reign of Alexis Mikhailovich], 3rd ed., St Petersburg, 1884. Kotoshikhin had personal reasons for dissatisfaction. He had been an official in the department of Foreign Affairs, and made a minor error in transcribing the Tsar's titles; for this he was beaten. Subsequently, during the second war with Poland, he disobeyed an order given to him by Prince Dolgoruky, commander-in-chief of the Russian Army. In order to escape Dolgoruky's anger Kotoshikhin fled to Poland, Germany and eventually to

Time of Troubles'. The Russian people who lived through these turbulent years, called them, and in particular the later period, 'the great destruction of the State of Muscovy'. The first signs of the Time of Troubles appeared immediately after the death of Fedor,[1] the last Tsar of the old dynasty. The Time of Troubles ended when delegates assembled in Moscow at the beginning of 1613,[2] and elected as Tsar, Michael, founder of the new dynasty.[3]

The Time of Troubles covers fourteen or fifteen years in Russian history from about 1598 to 1613. A monk, Abraham Palitsyn from the Troïtsa Monastery, and author of an account of a siege by the Poles of this monastery,[4] who lived during the Time of Troubles considered that they covered a period of fourteen years. What was the origin and significance of the Time of Troubles? Why did 'this Muscovite tragedy', this *tragoedia moscovitica* as it was called by contemporary foreigners, occur? The following is an outline of this tragedy.

In 1581, two years before his death, Ivan the Terrible, in one of his frequent moments of uncontrollable anger, brutally assaulted his pregnant daughter-in-law for being too lightly dressed when she entered his room – *simplici veste induta* – according to the Jesuit, Antonio Possevino,[5] who arrived in Moscow three

---

Sweden. During a drunken brawl he killed his landlord (who happened to be the husband of his mistress). Kotoshikhin died on a Swedish gibbet. See Zinaïda Schakovskoy, *Precursors of Peter the Great*, trans. J. Maxwell Brownjohn (Cape, 1964) pp. 31–2.

[1] Tsar Fedor reigned from 1584 to 1598, and was the last of the line of Rurik through Daniel. See J. L. I. Fennell, 'The Dynastic Crisis 1497–1502', *Slavonic Review*, vol. 39, no. 92 (Dec 1960) pp. 1–23.

[2] January 1613.

[3] Michael Romanov was elected Tsar in February 1613.

[4] No translation of this work exists. However there is a modern Russian edition, *Skazanie Avraamiya Palitsyna* (Moscow/Leningrad, 1955).

[5] Antonio Possevino was a Jesuit priest sent by Pope Gregory XIII in 1580 to mediate between Ivan the Terrible and Steven Batory. When peace was finally concluded on 6 January 1582 Muscovy lost the Baltic seaboard; it was not to be regained for one hundred and fifty years. See Ian Grey, *Ivan the Terrible* (Hodder & Stoughton, 1964) pp. 225–8. For a detailed discussion of Possevino's mission see S. Polčin, 'La Mission religieuse de P. Antoine Possevin, S.J., en

months after this event, and who soon heard the details from current rumours. Her husband, and heir to the throne, Tsarevich Ivan attempted to protect his wife; whereupon his father killed him with an unfortunately well-aimed blow on the head with an iron stick. Ivan the Terrible, almost out of his mind with grief for his son, would jump out of bed at night, wailing loudly, crying that he wished to renounce the throne and take monastic vows. Be that as it may, it was due to this unfortunate occurrence that his second son, Tsarevich Fedor succeeded to the throne. Fedor, last Tsar of the old Muscovite dynasty, is an interesting character. Ivan Kalita's descendants who had built the state of Muscovy had always distinguished themselves by their amazing ability in dealing with mundane affairs – even though they were overly materialistic. At the moment of its decline, however, the old dynasty completely renounced earthly pursuits. According to contemporaries, Tsar Fedor spent the whole of his life eschewing worldly vanities and vexations, and concerned himself with spiritual affairs. The Polish Ambassador, Sapieha,[1] describes Fedor as follows: 'The Tsar is small, fairly thin, with a quiet, almost humble voice, a simple countenance, a small mind, or, as I have heard from others, and noticed myself, no mind at all, because at an ambassador's reception he sat on his throne, smiling all the time, and admiring first his sceptre, and then his orb.' Another contemporary, a Swede called Petreius,[2] in his description of the State of Muscovy (1608–11) also mentions that Tsar Fedor was practically an imbecile, who only found pleasure in spiritual matters, and often went from church to church to ring the bells and listen to mass. Ivan the Terrible bitterly reproached him for this, saying that he was more like the son of a sexton than the son of a Tsar. These descriptions are undoubtedly exaggerated, and

Moscovie (1581–1582)', *Orientalia Christiana Analecta* (Rome, 1957). Possevino's other activities are discussed in P. Pierling, S.J., *Dimitri dit le Faux et Possevino* (Paris, 1914).

[1] This was Leo, Great Chancellor of Lithuania. Details of his role are discussed in Philip Barbour, *Dimitry* (Macmillan, 1967) pp. 14, 16–17 and 98–100.

[2] Peter Petreius, *Regni Muscovitiici Sciographia* (Stockholm, 1615). Olearius in his *Travels in Seventeenth-century Russia* borrowed extensively from Petreius.

are by way of being caricatures. Devout and loyal Russian contemporaries tried to depict Tsar Fedor as a familiar and well-beloved ascetic.

The esteem and respect that was attached in ancient Russia to the concept of 'fools for Christ's sake' has been discussed elsewhere.[1] The 'fools for Christ's sake', or the 'blessed ones', renounced all worldly possessions as well as spiritual comforts such as honour, glory, respect and family ties. Moreover, they challenged other people's rights to enjoy material and spiritual blessings. Poor and homeless, they wandered about barefoot and in rags, more like animals than people, despising seemly conversation, deliberately making themselves a laughing-stock, and mocking both the things that people love and value as well as the people themselves. Ancient Russia saw in this humility, carried to the ultimate in degradation, a practical fulfilment of the divine ordinance that the kingdom of heaven belongs to the humble in spirit. The secular conscience of the times considered that the spiritual abasement expressed by 'fools for Christ's sake' was the living image of humanity's passions and vices. Moreover, these people enjoyed extensive rights and complete freedom of speech. Men in high places and the Tsars, even Ivan the Terrible, would listen patiently to the audacious, derisive, and insolent speeches of these sacrosanct street mendicants, without daring to lift a finger against them.

This was the familiar and beloved image that his contemporaries bestowed on Tsar Fedor. He was, in their eyes, a holy occupant of the throne, humble in spirit, worthy of a heavenly, and not an earthly, kingdom. He was the sort of man the Church liked to include among its saints, a reproach to the evil thoughts and sinful frailties of the ordinary Russian. 'O! to be blessed in one's mother's womb, and bereft of any cares save one's spiritual salvation,' exclaimed a courtier, Prince Katyrev-Rostovsky[2] about

[1] The significance of 'fools for Christ's sake' is discussed in James H. Billington, *The Icon and the Axe* (Weidenfeld & Nicolson, 1966) pp. 59–60, and in G. Fedotov, *The Russian Religious Mind* (Harvard U.P., 1946) I 147–8, 411, and II 316–43.

[2] Prince Ivan Katyrev-Rostovsky lived until 1640. He was noted for his goodness and for weakness. He enjoyed the favour of Tsar Boris Godunov,

Fedor. According to another contemporary, Fedor combined monasticism with sovereignty, one serving as an embellishment for the other. He was known as 'the sanctified Tsar' ordained by heaven to sanctity and a heavenly crown. In other words, Tsar Fedor would, to use Karamzin's[1] phrase, have been better suited in a cellar or a cave than on the throne.

Towards the end of the nineteenth century Tsar Fedor became the subject of poetic works; Count Alexis Tolstoy devoted the second tragedy of his dramatic trilogy to him.[2] In fact the portrayal of Tsar Fedor in this play is remarkably faithful to the old Russian image of this Tsar. The poet must have drawn the character of this blessed Tsar from old Russian manuscripts. Delicate traces of Fedor's inclination for good-natured jokes which tempered the stern convictions held by the sanctified are apparent. But beneath all this piety which so moved Fedor's contemporaries, Tolstoy clearly shows the man's moral sensitivity. He was a prophetic simpleton who, by some unconscious, mysterious and instinctive process, could understand things which eluded men wiser than he. Fedor was grieved to hear about party disputes, or about the enmity that existed between the supporters of Boris Godunov and Prince Shuisky. He wanted to live to see everyone united in support of one Russia; he wanted to reconcile enemies; and strongly objected to Godunov's doubts as to the possibility of a general reconciliation.

> You do not understand this, No, no! Boris.
> You manage the state as you best know how;

---

played an equivocal role after 13 April 1605, was exiled by Tsar Vasili Shuisky, and finally returned to favour under Tsar Michael.

[1] Nicholas Karamzin (1766–1826) was the author of a monumental *History of the Russian State*. See Anatole Mazour, *An Outline of Modern Russian Historiography* (D. Van Nostrand, 1939) pp. 22–9, and Billington, *The Icon and the Axe*, pp. 262–4.

[2] Count Alexis Tolstoy (1817–75). The dramatic trilogy consists of: *The Death of Ivan the Terrible*, *Tsar Fedor*, and *Tsar Boris*. Philip Barbour lists twenty-one literary works devoted to Tsar Fedor, and states that this list is incomplete. See Barbour, *Dimitry*, pp. 375–6.

> You are clever in that: but here I think I know
>   more than you,
> Here one must know the heart of man . . .

Elsewhere he says to Godunov:

> What kind of Tsar am I? It is not difficult
> To confuse and deceive one in all affairs;
> But in only one thing am I not deceived;
> When I must choose between black and white
> I am not deceived . . .

The historical embellishments in these entertaining and poetic representations of an historical character, whether described by contemporaries or writers of a later era, must not be overlooked.

Tsarevich Fedor grew up in the Alexandrov suburb in the middle of the horrors and abominations perpetrated by the *Oprichnina*.[1] Early each morning, his father, a superior of a so-called monastery, would send him to the belfry to ring the bells for matins. He was weak from birth as a result of the fatal illness of his mother, Anastasia Romanov.[2] He grew up motherless, surrounded by the horrors of the *Oprichnina*, small, palefaced, and stunted; he had a tendency towards dropsy, and walked with unequal, slow and quasi-senile steps, the result of a premature weakness in the legs. This description is offered by the English ambassador Fletcher when he saw Fedor aged thirty-two in 1588–9.

With Tsar Fedor the dynasty was indeed dying out. His smile was fixed, but lifeless. It was with this very smile that Fedor tried to defend himself from his father's capricious anger, and it seemed

[1] It is impossible to translate this word. Michael Florinsky defines it as an 'entailed domain'. It was created by Ivan IV. To administer this domain, which was exempt from the jurisdiction of the general administration, a special household was created, and its members were called *oprichniks*. See D. Mirsky, *Russia* (Cresset P., 1931) p. 150; Florinsky, *Russia* (Macmillan, New York, 1953) I 199–202; Grey, *Ivan the Terrible*, pp. 161–7; Blum, *Lord and Peasant in Russia*, pp. 144–7.

[2] Anastasia Romanov died in 1580. Ivan the Terrible is reputed to have married seven women, of whom five were crowned as Tsaritsas.

that he was praying for pity and mercy. Through force of habit, and especially after his elder brother's terrible death, the deliberately pitiful expression on Fedor's face became an involuntary, automatic, grimace. Goaded by his father, he lost his will-power, but retained for ever an expression of beaten submissiveness. When he inherited the throne, he looked for a man to be the keeper of his will, and Boris Godunov, his astute brother-in-law, carefully took the demented Ivan the Terrible's place.

Ivan the Terrible solemnly declared on his death-bed that his successor, 'wrapped in humility', was incapable of governing, and appointed a council to help him: a regency was created of powerful noblemen. Immediately after the death of Ivan the Terrible, the most powerful of these regents was Nikita Yurev, the new Tsar's maternal uncle. But he fell ill and died, leaving power in the hands of the Tsar's brother-in-law, Boris Godunov. Taking advantage of the Tsar Fedor's weak character, and the Tsaritsa's support (Godunov's sister), he gradually ousted the other regents and asserted himself as Russia's real master ruling in his brother-in-law's name. He can hardly be called a prime minister, since he was a particular type of dictator or a co-ruler. According to Kotoshikhin, Godunov was appointed by the Tsar to administer the government while he gave himself up to 'humility and prayer'. In this way Boris Godunov exerted enormous influence over the Tsar and over the government. In the words of Prince Katyrev-Rostovsky, who has been quoted elsewhere, Boris Godunov was so powerful that 'people obeyed him as they would the Tsar'. He surrounded himself with royal pomp, and received foreign ambassadors in his palaces with all the glitter and grandeur of a real potentate, and 'was honoured no less than the Tsar'. He governed wisely and carefully, and the fourteen years of Tsar Fedor's reign were a period of respite from the pogroms and terrors of the *Oprichnina*.

'The Lord softened towards his people', wrote Prince Katyrev-Rostovsky, 'and gave them peace which enabled the Tsar to rule quietly in peace, so that the whole of Orthodox Christianity became comforted and lived in peace and quiet.' The successful war against Sweden did not affect these sentiments.

However, disturbing rumours suddenly began to circulate in Moscow. Ivan the Terrible had a younger son, Dimitri, to whom he left, in accordance with the old custom of Muscovite rulers, a small landed property, the town of Uglich and its environs. In order to prevent court intrigue and agitation at the beginning of Tsar Fedor's reign, Dimitri and his mother's relatives, the Nagoi, were banished from Moscow. It was said in Moscow that the seven-year-old Dimitri, son of Ivan's fifth and last wife (his uncrowned wives are not included in this count), was in canon law a dubious Tsarevich,[1] but that he resembled his father as he had been at the time of the *Oprichnina*. Moreover, it was said that his life was in danger from people close to the throne, who intended to seize it themselves in the likely event that Tsar Fedor died without issue. In 1591, as if to justify these rumours, the news spread through Moscow that the appanage Prince Dimitri's throat had been cut in Uglich in broad daylight, and that the enraged townspeople had killed his murderers, so that there were no witnesses to the event.

A committee of investigation was sent to Uglich presided over by Prince Vasili Shuisky, who was Godunov's secret enemy and rival. The investigation was stupidly and carelessly handled; painstaking enquiries were instituted into irrelevant trifles, and important facts were disregarded. Contradictory evidence was not clarified, and in general the commission merely confused the issue. It tried to persuade itself and others that the Tsarevich did not have his throat cut by others, but had cut his own throat by accident in an attack of epilepsy, to which he was subject, by falling on a knife with which he and other children were playing.[2] Therefore the townsmen of Uglich were severely punished for their unwarranted violence against the alleged murderers. When the Patriarch Job, a friend of Godunov's with whose assistance he had been made Patriarch two years before, received the report,

[1] This was because the Russian Church recognised the validity of no more than three marriages.

[2] This was the testimony given by Dimitri's nurse. See Barbour, *Dimitry*, p. 3; also A. M. Nikolaieff, 'Boris Godunov and the Ouglich Tragedy', *Russian Review*, vol. 9, no. 4 (Oct 1950) pp. 275–85.

he declared to the Holy Council that the Tsarevich's death was due to the judgement of God; and here, for the time being, the matter ended.

Tsar Fedor died in January 1598. There was nobody of the Kalita dynasty left to ascend the vacant throne. An oath was taken to his widow, Tsaritsa Irina, but she took the veil. The dynasty thus died out amidst confusion and unnatural death. Under the leadership of the Patriarch Job the Zemsky Sobor elected the ruler, Boris Godunov, as Tsar.

Once on the throne Boris Godunov was as wise and as careful as he had been during Tsar Fedor's reign. By birth he belonged to one of the important noble families, although not of the highest rank. The Godunovs were the cadet branch of an old and important Muscovite boyar family, who stemmed from Tchet, Mirza tribesmen who came from the Horde to Moscow during the reign of Ivan Kalita. The senior branch of the family, the Saburovs were prominent among the Moscow boyars; but the Godunovs became prominent only during the reign of Ivan the Terrible, while the *Oprichnina* undoubtedly assisted in their rise to power. Boris stood *in loco parentis* at one of Ivan the Terrible's many weddings during the time of the *Oprichnina*, and later married the daughter of Maliuta Skuratov-Belsky, head of the *Oprichniks*. Boris's position at court was strengthened even more when his sister, Irina, married Tsarevich Fedor. Until the creation of the *Oprichnina*, no trace of any Godunovs can be found in the *Boyar Duma*; their name only appears after 1573. After Ivan the Terrible's death their name appeared frequently, and always among the important noblemen and courtiers. But Boris himself was not inscribed in the lists of *Oprichniks* and therefore did no harm to himself, since they were considered outsiders by the people.

The beginning of Boris's rule was highly successful, and his early measures won general approval. Contemporaries wrote about him in flamboyant terms, saying that both in domestic and foreign policies he 'displayed a sober-minded and wise justice to his people'. They found in him 'much wisdom and good sense', and called him a wonderful man, courteous in speech, constructive

and conscientious in affairs of state. They commented enthusiasti-
cally on his looks and personal qualities, saying 'that nobody in
the Tsar's council could rival him in the splendour of his features
or in the wisdom of his judgements'. But they did comment with
astonishment that this was Russia's first illiterate Tsar, 'who was
never taught to read or write, and who did not even know the
simple letters of the alphabet'.

It was admitted that he was good-looking, wise, and accom-
plished much, that he was pure in heart, kind and good to the
poor; nevertheless, he was criticised for his lack of skill in military
affairs, and was found to have certain other faults. Virtuous he
might have been, and indeed, might have resembled the Tsars of
old, had not envy and malice overshadowed his virtues. Moreover, he had an insatiable love of power, a tendency to listen and
believe informers, and would indiscriminately persecute the
accused. He believed himself to be incompetent in military
affairs, and did not trust his military leaders; as a result Tsar Boris
pursued a vacillating and ambiguous foreign policy. He did not
take advantage of Poland's hostility towards Sweden to enter into
an alliance with the King of Sweden to take Livonia away from
Poland. He concentrated on internal affairs and as Abraham
Palitsyn put it, 'on improving what was necessary in his realm'.
Indeed, Palitsyn says that during the first two years of his reign
'Russia's blessings blossomed'. The Tsar was particularly concerned with the poor and needy, tried to alleviate their condition,
and because he pursued 'evil' people, became tremendously
popular, and 'was loved by all'. He displayed unusual daring in
his approach to internal policies. During a discussion on the
history of the peasants, it was argued that the belief that Boris
Godunov was responsible for the enserfment of the peasants was a
myth. In fact, the exact opposite was true: Boris Godunov was
ready to consolidate the freedom and prosperity of the peasants.
It seems that he was working on a law which was to have defined
precisely the obligations and taxes due by the peasants to the
landowners. This law was not implemented by the Russian
government until the emancipation of the serfs.[1]

[1] In 1861.

This then was how Boris Godunov's reign began. But, in spite of his long administrative experience, his generosity to all classes at his accession, and his genuine ability for government, which so astonished his contemporaries, his popularity was short-lived. Boris Godunov was all things to all men, who were attracted to him because of his obvious ability and intelligence, and repulsed by his heartlessness, and lack of scruple. He could evoke gratitude and admiration, but not confidence; he was always suspected of duplicity and low cunning, and held to be capable of anything. Undoubtedly, the terrible school of Ivan the Terrible through which Boris had passed had marked him for life. Even during the reign of Tsar Fedor he was considered intelligent and capable, but none the less untrustworthy and unprincipled.

Careful and objective observers of Boris such as Ivan Timofeev,[1] author of some curious notes on the Time of Troubles, vacillated between severe criticism and unashamed adulation. They could not decide whether his laudable actions were instinctive or the result of conscious determination to mask his real intentions. This 'Tsar from the slaves' was a curious mixture of good and evil, a gambler with a delicately balanced conscience. For such a man no odium or criticism was inconceivable. Rumour had it that he had allowed the Crimean Khan to threaten Moscow; that he had killed the kind Tsar Fedor together with his infant daughter, Theodosia, who happened to be Boris's niece; that he had poisoned Tsaritsa Alexandra, his own sister; that a one-time Grand Duke of Moscow, a half-forgotten protégé of Ivan the Terrible, Simeon Bekbulatovich,[2] who was so old that he could hardly see, was

[1] For Ivan Timofeev's social and political ideas see *A History of Russian Economic Thought*, ed. John M. Letiche (University of California Press, 1964) pp. 199–201.

[2] Ivan the Terrible once enacted a charade, and appointed Prince Simeon Bekbulatovich, a baptised Tatar, as Tsar in his place. Documents have even survived which were issued in the name of 'Grand Prince Simeon of All Russia'. He remained on the throne for two years, while Ivan lived quietly as a boyar. Suddenly Simeon was dethroned, and sent into honourable exile to Tver. See Grey, *Ivan the Terrible*, pp. 208–9; Jack M. Culpepper, 'The Kremlin Executions of 1575 and the Enthronement of Simeon Bekbulatovich', *Slavic Review* (Sep 1965) pp. 503–6.

blinded by Boris. Moreover, it was believed that he had deliberately
set Moscow on fire at the time of the murder of Tsarevich Dimitri
in order to divert the attention of the Tsar and the people of
Moscow from the crime at Uglich. Boris Godunov became the
target for every possible kind of political slander. Who, if not he,
had killed the Tsarevich Dimitri? At least, this was what rumour
decided had happened, and to some purpose. This rumour spread
throughout the country, and was to prove fatal to Boris Godunov.
He was, they said, implicated in the crime; he had sent the murderers to the Tsarevich in order to open the way to the throne
himself. For information on the part played by Boris in this affair,
contemporary chroniclers relied on hearsay and conjecture;
obviously circumstantial evidence did not, and could not, exist.
Influential men in similar situations can, and do, cover up their
traces. The chronicles avoid the contradictions and confusion
contained in the Uglich commission report. The chroniclers
appreciated the difficult position Boris Godunov and his supporters were in during Tsar Fedor's reign. He was forced to kill
in order not to be killed himself. Indeed the Nagoi family would
never have spared the Godunovs had Tsarevich Dimitri ascended
the throne. Boris Godunov was, after all, aware that those who
aspire to the throne have to be merciless, not magnanimous. The
only doubt raised by the chroniclers concerns the apparent frank-
ness with which Boris dealt with them; and they attributed to
him not only active and direct participation, but also the responsibility for initiating the murder. An unsuccessful attempt to
poison the Tsarevich, consultations between Godunov supporters
and friends on other ways of disposing of Dimitri, an unlucky
choice of agents, Boris Godunov's grief at their failure, being
reassured by Kleshnin, who promised to carry out his wishes – the
very mention of these details, seems somehow to be out of
character for habitual intriguers. For such an expert as Kleshnin,
a prime mover in the Uglich affair, who was also indebted to
Boris Godunov, explicit instructions would have been unnecessary; an allusion, an imperious gesture would have been sufficient.
In any case it is difficult to imagine that such a deed could have
been committed without Boris Godunov's knowledge; that it had

been organised by one of his creatures, who had read his mind and wanted particularly to ensure the position of the Godunov faction, is the likeliest explanation.

The subsequent seven years were peaceful, and the memory of the Uglich affair faded. On Tsar Fedor's death, however, widespread suspicions were uttered again. Rumour had it that Boris Godunov's election to the throne had been dishonest; that having dispatched Tsar Fedor, Godunov ascended the throne by police stratagems, which as rumours grew, turned into a widespread organisation. It was said that agents had been sent all over Moscow, and to other towns, and even monks from the monasteries, to urge the people to beg Boris Godunov to rule as Tsar. Even the widowed Tsaritsa helped her brother, bestowing judicious bribes and favours on the Streltsy officers on condition, of course, that they came out for Boris Godunov.

The police threatened to impose heavy fines on dissenters, and drove the people to the Novodevichi Monastery, humbly to beg the Tsaritsa, who had taken the veil, to persuade her brother to become Tsar. A large number of police saw to it that the national petition was presented amid loud cries and the shedding of many tears. Those whose tears did not flow easily avoided police batons by rubbing their eyes with saliva. When the Tsaritsa appeared at her cell window to see the extent of this widespread weeping and praying, the people, at a given signal, prostrated themselves; those who refused or were unable to so do, were hit on the neck until they did. Thereafter, they arose and howled like wolves. People's stomachs were distended from the crying and shouting, their faces turned purple with the effort, and ears had to be covered up. This performance was repeated several times until the Tsaritsa, touched by this spectacle of devotion by the people, blessed her brother.

Although exaggerated, the bitterness of these accounts, clearly indicates the resentment which Boris Godunov and his supporters instilled in the people. Finally, in 1604 the worst rumour of all was started. For three years already in Moscow there had been talk of an unknown man who called himself Tsarevich Dimitri. Now it was openly being said that Boris Godunov's agents had murdered a substitute child in Uglich, and that the real Tsarevich was alive, and was coming from Livonia to reclaim his father's throne. The Russian people were deeply perturbed by this news, and the Time of Troubles started. Tsar Boris died in the spring of 1605, having been badly shaken by the news of the false Dimitri's successes. The false Dimitri was crowned in Moscow, and assassinated shortly thereafter.

This then is how the Time of Troubles began. The groundwork was laid primarily by two circumstances. First, the violent and mysterious end to the old dynasty and, second, its artificial reappearance under the false Dimitri. The first was the basic reason for the Time of Troubles. The extinction of a dynasty is, of course, a misfortune in the history of a monarchy, but nowhere was it accompanied by such disruption and destruction as in Russia. On the extinction of one dynasty, another is chosen, and order is restored. Pretenders seldom appear, or if they do, they are unimportant and generally vanish of their own accord. But in Russia, following the example of the false Dimitri, Pretenders became a chronic, national disease. In fact, until the end of the eighteenth century few reigns existed without the appearance of a Pretender. Under Peter the Great the absence of a Pretender created the belief that the real ruler was in fact a usurper!

However, neither the extinction of a dynasty, nor the appearance of a Pretender is a sufficient condition in and of itself, to have caused the Time of Troubles. Other conditions existed which added to the destructive process. The multi-causal basis of the Time of Troubles must therefore be investigated further.

Chapter Two

★

A SURVEY of the complex background of the Time of Troubles will explain its latent origins. A distinctive feature of the Time of Troubles was the involvement of all classes of society, starting with the upper classes and subsequently continuing down the scale of the existing structure of society. At the top were the boyars; and they initiated the Time of Troubles.

Tsar Boris Godunov came to the throne legally, having been elected by a Zemsky Sobor.[1] On grounds of personality, and political merit he might have become the founder of a new dynasty. But the boyars, who had suffered patiently under Ivan the Terrible, were now subjects of a Tsar who had been elected from among themselves, and were no longer prepared to accept the simple customs on which their political status had depended under the old dynasty. They expected Boris Godunov explicitly to formalise their status. That is to say, they wanted Boris Godunov to accept a limitation of his own powers expressed in a formal act 'that he would swear allegiance to the state according to a prepared charter' – to quote the eighteenth-century historian, Tatishchev.[2]

---

[1] There is unfortunately no modern study of the Zemsky Sobor. The only full-length western European work is now out of date. However it is still useful if used carefully. See Félix de Rocca, *Les Assemblées politiques dans la Russie ancienne: Les Zemskié Sobors* (Paris, 1899). See also Maxime Kovalevsky, *Modern Customs and Ancient Laws of Russia* (London, 1891) pp. 162–208; and J. L. H. Keep, 'The Decline of the Zemsky Sobor', *Slavonic and East European Review*, XXXVI (1957) 100–22. It is now generally agreed that the first Zemsky Sobor was convened by Ivan the Terrible in 1550.

[2] Vasili Tatishchev (1686–1750) presented his *History of Russia* to the Academy of Sciences in 1739; it was the first example of a critical, scientific history by a

Boris Godunov reacted with his usual duplicity. Aware of the boyars' implicit expectations, he was prepared neither to satisfy nor deny them. Hence the comedy of stubbornly refusing to accept the power offered to him, as a subterfuge in evading the conditions on which that very power was based. In the expectation that Boris Godunov would discuss these conditions and the oath of allegiance with them, the boyars said nothing. Boris Godunov, however, also remained silent and refused to accept the throne, hoping that the Zemsky Sobor would elect him unconditionally. In the event, Boris Godunov held out longer than the boyars, and was elected unconditionally. Herein lay his mistake, for which he and his family were to pay a heavy price. For by so doing, he indulged in a completely empty demonstration of power. He should have emphasised his importance as a representative of the Zemsky Sobor, instead of trying to prove a connection with the old dynasty with the help of forged documents. The Zemsky Sobor's report confidently affirmed that Ivan the Terrible entrusted his son, Fedor, to Boris Godunov: 'In presenting you with him, we also present you with this realm.' It was as though Ivan the Terrible foresaw the deaths without issue of Dimitri and Fedor; and was Fedor on his death bed likely to 'entrust this realm' to Boris Godunov? In fact, these particular fanciful statements were the loyal effort of Patriarch Job who edited the Zemsky Sobor's report. Boris Godunov did not inherit the state of Muscovy; he was the people's elected representative. Moreover he was the first of a sequence of Tsars to enjoy an altered political significance. He could have avoided ridicule and hatred had he not slavishly imitated the customs, and adopted the prejudices of the old dynasty. Powerful boyars led by Prince Shuisky opposed the election of Boris Godunov, fearing, in the words of a document 'that they and the people would be persecuted by him'. Boris Godunov should have dissipated their fears, and, indeed, for some time the leading boyars expected him to do this. One of Tsar

Russian. See H. Rogger, *National Consciousness in Eighteenth-century Russia* (Harvard U.P., 1960) pp. 194–206. For a Soviet view of Tatishchev's economic thought see *A History of Russian Economic Thought*, ed. John M. Letiche (University of California Press, 1964) pp. 355–69.

Vasili Shuisky's protagonists wrote, at his instigation, that the great boyars, descendants of the house of Rurik and related to the old dynasty, had legitimate claims to the succession; but they did not want to choose a Tsar from among themselves, and were content to leave the decision to the will of the people. For had they not in any event been powerful and renowned both in Russia and in distant countries under the old dynasty? All that was necessary, however, was to safeguard their power and glory from an Autocrat who recognised neither the great nor the glorious. Indeed, the only effective guarantee would be to restrict the power of an elected Tsar, which was what the boyars anticipated. Boris Godunov should have taken the initiative, and transformed the Zemsky Sobor from an occasional assembly into a permanent national representative assembly, an idea that had occurred to the Muscovites under Ivan the Terrible. Boris Godunov himself had called for such an assembly so that he might be chosen by the nation. This could have reconciled the opposition and, who knows, might have averted the disasters that subsequently befell him and his family, and Russia; furthermore he might well have become the founder of a new dynasty.

However, 'this cunning dissembler', lacking political acumen, overreached himself. When the boyars realised that their desires would not be satisfied, and that the new Tsar intended to be as autocratic as Ivan the Terrible, they decided to oppose him secretly. Contemporary Russians were unanimous in explaining that Boris Godunov's misfortunes stemmed directly from the dissatisfaction of leading personalities who created serious problems for him. Aware of their smouldering discontent, Boris Godunov took the necessary measures to forestall any plot. He created an intricate network involving the boyars' own bondsmen who were to spy on their masters. Released felons were employed to roam the streets of Moscow and listen to what was being said about the Tsar; anybody who was critical was arrested. Denunciation and slander became a terrible social canker. Everybody denounced everybody else, irrespective of class, and even the clergy were involved; members of the same family hardly dared to talk to one another. The very mention of the Tsar's name resulted in arrest and torture. Denunciations were followed by disgrace, torture, death, and the destruction of homes. 'Never', according to contemporary writers, 'was there such misery as under this Tsar.' Boris Godunov dealt viciously with the group of powerful boyars led by the Romanovs, in whom, as cousins of Tsar Fedor, he saw evil-doers and rivals. Five members of the Nikitich family, together with their relatives and friends, their wives, children, sisters and nephews, were banished to different distant parts of the country. The eldest Nikitich, the future Patriarch Philaret, together with his wife, were forced to take monastic vows. Finally, in a panic, Boris Godunov decided that he ought to know what was being said within the confines of people's homes, and what people were thinking; he felt that he should be the guardian of their consciences. He had a prayer circulated to be read at table during the toast to the Tsar and his family. The only reaction to this hypocritical and fulsome prayer is compassion at the depths to which a man, albeit a Tsar, can sink. Not unnaturally, there only was one reaction to these measures: hatred. The boyars with their ancient traditions, were hidden away in their houses, estates and in far-flung prisons. Their places were taken by obscure Godunovs together with their kinsmen and supporters who crawled out from their holes to throng the court and surround the throne. The old dynasty was replaced by a family led by a man who had been elected by the Zemsky Sobor, but who in fact turned into a petty, authoritarian coward. He hid himself away in his palace, seldom appeared in public, and did not receive petitioners personally, as had done previous Tsars. Suspicious of everybody, tormenting himself with his memories and past horrors, he was, as a foreigner living in Moscow at the time so aptly put it, as frightened as a thief in danger of imminent arrest.

The idea of a Pretender probably occurred to those boyars led by the Romanovs who had been particularly persecuted by Boris Godunov. Although the Poles were blamed for the creation of a Pretender the idea was 'kneaded in Moscow even though baked in a Polish oven'. Boris Godunov had every reason for believing that the boyars upheld the Pretender, and as soon as he heard of the appearance of the False Dimitri he told them directly that it was their doing.

The unknown nonentity who succeeded to the throne after Boris Godunov has been the object of great anecdotal interest. In spite of all scholarly attempts his identity is still a mystery.[1] For a long time it was believed, following upon an idea emanating from Boris Godunov himself, that the Pretender was one Gregory Otrepev, son of an insignificant Galician nobleman. The adventures of this man are well enough known. It is only necessary to point out that while in Moscow he had been a serf belonging first to the Romanovs, and subsequently to Prince Cherkassky.[2] He later took monastic vows, and because of a certain literary ability and his eulogy of Muscovite miracle workers, became one of the Patriarch's scribes. It was at this time that he suddenly declared that he would be Tsar in Moscow. As a result he would have been incarcerated in some distant monastery, had not some powerful people protected him, and he was able to flee to Lithuania at the identical moment in which the group around the Romanovs fell into serious disfavour. The man who in Poland called himself Tsarevich Dimitri, confessed that his protector had been Vasili Shchelkalov, an important secretary who had also been persecuted by Boris Godunov. Whether or not the Pretender was, as seems likely, the same Gregory Otrepev, or somebody totally different, is irrelevant, since his actual identity is less important than the part he played. He was an unusual occupant of the throne of Muscovy. Young, below average height, physically unattractive with red hair, clumsy gestures, and sad, thoughtful, facial expressions, his external appearance belied his religious background. He was a gifted man with a lively intellect who, with almost a passionate fervour, easily resolved problems raised in the Boyar Duma. In times of danger he was courageous almost to the point of rashness, slightly abstracted, a gifted orator who displayed considerable erudition. He departed from the old Muscovite Sovereigns' pious approach to life, and dispensed with

[1] For the evidence and a comprehensive account see Philip Barbour, *Dimitry* (Macmillan, 1967).

[2] Prince Boris Cherkassky was related to the Romanovs.

their overbearing and condescending behaviour. He broke with other customs sanctified by Muscovite tradition: he did not go to sleep after dinner, nor frequent the baths, and with his simple unaffected manner behaved quite unlike a Tsar. From the beginning he showed himself to be a creative administrator, free from severity, personally enquiring into everything, attending the Boyar Duma daily, and training the soldiers in person. As a result, he became extremely popular among the masses, although in Moscow certain groups looked on him with suspicion, and openly accused him of being a Pretender. His best and most loyal supporter, one P. F. Basmanov, confessed to some foreigners that the Tsar was not the son of Ivan the Terrible, but that he was recognised as Tsar because no one better could be found. But the False Dimitri looked on himself in a totally different way. He considered himself to be the legal, natural Tsar, entirely convinced of his royal birth. Those closest to him never noticed him doubt this, and moreover he was convinced that everybody agreed with him.

When the Princes Shuisky were tried for spreading rumours that he was a Pretender, the False Dimitri handed, what was a matter of personal concern, over to the whole country, and summoned the Zemsky Sobor. It was the first to resemble a national representative assembly with delegates chosen from all classes or ranks. This assembly sentenced the accused to death, which was commuted to exile by the False Dimitri, who soon allowed the culprits to return and whom he restored to their former boyar status. No Tsar who admitted to himself that he was an impostor, and had illegally seized the throne, would have acted in such a daring or confident manner. Boris Godunov would certainly have confined them to a torture chamber and subsequently starved them to death. The reasons for the False Dimitri's opinions of himself remain a historical and psychological mystery. Be that as it may, he did not remain on the throne for long because he did not fulfil the boyars' aspirations. He did not wish to be their instrument, and acted independently, developing his own political ideas, which in foreign policy were often courageous and far-reaching. He planned to lead all the Catholic powers under

Orthodox Russia against the Turks and Tatars.[1] He criticised his advisers in the Boyar Duma for seeing nothing, learning nothing, and suggested that they should travel abroad to be educated – but he said all this politely and inoffensively. Much more irritating to the high-born boyars was the familiarity between the throne and the Tsar's ignorant and presumptuous relatives, and his weakness for foreigners, especially Catholics. The Boyar Duma included a certain Prince Mstislav, two Princes Shuisky, one Prince Golitsin as well as other boyars, five parvenu Nagois, while among the *okolnichi*[2] there were three former departmental secretaries. Even greater resentment was felt by both boyars and people of Moscow at the unruly and wandering Poles with whom the new Tsar had inundated the capital. The Polish hetman Zholkiewski, who was active in Muscovite affairs during the Time of Troubles, noted a minor incident in Cracow which clearly described the situation in Moscow at this time.[3] At the beginning of 1606, the False Dimitri sent an ambassador called Bezobrazov to Cracow to inform the Polish King of the accession of a new Tsar to the throne of Muscovy. After the celebration Bezobrazov indicated that he wished to confer with the Chancellor[4] in private; he repeated a message given to him by the Princes Shuisky and Golitsin in which they blamed the Polish King for having given them a low, superficial, cruel man, a dissolute spendthrift, totally unfit for the throne of Muscovy, who did not even behave decently towards the boyars. They did not know how to get rid of him, and were prepared to recognise as Tsar, the Polish King's own son, Vladislav. Clearly, the powerful magnates in Moscow were contemplating some plot against the False Dimitri and were afraid that the Polish King might interfere on behalf of his own nominee.

[1] See P. Pierling, S.J., *La Russie et le Saint-Siège* (Paris, 1901) III 423–9.

[2] The *okolnichi* were courtiers attached to the person of the Tsar, and were immediately below the rank of boyar in importance.

[3] No mention is made of this incident in Russian sources of the time. See Pierling, *La Russie et le Saint-Siège*, III 266 ff.; and Hetman Sholkiewski, *Expedition to Moscow: a Memoir*, trans. and ed. J. Giertych, Polonica Series no. 1 (London, 1959).

[4] The Grand Chancellor of Lithuania at this time was Leo Sapieha.

The False Dimitri's habits, his departure from, and frivolous attitude toward, ceremony, his individual initiatives and dispositions, particularly in foreign affairs, evoked criticism and displeasure among different classes of society in Moscow. However, beyond the capital his popularity among the masses was not noticeably impaired. His downfall, however, was caused by something totally different, and was clearly stated by Prince Shuisky, the ringleader of the boyar conspiracy against the Pretender. At a conspiratorial meeting on the eve of the rising, he explicitly said that he had recognised the False Dimitri only as a means of getting rid of Boris Godunov. The powerful boyars had had to create a Pretender in order to dislodge Boris Godunov, and then had to dispose of the Pretender in order to clear the way to the throne for one of themselves. This is exactly what they did, and furthermore they shared the responsibility for achieving their ambition. The Romanov faction initiated the action, which was then taken up by the group of titled nobles led by Prince Vasili Shuisky. Both groups considered that the Pretender was their puppet whom they kept on the throne for as long as he was needed before casting him aside. None the less, the conspirators did not hope for success without resorting to chicanery. It was primarily on account of the Poles that the Pretender was criticised. The boyars decided not to instigate popular disturbances simultaneously against both the Pretender and the Poles. Instead they created two distinct movements, and on 17 May 1606 they led the people to the Kremlin with the cry 'The Poles are killing the boyars and the Sovereign'. Their plan was to surround the False Dimitri, supposedly to protect him, and then to kill him.

The Pretender was succeeded by the Conspirator-Tsar, Prince Vasili Shuisky. He was an elderly boyar of fifty-four, small, plain, and partially blind; he was not stupid, but was crafty rather than intelligent, an inveterate liar and a compulsive intriguer. He had been through fire and water, and had come face to face with the execution block only to be saved by the merciful Pretender against whom he had conspired. He was also a great believer in informers, and was terrified of sorcerers. Tsar Vasili

Shuisky started his reign with a number of proclamations which were published throughout the country, and which contained at least one lie. Thus he wrote in the proclamation on which he had taken an oath: 'He who has sworn on the cross undertakes not to condemn a man to death without a fair trial by his boyars.' As will be shown, in fact, on taking the oath he said nothing of the kind. In another proclamation issued in the name of boyars and officials it is stated that upon the overthrow of Gregory Otrepev, the Church Council, the boyars and other personages had chosen 'for the whole State of Muscovy' a ruler, Prince Vasili Shuisky, to be Autocrat of all Russia. The proclamation unequivocally states that there had been an election when in fact none had taken place. It is true, however, that when the Pretender had been overthrown, the boyars had somehow considered organising a broadly-based meeting and summoning provincial representatives to Moscow in order to 'elect a Tsar in council who would be beloved by all'. Prince Vasili Shuisky was frightened of the townspeople, the provincial representatives, and he advised against calling a representative council. A few of his titled supporters secretly recognised him as Tsar, while in the Red Square, the same crowd who had risen against the Pretender and the Poles, now shouted for Shuisky. According to the documents, people even in Moscow were unaware of what had taken place. In his third proclamation the new Tsar did not hesitate to use forged Polish evidence concerning the Pretender's intention to massacre the boyars, and force all Orthodox Christians to convert to the Lutheran or Roman Catholic faiths. None the less the accession of Prince Vasili Shuisky to the throne was an important event in Russian political history. He agreed to a limitation of his powers which was embodied in a decree and proclaimed throughout the country, and which he swore to uphold.[1]

The document referred to above is condensed and vague, and resembles a rough draft. Towards the end of the document the Tsar gave a solemn undertaking to all Orthodox Christians that he would judge them 'honestly and by fair trial', according to the

[1] But see Michael Florinsky, *Russia* (Macmillan, New York, 1953) I 230, who maintains that the heritage of absolutism was fully upheld.

law, and not arbitrarily. But even this condition is expressed obscurely. As far as more serious offences punishable by death and the confiscation of property were concerned, the Tsar committed himself to consulting with 'his boyars', i.e. with the Boyar Duma. He thereby renounced his right to confiscate property belonging to the criminals' brothers and family who were themselves innocent.[1]

This statement was followed immediately by the Tsar saying 'I will not listen to false statements, but will discover the facts through search and confrontation'; he undertook to punish false witnesses with the same punishment that the alleged crime would have carried. But these statements seem to refer to lesser offences which the Tsar could decide without the Boyar Duma, and define more clearly the concept of a fair trial. The document therefore seems to envisage two types of superior trials: the first by Tsar and Boyar Duma, the second by Tsar alone. The document ends with a special condition: the Tsar 'will not proscribe any man without cause'.

The Tsar's proscription could be imposed on state servants who had incurred his displeasure for whatever reason. It resulted in temporary banishment from court, 'away from the Tsar's serene eyes', loss of privileges, demotion, and even confiscation of estates or town houses. In this instance the Tsar was acting in a disciplinary, and not in a judicial, capacity in order to maintain service interests and discipline. As an expression of the Sovereign's power, proscription did not have to be justified, and in accordance with accepted Muscovite standards, was often barbarous, and transformed a disciplinary affair into one subject to capital

[1] The coronation oath extracted from Tsar Vasili Shuisky in 1606 is quoted in part by Thornton Anderson, *Russian Political Thought* (Cornell U.P., 1967) p. 99.

I, the Great Sovereign, [obligate myself] not to sentence any man to death without having judged him with my boyars in a true court, and not to take his *votchina*, houses, or chattels from his brothers or wife or children if they were not of the same mind with him; and also among merchants and tradespeople, if, after judgement and investigation, any of them should be deserving of death, not to take houses or shops or goods from the wives and children left behind if they had no part in the guilt of the condemned.

punishment. Under Ivan the Terrible any doubts concerning an official's devotion to duty could result in execution. Tsar Vasili Shuisky was therefore extremely brave in that he undertook only to proscribe a man for a particular offence for which he had been found guilty, a promise which was naturally never kept; and in order to find out the truth he promised to set up a special disciplinary tribunal.

Obviously the proclamation was very one-sided. Tsar Vasili Shuisky undertook exclusively to protect the individual and his property from arbitrary authority. The proclamation said nothing about the basis of government, nor did it delineate the responsibilities between the Tsar and important administrative state institutions. The power of the Tsar was restricted by the Boyar Duma together with whom, as in the past, he acted.[1] But this limitation of power only affected the Tsar in judicial matters, and in his personal relations. However, the origin of the document sworn to by Tsar Vasili Shuisky was even more complex than its contents; and it has a secret history of its own. The chronicler explained that immediately following his proclamation as Tsar, Vasili Shuisky went to the Ouspensky Cathedral, and made a speech such as had never been heard before in the history of Muscovy. 'I swear by this cross *to the whole country* that I will do no ill *without council.*' The boyars and others told him not to take an oath on this subject since it was not the custom in Muscovy; but he declined to listen. The boyars believed that Tsar Vasili Shuisky's action was revolutionary. The Tsar would no longer rely on the Boyar Duma, hitherto his collaborator in affairs of state and justice, to assist him in judicial affairs, but on the Zemsky Sobor, a recent creation, which was only rarely summoned to discuss extraordinary state problems. The boyars believed that this was an unprecedented innovation, an attempt to replace the Boyar Duma with the Zemsky Sobor, and shift responsibility for government from the boyars to a representative national

[1] Information in English on the competence, functioning and composition of the Boyar Duma is practically non-existent. Although it refers to an earlier period see Gustave Alef, 'Reflections on the Boyar Duma in the reign of Ivan III', *Slavonic and East European Review* (Jan 1967) pp. 76–123.

council. The Tsar decided to govern with the help of the Zemsky Sobor, even though he had been afraid to seek their help to win the throne. Indeed, the Tsar knew precisely what he was doing.

On the eve of the rising against the Pretender, Tsar Vasili Shuisky had sworn in front of his colleagues to rule together 'with a general council'. Imposed on the country by a boyar clique, he appeared to be a boyar Tsar, partisan, ruling at the dictate of others. He looked to the Zemsky Sobor for support of his illegal position, and hoped that it would counterbalance the Boyar Duma. By taking an oath in front of the whole country not to punish without the advice of the Zemsky Sobor, he counted on extricating himself from the tutelage of the boyars, and becoming a representative Tsar, thereby consolidating his power through an institution which had none, or in other words, to free himself from all practical limitations. The proclamation as it was issued and sworn to, was the result of an agreement between the Tsar and the boyars. The Tsar had secretly agreed with the boyars that they would participate together in all legislative, judicial and administrative affairs. Having assured the pre-eminence of the Boyar Duma over the Zemsky Sobor, the boyars did not insist on the publication of all the concessions they had obtained from the Tsar. They even considered it unwise to show society that they had extracted their pound of flesh from the Tsar. The sworn proclamation clearly emphasised that the only importance enjoyed by the Boyar Duma was to advise the Tsar in matters of legal importance: which was all that the boyars had required. Throughout the sixteenth century, as the governing class, they had shared power with the ruler. But many of them had suffered from autocratic behaviour under Ivan the Terrible and Boris Godunov. Consequently, taking advantage of the situation, the boyars decided to restrict the ruler's autocratic powers, and protect individuals, i.e. themselves, from a repetition of past disasters. Having forced the Tsar to call upon the Boyar Duma to participate in political affairs the boyars were convinced that they would henceforth enjoy administrative power as of customary right.

For all its vagueness, Tsar Vasili Shuisky's proclamation constitutes a new and unprecedented document in Muscovite State Law. It was the first attempt to establish a political system on the basis of a formal limitation of autocratic power, which was subsequently changed in character and in structure. Not only did Tsar Vasili Shuisky circumscribe his own power, but the very oath he took imposed further limitations, and turned him not only into an elected Tsar, but also into one who had taken a legal oath. The oath was a negation of the personal power enjoyed by the Tsars of the old dynasty, which had evolved from the appanage attitudes of Sovereign-masters. Since when does a householder swear allegiance to his servants and guests? Furthermore, Tsar Vasili Shuisky renounced three prerogatives which particularly expressed the Tsar's personal powers. First, 'disgrace without guilt', or proscription by the Tsar without sufficient reason and resulting from his own investigations only. Second, confiscation of the property belonging to innocent relatives and the family of a criminal; the denial of this right resulted in the abolition of the ancient practice of holding a family responsible for the behaviour of its individual members. Third, extraordinary trials resulting from denunciations with their torture and false witnesses, the absence of eye witnesses, and their interrogation, as well as other normal legal procedures. These prerogatives constituted the essential basis for the power of Muscovite Sovereigns, and were expressed in the following maxims: Ivan III said 'I will create a Prince whomsoever I chose', and Ivan IV, 'as we may be merciful to our slaves, so may we punish them'. In rejecting these prerogatives Tsar Vasili Shuisky transformed himself from a master of slaves into a rightful Tsar with subjects, ruling according to law.

The unity of the boyar ruling class did not, however, last through the Time of Troubles, at which time it split into two factions. The majority of middle-ranking boyars together with the metropolitan nobility, senior departmental officials and secretaries broke away from the more powerful boyars. From the accession of Tsar Vasili Shuisky the first group of boyars played an active part in the Time of Troubles. They devised a new government structure, also based on restricting the Sovereign's powers, but which was to have a broader political base than had been provided for by Tsar Vasili Shuisky in his original manifesto.

The following circumstances were responsible for these proposals. Few people were satisfied with Tsar Vasili Shuisky, mainly because of the illegalities surrounding his accession, and his dependence upon a group of boyars, who, in a contemporary's words, had chosen him and toyed with him like a child. Discontent with the existing Tsar created a demand for a Pretender. Imposture was becoming a stereotype of Russian political thought which was the answer to public discontent. From the beginning of Tsar Vasili Shuisky's reign, there were rumours that the first False Dimitri, i.e. a second Pretender, had escaped, even before a second False Dimitri had come into being. The Northern Territory, the towns of the Oka region, Putivl, Tula and Ryazan rose in 1606 in the name of this phantom against Tsar Vasili Shuisky. Defeated by the Tsar's army near Moscow, the rebels took refuge in Tula, where they appealed for help to Pan Mniszek, asking him to send them any man called Tsarevich Dimitri from his stable of Russian Pretenders. Finally, a second False Dimitri was found, and in 1608, reinforced by Polish–Lithuanian and Cossack detachments, took up a position in the village of Tushino, a few miles from Moscow, thereby placing the heart of Russia between the Oka and Volga rivers under his 'thievish hegemony'.

The situation in Muscovy was further complicated by the state of its international relations. Mention has already been made of the existing enmity between Sweden and Poland as a result of Charles IX ousting his nephew, Sigismund III,[1] the elected King of Poland, from his throne. Because the Polish government supported the second Pretender, albeit secretly, Tsar Vasili Shuisky appealed to Charles IX for help against the Tushino rebels. Negotiations by the Tsar's nephew, Prince Michael Skopin-Shuisky, led to an auxiliary detachment of Swedish soldiers under General Delagarde being sent to Russia. In return Tsar Vasili Shuisky concluded a perpetual agreement with Sweden against Poland,[2] as well as agreeing to other heavy

[1] Sigismund III (1587–1632) was the first Swedish King of Poland.
[2] This agreement was signed in February 1609.

concessions.[1] Sigismund immediately retaliated by breaking off relations with Muscovy, and in 1609 he besieged Smolensk.

There were many Poles at Tushino led by Prince Roman Rozhinski, who was also the local hetman. Insulted and scorned by his Polish allies, the would-be Tsar managed to escape from their vigilant surveillance in a peasant's coat on a mud-spattered sledge to Kaluga. Prince Roman Rozhinski then concluded an agreement with the King which provided for the withdrawal of the Poles to Smolensk. The Russian detachments had to follow, and they chose a deputation to negotiate with Sigismund the election of his son Vladislav to the throne of Muscovy. The deputation included the boyar Michael Saltykov, some metropolitan noblemen and half a dozen powerful Muscovite departmental secretaries. Not one important name was included among the envoys although none of them were exactly from the lower classes. Nevertheless as a result of either personal ambition, or the general confusion, once outside the rebellious half-Russian half-Polish camp at Tushino, they took it upon themselves to act as representatives of the state of Muscovy, of the whole Russian land. This was, of course, clearly presumptuous, and gave them no right to expect recognition of their fictitious plenipotentiary powers. But this in no way detracts from the historical importance of their proceedings. Contact with the Poles, and an acquaintance with their freedom-loving concepts and customs, broadened the Russian adventurers' political understanding. They stated the conditions on which Sigismund's son would be elected Tsar, insisted on the preservation of the ancient rights and freedom of the peoples of Muscovy, and included new privileges which had never before been enjoyed by the people. As a result of these contacts, the Muscovites were carried away by the idea of a freedom imposed from abroad, but it also made them appreciate the religious and national dangers which would follow: Saltykov burst into tears when speaking to the King about the preservation of the Orthodox religion. This double-edged consideration

[1] Tsar Vasili Shuisky ceded to Sweden Russian territories on the shores of the Gulf of Finland. For the diplomatic and military manœuvring see Pierling, *La Russie et le Saint-Siege*, III 360–96.

resulted in the Tushino deputation attempting to safeguard their homeland from the power of a nation, alien in both religion and race, whose help they were seeking to invoke.

No other act of the Time of Troubles shows the tensions to which Russian political thinking was subjected as does the agreement between Michael Saltykov and his friends, and King Sigismund. The agreement, which was concluded on 4 February 1610 near Smolensk, laid down the conditions precedent for the recognition of Prince Vladislav as Tsar of Muscovy by the Tushino plenipotentiaries.[1] This political document provided for a fairly sophisticated government structure. First, it defined the rights and privileges of the whole population and its different classes; and second, it elaborated upon the structure of government. Above all, however, it provided for the inviolability of the Russian Orthodox religion, and explicitly defined the rights of the whole population and its different classes. This document elaborates in far greater detail than Tsar Vasili Shuisky's proclamation the measures guaranteeing the personal freedom of the individual. The concept of individual rights, which had hardly existed previously, is set out explicitly in the agreement of 4 February 1610. People were to be tried according to the law, and were not to be punished without trial. This is given particular

---

[1] And when Prince Vladislav, the son of Sigismund, is Sovereign of the Russian State he shall honour and adorn according to previous custom the Holy Churches in Moscow and in all the cities and towns in the whole Muscovite State . . . and the bishops, priests, and other ranks, and all Orthodox Christians shall be in the Orthodox Christian faith of the Greek law as previously; however, in the capital city, Moscow, there might be one Roman Church for the Poles and Lithuanians residing with His Grace the Lord Prince. . . . And without [Vladislav] having investigated the guilt and having deliberated with all the boyars, nobody will be punished, nor honour taken from anybody, nor anybody sent to prison, nor *pomestie, votchiny,* and houses taken away. . . . And all that the Sovereign does, he will do by the decision [*prigovor*] and counsel of the boyars and the entire Duma; and without counsel and a decision he shall not conclude such affairs. . . . His Sovereign Grace will command that the State revenues be collected as previously, as in the time of former Great Sovereigns; and beyond the previous customs he will not add anything without having consulted the boyars.

See Thornton Anderson, *Russian Political Thought,* pp. 99–100.

emphasis, and there are frequent repetitions to the effect that no person was to be punished unless he had been found guilty 'by all the boyars'. Evidently, the custom of punishment without a prior investigation and trial was a particular grievance which required as radical a solution as possible. As in Tsar Vasili Shuisky's proclamation, so this agreement also states that no guilt would attach to the innocent brothers, wives and children of political offenders, nor would their property be confiscated.

Two other conditions affecting individual rights are quite new: high-ranking officials were not to be demoted unless proven guilty, and low-ranking officials were to be promoted according to merit. All subjects of Muscovy were to be free to travel to study in other Christian countries, and the Sovereign was to refrain from confiscating property in their absence. The concepts of religious tolerance and freedom of thought appear momentarily. The agreement of 4 February 1610 committed King Sigismund and his son not to try to convert a Greek Orthodox believer to Roman Catholicism or any other religion, because faith was a gift from God, and was not to be abused by force; moreover, there was to be no religious persecution. The Russians were to follow their own religion, and the Poles were to continue in their faith.

The Tushino delegation, however, displayed less appreciation for freedom and justice in relation to the class structure. The agreement safeguarded and extended the rights and privileges of the clergy, the departmental officials, the metropolitan and provincial nobility, the children of boyars, and some of the merchants. The King forbade the movement of peasants from Russia to Lithuania and vice versa, and this was to apply equally to Russians of all ranks, as for instance, to landowners. Serfs were to remain in their existing dependent condition, and the King was not to free them. As has been mentioned above, the agreement established conditions precedent of government. The Sovereign shared his power with two institutions, the Zemsky Sobor, and the Boyar Duma. Because the Boyar Duma was incorporated into the structure of the Zemsky Sobor, the final version of the agreement of 4 February 1610 alludes to 'the Duma of the boyars and all the land'. For the first time the political jurisdiction of both institutions is defined. The Zemsky Sobor had two functions. First, it had the right to amend and supplement laws, such as the Codes, which emanated from the 'boyars and all the land' to which the Sovereign had given his assent. Custom and the Muscovite Codes, on which Muscovite justice relied, had the validity of fundamental laws. This meant that the agreement conferred upon the Zemsky Sobor the power (constituent authority) to make laws. The Zemsky Sobor could also initiate legislation. If, for instance, the Patriarch and the Church Council, the Boyar Duma, and persons of any rank were humbly to petition the Sovereign concerning matters not provided for in the agreement, the Sovereign would discuss them with the Church Council, the boyars and all his land, 'according to the custom of the State of Muscovy'. The Boyar Duma was to enjoy legislative power. The Boyar Duma together with the Sovereign were to concern themselves with current legislation, and were to issue ordinary laws. Questions of tax, petitions by officials, and problems concerning estates, whether held in service tenure or unencumbered, were to be decided by the Sovereign with the boyars and officials. The Sovereign was not to introduce new taxes, or alter the taxes imposed by previous rulers without the agreement of the Boyar Duma. Supreme judicial power was to be the responsibility of the Boyar Duma: the Sovereign was not to punish, dishonour, exile or demote, without prior investigation and trial by all the boyars. At this point the agreement sternly reiterates that the Sovereign had to decide on all these problems as well as on problems concerning the heirs of a man who died with no issue, in accordance with the advice and judgement of the boyars, and that no action was to be taken without them.

The agreement of 4 February 1610 was the work of a party or class, which even included a few of the middle class, although it consisted primarily of the metropolitan nobility and departmental secretaries. Circumstances, however, resulted in the agreement being given a wider meaning. Tsar Vasili Shuisky's nephew, Prince Michael Skopin-Shuisky, helped by Swedish detachments, seized some of the northern towns from the Tushino faction, and in March 1610 entered Moscow. The masses wanted this talented, young warrior to succeed his old, childless uncle; but he died suddenly.[1] Tsar Vasili Shuisky's army, which had been sent to Smolensk to fight against Sigismund, was routed at Klushino by the Polish hetman Zholkiewski;[2] whereupon the nobility, led by Zachary Liapunov, removed Tsar Vasili Shuisky from the throne and forced him to take monastic vows.[3]

Moscow acknowledged the Boyar Duma as a provisional government. The Boyar Duma had to choose between two competitors for the throne: Vladislav, for whom Zholkiewski, on his way to Moscow, demanded recognition, and the Pretender, also on his way to Moscow, who was relying on the support of the masses of Moscow. Afraid of the False Dimitri, the Moscow Boyars made an agreement with Zholkiewski, on conditions entered into by the King at Smolensk. However, the agreement which gave rise to the oath being taken by Vladislav on 17 August 1610, was not a repetition of the earlier agreement of 4 February 1610. Although many articles were a restatement, there were new ones, while others were condensed, extended, or omitted. The omissions and additions are especially characteristic. The most important boyars deleted the article affecting the promotion of ordinary people on merit, and replaced it by a new condition, that 'Muscovite princes and boyars are not to be squeezed out or demoted by foreigners who have come to Russia for their own honour'. They also deleted the article dealing with the right to travel abroad to study in other Christian countries. The Muscovite aristocracy considered this too dangerous for internal tranquillity. The ruling class of aristocrats was less understanding than the middle, servile class, who fulfilled their executive functions; but this is the common fate of a class that aspires to greater heights than its performance warrants. The agreement of 4 February 1610 laid the

[1] Prince Michael Skopin-Shuisky became ill towards the end of April 1610, and it was widely rumoured that he had been poisoned by jealous relatives.

[2] The Russian army was vastly superior in numbers, but was led by Tsar Vasili Shuisky's brother, Dimitri, who was a military incompetent.

[3] He was incarcerated in the Chudov Monastery; his wife was forced to take the veil, and his brothers were arrested.

basis for a constitutional monarchy; it provided a framework for the exercise of power, and also allowed for the enjoyment of basic rights by the people. Moreover, it was essentially conservative in outlook, safeguarding as it did the customs of earlier Tsars and the time-honoured practices of the state of Muscovy. People rely on a written law when they feel that a custom is slipping away from them. Michael Saltykov and his colleagues were more responsive to change than the aristocracy; they had suffered more from the deficiencies in the political system, as well as from excesses of power.

The upheavals and clashes they experienced with foreigners strongly encouraged them to find ways of avoiding these disturbances, which imbued their political ideas with greater scope and clarity. They strove to replace ancient and unstable custom with a new written law, thus making it more purposeful.

The ordinary, provincial nobility were drawn into the Time of Troubles following the participation by the upper and middle-ranking metropolitan nobility. Likewise, the role they played became apparent from the beginning of Tsar Vasili Shuisky's reign. The first move came from the nobility of the towns beyond the river Oka and the north, i.e. from the towns which merged into the Steppe. The disturbances and dangers of life on the Steppe inculcated the native nobility with a fearless and warlike spirit. The rising was started by the nobility of Putivl, Venev, Kashir, Tula and Ryazan. The Governor of distant Putivl, Prince Shakovskoy, who was titled but not of noble birth, rebelled as early as 1606.[1] He was followed by the descendants of ancient Ryazan boyars, now ordinary noblemen, such as Liapunov and Sunbulov. Prokofy Liapunov, a nobleman from Ryazan, was a typical representative of the bold semi-Steppe nobility; he was decisive, presumptuous, and impetuous. Before any of the others, he saw which way the wind was blowing; but he acted impetuously without stopping to think. He sent Prince Skopin-Shuisky a message congratulating him on becoming Tsar before he had even arrived in Moscow, and while Tsar Vasili Shuisky was still

[1] Prince Gregory Shakovskoy had been exiled by Tsar Vasili Shuisky on his accession. See Pierling, *La Russie et le Saint-Siège*, III 348-9.

Tsar, thereby ruining Prince Skopin-Shuisky's chances at his uncle's court. Already in 1609 Zachary Liapunov had engineered a rising in Moscow against the Tsar, when the rebels had shouted that the Tsar was stupid, impious, drunk and lecherous, that they were in revolt for the sake of their brethren, the nobility and the sons of boyars whom the Tsar, together with his fellow con-spirators, the important boyars, had allegedly immersed in water and beaten to death. It follows that this was a rebellion by the lesser nobility against the aristocracy. In July 1610 Prokofy Liapunov's brother, Zachary, together with a crowd of adherents, all from the lesser nobility, deposed the Tsar, thereby ensuring the opposition of the clergy and the powerful boyars. The political aims of the provincial nobility are not clear. Together with the clergy they had elected Boris Godunov to the throne, in spite of the boyar aristocracy, and were content with this Tsar chosen from among the boyars; but they were against the boyar aristo-cracy, and were also against Tsar Vasili Shuisky, who himself was a boyar. At first they wanted Prince Skopin-Shuisky on the throne, then Prince Vasili Golitsin. However, one action partially reveals the political aspirations of this class. Having taken an oath of allegiance to Vladislav, the boyar government of Moscow sent an embassy to Sigismund to ask his son to become Tsar, and because they were afraid of the Moscow mob whose sympathies lay with the second Pretender, they summoned Zholkiewski's forces to the capital. However, the death of the 'Tushino brigand' towards the end of 1610[1] unravelled the knot, and a powerful national movement rose against the Poles; towns united together to clear their homeland from foreigners. The first to revolt was, as has been mentioned above, Prokofy Liapunov with his Ryazan following. Before the massed contingents could reach Moscow, the Poles slipped away from the Muscovites and burned the capital (March 1611). Having besieged the fortified Kremlin and Kitaigorod, to which the Poles had withdrawn, the massed contingents elected a provisional government consisting of three people, the two Cossack leaders, Princes Trubetskoy and Zarutsky, and the leader of the nobility, Prokofy Liapunov. This 'troika'

[1] He was murdered in Kaluga on 10 December 1610.

was set up by the Decision of 30 June 1611. Most of the contingents consisted of provincial men of service, who had armed and fed themselves from moneys collected from the urban and rural taxpayers. The Decision was drawn up in these noblemen's camp; it was issued in the name of 'the whole land', and the 'troika' were allegedly elected by 'the whole land'. Thus, representatives of one class, volunteer-noblemen, declared themselves to be the representatives of the whole land, and of all the people. The Decision contained few political ideas; on the contrary, it mirrored the pretensions of one class. The 'troika' were committed to 'strengthen the country, and take every aspect of the nation and the war into account'. However, according to the Decision, nothing of any importance was to be done without the agreement of the 'national camp council', which emerged as the highest executive authority, and arrogated to itself more extensive powers than had the Zemsky Sobor in the agreement of 4 February 1610. The Decision was primarily concerned with safe-guarding the interests of the men of service, and regulating the relationship between landowner and peasant; it mentioned estates held in service tenure, unencumbered, heritable estates, but the only reference to peasants and house serfs related to decisions to return fugitives and deportees from the Time of Troubles to their previous owners. The contingents, who had been camped for about two months around Moscow, had done little to justify their existence, except to become the most powerful administration in the country. However, when Liapunov incurred the enmity of his Cossack allies, the nobility were unable to protect their leader, and were easily dispersed by Cossack sabres.[1]

Finally, the taxed and untaxed common people became involved in the Time of Troubles, following the participation by the provincial men of service. Originally they had followed the example of the provincial men of service, but subsequently they turned on both the boyars and the nobility. The prime mover behind the rising of the nobility in the south, Prince Gregory Shakovskoy, 'a full-blooded instigator' in the words of a contem-

[1] Liapunov was murdered by the Cossacks on 22 July 1611.

porary chronicler, chose as his ally a man who was not of noble birth. This was Bolotnikov[1] an adventurous and able bondsman, who had been captured by the Tatars, experienced hard labour in a Turkish prison, and had returned to his own country as the second Pretender's agent, while that Pretender was still only a figment of the imagination.

Bolotnikov appealed to the masses, from whence he had emerged, to join the rising, started by the nobility, which he now led. He was joined by poverty-stricken country folk, homeless Cossacks, fugitive peasants and bondsmen from the dregs of society, and turned them against officials, serf-owners and men in positions of power. Supported by detachments of the nobility from the south who had risen, Bolotnikov with his rabble reached Moscow in triumph without once having clashed with the Tsar's troops. However, now that a division appeared between these two incompatible classes, Bolotnikov was not to be thwarted. He arranged for proclamations to be put up throughout Moscow calling upon bondsmen to kill their masters, promising them their wealth and wives, and inciting them to kill and rob the merchants. Thieves and swindlers were promised the rank of boyar, and the position of governor, as well as honour and wealth.

As soon as they saw with whom they were dealing and the type of following enjoyed by Bolotnikov, Prokofy Liapunov and the other noble leaders deserted him and went over to the side of Tsar Vasili Shuisky, and helped his army defeat the rabble. Bolotnikov was killed, but his appeal found a response. Everywhere peasants, bondsmen, settlers from the Volga area, fugitives and other unfortunates rose in favour of the Pretender. This response prolonged the Time of Troubles and changed its character. Hitherto it had been a political struggle, a dispute over a system of government and a state structure. The revolt of the lower classes transformed the Time of Troubles into a social struggle, aimed at the destruction of the upper classes. The success

[1] The chaotic and violent uprising led by Bolotnikov in 1606–7 is considered the first of the great nation-wide peasant rebellions. See James H. Billington, *The Icon and the Axe* (Weidenfeld & Nicolson, 1966) pp. 198–9; and Jerome Blum, *Lord and Peasant in Russia* (Princeton U.P., 1961) pp. 258–9.

of the candidacy of the Pole, Vladislav, was due in part to the participation of the lower classes in the Time of Troubles; more reasonable people only agreed to accept the King's son in order to prevent the 'Tushino brigand', the people's choice, from ascending the throne. The Polish notables said in 1610 at the King's Council that the ordinary people of Muscovy had risen against the boyars and were practically all powerful. Then suddenly a social rift occurred, and every town became a battleground between the upper and lower classes. A contemporary chronicler said that the 'good' well-to-do people decided to serve the King's son rather than be killed by their own serfs, or be in a state of perpetual unrest, while the poor townspeople together with the peasants ran to the 'Tushino brigand' hoping to be quit of all their miseries.

The political aspirations of these classes are completely obscure; indeed it is difficult to attribute to them any capacity for political thought. They had nothing new to contribute, but were looking for a way out of their difficulties; they were looking for personal, and not class, immunities. The bondsmen rebelled in order to escape from bondage and become free Cossacks; the peasants to get rid of both the obligations which tied them to landowners, and taxes; the city dwellers to get rid of urban taxes, and to belong to the service of official classes. Bolotnikov rallied to his call all who sought freedom, honour and wealth. For all these people the real Tsar was the 'Tushino brigand', who, in the opinion of the law-abiding, was the embodiment of disorder and lawlessness.

The sequence of the Time of Troubles has been unfolded, attention must now be given to its principal causes and immediate effects.

Chapter Three

★

A PROPER understanding of the Time of Troubles can only be reached following an analysis of its causes, and the conditions which led to its prolongation. The immediate cause of the Time of Troubles has already been discussed: the violent, mysterious end of the old dynasty followed by its artificial re-creation by a series of Pretenders. The response they evoked was powerful because it fell on fertile ground which had been nurtured carefully, though improvidently, by Ivan the Terrible and Boris Godunov during Tsar Fedor's reign. The nation was troubled and confused by the shameless outrages perpetrated by the *oprichnina*, and the insiduous intrigues of Boris Godunov.

The development of the Time of Troubles revealed the underlying malaise. A fortuitous event, the end of a dynasty was the beginning. Whether forcefully or naturally, the extinction of a family or line is a common occurrence which barely merits attention. But the extinction of a dynasty is quite another matter. In Russia towards the end of the sixteenth century it led to a political and social struggle;[1] starting as a political struggle over the form of government it developed into a struggle between all classes of society. Conflicting political ideas were accompanied by a clash of economic interests. The supporters of the numerous

[1] It is worth mentioning that for two hundred years the Grand Princes of Moscow had tried to establish the system of primogeniture as against the right of the Khan to invest whomever he pleased with the throne. The full acceptance of this principle occurred in the sixteenth and seventeenth centuries, which helps to explain why the end of the old dynasty appeared as such a catastrophe to Russian society.

Tsars and Pretenders who fought for the throne represented many levels of Muscovite society. Each class had its own Tsar or would-be Tsar; and these Tsars or candidates were only symbolic, first of different political aspirations, and second, of the classes who held them. The Time of Troubles was unleashed by the aristo-cratic intrigues of the great boyars who were protesting against the unlimited powers of the new Tsars. Next to become involved were those noblemen who were in military service in Moscow, whose cause was the defence of an officer caste's political freedom against the oligarchic designs of the great boyars. The ordinary provincial noblemen, aspiring to rule the country, emulated the example of the metropolitan nobility, and embroiled themselves in the struggle. The landed classes, unencumbered by service obligations, were attracted by the cause of the ordinary provincial nobility, and rose in the name of anarchy, against any organised system of government to protect their personal privileges.

Each successive phase of the Time of Troubles was accompanied by the intervention of Cossack and Polish bands, outcasts from Muscovy and Poland, from the Don, Dnieper and Vistula regions, who welcomed the unsettled conditions as an opportunity for easy pillage. At the beginning, the boyars tried to unify all classes who were prepared to destroy society in favour of a new system of state organisation; however, their ideas did not conform with the ideas held by other classes. An attempt was then made to avert the catastrophe by finding a figure-head, and artificially restoring a dynasty which had recently perished, a dynasty which alone had successfully checked inter-class hostility, and maintained some form of balance between their different interests.

A Pretender provided the means to escape from a struggle be-tween irreconcilable interests. When this ploy failed, and it was fre-quently attempted, there remained no political union or interest which could have prevented the collapse of society. But society did not collapse: it was the structure of the state which became unstable. Although the political system crumbled, strong national and re-ligious ties were maintained, and in the end they preserved society.

The Cossack and Polish marauders gradually evoked a response from the very people they were in the process of ravaging, and forced a divisive society to unite, not in the name of any particular system, but for the sake of national, religious and civic unity, which were all being threatened. In this way, the Time of Troubles, which had begun and flourished as a result of an internecine social struggle, ended as a battle between the whole of society and forces who were alien and inimical to Russian nationalism, who had intervened in a domestic upheaval.

There were two conditions in particular which sustained the Time of Troubles – Pretenders and social dissension; and both phenomena need further investigation in order to arrive at a proper understanding of the Time of Troubles. Muscovite political theory suffered from the misconception that the state, as a union of peoples, could not belong to anybody except to the nation itself. But the ruler of Muscovy and the peoples of Muscovite Russia believed that the state of Muscovy was the unencumbered estate (*votchina*) of a princely dynasty, from whose property it had developed. In this *manorial dynastic concept of the state* lies one of the basic elements of the Time of Troubles.[1] This misconception was linked to the paucity of, and lack of sophistication in, political ideas which in any event were divorced from reality. It cannot be emphasised too strongly that most people believed that the state of Muscovy was the property of the Sovereign, the family holding of the Kalitas, who had created, expanded and consolidated it over three centuries. In fact, it had already become a union of the Greater Russians, and although the people had a concept of 'the whole Russian land', they failed to equate the people with an entity which was the state. The cohesive elements within the country continued to be subservient to the will and interests of the owner of the land. However, it is necessary to understand that this propertied approach to the state was not part of the dynastic claims of a Sovereign, but was consistent with contemporary political ideology, inherited from the appanage period. In Russia at this time, therefore, there was no concept of the state other than as an estate, the hereditary property of a particular dynasty. Had a typical Muscovite of that time been

[1] For an illuminating discussion of the concept and theory of the state see Michael Cherniavsky, *Tsar and People* (Yale U.P., 1961) pp. 33-45.

told that sovereign power carried with it obligations and responsibilities, and that in ruling his people the Sovereign was serving
the state for the common good, he would have been confused
by the sophisticated complexity of these ideas. As a result the
traditional understanding of the relationship between the
Sovereign and people to the state becomes at least comprehensible.
It was believed that the state of Muscovy in which they lived
belonged to the Sovereign, and not to the Muscovite or Russian
peoples. The inseparable factors were not the state and the people,
but the state and Sovereign of a particular dynasty; it was easier
to imagine a Sovereign without a people than a state without a
Sovereign. This attitude permeated the political life of the people
of Muscovy. People are prepared to support a government so
long as its policies are consistent with their welfare; when, however, they become dissatisfied with the government for acting
in a contrary spirit, they protest. A servant or lodger who has
entered into a mutually satisfactory relationship with an employer
or landlord usually leaves if mistreated. Subjects who rise up against
authority do not leave the state since they consider it their home;
whereas a servant or lodger who is discontented with his employer
or landlord leaves the house which he does not own. The people of
the state of Muscovy reacted like discontented servants or lodgers,
and not like unruly citizens. They frequently criticised their rulers;
but as long as the old dynasty was in existence they did not rebel
against it. The people of Muscovy devised a special type of
political protest: those who were unable to coexist with the
political system did not rebel, but simply left, 'wandered off',
and fled. It was as if the Muscovite felt himself to be a newcomer
in his own country, a transient in a strange house. When life
became too difficult he would consider escaping from his un-
congenial landlord, but would never rebel or try to alter the
system. Thus, the knot which tied together different opinions in
the state of Muscovy was not any consideration of public welfare,
but the representative of a given dynasty, and a viable state system
was held to be possible only under a ruler of this dynasty. Therefore, when this dynasty came to an end, and, as a consequence the
state appeared to belong to nobody, men lost their heads, ceased

to comprehend what and where they were, and were thrown into ferment and anarchy. It was as if they had become anarchists against their will, the result of an undefined obligation which was calamitous but inevitable. Since nobody was to blame, it was necessary to rebel!

The Zemsky Sobor had to choose a Tsar. Because of the novelty of elections the Zemsky Sobor lacked sufficient authority for its actions which were thrown into doubt and caused anxiety. The Zemsky Sobor foresaw that its decision to elect Boris Godunov would be objected to by the people who would say of the electors 'let us stand apart from them because they have appointed a Tsar for themselves'. The document giving effect to the Zemsky Sobor's decision branded those who said this as 'mad and accursed'. A widely distributed pamphlet of 1611 describes how its author had a miraculous vision which revealed that God himself would indicate who was to rule over Russia; a Tsar who was elected by other means would lead to 'there never being another Tsar'. Throughout the whole of the Time of Troubles men were unable to conceive of an elected Tsar; it was believed that he was no Tsar at all, and that the only true, legal Tsar had to be a descendant of Ivan Kalita. Consequently, it was held that the Zemsky Sobor had tried to associate the elected Tsar with the Kalitas by legal devices, genealogical inventions, and rhetorical exaggerations.

Boris Godunov on his election, was solemnly greeted by the clergy and people as a hereditary Tsar 'welcoming him to his estate'; while Vasili Shuisky, who was formally limiting his own power, was described as 'autocrat' in official documents, the term customarily bestowed upon hereditary Muscovite rulers. If the ruling classes propagated such a rigid view, it is no wonder that the masses believed that an elected Tsar was not a political necessity, albeit a sad one, but the negation of the laws of nature. Indeed, an elected Tsar was as incomprehensible as an elected father or mother. It was for this reason, therefore, that the masses were emotionally and intellectually incapable of accepting either Boris Godunov or Vasili Shuisky as their natural Tsar, and still less Vladislav, a Polish prince. These the people considered to be usurpers; whereas anybody, however unknown and tenuously connected to the dynasty, was a sop to their legitimistic qualms, and inspired them with confidence. Indeed, the Time of Troubles came to an end only when a Tsar was found who was related, although distantly, by birth to the extinct dynasty. Tsar Michael was established on the throne not so much because he was the nation's choice, but because he was a nephew of the last Tsar of the old dynasty.

Lack of confidence in a system based on the popular election of a Sovereign contributed in no small measure to the Time of Troubles. Moreover, this lack of confidence stemmed from the ingrained belief that a Sovereign could only be a Sovereign if he was a descendant of a particular dynasty. This inability to comprehend the idea of an elective Tsar was a derivative cause of the Time of Troubles.

Social dissension, one of the outstanding features of the Time of Troubles, has been mentioned above. This dissension was rooted in the tax structure of Muscovy, and was another fundamental cause of the Time of Troubles.

One of the basic precepts of any properly ordered society is that there should be a balance between the rights and obligations of individuals and classes. In the sixteenth century, Muscovy suffered from a heterogeneous conglomeration of social and political attitudes inherited from the past.[1] Neither freedom nor full rights existed, either for individuals or for classes. However, society did not consist of an indistinguishable mass, as in despotic Eastern countries, where equality for all meant the absence of rights for all. Society in Muscovy was fragmented, and divided into classes which had been formed during the appanage period. At this time classes had only a civic connotation based on their economic function, and were distinguishable by their occupations. Now, however, they acquired political characteristics. Special state obligations were imposed on different occupations. Classes as such did not really exist, and the simple division of responsibilities were imposed in official Muscovite terminology on

[1] See for instance Horace W. Dewey, 'Immunities in Old Russia', *Slavic Review* (Dec 1964) pp. 643–59.

ranks. There was no uniformity of state service. For some it meant either more or less power; for others it meant obedience in carrying out instructions. The responsibility for governing belonged only to one class; the rest were either instrumental in fulfilling instructions, serving in military capacities, or being burdened by tax obligations. The inequitable distribution of service obligations due to the state was reflected in social and political inequalities. The lower classes, upon whom the upper classes relied, carried the heaviest obligations which were, of course, unduly burdensome. Even the upper administrative class, who by virtue of state service had the power to command others, never had its political privileges legally confirmed. No legal basis existed for the power wielded by this class, which it had enjoyed from time immemorial according to custom. In general, Muscovite legislation concerned itself, either explicitly or implicitly, with defining and allotting state obligations; however, it neither defined nor guaranteed personal or corporate rights. The position of an individual or group was determined by the type of service performed. The apparent legislative privileges which seem to have conferred corporate rights were, in fact, nothing more than personal exemptions which provided inducements for a proper discharge of a man's duty. Yet even these privileges were not conferred equally on the individual members of a particular class, but depended on the particular situation of individual local communities. Certain urban or rural communities might obtain tax relief or immunities from legal liabilities, but it was not considered necessary to be explicit about rights for the urban and rural population. Even local self-government, where representatives were elected, was based on the same philosophy of obligations and their concomitant individual and general responsibilities. Moreover, as has already been mentioned, local government was the obedient instrument of the central authorities. The rights of individuals or classes generally have some legal basis. In Muscovy, however, the emphasis on individual and corporate state obligations left little room for personal or corporate rights, which were, in fact, sacrificed to the demands of state. As a result, there was a serious discrepancy between private rights and public duties. The threats of external danger, and a lack of individual and social purpose led to an acceptance of this inequitable system. However, the rule of Ivan the Terrible made people increasingly aware of its inherent defects. His arbitrary decisions, senseless executions, banishments and property confiscations evoked reactions, not only from the upper classes, but also from the masses, and provoked 'anguish and hatred against the Tsar throughout the land'; and tentative demands were made for legal protection of person and property from the ruler's caprices and inclinations.

None the less, neither these demands nor the burdens imposed by the state alone could have resulted in such profound internal disturbances had not the dynasty, which had built the state, come to an end. The dynasty itself served as the keystone of the main arch of state; when it disappeared the structure of political relations collapsed altogether. What previously had been patiently endured under a familiar Sovereign now seemed intolerable in his absence. In the writings of Ivan Timofeev there is a parable about a childless widow of a rich and powerful man whose house was plundered by the dead man's servants, who broke away from 'their servile station', and ran amok. Timofeev uses the story of the widow as an analogy for his own country without its natural born Tsar and master.[1]

All classes of society started to make known their own particular demands and ambitions in order to improve their relative situation. The upper classes, however, proceeded to act differently from the rest. They tried to legislate as a class in their own interests and extend their privileges at the expense of others. The lower classes do not seem to have acquired a feeling of unity amongst themselves; equally absent were a desire for privilege, and a determination to lighten the general burden. It was a case of every man for himself, hurrying to escape his rigorous and inequitable state responsibilities, in order either to rise to a more favourable situation, or to acquire someone else's wealth. Observant contemporaries all emphasise that the most noticeable characteristic of the Time of Troubles was the way the very

[1] Ivan Timofeev's views on legitimacy are discussed in Cherniavsky, *Tsar and People*, pp. 53–9.

dregs of society forced their way to the top. Abraham Palitsyn wrote that people wished to rise above their station: serfs wished to become masters, bondsmen wanted to be free, ordinary soldiers aped the boyars, while intelligent people had no ambitions and consequently were 'looked on as of no account' by the self-seekers whom they were frightened to offend. The clash of many conflicting ambitions between, and within, the upper and lower classes led to inevitable and fierce hostilities. These hostilities contributed also to the Time of Troubles, and initiated the next phase. Contemporaries blamed the destruction of the social order on the upper classes, and particularly on the new non-hereditary rulers, although Ivan the Terrible had already set an example with his *oprichnina*. Tsar Boris Godunov was severely strictured for his arrogant intention to reorganise the territorial structure and reform the administration of state. But he was also blamed for rewarding informers by giving them high office. These were men of low birth, ignorant of government business, and so illiterate that they were barely able to sign official documents, which they did painfully by guiding a trembling hand across the paper. This policy earned Tsar Boris Godunov the hatred of able and experienced statesmen. The other non-hereditary rulers who followed Boris Godunov continued this practice. Contemporaries were highly critical of these policies, and recalled with sadness previous hereditary Tsars who knew the appropriate reward for services rendered even by 'men of lowly birth'. Tsar Boris Godunov caused even greater confusion in society by his system of informers which encouraged bondsmen to rise against their masters, and by disgracing the boyars drove hordes of their dependants onto the streets who were then forced to rob and pillage.

Similarly, Tsar Vasili Shuisky sowed the seeds of social confusion with both hands; he first issued a ukase making serfdom even more restrictive, and then proceeded to restrict the masters' powers over their serfs. The upper classes diligently assisted the government in fomenting social confusion. According to Abraham Palitsyn, powerful magnates, and in particular the family and supporters of Boris Godunov in the reign of Tsar Fedor, were obsessed by a terrible passion for enserfment, and a desire to enserf any available individual; and, of course, their example was followed by others. However, there was a famine from 1601–6, and serf-owners became unwilling and unable to feed the serfs whom they had impressed; so they were turned out without proper release documents, and when the hungry serfs went elsewhere, they were persecuted for having run away.[1]

The imprudent actions of government and society, so regrettably nurtured, revealed such a welter of confusion in social relations, as well as such disorder, that with the extinction of the dynasty, it became difficult to rule by accepted government procedure.

A social-political situation was the second contributory reason for the Time of Troubles, which, when allied with the dynastic problem, powerfully, albeit indirectly, perpetuated the Time of Troubles by intensifying the effect of the former, as evidenced by the success of the Pretenders. Therefore, the phenomenon of Pretenders must be added to the reasons mentioned above. The problem of how the idea of Pretenders could arise at all does not involve much national-psychological perception.[2] The mystery surrounding the death of Tsarevich Dimitri resulted in conflicting rumours, with people believing the one that suited them best; above all they wanted a satisfactory outcome so that a Tsarevich could appear and thereby lift the oppressive uncertainty that clouded the future. As always, the people were inclined to believe that evil had failed, that providence had acted as guardian of universal truth, and had provided retribution against evil. The

[1] The situation became so critical that contemporary reports told of people eating grass, tree bark, and even one another. See Jerome Blum, *Lord and Peasant in Russia* (Princeton U.P., 1961) p. 161.

[2] Peasant rebellions were animated by one recurring political ideal: belief in a 'true tsar'. In the seventeenth century there were fourteen serious Pretenders, in the last thirty years of the eighteenth century there were thirteen, and there were even some in the early nineteenth century. The fundamentally conservative nature of the belief in a 'true tsar' may be seen from the fact that each of the major Pretenders gained national support through his ability to serve as a focus for a variety of forces resisting change. See James H. Billington, *The Icon and the Axe* (Weidenfeld & Nicolson, 1966) pp. 198–201.

terrible fate of Tsar Boris Godunov and his family[1] had been, in the opinion of the harassed people, a striking revelation of the eternal Truth of God, and helped to bring about the success of the Pretenders. Morality was supported by an unconscious political instinct, and was, for this reason, acceptable to the masses. Usurpation was a convenient way out of the struggle of irreconcilable interests which appeared at the extinction of the dynasty. Usurpation, therefore, naturally and forcefully united a society in a state of disintegration under a familiar, though counterfeit, structure of authority.

It is possible now to understand the origin of the Time of Troubles. A discontented people heavily burdened by state obligations, which had been barely tolerated under Ivan the Terrible, was further exasperated by Tsar Boris Godunov. The immediate circumstances leading to the Time of Troubles was the extinction of the dynasty, and its artificial resuscitation through the medium of Pretenders.

Fundamentally, however, consideration must be given to the popular attitude concerning the relationship between the old dynasty and the state of Muscovy, an attitude which clearly inhibited the acceptance of the idea of an elected Tsar. Attention must also be paid to the structure of the state with its oppressive taxes and inequitable distribution of obligations which resulted in social discord.

The first of these conditions evoked and sustained the necessity to resurrect the extinct dynasty, and this, of itself, ensured the success of the Pretenders. The second, converted dynastic intrigue into social and political anarchy. Other circumstances, however, also contributed to the development of the Time of Troubles. These were the actions of those who governed after Tsar Fedor; the constitutional aspirations of the boyars which were diametrically opposed to the character of Muscovite supreme power and the popular opinion of that power; the low standard of public morality as described by contemporary observers; sentences of court banishment imposed on the boyars; famine and plague which occurred under Tsar Boris Godunov; provincial agitation,

[1] Boris's brother, Fedor, was murdered, and their mother was strangled.

and the interference of the Cossacks. These were symptoms of the Time of Troubles, not its causes, which flourished, and which in turn created new problems.

The Time of Troubles stands at the watershed between two periods in Russian history, connected to the first by its causes, and to the second by its effects. The Time of Troubles came to an end with the accession of a Tsar who founded a new dynasty: this was the first immediate consequence of the Time of Troubles.

Towards the end of 1611, Muscovy seemed to be disintegrating. The Poles had taken Smolensk; a Polish detachment had burned Moscow, and entrenched itself within the Kremlin walls, which, together with Kitaigorod had been left standing. The Swedes occupied Novgorod, and selected one of their princes as candidate for the throne of Muscovy; in Pskov, a third Pretender, a man called Sidorsk, replaced the murdered second False Dimitri; the first provincial noble force near Moscow was destroyed upon the death of Liapunov. Meanwhile the country had no administration. The Boyar Duma, which had taken power after the downfall of Tsar Vasili Shuisky, dispersed when the Poles took the Kremlin, where some boyars still remained led by Prince Mstislav. Its centre having disintegrated, the country began to break up into constituent parts; nearly every town acted independently or only in conjunction with other towns. The country began to resemble an amorphous, decrepit federation. From the end of 1611 with the exhaustion of all political participants, a religious and nationalist spirit emerged which assisted in the salvation of the ruined country. Archimandrite Dionysus and Abbot Abraham issued proclamations from the Troïtsa Monastery to the people of Nizhni–Novgorod to unite under their *starosta*, a butcher, called Kuzma Minin. Their call was answered by the unemployed and unsalaried, those who had lost their lands, as well as by urban noblemen and sons of boyars. Minin also found a leader for them, Prince Dimitri Pozharsky. In this way a second detachment of noblemen was formed against the Poles. Militarily it was no better than the first, although it was better equipped, due to a full Treasury which had been selflessly collected by the people of

Nizhni–Novgorod and other towns who had joined forces. It took about four months to organise the troops, and six months later they moved towards Moscow, being constantly reinforced *en route* by crowds of men of service who asked to be taken on in return for future land grants. A Cossack detachment under Prince Trubetskoy, the remnant of the first force, was still encamped near Moscow. The detachment of noblemen was far more frightened of the Cossacks than of the Poles. In reply to Prince Trubetskoy's suggestion that they join forces, the noblemen replied 'in no circumstances will we join the Cossacks'. It soon became obvious, however, that nothing could be achieved without the Cossacks, and during the three months that were spent encamped near Moscow nothing significant was achieved.

Although Prince Trubetskoy had in his formation more than forty prominent men of eminent extraction, in fact only two did anything significant, and they were not of the same social background. These were Abraham Palitsyn, a monk, and Kuzma Minin, a butcher. At Prince Dimitri Pozharsky's request, Palitsyn persuaded the Cossacks to support the detachment of noblemen at a critical moment; and Kuzma Minin persuaded Prince Dimitri Pozharsky to let him have three or four companies. With their assistance Kuzma Minin then attacked successfully a small group led by Hetman Khotkevich, who was making for the Kremlin with food for his starving compatriots. This bold action encouraged a detachment of noblemen who forced the Hetman to retreat towards the waiting Cossacks.

In October 1612 the Cossacks took Kitaigorod by storm. But the detachment of noblemen was still trying to decide whether or not to storm the Kremlin; however, the remaining Poles, who from hunger had been driven to cannibalism, then surrendered. Moreover, it was the Cossacks and not the noblemen who finally drove King Sigismund, who was on his way to Moscow to restore it to the Poles from Volokalamsk, and made him turn for home. Once more during the Time of Troubles the noblemen had shown complete incompetence in their chosen professional field, as well as a lack of responsibility to their country.

The leaders of the joint forces, Princes Trubetskoy and

Pozharsky, sent a circular to all towns inviting ecclesiastical leaders and elected representatives from all ranks to Moscow to attend a territorial assembly and elect a Sovereign. At the beginning of 1613 members began to arrive in Moscow. It will be shown later that this was without doubt the first representative assembly in which urban and even rural interests participated. A three-day fast was observed when all the representatives had arrived, so as to cleanse themselves from the sins of the Time of Troubles, before undertaking a task of such importance. At the end of the fast the meeting began.

The first question to be put to the assembly was whether a Tsar was to be elected from any of the foreign royal families; this was firmly rejected. No Polish or Swedish Prince, nor a person of non-Orthodox faith, nor a foreigner could be elected. This eliminated the infant son of Marina, and upset the supporters of Prince Vladislav.

However, the election of a Sovereign of true Russian birth was not easy. Contemporaries draw a very gloomy picture of this session. There was no unanimity; instead, there were serious disagreements. Everybody wanted his own way, and men spoke only for themselves. Some suggested this, others that, and everybody contradicted everybody else. Lists of the great families were examined, but no agreement on any name could be reached, and this was a time-wasting occupation. Noblemen and commoners alike tried to bribe the electors with gifts and promises.

When Michael was elected the electors asked his blessed mother to bless her son on the throne; when she reproached the Muscovites for 'their lack of spirit', they replied that they had been 'sufficiently punished', and that they had at last seen reason and come to an agreement.

The Zemsky Sobor's intrigues, machinations, and dissensions in no way justified the complacent assurances given by the electors. The Zemsky Sobor had split into factions led by different highborn claimants, among whom annals of a later date named the Princes Golitsin, Mstislavsky, Vorotynsky, Trubetskoy and Michael Romanov. It was later said that Prince Pozharsky, a man of humble birth and modest character, coveted the throne, and distributed large bribes. The likeliest candidate was the able and highly born Prince Golitsin, but he was a prisoner in Poland. Prince Mstislavsky declined the nomination; the remainder were nonentities. Muscovy emerged from the horrors of the Time of Troubles without any heroes, and it was men of mediocrity, albeit brave, who had led the country out of its misfortunes. Prince Pozharsky was no Boris Godunov, nor was Michael Romanov a Prince Skopin-Shuisky. The absence of a strong candidate meant that a decision rested on prejudice and intrigue. While the Zemsky Sobor was divided into factions, not knowing whom to elect, petitions favouring Michael began to arrive from noblemen, wealthy merchants, the towns of the Seversky region, and even the Cossacks; in fact it was the Cossacks who were decisive in the choice of Michael.

Seeing the weakness of the nobility the Cossacks ran amok through the Moscow they had liberated, behaved as they wished, and were not in the least afraid of the temporary government of Trubetskoy, Pozharsky and Minin. However, when it came to the election of a Tsar they showed themselves to be true patriots. They decisively opposed the idea of a foreign Tsar, nominated and 'investigated' genuine Russian candidates, the infant son of the Thief of Tushino, and Michael Romanov, whose father, Philaret, had supported both Pretenders, and had been made Metropolitan by the first, and elevated to the Patriarchate by the second in his camp near Moscow.

The Cossacks, who had been the Pretenders' main supporters, naturally wanted either the son of the Thief of Tushino or the son of the Tushino Patriarch on the throne of Muscovy. In fact the son of the Thief of Tushino was nominated, but it was not a serious move, and it was done to please the Cossacks, who did not insist when he was turned down by the Zemsky Sobor. Michael himself was an undistinguished, sixteen-year-old boy, and would have had few pretensions to the throne. Yet both hostile parties, the Cossacks and the noblemen agreed on him. This unexpected coalition had a considerable effect on the Zemsky Sobor. At the height of the argument between the factions a nobleman from

Galicia, where the First Pretender had come from, handed the Zemsky Sobor a written Memorandum which stated that M. F. Romanov was the last real Tsar's nearest kin, and that therefore he should be elected Tsar. None the less, Michael was opposed by many, although he had been considered as a candidate for some time. Patriarch Hermogen suggested that he was a desirable successor to Tsar Vasili Shuisky. But the Galician Memorandum had offended many. Angry voices were heard saying, 'who has brought this document, and from where?' At this stage, a Don Cossack stepped out from the ranks of the electors, went up to the table and placed a written document on it. 'What is this document?' asked Prince Dimitri Pozharsky. 'It concerns the natural born Tsar Michael Fedorovich,' the Cossack replied. And this Cossack more or less decided the matter there and then. 'When the Cossack's document was read, everyone was agreed and of one accord,' wrote a chronicler. Thus was Michael proclaimed Tsar.

However, this was only a nomination by the Zemsky Sobor's delegates. It had to be confirmed by the whole country. Loyal emissaries were sent secretly to every town to find out what people felt, and whom they wished to have as Sovereign of the state of Muscovy. The people seemed to have made up their minds. The emissaries returned to report that everybody, rich and poor alike, were of one mind: they wanted Michael Romanov to be their Tsar, and no one else. This secret investigation, possibly together with much propaganda, was the Zemsky Sobor's way of conducting an electoral plebiscite.

The first Sunday in Lent of the Orthodox calendar, 21 February 1613, was chosen for the decisive election. Every person was given a note with only one name – Michael Fedorovich. Some clergy, together with a boyar, were sent to the Red Square; they had barely time to ask the crowd whom they wanted as Tsar when the Square resounded with cries of 'Michael Fedorovich'.

In this way, Michael's election was organised and confirmed by the Zemsky Sobor, and the people by different methods: pre-election propaganda assisted by numerous Romanov relations, pressure from the Cossacks, a secret national opinion poll, and by acclamation in the Red Square. But these were only successful because the Romanov family had popular support. Michael's victory was due to the popularity of his family, rather than to personal qualities or propaganda. He belonged to a boyar family well-loved in Moscow. The Romanovs were a recent offshoot of the Koshkins, an old boyar family. As early as the reign of the Great Prince, Ivan Kalita, a distinguished person, as a genealogist put it, left 'the lands of Prussia' for Moscow, where he became known as Andrew Ivanovich Kobyla. He became a prominent boyar at court. According to the chronicles, his fifth son, Fedor Koshkin was the founder of the Koshkin line. During the fourteenth and fifteenth centuries this family flourished at court. It was the only untitled boyar family to maintain itself amidst the newly-titled men of service who flocked to the court in Moscow during the second half of the fifteenth century. Amidst the Princes Shuisky, Vorotynsky and Mstislav, the Koshkin family managed to keep in the forefront of the boyars.

At the beginning of the sixteenth century, boyar Roman Yurevich Zakharin occupied an eminent place at court; he was descended from Koshkin's grandson, Zacharias. It was he who became the founder of a new branch of the family, the Romanovs. A son of Roman Zakharin was called Nikita, and he was the brother of the Tsaritsa Anastasia. Moreover, he was remarkable for being the only Muscovite boyar of the sixteenth century who had a good name among the people. His name was commemorated in a popular folk song, which described him as a benevolent mediator between the people and an angry Tsar, Ivan the Terrible. Of Nikita's six sons, the eldest, Fedor was particularly distinguished. He was a kind, gentle boyar, a dandy, who also had an enquiring mind. An Englishman, Jerome Horsey, who was then living in Moscow, wrote in his memoirs that Fedor wanted especially to learn Latin, and that he, Horsey, had compiled a Latin grammar for him writing the Latin words in Russian characters.

The Romanovs' popularity was acquired because of their qualities, and was undoubtedly strengthened by their persecution by Tsar Boris Godunov. Abraham Palitsyn even goes so far as to

include this persecution among the three sins for which God had
punished Russia during the Time of Troubles. Their feud with
Tsar Vasili Shuisky was also taken into account, as were their ties
with the camp at Tushino, which acquired for them the protection of the second False Dimitri, and their popularity with the
Cossacks. In this way the equivocation of the Romanovs during
the Time of Troubles prepared the way for Michael's support
from both sides, from the Zemsky Sobor and the Cossacks. Most
of all, however, Michael was helped during the election by his
family ties with the old dynasty.

During the Time of Troubles the Russian nation was so unsuccessful in its choice of new Tsars that the only safe thing to do
was to choose a person who was somehow connected with the
old ruling family. Tsar Michael was not considered an elective
Tsar; as a nephew of Tsar Fedor, he was held to be a natural and
hereditary Sovereign. Contemporary chronicles clearly state that
Michael was asked to ascend the throne 'because of his family
ties with the Magnificent Tsars'. It was not without reason that
Abraham Palitsyn called Michael 'the chosen of God before birth';
and Ivan Timofeev, in his enumeration of the direct line of
hereditary Tsars, puts Michael immediately after Tsar Fedor,
thereby ignoring Boris Godunov and Vasili Shuisky as well as all
the Pretenders. Indeed, Tsar Michael habitually referred to Ivan
the Terrible in all documents as his grandfather.

It is difficult to know to what extent Michael's election was
helped by a rumour current at the time that Tsar Fedor on his
death-bed verbally promised his throne to another Fedor, his first
cousin and Michael's father.[1] Be that as it may, the noblemen who
supervised the election may have been influenced in Michael's
favour by another consideration they could not afford to disregard. Sheremetiev was supposed to have written to Prince
Golitsin in Poland stating that 'Michael Romanov is young; as
yet he has shown little intelligence, and can be guided by us'.
Sheremetiev knew, of course, that the throne could not prevent
Michael from growing up, and that he would not always be a
youth. None the less, there were already signs that he would

[1] Fedor was Philaret's secular name.

resemble his uncle, Tsar Fedor, that he would be weak both mentally and physically, but kind and gentle, and would not re-create circumstances similar to those endured during the reigns of Ivan the Terrible and Boris Godunov. It was desirable to elect an amenable Tsar, not an able one.

This was how a new dynasty was founded which put an end to the Time of Troubles.

Chapter Four

★

ATTENTION MUST now be paid to the immediate consequences of the Time of Troubles which created the political and intellectual climate through which Tsar Michael had to manœuvre. Fourteen years of turbulence had not passed without leaving their influence on the state. This was apparent from the inception of Tsar Michael's reign. The Time of Troubles had brought about two fundamental changes. First, there had been a complete disruption in the political traditions on which the administration of sixteenth-century Muscovy rested. Second, the Time of Troubles had created relationships between Muscovy and her neighbours such that an even greater proportion of the country's resources had to be devoted to war than in the sixteenth century. From these two changes there emerged a series of new political ideas which received the support of the people, as well as a new set of political realities which determined the course of Russian history in the seventeenth century.

The devastating effect exerted by the Time of Troubles on the people of Muscovy led to the formulation of political ideas which would have been alien to sixteenth-century Russians. This is the sad benefit of a turbulent era: peace and prosperity are exchanged for the acquisition of experience and ideas. As during a storm the leaves on a tree are swept back revealing the trunk, so unsettled periods destroy all façades and reveal what lies behind them. Similarly, people, who had been accustomed to seeing only the obvious, unconsciously realised that they had been suffering from defective vision. This realisation is the beginning of political thinking.

National revolution creates the most favourable conditions for stimulating political thought; and this explains the wealth of political ideas which invariably are formulated during, and immediately after, national disturbances. The wealth of ideas which enriched Muscovy during the Time of Troubles completely altered traditional attitudes towards Sovereign and state, which have been discussed elsewhere. Sixteenth-century Muscovites considered that their Sovereign was less the guardian of the national weal than the proprietor of the territory which was the state of Muscovy; and although they had lived on this land from time immemorial they none the less considered themselves to be strangers, the result of a political accident.

The Sovereign's personal will was the mainspring of the state's existence, and his personal or dynastic interests were its only *raison d'être*. The state and the people were of no account: only the Sovereign mattered. These opinions were altered by the Time of Troubles. During these difficult years the people of Muscovy had more than once to choose a Tsar for themselves; at other times the country remained without a Sovereign, and the nation was left to its own devices. From the inception of the seventeenth century the people of Muscovy lived through situations, and witnessed events, which would have been considered impossible and beyond the comprehension of the generations immediately preceding their own. Seventeenth-century Muscovites saw Tsars fall who did not have the support of the nation; whereas the nation without a Sovereign did not disintegrate but, rallying its forces, elected a new Tsar for itself. That events such as these could have occurred would have been completely beyond the understanding of sixteenth-century Muscovites.

Hitherto, the concept of a state had been equated with the physical existence of a Tsar, and therefore was embodied in his person. During the Time of Troubles, however, when either there was no Tsar, or his identity was uncertain, it became possible, for the first time, to think in terms of abstractions. During the Time of Troubles, documents referred to the *State of Muscovy*, which was a concept intelligible to all as something which existed in fact, independent of the existence of Tsars. Indeed, the concept of a state as an entity distinct from that of the person of the ruler became equated with the idea of a nation. Hence, documents from the Time of Troubles refer increasingly to 'the people of the State of Muscovy' instead of to 'the Lord Tsar and Grand Prince of All Rus'. That the Muscovites found it difficult to get accustomed to the idea of an elected Tsar has already been mentioned. The cause of the difficulty, however, was the lack of appreciation that, if so required, the will of the people could be considered a sufficient source of supreme legal authority. That this was not appreciated was because the concept of the people as a political force did not exist.

All the Tsar's subjects were considered his *kholops*, his manorial servants, or simply as *orphans*, parentless and homeless, who lived on his land. Given this situation what political power could emanate from *kholops* and *orphans*, and how could it become the source of the divinely appointed authority of the Lord's Anointed? The Time of Troubles administered the first and most serious attack on the stagnant political beliefs of the time, and drew attention to the gulf that existed between the urgent and devastating problems created by events, and the nation's intellectual capacity to solve them.

During the Time of Troubles, the community was left very much to its own devices, and had, perforce, to act independently and deliberately. During this period it was realised that neither the community nor the individual was a political accident, as the Muscovites had previously regarded themselves, nor were they interlopers or temporary residents of a particular state; rather, it was the dynasty itself which was a political accident. In the fifteen-year period following Tsar Fedor's death there had been four unsuccessful attempts to found a new dynasty, and success was only achieved at the fifth attempt.

The Time of Troubles evoked a political force which acted sometimes in concert with, and sometimes independently of, the authority of the Sovereign: the will of the people. It was expressed in the declarations of the Zemsky Sobor, at popular rallies in Moscow which, for instance, acclaimed Vasili Shuiski as Tsar, and during meetings of urban representatives who declared themselves against the Thief of Tushino and the Poles. As a result, the concept of a proprietor-Tsar gradually lost its validity, and a new political idea was superimposed on the old idea of a Sovereign elected by the people. In this way the basis of what constituted a state became acceptable politically: *a Sovereign, the State,* and *the Nation.* Whereas previously it was held that no state or nation could exist apart from the Sovereign, and men could believe in a Sovereign without a nation rather than in a state without a Sovereign, so now experience led people to believe that, for a time at least, a state could exist without a Sovereign, but that neither Sovereign nor state could manage without a nation. The same conclusions were reached, using different arguments, by contemporary observers of the Time of Troubles, such as Abraham Palitsyn, and Ivan Timofeev, as well as other anonymous chroniclers. These writers believed that the misfortunes were due entirely to the absence of determined and vigorous efforts by society to unite against the powers who were intent on the destruction of law and order. When Boris Godunov had successfully breached existing legal foundations, and had destroyed the edifice which maintained law and order 'all the well-born were struck dumb as fish, and there was no strength in Israel, no one brave enough to tell the mighty the truth'. 'For this national apathy,' wrote Palitsyn, 'for the thoughtless silence of the whole land, the country was punished.'

It is none the less true that at the Zemsky Sobor of 1613, amidst general confusion and dissension, the ancient, customary idea of a 'natural' Tsar triumphed; it was to this concept that Michael owed his election. This retrograde movement was a sign that the nation, represented at the Zemsky Sobor by elected delegates, was unable to adjust to the new situation, and preferred to return to the system that had obtained previously, to 'the thoughtless silence of the whole land'. Time and again, as will be shown elsewhere, a newly-found national awareness was stifled by the country's extremely conservative historical development.

None the less, during the Time of Troubles more than one section of society believed, sometimes forcefully, in an active and well-organised national participation in the affairs of the country. The essence and significance of this idea can be brought into proper perspective by realising the difficulty with which new political ideas find acceptance. With this in mind, it must be obvious that such a fundamental change in attitudes could not be without effect. Indeed, during the Time of Troubles more than one event was influenced by these new ideas.

In 1609 one Sunbulov, a rebellious nobleman from Ryazan, gathered together a crowd in a square in Moscow, and demanded that Tsar Vasili Shuisky should be deposed. However, there were people in the crowd who answered the insurgents, saying: 'Although the Tsar has offended you we cannot depose him without the great boyars and *a council of all the people.*' It follows that a Zemsky Sobor led by the boyars was considered the only institution authorised to decide such an important matter. Subsequent governments recognised and supported the competence of national representatives to decide fundamental political questions. Tsar Vasili Shuisky himself expressed the self-same idea which the more reasonable citizens had raised in the Moscow square. When Sunbulov and his fellow-insurgents had broken into the Palace they were met by the Tsar who said: 'Wherefore, accursed ones, do you come to me with so much noise and impudence? If you wish to kill me, I am ready to die; if you wish to drive me from the throne it were not lawful for you so to do until there be gathered all the great boyars and the men of all ranks. Whatsoever petition be agreed upon by all the land, to it will I submit.'

The idea also occurred to those who were frequently invited to participate in the decision-making processes of state, that a properly constituted assembly not only had the right to choose a Tsar, but also on occasion, to judge him. Indeed, this idea was officially enunciated on behalf of Tsar Vasili Shuisky's government. A Prince Gregory Volkonsky was sent to Poland at the beginning of Tsar Vasili Shuisky's reign in order to justify to the Polish Government the extermination of the First Pretender and the massacre of his Polish adherents. In accordance with his official instructions, Prince Gregory Volkonsky told the King and his magnates that the people of Muscovy 'gave all a fair hearing, and they had the right to punish evil and sacriligious acts such as those which had been perpetrated by any Tsar as the False Dimitri'. Prince Gregory Volkonsky was even more daring when he began to develop his ideas on punishment to the Polish government and stated that 'although the Tsarevich Dimitri had appeared as a natural born and true Sovereign, if he were not wanted then it would be impossible to force him onto the country'. This view would have seemed like political heresy even to that great liberal of the sixteenth century, Prince Andrew Kurbsky.[1]

The events of the Time of Troubles were not only responsible for creating conditions in which new political ideas could flourish, but they also altered the structure of the ruling class with whose assistance the Tsars of the old dynasty had ruled. This change also contributed to the successful acceptance of the new ideas. The old Muscovite Sovereigns had ruled with the assistance of the boyar class, who had been well organised, permeated with an aristocratic spirit, and inured to power. The political importance of the boyar class was not derived from any law, but rested solely on ancient custom, which was justified by two considerations. First, an article in the Sudebnik[2] of 1550 assured the Boyar Duma of legislative authority, in which the boyars played a preponderant

---

[1] Prince Andrew Kurbsky, a boyar and general, deserted to the Polish–Lithuanian forces on 30 April 1564. From Wolmar Kurbsky wrote the first of his five letters to the Tsar, Ivan the Terrible. This correspondence is one of the most important historical documents of sixteenth-century Russia. See *The Correspondence between Prince A. M. Kurbsky and Tsar Ivan IV of Russia 1564–1579*, ed. and trans. J. L. I. Fennell (Cambridge U.P., 1955); also *Kurbsky's History of Ivan IV*, ed. and trans. J. L. I. Fennell (Cambridge U.P., 1965). This History describes events in the reign of Ivan IV from 1533 to the early 1570s, and is the first attempt at an historical monograph in Russian. For a brief summary of the arguments developed by Prince Kurbsky see Thornton Anderson, *Russian Political Thought* (Cornell U.P., 1967) pp. 91–5.

[2] A Sudebnik was a code of laws. Article 98 of the 1550 Sudebnik provided that new laws would be enacted only 'by announcement of the Sovereign and the decision of all the boyars'. See Thornton Anderson, *Russian Political Thought*, p. 86. On the 1550 Sudebnik see Horace W. Dewey, 'The 1550 Sudebnik as an Instrument of Reform', *Jahrbücher für Geschichte Osteuropas*, n.s., x (Jul 1962) 161–80.

role. Second, the system of precedence (*mestnichestvo*) subordinated all official government positions to genealogical relationships thereby increasing the upward mobility of the boyar class. The first of these considerations upheld the boyars as the supreme administrative institution, while the second upheld them as the ruling class.

In Tsar Michael's reign one of the leading representatives of the boyar class, Prince Vorotynsky, defined the ancient predominant situation of the boyars as follows: 'Previous Tsars may have disgraced us, but they never removed from us the right to govern; we held privileges of every sort and were never dishonoured by men of low birth.' Prince Vorotynsky wished to say that though individual boyars suffered from the caprices of the ancient Tsars, the boyars as a class were never deprived of their significant role in government, nor were they ever superseded by men of low birth. By this statement Prince Vorotynsky formulated clearly the administrative strength of the boyars as a class, and their political weakness as individuals. The disintegration of this class, which had enjoyed every privilege, started at the beginning of the Time of Troubles, although the original impetus was given by Boris Godunov. The ranks of the boyars, built on a system of precedence, were being depleted; the vacancies were filled by men of obscure origin who were unaccustomed to power, and lacked any family tradition and political skills. The Tsars of the new dynasty were no longer surrounded by the serried ranks of the old aristocratic families who previously had enjoyed high office. Under Tsars Michael and Alexis there were no longer any Princes Kurbsky, Kholmsky, Mikulinsky, or Penkovy; and the Princes Mstislavsky and Vorotynsky were to disappear not long after. In a list of boyars and members of the Duma for 1627 a Prince Shuisky is mentioned, but no Prince Golitsin. Moreover, not one of the old untitled Muscovite boyar families was named: the Tychkovs and Cheliadnins, the Saburovs and Godunovs are not mentioned at all. Instead, the representatives of recent families are named, about whom little or nothing was known in the sixteenth century: the Streshnevs, Naryshkins, Miloslavskys, Lopukhins, Boborykins, Yazykovs, Chaadaevs,

Chirikovs, Tolstoys, Khitrys and others. Mention must be made of the remaining titled families: the Princes Prozorovsky, Mosalky, Dolgoruky and Urussov; as far as other titled families were concerned only a few, insignificant representatives remained.

This change in the structure of the ruling class was noticed both by foreigners and by Russians. At the beginning of Tsar Michael's reign the remnants of the original Muscovite boyar class complained that during the Time of Troubles many low-born men had risen to the top, including merchant-traders, and young boyar children of low extraction, who had originated from the provincial nobility, and on whom successive Tsars and Pretenders had bestowed high service ranks creating them *okolnichi*, duma noblemen and secretaries. In 1615 the Polish plenipotentiaries who were negotiating with the Muscovite envoys taunted the Muscovite boyars by saying that Muscovy was indeed paying for her sins since ordinary peasants, priests' children, and butchers, all quite unqualified to manage important provincial and national affairs, had been advanced over the heads of the great princely and boyar families. Under the new dynasty these political novices moved increasingly into positions of power, penetrating even the Boyar Duma, which became even less representative of the boyars as a class. These political novices were the precursors and predecessors of the eighteenth-century state officials who were so aptly described by their contemporaries as 'occasional men', i.e. men appointed for a particular occasion. As has been seen, therefore, the Sovereigns of the old dynasty ruled with the assistance of an entire ruling class, whereas seventeenth-century Sovereigns began to rule with the help of individuals who had risen to the top quite fortuitously. These newcomers, unhampered by tradition, became the exponents and protagonists of new political ideas which had developed during the Time of Troubles.

Having permeated the ruling circles, these newcomers made a complete nonsense of considerations of precedence. The system of precedence had created a tightly-knit closed circle of individuals and families, which during disputes over precedence created tangled professional and genealogical relationships. Two officials, in doubt as to their relative standing, would decide who took precedence over whom by referring to relationships at third, fourth and fifth remove; should one of the disputants through an oversight or inadvertently make a mistake, the honour of the other would be offended, and all the distant relatives would interfere in order to clear themselves of this attack upon their dignity! On one occasion Prince D. M. Pozharsky was appointed to a post at a lower grade than B. Saltykov. The discussion at a meeting of the Boyar Duma went as follows: the Pozharsky family and those of Prince Romodanovsky all descended from the Princes of Starodub; but the Romodanovskys were inferior to M. Saltykov, and M. Saltykov was inferior to B. Saltykov; therefore Prince Pozharsky was inferior to B. Saltykov.

The newcomers broke this chain of precedence, and penetrated the ranks of the old nobility either through direct services or through services they had professed to have rendered to the country. The system of precedence, however, took no account of advancement through individual effort. What did services rendered to the state matter? What did matter was ancestry, which was determined by reference to genealogical tables and lists of the service nobility. The system of precedence did indeed recognise a higher allegiance – ancestral honour! The newcomers, however, were not prepared to forgo any merit or reward, and no period in the history of Muscovy was so congested with quarrels over precedence as the reign of Tsar Michael. The brunt of clashes over precedence fell on Prince B. M. Pozharsky, one of the most distinguished newcomers. It was to no purpose that he had cleared Muscovy of Cossack thieves and Polish traitors; that he had been promoted from courtier to boyar and acquired 'a great estate in perpetuity'; the boyars took every opportunity to quarrel with him saying that the Pozharskys were not a first-class family, and that the only positions they had ever occupied had been as town governors or village councillors. When he was given precedence over Prince Saltykov, Prince Pozharsky raised no objections whatever but merely ignored the Tsar's ukase and the Boyars' decree dealing with the matter. Whereupon Prince Saltykov brought an action against him for having impugned his honour, and the saviour of the country was forced to 'yield pride of place' to his insignificant, but better-born rival. Prince Pozharsky was degraded, and was led on foot, under escort, from the Tsar's palace to his rival's house. Following this incident, Tatishchev, who had treated Prince Pozharsky with excessive deference, was flogged to death, and his head delivered to Prince Pozharsky's home.

The decline of the system of precedence, which began as soon as service was opposed to lineage, proceeded to deny lineage as any basis for position. A high rank, conferred for meritorious service, was not rewarded with a patent of nobility. A fundamental rule of the system of precedence was that the Sovereign could bestow money or land in service tenure, but not ancestral honours. As disputes over precedence grew fiercer, and few appointments went unchallenged, the government found a way of eliminating the harm that was being done: it began to appoint men who were disinterested in problems of precedence to posts hitherto only occupied by men whose names were inscribed on the lists of the well-born. However, no sooner were the newcomers appointed to these posts than they assumed that they too were to be included in the lists of the well-born, and began to argue among themselves, and even with those who were on the lists, about precedence. As a result the government often deprived them of rank, imprisoned them and had them knouted. This was not sufficient and on one occasion, during a meeting of the Boyar Duma, a secretary and a boyar became so incensed at having to consider interminable claims over precedence that they beat up one quarrelsome fellow saying: 'You do not petition us about the matter in hand; know then what is due to you.'

The Time of Troubles completely changed the standing of service families, raising some, degrading others. Although service ranks were of no account in the system of precedence, and did not carry any aristocratic connotation, a man of good birth was, in fact, usually promoted to a higher rank as an indication of his aristocratic background. Men with less eminent backgrounds who achieved high rank during the Time of Troubles tried to argue that this attribute of good birth was proof that they too were well-born; moreover they stated that in granting them high rank the Sovereign had also created noblemen. This idea, which was the very negation of the system of precedence, was typical of the new political ideas which had arisen during the Time of Troubles. It was pithily expressed by a poor official in an argument with a well-born rival: *'both great and small men live by favour of the Sovereign'*. It was this notion which finally resulted in the abolition of the system of precedence in 1682, and later, in 1722, formed the basis for Peter the Great's Table of Ranks, which completed the absorption of the old boyar aristocracy by the newer bureaucracy of court officials.

The new political ideas which stemmed from the Time of Troubles had a direct and significant effect upon the administrative structure under the new dynasty. The actual changes were a continuation and development of trends which had appeared during the Time of Troubles. As was stated above, the mutual relationship between the Sovereign and the boyar class had been established by custom, and not by law, and depended on chance, or arbitrary arrangements; and that between the Muscovite Tsar-proprietor and the boyar-servitors within the manor it was possible to have a dialogue about the conditions of service, though not about the system for ruling the manor.

When the old dynasty came to an end these manorial relations were transferred to a political basis: a Tsar elected by his own people as well as by foreigners could no longer consider the state as his own patrimony; furthermore, the boyar-officials wished to participate in its administration. Already during the Time of Troubles the boyars and great magnates had, on more than one occasion, attempted to create a system based on a written agreement with the Tsar, or in other words, on a system based upon the formal limitation of the supreme power. One such attempt was made at the accession of Tsar Vasili Shuisky, and another during the negotiations with Michael Saltykov on 4 February 1610. All these efforts were a consequence of the break in the Muscovite political tradition caused by the extinction of the old dynasty. The boyars were not prepared to desist in their aims even when the Time of Troubles had ended. On the contrary, the political agitation which had stemmed from the days of Ivan the

Terrible and Boris Godunov merely led to an intensification of the boyars' demands.

When Tsar Michael's father, the Metropolitan Philaret, heard that an electoral council was being called in Moscow, he wrote from his Polish prison to say that a restoration of the powers of previous Tsars would expose the country to ultimate ruin, and that he would prefer to die in a Polish prison rather than witness, as a free man, such a calamity. He did not suspect, on returning to his own country where he was to share with his son the power and title of Tsar, that he would have to change his constitutional views. As it was, an event occurred at Michael's accession which echoed Philaret's original views, and which is mentioned by a number of different witnesses. A chronicler from Pskov, who wrote an intelligent account of the Time of Troubles and Tsar Michael's election, described with indignation how, during the latter event, the boyars who were masters of Russia, neither respected nor feared the Tsar. The chronicler went on to say that on his accession to the throne the boyars forced Michael to swear by the cross that he would not impose the death sentence for whatever reason on any boyar or magnate, but would only imprison them.

A more detailed account is given by a writer of a later generation, Gregory Kotoshikhin, who was Secretary at the Office of Foreign Affairs. Kotoshikhin fled from Russia in 1664 to Sweden where he wrote an account of the State of Muscovy. That he left Moscow nineteen years after Tsar Alexis' accession would enable him to recall, either through personal memories or contemporary accounts, the whole of Tsar Michael's reign. Kotoshikhin included Tsar Michael among the Sovereigns of the old dynasty who did not accede to the throne by right of hereditary succession but through popular election. Kotoshikhin maintained that all these elected Tsars came to the throne with limited powers. The obligations they assumed, or in Kotoshikhin's words 'for which signatures were taken', consisted of an undertaking that 'they would not be cruel and unmerciful, that they would not punish without a trial or proof of guilt, and that they would deliberate on all matters with the boyars and members of the Duma, without whose knowledge they would do nothing either overtly or secretly'. Kotoshikhin added that although Tsar Michael styled himself as Autocrat, he could, in fact, do nothing without the boyars' advice.

This point of view is maintained in eighteenth-century accounts. An eighteenth-century Russian historian, Tatishchev, who used documents which are no longer extant, wrote a short historical–political treatise *On Sovereigns* in 1730, in which he stated that although Tsar Michael's election to the throne was 'in order with the people', i.e. his election was legal, he was forced to sign a document similar to the one Tsar Vasili Shuisky had to sign, which forbade him to take any initiative, and forced him to rely entirely upon the boyars.

Tatishchev wrote another treatise, however, doubting the existence of such a charter. He arrived at this conclusion after examining the writings of a Swede called Stralenberg[1] who lived in Moscow during the reign of Peter the Great. Tatishchev stated that he had no evidence, either oral or documentary, that such a charter had ever existed. In his description of Russia, which was published in 1730, Stralenberg relied upon the recollections and stories of the seventeenth century which were still fresh in Russian minds. Based upon these recollections he learned that Tsar Michael, on his accession, had to give a written and verbal undertaking that he would safeguard and cherish the Orthodox faith, forget old family differences and disputes, make no new laws or alter old ones on his own initiative, and make no declaration of war or negotiate peace. He also had to agree to try all

---

[1] Philip J. T. von Stralenberg wrote that Michael had

I. To maintain and protect the Religion of the country. II. To forget and forgive all that had happened to His Father, and not to think further in any Personal Enmity whatsoever. III. To make no new Laws nor to alter the old ones. In high and weighty causes not to judge for Himself, but according to the Law, by ordinary and usual Process. IV. To make no peace, nor war, with his Neighbours, of His own Head. V. To resign His Estates to His family, or to incorporate them with those belonging to the Crown, as Proof of His Justice and to avoid all Manner of Process with private Persons.

See Philip J. T. von Stralenberg, *An historico-geographical description of the north and eastern parts of Europe and Asia* (London, 1738).

important legal cases according to the established law, and bequeath his estates to his relatives or add them to existing state land. No trace of a document sealed by Tsar Michael has ever been found, and no mention is made in contemporary documents of any of the obligations he is purported to have assumed.

In the extensive Charter of Establishment by which the Zemsky Sobor confirmed Michael's election, and in the document which embodies their oath of allegiance, there are three points which can help in estimating the power of the new Tsar. First, he was elected to the throne because he was the nephew of Fedor, last Tsar of the old dynasty. Second, the Zemsky Sobor took an oath of allegiance not only to the Tsar they had elected, but also to the future Tsaritsa and their progeny, thereby admitting that they had elected if not a hereditary, then a potentially hereditary, Sovereign. Third, the men of service promised 'to behave without contradiction in all affairs of state', and obey the Tsar's officials.

It is possible to doubt whether any restrictions had been placed upon Tsar Michael's powers. However, contemporaries of Tsar Michael believed that his powers were restricted, and this belief was held for more than a century. Some obscure hints in the literature of the time might assist in uncovering the truth. The most reliable source is a Pskov chronicle which dealt with the problem before it had time to grow into fiction or political legend. For the first five years of Tsar Michael's reign, and before his father had returned from captivity, in Poland the leading courtiers were Romanovs, Saltykovs, Cherkasskys, Sitskys, Lykovs, and Sheremetievs. The great boyar families of Golitsin, Kurakin and Vorotynsky were still in existence, and it was these families who had concluded an accession agreement with their fellow-boyar, Vasili Shuisky, and who later, led by Mstislavsky, had recognised as Tsar, the son of the Polish King, Vladislav. These families represented a real danger to the Romanovs, and could have stirred up a new Time of Troubles had they been denied their share of privilege. Even Michael's supporters might have found power, obtained fortuitously or by intrigue, a bone of contention over which at the right time they were quite prepared to quarrel. It was therefore in the interest of both factions to prevent a repetition of the misery which had been experienced when the Tsar or his favourite treated the boyars as slaves.

Behind the scenes of the Zemsky Sobor a secret agreement was made, which resembled the one broken by Boris Godunov, and respected by Vasili Shuisky. The object of this secret agreement was to safeguard the boyars against an arbitrary Tsar. However, it was not worth obtaining a commitment from the weak-willed Michael with a compact of this nature, particularly in view of the existence of his mother, the Abbess Martha, a confirmed intriguer who dominated her son.

The difficulty that has to be resolved is whether or not a written commitment was obtained from Tsar Michael. The chronicle makes no mention of such a document and refers only to the oath. The early years of Michael's reign would seem to confirm that a written document did exist. During these years it was quite apparent, and frequently repeated, that the ruling classes lorded it over the whole country, 'disdaining' their Sovereign, who was forced to ignore their activities. It is not difficult to understand why a written commitment was never published, if it existed at all. From Tsar Vasili Shuisky's time an elected Tsar with restricted powers was considered to be a partisan Sovereign, an instrument of the boyar oligarchy. It would therefore have been particularly awkward to display an excessively partisan document in front of the Zemsky Sobor. An implicit limitation of power of whatever nature did not prevent Tsar Michael from retaining the title of *Autocrat* or even from using it in the seal which he had specially made.

The highest administrative body had, by the tacit agreement of the ruling class, been the Boyar Duma. During Tsar Michael's reign the Boyar Duma no longer remained the sole repository of power which it frequently began to share with the Zemsky Sobor. The extent to which the structure of the Zemsky Sobor changed at this time to become a genuine representative assembly will be discussed below.

Tsar Michael's reign represented a period of intense activity for the government in conjunction with the Zemsky Sobor. Neither before nor after this reign did the elected representatives of all ranks within the State of Muscovy meet so frequently. The government was forced to call on the assistance of the country to consider practically every important issue of domestic and foreign policy. Contemporary documents reveal that during Tsar Michael's reign the Zemsky Sobor was convened ten times. Even more important, the Zemsky Sobor emerged during this period with greater powers than it had ever previously enjoyed, and greater authority than it had been granted by the Saltykov declaration. During Michael's reign the Zemsky Sobor discussed problems which previously had been the prerogative of the Boyar Duma. For instance, it considered matters of immediate state concern, such as taxation, which in accordance with the Saltykov declaration was to be dealt with jointly by Tsar and Boyar Duma. By so doing, the Zemsky Sobor was participating directly in affairs until recently the prerogative of the Boyar Duma. From the beginning of his reign, the Zemsky Sobor enjoyed a very special relationship with the Tsar. Until the newly-elected Tsar had arrived in Moscow the Zemsky Sobor acted as a provisional government, headed by the boyars, and ruled over the whole country. None the less, the Zemsky Sobor did not dictate terms to the Tsar. During the discussions the Tsar, or more specifically his advisers, began to sound more and more peremptory: 'You have appointed us Tsar, it was not of Our seeking. We have been elected Sovereign by the whole country; you have sworn fealty to Us of your own free will; you have promised to serve and uphold Us and be as one with Us. Notwithstanding these promises there are killings and pillage and other disorders, which do offend Us. Expunge these offences and restore order.' Sometimes similar speeches were made to the representatives 'with great anger and tears'. 'You have yourselves elected Us Tsar; give Us the means withal to rule, and do not burden Us unnecessarily with troubles.'

A subtle administrative change took place: the body which had elected the Tsar in 1613 became an executive instrument responsible to the very man on whom it had conferred power. A consideration of the situation described above leads to the assertion that Tsar Michael's powers were restricted by obligations similar to those imposed upon Tsar Vasili Shuisky. In other words, a restraint was exercised by the Boyar Duma. After the Time of Troubles, however, when it became imperative to re-establish order, the Boyar Duma found that it was incapable of dealing with current problems, and was forced, *nolens volens*, to turn to the Zemsky Sobor. The direct participation in the administration of the country enjoyed by the elected representatives could not be stopped with the ending of the Time of Troubles. The very fact that the Tsar had been chosen by the will of the people, as represented by their elected representatives, compelled him to continue ruling through the Zemsky Sobor. If the Boyar Duma restricted the powers of the Tsar, then the Zemsky Sobor, in assisting the Boyar Duma, tended to act as a check upon its powers. In this way, influenced by the exigencies and political ideas which had emerged during the Time of Troubles, and which continued to exist after this period had ended, the Tsar's power became both complex and restricted. There were two considerations which determined its content and its basis.

The Tsar's power derived directly from the electoral process, although it was camouflaged as a result of the political fiction which maintained that power was inherited as part of the Sovereign's birthright. Tacitly, power was exercised, by agreement with the upper administrative classes, through the Boyar Duma. As far as the nation was concerned, however, all official documents referred to an Autocratic power; but this was used in a titular, rather than in a juridical sense, which did not prevent even Tsar Vasili Shuisky from referring to himself in official documents as Autocrat. The concept of power as enjoyed by the new Tsar was therefore ambiguous. Hereditary, but elective in origin, it was restricted but autocratic in form. Supreme power, on this basis could be neither lasting nor conclusive. Indeed, it could only be maintained so long as the mutually inconsistent interests and relationships created and confused by the Time of Troubles, continued, and which was a purely fortuitous occurrence in the history of Muscovy. Gradually, the Sovereign consolidated his powers, and its heterogeneous elements were rationalised. The political obligations assumed by Tsar Michael were, as far as can be judged now, respected throughout his reign. Although his father, having returned from captivity and been made Patriarch and co-equal Tsar,[1] governed with a firm hand, and did not always consult the boyars, none the less for as long as he lived government was carried on through the combined efforts of both Sovereigns and with the help of the Boyar Duma and Zemsky Sobor.

The dual authority was a compromise between family and political considerations. It was difficult for a parent to become his son's subject; however, the son needed a permanent regency, which was naturally entrusted to his father with the title of co-Tsar. The concept of a unified authority, was, in this context, justified with the help of dialectics. Which Tsar took precedence over the other was decided in the following manner: 'Whatever the Tsar might be, the same will be his father; their Sovereign power is indivisible.'

Tsar Michael died intestate, and indeed he could not have done otherwise. Under the new dynasty the state ceased to be the Tsar's personal patrimony, so that the old judicial system of handing over power by testament was no longer valid. Moreover, no law of succession existed. Therefore, Tsar Alexis, like his father, acceded to the throne by a method which was totally different from the one used by the Tsars of the old dynasty. Alexis acquired power as it were, through two legal processes: succession without testament, and election by the Zemsky Sobor.

In 1613 the nation had sworn allegiance to Michael and his progeny. Tsar Alexis ascended the throne as his father's successor, and contemporaries referred to him as the 'natural' or hereditary Tsar. The Zemsky Sobor had been convened three times to elect a Tsar (Fedor, Boris Godunov and Michael). Election by council

---

[1] Temporal power was shared between Tsar Michael and his father, Philaret, Patriarch of Moscow. Philaret assumed the title Great Sovereign which hitherto had belonged to the Tsar alone. All State papers were issued in both their names. It must however be realised that this relationship was personal and practical rather than formal and theoretical. See J. L. H. Keep, 'The Regime of Philaret (1619–1633)', *Slavonic and East European Review*, XXXVIII (Jun, 1960) pp. 334–60.

instead of nomination by testament became the acknowledged procedure, and for a fourth time recourse was had to election by council, thereby transforming an accidental occurrence into an accepted convention. Indeed, election by council ensured the legal succession which had been established by oath at the Zemsky Sobor of 1613.

Contemporaries testified that the Zemsky Sobor was duly convened at Tsar Michael's death, and that his sixteen-year-old son was elected. In his descriptions of the State of Muscovy, Olearius,[1] envoy from Holstein, wrote that Tsar Alexis acceded to the throne by the unanimous vote of all the boyars, magnates and people. Gregory Kotoshikhin also quite clearly recalled that a council had been convened. As soon as Tsar Michael had died 'the clergy, boyars, noblemen, sons of boyars, leading merchants, commercial men of all ranks, and the populace of the capital' were, as in 1613, questioned on their choice for Tsar. However, Tsar Alexis did not assume the obligations agreed to by his father. Kotoshikhin noted that 'the present Tsar was elected to the throne but he gave no undertakings similar to those given by the previous Tsar. He was not asked to do this because he had the reputation of being a peaceful man, which is why he signs as *Autocrat* and rules the country according to his will.'[2] The Zemsky Sobor could not limit the Sovereign's power; only the boyars could extract an undertaking of this nature from Tsar Alexis. Though it is clear that a repetition of the secret understanding of 1613 was thought possible in 1645, it was deemed to be un-

[1] Adam Olearius (1603–71). His real name was Adam Oelschlager. He served as secretary to successive embassies sent by the Duke of Holstein to the Tsar of Russia and the Shah of Persia to negotiate trade agreements. Olearius' *Travels* cannot be ignored since this book contributed largely to the formulation of the European image of Muscovy. See *The Travels of Olearius in Seventeenth-century Russia*, trans. and ed. Samuel H. Baron (Stanford U.P., 1967). This edition is the first English translation since 1669.

[2] Historians are generally agreed that Tsar Alexis was a kind, gentle and humane Tsar. However, the epithet 'most gentle' was a translation of the Byzantine *galenotetos*, and did not form part of official diplomatic style! Moreover Tsar Alexis was the Autocrat, and in fact, had an explosive temper. See Michael Cherniavsky, *Tsar and People* (Yale U.P., 1961) pp. 61–4.

necessary. Tsar Alexis justified the boyars' confidence in not extracting undertakings from him at his accession. Tsar Alexis refrained from abusing his power, and lived in peace with the boyar class. Moreover, the younger generation of boyars with whom Tsar Alexis had to deal no longer manifested the political tendencies which had emerged from the Time of Troubles, and which had culminated in the agreement of 1613. The political obligations assumed by the new dynasty at its inception were being eroded, and Tsar Alexis tried to convert the election by council into a symbolic ceremony.

Eighteen months before he died (1 September 1674), the Tsar solemnly *proclaimed to the people* his eldest son as the successor to the throne. The proclamation was made in the Red Square in Moscow in the presence of the high clergy, members of the Duma, and foreigners living in Moscow. This solemn presentation of the heir to the people was the form used by the Tsar to transmit his authority to his son after his death. This single act legalised Fedor's accession, to whom, as Tsar Michael's grandson, the oath of allegiance given by the Zemsky Sobor in 1613 did not apply. This unprecedented method of transmitting supreme authority in the presence of the people, and their tacit consent, was not consolidated, since Fedor died childless. A real election had to take place because circumstances made it necessary, even though the procedure was simplified. When Tsar Fedor died in April 1682, the Patriarch, archbishops and boyars who had assembled to pay their last respects to their late Sovereign, met in another part of the Palace to debate which of Tsar Alexis' other two sons should be Tsar. It was agreed that the people, with no distinction as to rank, should choose. People of all ranks were ordered to assemble in the palace forecourt, and the Patriarch made a speech in which the question was put. Unanimity was not obtained, but the majority decided they wanted the younger, ten-year-old Peter, instead of the older Ivan who was weak-minded. The Patriarch put the identical question to the clergy and boyars who were standing with him, and they too chose Peter. The Patriarch then went towards Peter and formally blessed him as Tsar. This detailed description will show how simply an affair of great importance was dealt with. The gathering did not consist of elected representatives, nor was a Zemsky Sobor held. The crowd in front of the Palace who took the decision happened to be in the Kremlin because of the death of Tsar Fedor. Moreover, it is obvious that the people who shared in the decision-making process with the Patriarch did not have any understanding of law, of councils, or indeed of what constituted a State; possibly they considered such ideas could be dispensed with on such an occasion.

The Streltsy, however, at the instigation of a faction who favoured the Tsarevna Sophia, reacted against the decision taken by the authorities, and after the revolt of 15 May 1682, forced them to convene a parody of a council to elect both Tsareviches to the throne. In the proclamation issued by this secondary revolutionary gathering it is stated 'that all ranks in the country petitioned for the sake of appeasement, that the two brothers be proclaimed Tsars on the throne, and that both of them rule as Autocrats'.[1]

The changes that were effected in the power structure during the first three reigns of the new dynasty, and the results produced by these changes after the death of Tsar Fedor have been discussed above. The century had opened with the ruling classes evincing concern over the evolution of fundamental laws, and the establishment of a constitutional framework for the exercise of power; the century closed leaving the country without any fundamental laws, without a defined administrative structure, and even without a law of succession to the throne. Incapable of making a law dealing with the succession, men resorted to court intrigue, to symbolic ritual, to spurious Zemsky Sobors, and finally, to armed riot. Yet the boyars never wholly abandoned their political traditions.

Towards the end of 1681 a discussion took place concerning the abolition of the system of precedence, which would have led to the political destruction of the boyars; as a result they made a

---

[1] Details of the events of 15 May 1682 and the role of the Streltsy can be found in C. Bickford O'Brien, *Russia under Two Tsars 1682–1689* (University of California Press, 1952) pp. 24–7.

concerted and surreptitious effort to retrieve their position. Realising that their power base in the central government was crumbling, they tried to establish themselves in the provinces. They planned to divide the country into large regions which would include formerly independent kingdoms. Surviving members of the great magnates of Muscovy were to be appointed in *perpetuity* as irremovable viceroys (*namestniks*) to govern these regions. This effectively would have created plenipotentiary local governors who would, as it were, become 'boyars and Princes' of the Tsardoms of Kazan, Siberia, etc. Tsar Fedor had already given his approval to this plan of aristocratic administrative decentralisation; however, the Patriarch, to whom the plan had been submitted for approval, completely destroyed it by pointing out the dangers inherent to the country as a whole.

One of the most important effects of the Time of Troubles had been to change the structure and significance of the Zemsky Sobor. Sixteenth-century councils were attended only by officials representing the central and provincial governments. The Zemsky Sobors of 1598 and 1605 were, however, already being attended by the elected representatives of the ordinary or common people. The Time of Troubles created conditions in which the elected representatives had a numerical preponderance over the officials, which gave the Zemsky Sobors characteristics of a truly representative assembly.

Circumstances forced the community to participate directly in public affairs, which the government encouraged by exhortations to stand firm for the Orthodox faith. Pamphlets dealing with current affairs, spiced with a touch of the miraculous, were solemnly read to all those assembled in the council chamber. Words, hitherto unfamiliar, were incorporated into phrases which were commonly used to express new ideas: '*council of all the land*', '*the common council of all the land*', '*gathering of all the people*', '*the united assembly of the local communities*'. The idea most commonly accepted was that the Sovereign should be elected by '*a council of the whole land*', and it was expanded even further to embrace everything dealing with domestic affairs. It was considered necessary to appoint 'a strong general council' to deal with every domestic issue, and to this end the towns organised meetings in order to choose '*the best men*' among them from all ranks. As the country became divided over the rivalry for the throne between Vasili Shuisky and the second False Dimitri, men started to remember the miseries endured during the appanage period, with the result that the concept of a united and integrated state came into vogue. This in turn led to the decision that nothing of any importance could be achieved without the elected representatives of all ranks. A mission to Sigismund in 1610, led by Metropolitan Philaret and Prince V. V. Golitsin, was accompanied by more than 1,000 elected representatives from all ranks. Similarly, on his march towards Moscow, Prince Pozharsky summoned representatives from all ranks to attend upon him at his camp. It was considered desirable that every transaction of national importance should be taken, whenever possible, in the presence of the country's elected representatives, who could then testify that decisions had been arrived at honestly and openly, and not by any secret or tortuous agreement which would mitigate against the national interest, as had decisions taken by Malyuta Skuratov, Boris Godunov and even Vasili Shuisky. It was realised at last that these secret agreements had been the cause of miseries which had afflicted the whole country. In this way, tentative experiments led to the development of the elective composition of the Zemsky Sobor, even before the convocation of the electoral council of 1613, which was the first authentic attempt at national representation.

Having rid Moscow of the Poles, the boyars and leaders of the second levy summoned delegates from the 'best and most intelligent' men of all ranks to attend a general council to elect a Sovereign; included in this summons were urban and rural representatives, merchants and manufacturers from the provincial towns, as well as peasants. These groups had not been represented at the Zemsky Sobors of the sixteenth century. The leaders of the second levy wished to give practical effect to the ideas which had arisen during the Time of Troubles dealing with 'pan-national councils', or 'universal councils', the expression used in contemporary documents. The change in composition was accompanied by a change in the Zemsky Sobor's relative importance.

During the sixteenth century the government convened an official council to find men who would be responsible for giving effect to council agreements or ukases emanating from the Tsar. In a proclamation circulated through the towns the leaders of the second levy pointed out that a country without a Sovereign could never be properly organised. Mention has already been made of the electoral council of 1613 which, having completed its task of electing a Tsar, immediately converted itself into an administrative commission. By order, and at the instigation of the newly elected-Tsar, it then proceeded to adopt a number of preliminary measures to deal with the reorganisation of the country, until such time as a permanent government might be formed.

In 1619 it was decided to summon to Moscow elected representatives, 'wise and good men', as they were called, from all ranks to consider the reorganisation of the state, who could state what wrongs, injustices and injuries had been suffered by their communities. Having listened to their petitions dealing with needs, damages, and complaints of every kind, the Tsar was, together with his father the Patriarch, 'to see that everything was put right'. In this way, through the presentation of petitions, a type of legislative initiative was entrusted to the delegation, although the Tsar reserved the right to decide which policy was to be adopted. From being an instrument of the nation's will, the Zemsky Sobor was transformed into an assembly which voiced public grievances and aspirations. An examination elsewhere of the events of the seventeenth century will reveal that the subsequent structure, activity and fate of the Zemsky Sobor was determined by the two functional changes discussed above.[1]

The effects of the Time of Troubles, together with new political ideas, a new structure of the ruling class, a revision in the powers of the Sovereign, and alterations in the character of the Zemsky Sobor, all augured well for a favourable development of state and society, and provided the new dynasty with a spiritual and political

[1] See J. L. H. Keep, 'The Decline of the Zemsky Sobor', *Slavonic and East European Review*, XXXVI (1957) 100–22, and Maxime Kovalevsky, *Modern Customs and Ancient Laws of Russia* (London, 1891) ch. 5.

dynamic never enjoyed by the old dynasty. Unfortunately, there are dangers inherent in abrupt intellectual and structural changes: can a new situation be dealt with without creating a further series of problems? The Time of Troubles had indeed created a break in political traditions and customs, but the creation of new traditions and customs having the confidence of the people, is a function of time. It was this lack of confidence, for instance, in the changes effected towards the end of the seventeenth century in the powers of the Sovereign, that presented a serious threat to the stability of the state of Muscovy. There were, of course, other consequences of the Time of Troubles which were equally harmful.

The violence engendered by the Time of Troubles had destroyed both the economy of the country and the self-confidence of the people. The country was completely ruined. Foreigners who arrived in Moscow in 1615 soon after Tsar Michael's accession painted a terrible picture of devastated and deserted villages, and settlements with abandoned huts containing the corpses of soldiers. The stench forced the winter travellers to sleep outside in freezing temperatures. Those who had survived the Time of Troubles simply wandered about; all semblance of law and order had collapsed, and relations between people were in chaos. Powerful and continuous efforts had to be made to restore order, to collect the scattered populace, resettle them in their previous locations, and force them to adopt the daily habits they had abandoned during the Time of Troubles.

Some documents dating from Tsar Michael's reign have been preserved. These were primarily district lists of the men of service, the tenths (*desyatins*), and the cadastral registers which illustrate the economic situation of the service landowners and peasant population. They describe the economic chaos that was prevalent in the country and among the people during the first reign of the new dynasty. Most noticeable was the change in the composition of the rural peasant population who provided the state with its main sources of income.

The cadastral registers of the sixteenth century divided the peasants into two classes based on their holdings: there were the peasants proper, and there were the landless peasants, the *bobili*.[1] The latter were also peasants, except that they were poorer, and either cultivated smaller plots than other peasants or owned no land at all, and, in fact, only owned the homestead which they occupied. During the sixteenth century there were more peasants than *bobili*; however, the cadastral registers of Tsar Michael's reign show that after the Time of Troubles, the situation was reversed.

In 1622, on land belonging to the rural men of service, there were in the districts of Beleev, Mtsensk and Elets 1,187 peasants and 2,563 *bobili*. It follows, therefore, that the Time of Troubles had forced a significant number of peasants either to give up their land entirely, or to accept a reduction in the size of their holding. Furthermore, the increase in the number of *bobili* was a sign that land was being increasingly abandoned. In the district of Ryazan, for instance, in 1616, the ratio of waste land to cultivated land was 22 : 1. This was not exceptional. Abraham Palitsyn, an efficient monasterial landlord who was well acquainted with the country's economic situation, confirmed, somewhat quaintly, the extent to which land had simply been abandoned. He wrote that notwithstanding the three consecutive harvest failures in the reign of Tsar Boris Godunov, many people had vast quantities of stale grain, that the threshing floors were overflowing with straw and hay, and that this fed the people throughout the fourteen years of the Time of Troubles, during which 'no ploughing, sowing or reaping took place because of the threat of the sword'. This information indicates that agriculture was well developed before the Time of Troubles, but that during this period harvests were insufficient, and agriculture in a state of decline. The disruption in agriculture together with the changes brought about in the economic situation of the rural population seriously affected private landholding, and in particular the economic situation of the provincial nobility. Some examples based on the *tenths* of 1622, when the effects of the Time of Troubles were becoming noticeable, will serve as an illustration.

[1] See Jerome Blum, *Lord and Peasant in Russia* (Princeton U.P., 1961) pp. 240–2; and A. Miller, *Essai sur l'Histoire des Institutions Agraires de la Russie Centrale du XVIe au XVIIIe siècles* (Paris, 1926) pp. 141–6.

The efficiency of the service class depended on the profit extracted from its properties, and on the number and comparative affluence of the peasants who lived on the *votchina* and *pomestie* estates. A few noblemen owned their estates outright, but the majority lived on the incomes derived from their estates held in service tenure. Thus in the district of Beleev, one-quarter of all land held by the rural nobility was held outright, in Tulsk a little more than one-fifth, in Mtsensk one-seventeenth, in Elets one-157th, and in Tver among the wealthiest provincial noblemen, one-quarter.

The estates held in service tenure by the rural nobility were generally small and sparsely populated. An average estate held in service tenure in the district of Tula comprised 135 *desyatin*[1] of arable land, in Elets 124 *desyatin*, in Beleev 150 *desyatin*, and in Mtsensk 68 *desyatin*. There were in these four districts two tax-paying agricultural labourers, whether peasants or *bobili*, to every 120 *desyatin* of land held in service tenure, or one agricultural labourer to every 60 *desyatin*. It must not be assumed that all this land was tilled by the peasants and *bobili*; only a small portion was worked, and not all of that was under cultivation. In the district of Tver there was a well-to-do nobleman who owned 900 *desyatin* of *votchina* and *pomestie* land of which only 95 *desyatin* was cultivated. Of the 95 *desyatin* 20 was cultivated by the domestic serfs, while the remaining 75 *desyatin* was leased to 28 peasant and *bobili* families who lived on 19 homesteads. This meant each household had about 46 *desyatin* attached to it. Peasant tillage on a large scale was comparatively rare.

In the district of Elets, and the other southern districts already mentioned, there were many landless noblemen, noblemen with only one farm, noblemen who owned land but no peasants and *bobili*, and noblemen who only owned manor houses without land. For instance, in the district of Elets there was a total of 878 noblemen and boyars' children; of these 133 owned no land, and 296 either owned one farm or just a manor house. Some noblemen abandoned their estates, and joined the Cossacks, or became serfs under contract to a boyar, or became monasterial servants,

[1] One *desyatin* equals 2·7 acres.

or simply 'lay about in taverns'. The greater the decline in service land ownership the greater the necessity to increase the monetary salaries payable to this class in order to make its members fit to serve. Salary increases led to an increase in land taxes which were levied on the peasants. Because the taxes were assessed according to the area of tilled land, the peasants, who were unable to bear the ever increasing tax burdens, reduced the dimensions of tilled land in order to pay less. Consequently, the Treasury became trapped in a vicious circle.

Finally, the government's domestic problems were exacerbated by a change in national attitudes. The new dynasty had to deal with a society which was totally different from the one ruled over by the previous Tsars. The anxieties which stemmed from the Time of Troubles had a deleterious influence on the political development of the people. From the accession of Tsar Michael, and throughout the seventeenth century, each class was endlessly complaining about its misfortunes, its impoverishment and ruin, and about the abuses of power. Although at the time people had remained silent, now they were forever discussing their sufferings. Dissatisfaction developed steadily throughout the century, until towards the end it came to dominate the attitude of the people.

The people emerged from the turbulence of the Time of Troubles angrier than they had ever been before. They had quite lost that political passivity which had so amazed foreigners in the sixteenth century, and they were no longer a passive, obedient, instrument in the hands of the government.

This change manifested itself in a phenomenon which was new in the history of Muscovy: the seventeenth century was a century of national uprisings. That this was so was quite unexpected, given that they occurred under Tsars whose personal qualities and manner of ruling seem least of all to have justified them.

Chapter Five

★

THE EFFECT the Time of Troubles had on internal development and on society has been discussed in an earlier chapter. What influence however, did the Time of Troubles have on foreign affairs?

The country's international position changed considerably as a result of the Time of Troubles, and became extremely complicated. For one hundred and fifty years the old dynasty had consistently pursued an expansionist policy, slowly but determinedly acquiring territory, and bringing remoter parts of the country under its influence. New problems appeared with the political unification of Greater Russia.

Concurrent with the incorporation of the remaining independent territories into Muscovy the Great Prince Ivan III[1] declared during his war with Poland, that a united greater Russia would not lay down her arms until she regained every piece of Russian territory which had been seized by her neighbours, and its people had been reunited. His grandson, Tsar Ivan the Terrible, tried to extend the borders of the Russian nation to its natural geographic boundary at the edge of the Russian plain which was then occupied by hostile tribes. Two problems in foreign policy arose as a result: *how to unify politically all the Russian peoples, and how to extend the country's frontiers to the edge of the Russian plain.*

Neither was resolved by the old dynasty, even though some success was achieved. Ivan the Terrible's father and grandfather regained the provinces of Smolensk and Seversk, thereby

[1] For details of Ivan III's policies see Ian Grey, *Ivan III and the Unification of Russia* (English U.P., 1964) pp. 88–95 and pp. 116–42.

penetrating as far as the Dnieper. Ivan the Terrible at first turned in the opposite direction, seized the middle and lower Volga regions, and extended his eastern frontier to the Urals and the Caspian.[1] His subsequent move towards the west was less successful.[2] He hoped to capture Livonia, thereby extending his borders to the eastern shores of the Baltic, and provide a natural boundary; but he failed to control the length of the Western Dvina. During the war with Batory[3] he even lost control of the ancient Russian towns on the Gulf of Finland and Lake Ladoga: Yam (Yamburg), Konopri, Korela (Keksholm) and Ivangorod. After the Swedish war of 1590–5, Tsar Fedor, Ivan the Terrible's son, regained these towns, and established a foothold on the Gulf of Finland in the region of Votski.[4] During the Time of Troubles, Muscovy for the second time lost the western positions it had occupied in the sixteenth century. The Poles seized the regions of Smolensk and Seversk, severed Moscow from the Dnieper, while the Swedes drove the Russians from the shores of the Baltic. In 1617, by the Treaty of Stolbovo,[5] the first Tsar of the new dynasty ceded to Sweden the towns mentioned above, as well as Oreshok (Schlusselberg), and in 1618 by the Agreement of Dulino he had to relinquish Smolensk and Seversk to the Poles. Once again Muscovy had to retreat from her cherished western boundaries.

[1] Details of the conquest of Kazan in 1551–2 can be found in Ian Grey, *Ivan the Terrible* (Hodder & Stoughton, 1964) pp. 92–102; and Alton S. Donnelly, *The Russian Conquest of Bashkiria 1552–1740* (Yale U.P., 1968) pp. 12–20.

[2] Ivan the Terrible's determination to recover Russian lands in the west and revive Muscovite trade with the west through the Baltic is discussed in T. S. Willan, *The Early History of the Muscovy Company 1553–1607* (Manchester U.P., 1956) pp. 11–14; in Grey, *Ivan the Terrible*, pp. 126–37; Thomas Esper, 'Russia and the Baltic 1494–1558', *Slavic Review* (Sep 1966) pp. 458–74.

[3] Steven Batory, a Hungarian by birth, was a national hero in Hungary and Transylvania as a result of his struggle against the Emperor Maximillian. Batory was elected to the throne of Poland–Lithuania by the Polish gentry on 14 December 1575. See Grey, *Ivan the Terrible*, pp. 215–28.

[4] Nevertheless Narva remained under Swedish control, thereby denying Russia an outlet on the Baltic Sea.

[5] Russia also had to pay an indemnity to Sweden. However, Russia did recover Novgorod, and Philip of Sweden, Gustav Adolphus' brother, formally dropped his claim to the throne of Russia.

The new dynasty began badly: it not only abandoned the old dynasty's foreign policy, but it lost many of the gains it had inherited. Moreover, the country's international position deteriorated due to the contempt her neighbours showed her during the Time of Troubles. In 1612 Muscovite noblemen wrote a circular which was distributed throughout the towns saying 'the State of Muscovy is harassed from all sides by enemies; neighbouring countries believe we have fallen into degradation and shame'. The new dynasty had to subject the country to even greater efforts in order to regain what had been lost; this was its responsibility and the basis of its power. From its inception the new dynasty had to fight a series of wars to defend what was theirs or regain what had been lost. The national effort was intensified even further when wars of defence turned, in spite of the politicians, into wars of offence, and a continuation of the previous dynasty's policy of unification; it was a struggle also over land which had never belonged to Muscovy. The Eastern European situation was such that Muscovy was unable to recover from her first unsuccessful efforts and initiate new preparations for war.

In 1654 Little Russia rose up against Poland, and placed herself under the protection of Moscow. This embroiled Muscovy in a new war with Poland, which in turn created a new problem, that of Little Russia, which complicated even further the relations between Moscow and Poland over Smolensk and Seversk. The problem of Little Russia was fundamental to Muscovite foreign policy during the second half of the seventeenth century.

It now becomes imperative to consider the history of Western Russia, although this will be limited to an explanation of the background to the problem of Little Russia. The problem stemmed from an event which revealed the difficulties.

In 1648 Bogdan Khmelnitsky,[1] a commander of Little Russian

---

[1] Bogdan Khmelnitsky had been a faithful Polish subject. However, in 1647 a Polish nobleman abducted and subsequently married Khmelnitsky's mistress. Unable to obtain satisfaction from the Polish courts Khmelnitsky made his way to Zaporozhie, and was soon proclaimed Hetman of the Zaporozhian Cossacks. See C. Bickford O'Brien, *Muscovy and the Ukraine* (University of California Press, 1967) pp. 12–20.

regulars, led a rising of Zaporozhie Cossacks against the Poles. He was supported by the peasantry of Little Russia, who had rebelled against their Polish and Polonised Russian masters. Other registered Cossacks joined Bogdan Khmelnitsky, who by now commanded a large force, and within five or six months they had mastered practically the whole of Little Russia. What was behind this movement of 1648? What was the *Retch Pospolita*? What part did Little Russia play in it? How did Polish magnates come to be in Little Russia? Where did the Little Russian Cossacks come from? Why did the Ukrainian peasantry join them in the rebellion?

The reunification of Western Russia was the most difficult problem facing Muscovite foreign policy in the seventeenth century.[1] It was a problem which stemmed essentially from the political agreement between the Polish landowners and the Grand Prince Jagiello of Lithuania towards the end of the fourteenth century. This agreement, the Privilege of 1386, provided Jagiello with the Kingdom of Poland and the land of the Polish Princess Yadviga. The Privilege was one of mutual self-interest. Jagiello having become King and converted to Catholicism together with his people, hoped that the Pope would support him against the dangerous Teutonic knights.[2] The Poles calculated that through Jagiello they would be able to control the wealth and forces of Lithuania, and particularly Western Russia, Volynia, Podolia and the Ukraine.

In this way the neighbouring countries of Poland and Lithuania became united dynastically. It was an artificial union of two alien and even hostile states, a diplomatic intrigue based on mutual misunderstanding, rather than a political act based on unity of common interests. Nevertheless, this event fundamentally altered the situation of Western Russia. Its subjugation by Lithuanian Princes was accompanied by the subjection of

[1] See L. R. Lewitter, 'Poland, the Ukraine and Russia in the Seventeenth Century', *Slavonic Review*, vol. 27, no. 68 (Dec 1948) pp. 157–71, and no. 69 (May 1949) pp. 414–29.

[2] On his conversion to Roman Catholicism Jagiello took the name of Vladislav II.

Lithuania to Russian influence. At the beginning of the fifteenth century, those Russian regions which became part of Lithuania, Volynia, Podolia, Kiev, Seversk, Smolensk and others, exceeded the rest of Lithuania in size and population. Ethnically, and culturally this Lithuanian–Russian principality was more Russian than Lithuanian.[1] The Russian language, law, customs and religion had been known among the pagan, semi-barbarous Lithuanians for nearly one hundred years.

The cultural assimilation of the united peoples influenced predominantly by the more developed Russians was so successful that after three or four generations, towards the beginning of the sixteenth century, a fusion of Lithuania and Western Russia might have been expected. However, after the unification of Poland and Lithuania Russian influence was replaced by an all-pervading Polish influence.

The *sejm* or diet, which was concerned with general problems affecting both states, was particularly influential. Lithuanian and Russian magnates mingled with Polish magnates at the *sejm*, and became acquainted with their political ideas and organisation. On the other hand, Polish influence was also felt in Lithuania–Russia through the Charters of the Lithuanian Grand Princes, which were called *privileyi*, and which established similar laws, class structure and administration as in Poland. Thus, Polish influence substantially altered the legal structure and shape of society in the Russian regions which were absorbed into the Lithuanian principality.

The Russian princes who held these regions, as their forefathers of the eleventh and twelfth centuries had done by right of succession, were now obliged to submit to the Lithuanian Grand

[1] Oswald P. Backus has assessed the impact of minority peoples upon Russian institutions and ideas, and has provided an invaluable guide to the political, religious and economic organisation of Lithuania. See Oswald P. Backus, *Motives of West Russian Nobles in Deserting Lithuania for Moscow 1377–1514* (University of Kansas Press, 1957). See also Oswald P. Backus, 'The Problem of Unity in the Polish-Lithuanian State', *Slavic Review* (Sep 1963) pp. 411–31 and 450–5; Oscar Halecki, 'Why was Poland Partitioned', *Slavic Review* (Sep 1963) pp. 432–41; Joseph Jakstas, 'How firm was the Polish Lithuanian Federation?', *Slavic Review* (Sep 1963) pp. 442–9.

Prince, to serve him loyally, and pay tribute from their domains. In return they were allowed to hold their domains in hereditary tenure, or sometimes as temporary owners for 'as long as the Sovereign wishes'. This destroyed the hereditary system of tenure of the Russian Princes. At the beginning of the sixteenth century they became men of service, owning domains, and together with powerful Russian boyars and Lithuanian noblemen formed a land-owning aristocracy, similar to the one in Poland, although more influential.

The members of this aristocracy, the *pani*, were the Grand Prince of Lithuania's administrative council or *rada*, which, of course, increased their influence.[1] A Privilege issued by the Grand Prince Alexander in 1492 stated that Lithuanian Sovereigns would not have anything to do with other countries without the consent of the administrative council: they could not promulgate laws, alter existing ones, dispose of state taxes or revenues, nor could they make official appointments.[2] The King recognised the binding nature of the administrative council's decisions, and even when he disagreed would accept their view 'for the sake of himself and the common weal'.

Lithuania followed the Polish example and introduced the same type of administrative positions (*uryadi*) which in time were held for life. These were the offices of *hetman*, commander-in-chief, *kantsler*, keeper of the Seal, two *nodskarbi*, ministers of finance, a *zemski*, a supervisor of public revenues and expenditure, and a *nadvorni*, a court chamberlain; governors of provinces which previously had been ruled by Russian Princes in agreement with the popular assemblies (*veche*) were called *voevodas*. Under them came the *kashtelyani*, town prefects, and *starosti povetov*, district wardens; districts were administrative circumscriptions into which all provinces were divided. In this way the central and provincial administration of Lithuania–Russia resembled the Polish system and acquired an aristocratic structure.

[1] For the powers of the *rada*, and the predominance of Catholic Lithuanians in the *rada* see Backus, *Motives of West Russian Nobles in Deserting Lithuania for Moscow 1377–1514*, pp. 8–9.

[2] For details of the Privilege of 1492, ibid. pp. 42–5.

Privileges which were conferred on provinces, as well as Privileges which covered districts and smaller circumscriptions, established similar attitudes and class privileges to those which obtained in Poland. The Diet of Grodno of 1413 which confirmed the unification of Poland and Lithuania, passed a decree which said that Lithuanian boyars who became Catholics were to enjoy the same rights and privileges as the Polish gentry.[1] A Privilege of Casimir in 1447 extended these rights to the nobility of Ortho-dox persuasion, and gave the Lithuanian–Russian landowners an equal status with the Poles as far as heritable properties and land held in service tenure were concerned.[2] They were also exempted from taxes and state responsibilities, with the exception of some trivial ones, which were retained for symbolic reasons rather than financial advantage as a mark of citizenship. Peasants were re-moved from the Grand Prince's jurisdiction and were subjected to their masters' jurisdiction. Furthermore, Casimir's Privilege forbade the movement of peasants from the lands of private owners to the Grand Princes and vice versa. These prohibitions laid the foundation for enserfment in the Lithuanian Principality, in the same way as in Poland, where serfdom dated from the fourteenth century. In the matter of rights and liberties, the general and local privileges gradually placed the Lithuanian–Russian nobility on an equal footing with the Polish gentry. They acquired the status of a ruling class in the Principality with vast powers over the peasants living on their lands, and were influential in legislation, the dispensation of justice, and general administration.

The position of the Lithuanian–Russian nobility was strengthened further in the sixteenth century by the legislative Code of the Lithuanian Principality, known then as the Lithuanian State. Sigismund I laid the basis of this Code when he issued his Statute of 1529.[3] This first Statute was frequently revised and supplemented to conform with Polish legislation. Polish legal

[1] Ibid. pp. 37–8.

[2] For details of the Privilege of 1447, ibid. pp. 40–3.

[3] For details of this collection of laws see Michael Hrushevsky, *A History of Ukraine* (Yale U.P., 1941) pp. 169–72.

influence on the Statute was fundamental, and was merged with medieval Russian legal customs which had survived in Lithuanian Russia since the Russian *Pravda*.[1]

The final version of the Lithuanian Statute was published by Sigismund III in 1588 in Russian. The second Statute which was confirmed by the Diet of Vilna in 1566 was responsible for introducing minor diets into the Lithuanian Principality similar to those which existed in Poland; these met in every district to choose local judges for the district courts, and also to elect two representatives for the general diet.

The Diet of Grodno created the Lithuanian Diet which originally had consisted only of Lithuanian Princes and noblemen. The privileged position of the predominantly Catholic and non-Orthodox Lithuanian nobility, however, caused the Russian regions which had been united with Lithuania to take advantage of a feud which developed between the descendants of Gedinim[2] on the death of Vitovt in 1430,[3] to rebel against the Lithuanian government. As a result, Russian princes and noblemen won for themselves the same privileges as the Lithuanians, and during the middle of the fifteenth century they were represented at the Diet which had become a general Diet. But the Diet still retained its aristocratic character: from the Russian districts only noblemen were personally summoned and had a decisive voice. Under Sigismund I, in the first half of the sixteenth century, the Russian gentry were involved in a violent struggle with their own aristocracy which resulted in individual summonses to the general Diets. The Statute of 1566 stated that the Russian–Lithuanian gentry could be represented as were their equals in Poland. As far as the question of the continuation of Russian–Lithuanian union was concerned the Diet favoured an eternal union with Poland. When in 1569 the Lublin Decree fused the diets of Russian

[1] For an English translation of the first Russian code of laws known as the *Pravda Russkaya*, see George Vernadsky, *Medieval Russian Laws* (Columbia U.P. 1947) pp. 26–56.

[2] Gedinim (1316–41).

[3] Vitovt, Grand Duke of Lithuania 1392–1430. See Backus, *Motives of West Russian Nobles in Deserting Lithuania for Moscow 1377–1514*, p. 51.

Lithuania and Poland, the gentry received the same political privileges as the Poles.

The increased privilege of the nobility in the Principality was accompanied by a decline of the ancient towns of Western Russia. In ancient Kievan Rus provinces consisted of districts with their small towns; these came under the authority of the popular assemblies of the oldest towns. As official positions were allocated among members of the aristocracy, so towns were divorced from their districts. The assembly was replaced by a *voevoda* nominated by the Grand Prince together with the other officials. The provincial administration was replaced by the Crown. At the same time land hitherto devoted to the common use of towns was distributed by the Grand Prince to private owners in return for compulsory military service. The service landowners, the boyars and *zemiani*,[1] who previously had been part of the urban community were now divorced from the commercial urban population because of their privileged gentry status; moreover, they began to leave the towns in order to settle on their estates and land given to them for good service. The old districts which had been governed by Assemblies were gradually broken up and transformed into hereditary estates belonging to Princes and noblemen. Deserted towns stood isolated among foreign, and often hostile, landowners, who had plundered the ancient districts. The Assembly remained confined within the town walls and could not reach the outlying land; while the Grand Prince's officers, the *voevodas*, *kashtelyani* and *starostas* oppressed the townspeople.

In an attempt to save the towns of Western Russia from decline, the Polish–Lithuanian rulers gave them municipal self-government based on the German *Magdeburg Law*, which had come to Poland in the thirteenth and fourteenth centuries together with German settlers who poured into Polish towns.[2] During the fourteenth

---

[1] This was the name given to boyars from Volynia.

[2] Germans who settled in Poland were governed by German Law. German municipal law was granted to Polish and Russian cities in Poland because of fiscal advantages which accrued to the kings. There were several variations of the German municipal codes, the most popular in Poland being the Magdeburg

century this system of self-government was introduced to the towns of Galicia, which had been joined to Poland by Casimir the Great in 1340. After the middle of the fifteenth century *Magdeburg Law* spread throughout other towns of Western Russia.[1] Under *Magdeburg Law* the commercial classes received certain trading privileges and exemptions from certain fiscal obligations; they were also freed from the jurisdiction of the *voevodas* and other government officials.[2]

Magdeburg Law provided for towns to be administered by two councils or boards; the first was the *lava*, whose members were presided over by a *voit* (from the German Vogt)[3] appointed by the King, and, the second was the *rada*, whose councillors were chosen by the townspeople presided over by a *burmistr* who dealt with industry, trade, public services and order.

The political influence of Poland in Lithuania led to the Polish system being introduced into Russian Lithuania. As a result, during the fifteenth and first half of the sixteenth centuries, the dynastic union of both countries was somehow maintained and renewed by new agreements. At times, these countries were ruled by separate Sovereigns, at others they were united under one Sovereign. A new combination of circumstances took place in the sixteenth century which strengthened the Polish–Lithuanian union and increased their solidarity. These circumstances were extremely important for the whole of Eastern Europe, and especially for South-West Russia. What is being referred to here

---

law and the Kulm law. From Poland German municipal law penetrated into the Grand Duchy of Lithuania, where it was usually known under the name of the Magdeburg law. See George Vernadsky, *Russia at the Dawn of the Modern Age* (Yale U.P., 1959) pp. 210–14.

[1] Magdeburg law was extended to the towns of Troki, Brest, Lutsk, Kremenets, Vladimir-in-Volynia, Polotsk, Smolensk, Kiev, Minsk and Novgorod–Litovsk. The last Russian city to receive it was Vitebsk in 1593. Ibid., p. 210.

[2] The Magdeburg law was intended for Christian burghers only; the Jews were excluded from municipal self-government. Ibid. pp. 214–16.

[3] The West Russian term *voit* is usually considered a derivation from the German *vogt*. It seems, however, that both the Slavic and the German terms (*voit*) derive from the Greek *boethos* 'assistant, defender' (pronounced *voithos* in medieval and modern Greek). Ibid. p. 211, n. 70.

is the schism of the Church in Western Europe in the sixteenth century – the Reformation.

It is difficult to believe that Eastern Europe could have been affected by the affair of Dr Martin Luther, who in 1517 began his discussion over what constituted true sources of salvation, the problem of salvation through faith, and other theological issues. The Reformation in Western Europe was not noticed in Eastern Europe.[1] Although its religious influence was non-existent, indirectly it was extremely important. In the sixteenth century there were free-thinking movements within the Russian Church community which were fairly closely linked to the Reformation, and which were supported by ideas from the Protestant West. It would be difficult to know whether the Reformation affected diplomatic relations more strongly in Eastern Europe or in Western Europe. In fact it played a very important part in the history of Russia. It is only with reservations that the writer accepts the idea that ancient Russia was completely isolated from Western Europe, ignoring it and ignored by it, having no influence over the West and being uninfluenced by the West. Western Europe knew ancient Russia no better than it knows modern Russia. If four centuries ago, as today, Russia did not understand events in the West as well as it might, it was certainly affected more fundamentally than necessary by the West. Indeed this was the case in the sixteenth century.

In order to consolidate the dynastic union between Lithuania and Poland, the Polish government, together with the clergy, launched a vigorous Catholic propaganda among the Orthodox Lithuanian Russians. It was particularly fierce under Casimir, the third Jagellonian ruler, in the middle of the fifteenth century, and was strongly resisted by the Orthodox population of Lithuania. As a result, the Lithuanian Principality began to disintegrate towards the end of the fifteenth century. Orthodox Russians and

[1] Although their influence was not at first significant, Protestant currents reached Poland and Lithuania from Bohemia through the Hussite and post-Hussite movements before the onset of the Reformation. For the influences exerted by the Bohemian Brethren see P. Brock, *The Political and Social Doctrines of the Unity of Czech Brethren* (The Hague, 1967).

THE RISE OF THE ROMANOVS

even Lithuanian princes left Lithuania to serve the Grand Duke of Moscow.[1]

The Reformation abruptly altered international relations. Protestant teaching was well received in Poland where cultural links with Germany were very close. Many young Poles had studied in Wittenberg and other German Universities. In 1520, three years after the Wittenberg dispute, the Polish clergy gathered in Pertrokov, and forbade the Poles to read German Protestant writings, which was an indication of how quickly and successfully these writings had spread. In support of the clergy, the Polish government at the Assembly at Torun in 1520 published a decree threatening property confiscation and permanent exile to any person introducing, selling or distributing in Poland the works of Luther or other Protestants. Prohibitions increased, and capital punishment replaced property confiscation. All this was of no avail, Protestantism became firmly entrenched in Poland, and even the Bishop of Kiev, Pats, openly preached Lutheran doctrines. Protestantism penetrated Lithuania from Poland and other neighbouring countries. In the middle of the sixteenth century Catholics numbered one in every thousand in the seven hundred Catholic parishes, the remainder having been converted to Protestantism. In 1525 the Prussian order of Teutonic Knights led by Albert, who took the title of *Hertzog*, broke away from the Roman Church.[2] Translations of Protestant writings began to appear among the Teutonic Knights in Lithuania. The chief propagandist of Protestantism in Lithuania was the Lithuanian, Abraham Kulva, who had studied in Northern Germany and received a doctorate, and was later followed by Winkler, a German parson. Both of them spread the doctrine of Protestantism.

Calvinism was even more successful. It was supported by an influential Lithuanian magnate, Nicholas Radivil Chorny,[3]

[1] For the position of the Orthodox Church in Lithuania, see Backus, *Motives of West Russian Nobles in Deserting Lithuania for Moscow 1377–1514*, pp. 79–93.

[2] Albert's repudiation of the Pope was important politically, since, as a result, he became the Polish King's vassal.

[3] Radivil Chorny accepted Calvinism in 1553. His conversion, followed by

cousin of Queen Varvara, who was the wife, first secretly, and then openly, of King Sigismund II August. By the beginning of the second half of the sixteenth century the majority of Catholic noblemen had converted to Protestantism, thereby influencing many of the Lithuanian Russian Orthodox nobility such as Vishnevetsky and Khodkevich. The Lithuanian Union of 1569 was brought about by the success of Protestantism, which weakened the effect of Catholic propaganda in Lithuania–Russia. Sigismund I and Sigismund II August (1506–72), the last Jagellonian representatives on the Polish throne, were indifferent to the religious struggle within their country. Sigismund II August, an easy-going, useless idler, who had been subjected to the new ideas, secretly protected the new doctrines in so far as his position permitted, and distributed Protestant books from his own library, and allowed Protestant sermons to be preached in the Palace church. He was indifferent which church he attended when he left the Palace on festival days. While protecting the Protestants he also favoured the Orthodox. In 1563 he interpreted a decree of the Grodno Diet which forbade Orthodox believers from holding state or public office, in such a way as to nullify it. As Catholic propaganda supported by previous rulers abated, so the Lithuanian Orthodox population grew less afraid of, and hostile to, the Polish government. This change of opinion prolonged the political union of Poland and Lithuania, but when Sigismund II August died with no issue, the Jagellonian dynasty died with him, and the dynastic union came to an end.

As long as Catholic propaganda, protected by the Polish government, continued with such intensity in Lithuania, the Orthodox Lithuanian and Russian population had no desire to continue the union. Thus, future relations between Lithuania and Poland could have been difficult. But because Sigismund II August was tolerant or even indifferent, the Orthodox were no longer afraid of union. Opposition to union could only come from the Lithuanian nobility who were frightened of being crushed by

that of many others, made Calvinism an influential factor in the council of lords. See Vernadsky, *Russia at the Dawn of the Modern Age*, pp. 274–5.

the Polish gentry; and it was for this very reason that the Lithuanian–Russian nobility wanted a permanent union with Poland.

In January 1569 the Diet met in Lublin to decide the question of union.[1] When the Lithuanian nobility objected, the King managed to convince two of the most influential magnates of South-West Russia. They were Prince Constantine Ostrozhsky, a Gedinim and Voevoda of Kiev, and Prince Alexander Czartoryski, Voevoda of Volynia. These noblemen were both leaders of the Orthodox Russian–Lithuanian nobility and might have caused the King serious problems. Prince Ostrozhsky was a powerful, private landowner who considered himself the King's subject, even though he was richer and more influential than the King. Prince Ostrozhsky owned extensive properties which included almost the whole of the present-day province of Volynia, and large parts of the provinces of Podolia and Kiev, where he owned thirty-five towns and over seven hundred villages which produced an income of about 10 million zlotys (over 10 million late nineteenth-century roubles). Both magnates were supported by the Russian nobility of the South-West, and the Lithuanian nobility, who preferred them to the Polish gentry. These considerations decided the question of union.

Despite the end of the Jagellonian dynasty, the Diet of Lublin recognised the political union of both countries as something permanent. The Diet also determined the final structure of the united state. Poland and Lithuania were united as two halves of a single state, enjoying equal rights, the first being called a Crown State, the second a Principality, while together they were called the *Retch Pospolita* (res publica). This was an elective monarchy organised as a republic. The King, chosen by the General Diets of the Crown State and Principality was head of state. Legislative powers belonged to the Diet, which consisted of deputies from the gentry alone, and the Senate, which consisted of powerful lay and clerical dignitaries from both parts of the Union. The general administrative body was the Diet, the Senate and the

[1] For the basic principles of the Treaty of Union, signed on 15 July 1569, ibid. pp. 246–9.

King. But each part of the *Retch Pospolita* maintained its own separate administration, with its own ministers, armies and special laws.

The most important features in the history of South-West Russia were those decrees of the Lublin Diet, which provided for some districts of the area being incorporated into the Crown State. These were: Podliashie (the western part of Grodno), Volynia and the Ukraine (the provinces of Kiev, Poltava, and part of Podolia, in particular Braslov and part of Chernigov). Essentially these circumstances created the Union at Lublin in 1569. Union was accompanied by vital political, national and religious consequences for both South-West Russia, and the whole of Eastern Europe.

The decrees of the Lublin Diet meant an end of the rule of the Gedinims in Western Russia, and to Polish influence in this area. The Poles obtained what they had been striving for for nearly two hundred years: permanent union with Lithuania, and the annexation to Poland of the naturally rich and desirable south-west provinces.[1] Polish influence had helped the Gedinims to destroy many of the ancient customs, but they were also responsible for introducing innovations into the life and organisation of the area. Descendants of the house of Rurik with their retainers ruled the provinces of old Kievan Rus with the agreement of the older urban local assemblies. Because private land ownership was slow to develop, their social and economic ties with the districts were not durable.

Under the Gedinims this unstable ruling class was replaced by a more settled aristocracy of powerful landowners which included Russian–Lithuanian Princes and their boyars. This aristocracy, consolidated by the Diet, was superseded by a military class of small landowners, the ordinary nobility and the gentry. The old provinces of Kievan Rus, whose political centres were in the older towns, were broken up by Lithuanian Russia into administrative units under officials of the Grand Prince, and were not united by

[1] However, full incorporation of Lithuania into Poland was not achieved, and Lithuania retained her autonomy even after the Union of Lublin. Ibid. pp. 247–9.

a series of local administrations but by one government centre. Finally, the oldest provincial towns which represented their district committees through the assemblies before the Prince, were isolated from these communities by private landowners and the Grand Princes' administrative system. *Magdeburg Law* was substituted for the assemblies which became narrowly-based commercial societies hemmed in by urban inertia, deprived of provincial importance and participation in the political life of the country. Supremacy of the gentry, official positions conferred for life, and sometimes made hereditary, and *Magdeburg Law* were three changes brought to Lithuanian Russia by Polish influence. The Union of Lublin precipitated a further development for which Polish influence was responsible: serfdom.

The settlement of the hitherto empty central Dnieper region started in the middle of the sixteenth century. The vast Steppes attracted settlers; and the spread of serfdom in Lithuania encouraged emigration to this area. At the beginning of the sixteenth century, different types of agricultural settlers appeared; they varied from migrant peasants who settled with or without assistance from their owners, and who had retained their freedom of movement, to indentured domestic quasi-agricultural serfs. From 1529 to 1566, the period between the first and the second Statutes, as the gentry's political power increased so the peasants became more equal, in the sense that they gradually all became unfree, a process speeded up by the Union of 1569.

Under the elected Kings of the *Retch Pospolita*, legislation, as well as the political life of the country was directly influenced by the Polish–Lithuanian gentry, who were the ruling class. They did not fail to take political advantage of their position to oppress the rural population. When the Russian regions on both sides of the central Dnieper were united with the Crown State, Polish administration took the place of native Russian institutions; and the Polish gentry followed, acquiring land and introducing Polish serfdom with its own peculiar features.

The native Russian–Lithuanian nobility eagerly copied the landowning customs and ideas of their new neighbours from the Vistula and Western Bug. If government and law showed any

concern for the fiscal relations between the peasants and the landowners it was solely in the interests of the Treasury; because
otherwise the peasant was entirely at the mercy of his new landowner. The gentry had the power of life and death over their
peasants.[1] Contemporary Polish writers said that they were indifferent as to whether they killed a peasant or a dog. It was to
escape from serfdom, which was stifling them, that an increasing
number of peasants fled from the interior of the Crown State
Principality into the vast Steppes of the Ukraine, descending
along the River Dnieper and the Eastern Bug where there were
as yet no gentry.

Eventually, however, land speculators moved in. The gentry
began to solicit positions with life tenure in the border towns of
the Ukraine such as Braslov, Kanev, Cherkassy, and Pereyaslav,
together with their surrounding wastelands; they grabbed large
areas of the Steppe and hurriedly settled them with peasants and
artisans whom they had bribed. The Ukrainian Steppe was
disposed of in the same way as the lands and grazing rights of the
Bashkirs on the eastern shores of the Black Sea. Eminent men of
high position such as the Princes Ostrozhky and Vishnevetsky, as
well as Polotski and Zamoiski, quite unashamedly took part in
the scramble for the wastelands along the Dnieper and the banks
of its tributaries. However, these speculators behaved more
responsibly than did their successors in the Urals and Caucasus.
It was entirely due to them that the Steppes of the Ukraine came
alive. In a very short time scores of new small towns, and hundreds
of thousands of hamlets and agricultural settlements came into
being. Simultaneously the Steppe was fortified, without which
settlement would have been impossible. Newly-built forts
protected the old towns of Braslov, Korsun, Kanev and
Pereyaslav, and around them the peasants developed small towns
and villages. The continuous struggle with the Tatars turned

[1] 'The Peasants in Ukraine and the neighbouring Provinces are like Slaves
the same as they are in almost all places of Poland. . . .' Pierre Chevalier, *A
Discourse of the Original Country Manners, Government and Religion of the
Cossacks with Another of the Precopian Tartars, and the History of the Wars of the
Cossacks against Poland* (London, 1672) pp. 20–1.

these settlements into military communities reminiscent of the 'heroic outposts' of the tenth and eleventh centuries which protected the Steppe frontier of Kievan Rus. These communities became the Cossacks of Little Russia.

The Cossacks were a section of Russian society, which at one time had existed throughout the whole of Russia. In the sixteenth century, the casual labourers who worked their way from one peasant household to another were called *cossacks*.[1] They had neither definite occupations nor settled homes. This was the original meaning of the word. However, subsequently in Muscovite Russia the phrase 'free wanderers' was used. They found the southern borderlands of Russia which merged with the Steppe particularly suitable, and here they developed their special characteristics. When the danger of a Tatar invasion had diminished, a series of minor struggles developed between the inhabitants of the borderland Steppe, Russia and the nomadic Tatars. The fortified frontier towns were the focal point of the struggle. As a result, a class of armed men appeared who went into the Steppe to fish and hunt.[2]

Courageous and poor, these armed fishermen and hunters must have obtained payment for their dangerous occupation from the local traders, who were the beneficiaries. In this type of situation they remained hired labourers working for a master. As warriors, familiar with Steppe warfare, they could be supported by the administrations of the local principalities. The term

[1] The term *kozak*, probably of Turkic origin, had different connotations in different languages. For the Turk and Tatar the word signified 'free warrior' or 'freebooter', for the Poles a 'rebel' and 'pillager', and for the Ukrainian a 'brave warrior' and 'defender of a national cause'. See Bickford O'Brien, *Muscovy and the Ukraine*, p. 6; and Vernadsky, *Russia at the Dawn of the Modern Age*, pp. 249–50.

[2] In 1590 a Polish writer described the Ukraine as 'the richest part of the Polish state. Its fields are as blissful as the Elysian. There are so many cattle, wild animals, and various birds in the Ukraine that one could think her the birthplace of Diana and Ceres. In the Ukrainian apiaries so much honey is produced that one forgets the Sicilian Gela and the Attic Hymettas. It is hard to count the Ukrainian lakes teeming with fish. In short, the Ukraine is like that land which God promised to the Hebrews, flowing with milk and honey.' Quoted in Vernadsky, *Russia at the Dawn of the Modern Age*, pp. 251–2.

'cossack' was applied to those people who were constantly fighting the steppe Tatars, and this term was later used to include the free, nomadic, labourers of Northern Russia.

Clashes between Cossacks and Tatars started first of all in the eastern strip of the southern Steppe. This probably explains why the earliest account of the Cossacks mentions the Ryazan Cossacks who defended their town against the Tatars in 1444. In Muscovy during the sixteenth and seventeenth centuries events took place which could only have happened with the creation of Cossacks. Some sixteenth-century documents mention that sons of impoverished boyars took themselves off to the Steppe and joined up with the Cossacks. This does not imply that they joined a permanent community, such as the Don Cossacks; but simply that a group of men congenial to one another left their occupations and estates to wander freely in the Steppe, fighting the Tatars, and subsequently returning to their own country and settling. In a document of 1622 from Elets, mention is made of a group of landowners of that area who abandoned their estates, joined the Cossacks, and subsequently joined noble households as serfs, or monasteries as servants.

The original Cossack country lay along a line drawn through the frontier towns of the central Volga to Ryazan and Tula, and then, curving sharply southward, extended as far as the Dnieper through Putivl and Pereyaslav. The Cossacks achieved another objective in their offensive on the Steppe during the decline of the Tatars and the disintegration of the Horde. Urban Cossacks, particularly those from Ryazan, began to settle in military-trading posts on the open Steppe in the region of the Upper Don. These Don Cossacks were the virtual prototype of the Steppe Cossacks. At all events, during the second half of the sixteenth century while the Zaporozhie Cossacks along the Dnieper were just becoming a military community, the Don Cossacks had already become one. Converted Tatars also joined the Cossacks, and a petition from a converted Christian Crimean Tatar has been preserved. He had left the Crimea for the Don in 1509, where he served the Muscovite sovereign for fifteen years; he 'fought against the Crimeans, and often went with the Don

Cossacks to attack the Crimean peoples and nomads, and he went from the Don to Putivl'. He now asked the Sovereign to exempt his house in Putivl from taxes and duties 'to whiten or untax him', and to allow him to do military duty on the same terms as the local landowners.

Information about the Dnieper Cossacks stems from the end of the fifteenth century, which is much later than the information which exists about the Ryazan Cossacks. Their origin and social structure was just as simple as elsewhere. Groups of adventurers from the towns of the regions of Kiev, Volynia, Podolia and even the upper reaches of the Dnieper set out for the wild Steppe to bee-keep, fish, hunt, and harry the Tatars. In spring and summer these new migrant Cossacks worked their productive, arable land along the Dnieper and its tributaries, and in winter they gathered with their goods in the towns along the Dnieper where they settled. Kanev and Cherkassy became important Cossack winter quarters almost immediately. As in Northern Russia, some hired themselves as labourers to landowners and traders.

Local geographical and political conditions complicated the lives of the Ukrainian Cossacks. They became involved in the international conflicts of Russia, Lithuania, Poland, Turkey and the Crimea. Because of the part they were forced to play in these events, the Dnieper Cossacks were historically extremely important. Mention has been made of the colonisation of the lower Dnieper, which increased the local Cossack population. Although this was necessary for the development of the region, and the state, these people were restless and created difficulties for the Polish government. Steppe traders, accustomed to fighting, were the best defence against Tatar attacks. But the weapon was double-edged! Their main occupation consisted in retaliatory raids against the Tatars and Turkish territory. They attacked by land and sea; at the beginning of the seventeenth century light Cossack canoes raided Tatar and Turkish towns along the northern, western and even southern shores of the Black Sea, penetrating through the Bosphorus to Constantinople. In return the Turks threatened to go to war with Poland; and indeed, the Poles were frightened of the Turks. As early as the beginning of the sixteenth century a plan had been drawn up in Warsaw to neutralise the Cossacks, without diminishing their utility. This consisted in separating the most trustworthy Cossacks from the unruly, growing mass, taking them into salaried state service, and giving them the responsibility for defending the Ukraine. The rest were to be allowed to live as they wished. There is some evidence as early as the beginning of the sixteenth century of attempts to recruit Cossack companies to act as frontier guards. Indeed, this was probably only one of many attempts to create frontier guardsmen from these armed ruffians. It was only in 1570 that a permanent force of 300 men was formed of regulars and registered Cossacks. Later, under Steven Batory, these numbers were increased to 500, until in 1625 there were 6,000. But the growth of a regular Cossack force in no way diminished the numbers of unregistered Cossacks.

Local governors and officials tried to persuade these 'illegal' Cossacks, who were mostly peasants, to revert to their peasant occupations, and previous responsibilities. Having tasted Cossack freedom, they were reluctant to do so, and felt that they were entitled to disobey a government from whom they had fled, who had not protected them from subjugation, and who now, in time of war, wanted their help, and called for them in their tens of thousands.

This Janus-like policy by the government created bitterness among these stateless people, who were likely to rebel as soon as a dynamic leader appeared. Meanwhile, on the lower Dnieper a Cossack camp was built where the discontented Ukrainian Cossacks took refuge, and which became a breeding ground for insurrection: these were the Zaporozhie.

The Zaporozhie Cossacks developed imperceptibly from the trading Cossacks of the Steppe. The inhabitants of the Ukrainian border towns, who had become Cossacks, slipped down the Dnieper to the rapids. Professor Lyubavsky[1] has claimed that they

[1] Professor Matvei Lyubavsky (1860–1937) belonged to a senior group of V. Klyuchevsky's pupils. He wrote on the past of Lithuania for both his master's and his doctor's dissertations. Lyubavsky held that Lithuanian Russia, like Moscow, arose as a direct offspring of Kievan Russia. See Anatole G. Mazour, *An Outline of Modern Russian Historiography* (D. Van Nostrand Co. Inc., 1959) pp. 54–5.

had existed here as early as the fifteenth century. When the Polish government began to put pressure on the urban Cossacks, they fled to familiar places on the other side of the rapids where neither Polish commissaries nor expeditionary forces could penetrate. On islands formed by the Dnieper where it issues from the narrows into the open Steppe, and expands into a broad, open reach, the fugitives built themselves fortified camps.

In the sixteenth century the main stronghold of the Zaporozhie was at Khortitsa, the island nearest the rapids, and this was, in its day, the famous Zaporozhie Sich.[1] Later on the Cossacks moved to other islands near the rapids. The Sich was a fortified camp enclosed by wooden ramparts. It possessed artillery of a kind, consisting mainly of small cannon, captured from Tatar and Turkish forts. A military-trading association which called itself 'the knighthood of the Zaporozhie Host' was created from unnamed newcomers from different tribes. The inhabitants of the Sich lived in brushwood huts covered with horse hide.[2] They had different occupations. Some were essentially brigands and lived on their booty, others were fishermen or hunters, and supplied the food. Women were not allowed into the Sich, and married Cossacks lived apart in winter huts; they were responsible for growing grain to supply the Sich.

Until the end of the sixteenth century the Zaporozhie Cossacks remained a mobile society with a varied structure. In winter they dispersed to different Ukrainian towns leaving a few hundred men behind in the Sich to protect the artillery and other property. In peace-time in summer as many as 3,000 men lived in the Sich; but it became overcrowded whenever the Ukrainian peasants were unduly provoked by either the Tatars or Lithuanians, or whenever there was trouble in the Ukraine. At such a time every malcontent, exile or victim of oppression escaped beyond the rapids. A newcomer was never asked his identity, his domicile, his

[1] Zaporozhie means the region 'beyond the Cataracts'. The term *sich* derives from the verb meaning 'to hew', 'to cut': a place protected by cut trees, a 'wooden fortress'. See Vernadsky, *Russia at the Dawn of the Modern Age*, p. 256; Hrushevsky, *A History of Ukraine*, pp. 156–9.

[2] Each hut housed 150 men.

religion or his tribe; everyone who was considered suitable was taken in.

By the end of the sixteenth century there were signs of a military organisation in Zaporozhie, although it was far from stable, which it was not to become until later. This military brotherhood of Zaporozhie, known as the *kosh*[1] was commanded by a *kosh ataman* or chief, elected by the military council, who together with elected *asauls* or adjutant-generals, judges and secretaries was the government of the Sich. The brotherhood was divided into detachments, *kuren*,[2] of which there were thirty-eight under the command of a detachment *ataman*, who were attached to the government. The Zaporozhie Cossacks valued their fraternal equality above all else, and every problem was decided by the *sich, rada* or Cossack *kolo*.[3] This *kolo* treated its government without formality in so far as elections or replacements were concerned. Undesirable Cossacks were drowned.

In 1581 a nobleman from Galicia, a reckless adventurer called Zborovski, appeared in the Sich to incite the Cossacks to attack Moscow. Bored by inaction and lack of funds the Brotherhood accepted the proposal and elected him *hetman. En route* to Moscow the Cossacks enquired whether, if they returned safe and sound, he would be able to find them similar work from which they could profit. When he turned back from Moscow and suggested they should march to Persia, he was almost killed in the ensuing controversy. This search for work, or rather for pillage and loot, became more serious as Cossack numbers increased towards the end of the sixteenth century. They were unable to satisfy their needs by fishing and hunting in the Steppe; and they began to roam the Steppe on the right bank of the Dnieper in their thousands, despoiling the countryside.

[1] The word *kosh* was a term meaning 'camp' in Old Russian, and apparently deriving from Turkic. See Vernadsky, *Russia at the Dawn of the Modern Age*, p. 257.

[2] This term derives from the Mongol language in which a *kuriyen* is a camp of tents pitched in a huge circle. See George Vernadsky, *Mongols and Russia* (Yale U.P., 1953) p. 14.

[3] *Rada* means council, and *kolo* means circle.

The local authorities were unable to rid themselves of marauding Cossacks, who themselves did not know where to go. They willingly followed the first leader who summoned them to the Crimea or Moldavia. It was from these Cossacks that marauding groups were formed during the Time of Troubles, to attack Muscovy. Cossack raids on neighbouring countries were known in the Ukraine as 'Cossack bread'. They had nothing else to do except loot, and answered Zborovski's speech about submitting to the King and their fatherland, with a popular saying: 'while men live they must be fed'. But the Cossacks did not only turn on foreign countries such as the Crimea, Moldavia or Moskalia. In the sixteenth century they turned on their own country. Increasing in numbers the Zaporozhie Sich became a breeding-ground for Cossack insurrections against Poland.

Thus, the Lublin Union resulted in three, closely interlocking, developments in South-West Russia: serfdom, increased peasant colonisation in the Ukraine, and the transformation of the Zaporozhie Sich in a rebellious refuge for the oppressed Russian people.

Chapter Six

★

THE HISTORY of the Little Russian Cossacks and their connection with Lithuania–Russia has been discussed in general terms to the beginning of the seventeenth century, at which time fundamental changes occurred. The previous chapter showed how the Cossacks evolved; how groups of Steppe traders formed themselves into military associations who raided neighbouring countries, and from whom the government recruited a frontier guard. All Cossacks hoped that the Steppe would provide them with a living of one sort or another, which was why they were prepared to defend the threatened south-east frontiers. After the Union of Lublin the Little Russian Cossacks turned on the very state they had defended. The international position of Little Russia completely demoralised the motley rabble and strangled at birth any feeling of nationality.

The Cossacks customarily considered the neighbouring countries of Crimea, Turkey, Moldavia, and even Muscovy as places to plunder, as 'Cossack bread'. They extended this attitude to their own country, which was reinforced when the gentry began to settle in the outlying regions of the south-east bringing with them their serf laws. At this stage the Cossacks realised that their own country was a more formidable foe than either the Crimea or Turkey, and from the end of the sixteenth century they 'plundered it with increasing vigour'. Conceptually Eastern European morality embraced nationality and faith, and consequently the Cossacks of Little Russia were made stateless and denied any formal religious affiliation. The *Retch Pospolita* provided neither: Orthodoxy belonged to a blurred memory of childhood, an abstract idea to which they felt no commitment, and which was irrelevant to Cossack life. In wartime the Cossacks did not discriminate between the Russians and the Tatars; indeed they behaved worse than the Tatars towards the Russians.

In 1636 the government's emissary to the Cossacks, Adam Kissel, who was Orthodox, wrote that they were strongly attracted to the Greek Orthodox religion and its clergy, even though they behaved more like Tatars than Christians in religious matters. The Cossacks were definitely amoral, and it would have been difficult to find another group in the *Retch Pospolita* with such low standards of morality and social consciousness; possibly only the hierarchy of the Little Russian Church before the Union of the Churches was as ignorant and backward as the Cossacks. The Cossacks never felt that the Ukraine was their fatherland, possibly because they were intellectually incapable of so doing; certainly, their heterogeneous structure mitigated against it. The detachment of five hundred registered Cossacks recruited by Stephen Batory was made up of men from seventy-four towns and districts of Western Russia and Lithuania; from far-off Vilna and Polotsk, as well as from seven Polish towns including Poznan and Cracow; there were also Muscovites from Ryazan and other places along the Volga, Moldavians, a Serb, a German, and a non-Christian Tatar from the Crimea. What was there to unite this rabble? Oppressed by the Polish gentry, they carried sabres, with which to kill and bury the Polish gentry, and with which they bargained. Their political awareness and social consciousness were confined to these two activities, which were propagated by that Cossack academy, the Sich, which was every deserving Cossack's superior training ground; the Poles called it that den of mutiny. For suitable rewards the Cossacks offered their military services to the German Emperor against the Turks, to the Polish Government against Muscovy and the Crimea, and to Muscovy and the Crimea against their own Polish government. Early Cossack risings against the *Retch Pospolita* were of a purely social, democratic nature, devoid of religious or nationalist overtones. Naturally, they were all initiated in the Zaporozhie Sich.

Originally even their leader, one Christopher Kosinski, was a foreigner. He came from a background hostile to the Cossacks, and had abandoned his own country and class.[1] He joined the Zaporozhie, and with a band of Cossacks, was hired by the King of Poland. In 1591, because their wages had not been paid on time, he gathered together the Zaporozhie Cossacks and other riff-raff to destroy and burn Ukrainian towns, villages and estates belonging to the local nobility and gentry, concentrating on the possessions of Prince Ostrozhsky,[2] the wealthiest of them all. Prince Ostrozhsky finally defeated him, took him prisoner, but pardoned both Kosinski and the Cossacks on condition that they remained peacefully beyond the cataracts.[3] After two months Kosinski raised a new rebellion, swore fealty to the Tsar of Muscovy, and boasted that, together with the Turks and Tatars, he would destroy the Ukraine and kill all the gentry; he besieged the town of Cherkassy, intending to slaughter its inhabitants, including Prince Vishnevetski, the town governor who had pleaded for Kosinski's life with Prince Ostrozhsky. Kosinski lost his life during this encounter. He was succeeded by Loboda and Nalivaiko,[4] who continued to harass the Ukraine west of the Dnieper, until 1595. Eventually, these godless and stateless mercenaries were forced to unite under a religious and national banner, and were destined to become the stronghold of Western Russian Orthodoxy.

This unexpected development had come about as a result of a church union which took place twenty-seven years after the

[1] Christopher Kosinski is presumed to have been a minor nobleman from Podliashie.

[2] Prince Constantine Ostrozhsky was head of the nobility of Volynia.

[3] The Cossacks are said to have lost two thousand men and twenty-six cannon during this engagement which took place near Zhitomir in January 1593.

[4] Severin Nalivaiko built up a strong force of Cossacks in Podolia, presumably with the help of money sent by Pope Clement VIII as advance payment for equipment to be used against Turkey. According to some sources Nalivaiko was a Volynian burgher, while others state that he was a minor nobleman. Gregory Loboda was hetman of the Zaporozhie Cossacks, and an Ukrainian landowner. See George Vernadsky, *Russia at the Dawn of the Modern Age* (Yale U.P., 1959) pp. 264-7.

political union. The events leading to union can be summarised briefly.[1] Catholic propaganda, invigorated by the Jesuits who appeared in Lithuania in 1569, speedily disposed of Protestantism, and turned on Orthodoxy. The Jesuits were resisted from the beginning by the Orthodox magnates led by Prince Ostrozhsky, the urban population, and the guilds. The old idea of union with the Roman Church reappeared among the demoralised, despised and oppressed members of the Orthodox hierarchy; moreover the Brest Union of 1596 had divided the Russian Church into two hostile sections, the Orthodox and the Uniates. The established religion was no longer Orthodox, and the clergy were left without prelates when the two bishops who had opposed union died. The Russian merchants lost any political support they might have enjoyed on the mass conversion of the nobility to union and Catholicism. The clergy and merchants could appeal only to the Cossacks and their supporters, the Russian peasants, and faced by a common enemy, these four classes forgot their differences.

Although Church Union did not unify these classes it provided their joint struggle with a new stimulus, and helped towards a better, mutual understanding. It was easy to persuade the Cossacks that Church Union was an alliance between the Polish King, the Polish gentry, the Catholic priests and their common agents, the Jews, against the God of Russia, whom every Russian was bound to defend. To oppressed serfs and free Cossacks eager to see the downfall of the Polish gentry on whose lands they lived, the idea that a massacre would placate the offended Russian God was pleasing, and killing therefore was something they could undertake with an easy conscience.

The early Cossack insurrections of the late sixteenth century had neither religious nor nationalist characteristics. From the beginning of the seventeenth century, however, the Cossacks gradually became embroiled in the Orthodox opposition. Hetman Sahaidachny, together with all the Zaporozhian forces,

[1] The historical background to the Union of Brest of 1596 is extremely complex. For one of the clearest expositions, ibid. pp. 269–92; also P. Pierling, S.J., *La Russie et le Saint-Siège* (Paris 1897) II 361–5; and Oscar Halecki, *From Florence to Brest (1439–1596)* (Rome, 1958).

joined the Orthodox brotherhood of Kiev, and in 1620, with the agreement of the Patriarch of Jerusalem who was acting without authority, re-established and gave their protection to the supreme Orthodox hierarchy. In 1625 the Metropolitan of Kiev who was the head of the Orthodox hierarchy, summoned the Zaporozhian Cossacks to defend the Orthodox population of Kiev, where the town prefect was killed for having illtreated them.

In this way the Cossacks acquired a cause which, on the one hand summoned them to protect the Russian nation and the Orthodox religion, and on the other to destroy and expel the Polish gentry and landowners from the Ukraine. Not all Cossacks rallied to this cause. In the sixteenth century there was a certain amount of economic diversification, and those Cossacks who had settled in the frontier towns and who hunted on the Steppe, proceeded to cultivate and acquire farms, with good arable land. By the beginning of the seventeenth century the density of Cossack farms was high in other borderland areas, such as Kanev, and as generally happens when waste land is settled, the land was simply appropriated. Registered Cossacks, who were paid by the government, were mainly recruited from these settler Cossacks.

Eventually, the registered Cossacks were based on towns which became their administrative centres, and were divided into territorial regiments. The regular Cossack army was fixed at 6,000 men by agreement between the Cossacks and the Crown Hetman Konetspolski in 1625. It was subdivided into six regiments (Belotserkov, Korsun, Kanev, Cherkassy, Chigirin and Pereyaslav). Under Bogdan Khmelnitsky the regiments were increased to sixteen, and consisted of more than 230 squadrons.

The division into regiments dates from Hetman Sahaidachny, who died in 1622, and who was the general organiser of the Cossacks of Little Russia. His actions revealed the dissensions which existed among the Cossacks. Sahaidachny wanted to distinguish between the registered Cossacks and the peasants who had joined them. The attempt to create a privileged class caused the peasants to complain. Sahaidachny was himself a nobleman, and he tried to impose on the Cossacks the ideas of his class. It followed that the struggle between the Cossacks and the Ukrainian nobility acquired a specific character; not only did the Cossacks wish to free the Ukraine from these immigrant and foreign noblemen, they also wished to replace them by their own privileged class. A future Cossack aristocracy was being created by the Cossacks themselves. However, the Cossacks' real strength did not lie with those who were registered, who numbered some 6,000, and represented only one-tenth of those who thought of themselves as Cossacks, and had acquired their customs; it lay with the poor and homeless, who lived on the estates belonging to landowners and gentry, and who, as free Cossacks, declined to accept peasants' obligations. On the other hand, the Polish government and landowners were not prepared to recognise their freedom, and tried to turn them into real peasants.

Whenever the Polish government needed their military assistance, it enrolled both registered and unregistered men into the Cossack contingent; as soon as they were no longer required the unregistered men were struck off the lists and returned to their former status. These unregistered men, who were threatened with enserfment, gathered at Zaporozhie and organised rebellions. This state of affairs developed in 1624 and lasted for about fourteen years. The leaders of the unregistered Cossacks were men like Izmail, Taras, Sulim, Pavlyuk, Ostranin and Guna. The registered Cossacks either took separate sides, or went over as a whole to the Poles. These uprisings were all unsuccessful, and ended in 1638 with the Cossacks losing all their important privileges. The registered Cossacks were put under the command of Polish noblemen, and the Hetman was replaced by a government commissar. The Cossack settlers were deprived of their farms, and the unregistered Cossacks reverted to serfdom under the Polish gentry. The free Cossacks were abolished. According to a Little Russian chronicle, every vestige of freedom was taken from the Cossacks, unprecedented heavy taxes were imposed, and churches and church positions were sold to the Jews.

Poles and Russians; Russians and Jews; Catholics and Uniates; Uniates and Orthodox; Guilds and bishops; gentry and commoners; commoners and Cossacks; Cossacks and merchants; registered Cossacks and Cossack rabble; urban Cossacks and the

Zaporozhie Cossack elders and Cossack rabble; Cossack Hetmen and Cossack elders – these were all in latent or open conflict with themselves and each other. Their relations became so confused, and life in Little Russia so complex as a result, that neither the government in Warsaw nor in Kiev could unravel the situation.

Bogdan Khmelnitsky's uprising was an attempt to cut this knot with Cossack sabres.[1] It is difficult to ascertain whether or not Moscow foresaw this uprising, and the necessity for her to interfere in it. Moscow was concentrating on the provinces of Smolensk and Seversk, and after the abortive war of 1632-4, preparations were quietly proceeding to retrieve their loss. Little Russia still lay beyond the horizon of Muscovite politics, and the memory of Lisowski and Sapieha were still fresh in Muscovite minds. It is true that information was sent from Kiev to Moscow stating that Kievans were willing to serve the Orthodox Sovereign of Muscovy, accompanied by a petition that He should put Little Russia under His protection, since they had nowhere else to turn. Moscow replied cautiously, saying that only when the Orthodox were oppressed by the Poles would she consider saving her co-religionists from oppression. Thus, from the very start of Khmelnitsky's rebellion relations between Muscovy and Little Russia remained ambiguous.

To begin with Khmelnitsky's successes exceeded his expectation. He had never considered breaking away from the *Retch Pospolita,* but had only intended to frighten the conceited gentry away from the area. But after three victories he occupied almost the whole of Little Russia. He recognised that he had achieved more than he had intended. And success went to his head, particularly after dinner! He had visions of an Ukrainian Principality stretching to the Vistula, led by Grand Prince Bogdan; he called himself 'Absolute Russian Autocrat', threatened to get rid of the Poles and exile all the gentry beyond the Vistula. He was angry with the Tsar of Muscovy for not having helped him

[1] For details of Bogdan Khmelnitsky's uprising see in particular George Vernadsky, *Bohdan, Hetman of Ukraine* (New Haven, 1941); and C. Bickford O'Brien, *Muscovy and the Ukraine* (University of California Press, 1963) pp. 12–20.

from the beginning, and for not attacking Poland. In a rage, he told the ambassadors from Muscovy some unpleasant truths, and towards the end of the banquet threatened to destroy Moscow, and show them who was ruling there. The boasting was succeeded by humble, but far from innocent, repentance.

The change in attitude was not only due to Khmelnitsky's personality, but also because he realised how false his situation really was. After all, he could not deal with Poland alone, and the necessary help was not forthcoming from Moscow. Therefore, he would have to rely on the Crimean Khan. After his initial victories he hinted that he was ready to serve the Tsar of Muscovy if he would support the Cossacks; the Muscovite government procrastinated, and not having a plan, hoped that events would suggest one. The Muscovites did not know how to deal with the rebellious Hetman, whether to accept his fealty or support him secretly against Poland. Khmelnitsky was more convenient as a secret ally than as a subject. After all, a subject had to be protected, whereas an ally could be abandoned when he had served his purpose. Then again, open support of the Cossacks could only lead to war with Poland, which would thoroughly confuse relations with Little Russia. Yet to remain inactive would mean abandoning the Orthodox people of the Ukraine to the enemy, and making an enemy of Bogdan Khmelnitsky. Indeed, in the absence of help from Muscovy, Khmelnitsky threatened either to attack Moscow in alliance with the Crimean Tatars, or to make peace with Poland and in alliance turn against Muscovy.

However, soon after the Treaty of Zborov,[1] Khmelnitsky recognised that another war with Poland was inevitable. He told the Tsar's ambassadors that he wished, if he lost the war, to cross into Russian territory with his Zaporozhian forces. It was a year and a half later, when Khmelnitsky had lost his second campaign against the Poles and had to concede his earlier gains, that Muscovy

[1] The Treaty of Zborov (August 1649) was a serious reversal for Poland in its struggle with the Cossacks. Poland had to pay an annual tribute to the Crimea and agree to 'an eternal peace'. Poland had to reinstate the rights and privileges of the Cossacks, and agree to the registration of nearly 40,000 Cossacks. Ibid. pp. 16–17.

recognised that this idea might have some merit. The government proposed that Khmelnitsky and his Cossack army should settle on the rich and extensive territory along the rivers Donets and Medvedets, and in other suitable areas. This resettlement neither involved war with Poland, nor did it drive the Cossacks into seeking the allegiance of the Turkish Sultan; but it did provide Muscovy with an excellent frontier protection along the Steppe.

Unfortunately, events did not proceed at the same pace as Muscovite politics. Khmelnitsky was forced into a third war with Poland in very unfavourable circumstances.[1] He begged the Tsar to accept his fealty since otherwise he would have to accept the protection offered by the Turkish Sultan and the Crimean Khan. Finally, at the beginning of 1653, Muscovy decided to annex Little Russia and go to war with Poland. All this took time, and Khmelnitsky only heard of this decision in the summer; moreover, the Zemsky Sobor only met in the autumn to ratify this decision. Then there was more waiting while Khmelnitsky was defeated near Zhvanets, betrayed once again by his Tatar allies, and it was only in January 1654 that the Cossacks ceased to be in jeopardy.[2] They had to wait for thirteen years after the capitulation of Smolensk in 1654 for an opportune moment to efface their disgrace.

In 1648 the Little Russian Cossacks had rebelled. Poland was in a precarious situation. The Ukraine sought Muscovy's assistance rather than an alliance with the perfidious Tatars, and begged her to annex the Ukraine. Once again Muscovy hesitated; she was afraid of breaking the peace with Poland, and for six years remained an onlooker, while Khmelnitsky, defeated by the Tatars near Zborov and Berestechko, was verging on total collapse; Little Russia, overrun by her Tatar allies, was being

[1] The Poles renewed their war against the Cossacks in February 1651. In September 1651 a new agreement was signed between Poland and the Cossacks at Belaya Tserkov. For details of this agreement, ibid. pp. 19–20.

[2] The text of the Charter of Annexation can be found in *Documents Historiques sur l'Ukraine et ses relations avec la Pologne, la Russie et la Suède (1569–1764)* (Lausanne, 1919) pp. 36–8. The diplomatic details of the negotiations which culminated in the Pereyaslav Agreement of 1654 are discussed in Bickford O'Brien, *Muscovy and the Ukraine*, pp. 20–7.

devastated by them as well as by a ferocious internecine war. Finally, with the country utterly exhausted and helpless, Muscovy extended her powerful protection and turned the ruling Ukrainian classes from Polish rebels to embittered Muscovite subjects.

This situation could only have arisen from mutual misunderstanding. Muscovy wanted the Cossacks, even without their territories, but if the Ukrainian towns were to be annexed then it was on condition that they were to be ruled by Muscovite governors and officials. Bogdan Khmelnitsky himself counted on at least becoming something like a Regent of Kirgin, ruling Little Russia under the distant surveillance of the Muscovite Sovereign, together with the Cossack aristocracy and other officials. But neither side trusted or understood the other, nor said what they really thought, and therefore neither achieved their objectives. Khmelnitsky expected Moscow not only to break with Poland but to attack her from the east to liberate Little Russia, and extend Muscovy's protection over her. Muscovy, however, did not actually break off relations with Poland, but cunningly waited for the Cossacks to defeat the Poles, and force them to retreat, so that Muscovy could legally and without endangering the peace treaty, annex Little Russia to Greater Russia.

Two months before the Zborov affair, which sealed the fate of Poland and Little Russia, Khmelnitsky begged the Tsar 'to give his blessing to his troops to attack' their common enemy, while he in good time would attack them from the Ukraine, praying to God that the upright and Orthodox Sovereign would become Tsar and Autocrat of the Ukraine. Muscovy's reply to this apparently sincere request was a cruel mockery. 'We cannot break our eternal peace with Poland, *but if the King of Poland frees the Hetman and the Zaporozhian forces, then the Sovereign (of Muscovy) will favour the Hetman and the Zaporozhian forces, and command that they be accepted under his mighty hand.*'

This mutual misunderstanding and mistrust caused them both to be hurt by their own shortsightedness. Khmelnitsky was a brave Cossack warrior, a resourceful diplomat, but a mediocre politician. He once jokingly described his political philosophy to the Polish Commissioners as follows: 'If a Prince be at fault, cut off his head; if a Cossack be at fault cut off his head also; and that will be justice.' He considered his own rebellion to be a struggle between the Cossacks and the Polish gentry, whom he despised, and confessed that he and his Cossacks wanted to kill them all. Khmelnitsky did nothing to alleviate the social discord among the Cossacks, which was to become even more acute later on, and which was the extreme hostility between the Cossack elders and the ordinary Cossacks, the 'town and Zaporozhie rabble'. This hostility led to endless trouble in Little Russia, and resulted in that part of the Ukraine which lay on the west bank of the Dnieper falling to the Turks, and becoming a wilderness. Such were the effects of Muscovy's cautious and subtle diplomacy.

The annexation of Little Russia was looked at from a traditional political viewpoint, as a continuation of the territorial gathering-in of Russian lands, recovered from hostile Poland, and returned to the estate of the Sovereigns of Muscovy. When in 1655 White Russia and Lithuania were conquered, the Muscovites lost no time in expanding the Tsar's title to 'Autocrat of all Great, Little and White Russia, Lithuania, Volynia and Podolia'. The Muscovites, however, showed little understanding of internal Ukrainian social affairs, and, believing them to be quite unimportant, more or less ignored their existence. Muscovite boyars could not understand why the envoys of Hetman Vygovsky were so contemptuous of the Zaporozhians, as if they were drunkards or gamblers, or indeed why the Cossacks and their Hetman were referred to as 'the Zaporozhian forces'. The boyars were, however, curious enough to ask the envoys whether Hetmen lived in Zaporozhie or in other towns, from whom they were chosen, and how Bogdan Khmelnitsky had been elected. Having annexed Little Russia, the Muscovite government seemed quite prepared to remain ignorant of even the most elementary facts.

For several decades this tortuous Little Russian problem complicated and interfered with Muscovy's foreign policy, which became embroiled in Little Russian squabbles; moreover, Muscovy was weakened by her struggle with Poland, and was forced to abandon Lithuania, Little Russia, Volynia and Podolia, and barely managed to retain the Eastern Ukraine and Kiev. These losses might well have impelled the Muscovites to repeat Khmelnitsky's sentiments when he criticised them for not coming to his assistance in time: 'I did not want this, and it did not have to turn out like this.'

The Little Russian problem bedevilled Muscovy's foreign policy both directly and indirectly. Tsar Alexis, who went to war with Poland in 1654 because of Little Russia, quickly conquered the whole of White Russia and a large part of Lithuania including Vilna, Kovno and Grodno. While Muscovy was busy occupying the eastern regions of the *Retch Pospolita*, the Swedish King, Charles X, attacked from the north, and with equal rapidity captured Great and Little Poland, including Cracow and Warsaw. Charles exiled Jan Casimir, King of Poland, proclaimed himself King, and even wanted to take Lithuania away from Alexis. Thus, two enemies who had attacked Poland from different directions met and quarrelled over the spoils.

Tsar Alexis had not forgotten Tsar Ivan's ambition to control the Baltic coast and Lithuania, with the result that in 1656 the struggle with Poland was interrupted by a war with Sweden; once again the problem of extending Muscovy's frontiers to her natural boundary along the Baltic came to the fore. However, no progress was made; the Muscovites failed to capture Riga, Tsar Alexis stopped all military operations, and in 1661, was forced to make peace with Sweden, and by the Peace of Cardis, abandoned all his conquests.

For Muscovy the war was fruitless and harmful; it gave Poland the opportunity to recover from Swedish ravages; it prevented Poland from being annexed to Sweden; and although both were hostile to Muscovy both had been weakened by their mutual hostility.

Khmelnitsky, who died in 1657, left a legacy both to his friends, whom he had betrayed, and to his enemies, to whom he had sworn allegiance. Frightened by the *rapprochement* between Muscovy and Poland, Khmelnitsky had concluded an agreement with Charles X of Sweden and Prince Raguza of Transylvania to divide the *Retch Pospolita*. A typical Cossack, accustomed to serving all and sundry, Khmelnitsky had at one time or another been servant, ally or traitor to the Polish King, the Tsar of Muscovy, the Crimean Khan, the Turkish Sultan, the Moldavian Sovereign and the Transylvanian Prince. Towards the end he intended to become a free, independent Prince of Little Russia under the protection of a Polish–Swedish King, which was an ambition of Charles X. It was these intrigues that forced Tsar Alexis to bring the war with Sweden to an end. Little Russia also involved Muscovy in her first direct clash with Turkey.

An overt struggle between the registered Cossacks and the Cossack rabble broke out on Khmelnitsky's death.[1] His successor, Vigovsky, went over to Poland, and with the assistance of the Tatars annihilated Tsar Alexis' army at Konotop in 1659. Encouraged by this victory, and freed from the Swedes through the assistance of Muscovy, the Poles were not prepared to cede any conquests. This precipitated a second war between Poland and Muscovy, and further disasters ensued. Prince Khovansky was defeated in White Russia, and Sheremetiev was forced to surrender as a result of Cossack treachery near Chudnov in Volynia. Muscovy lost Lithuania and White Russia. Vigovsky's successors, Khmelnitsky's son Yury, and Teteri[2] changed sides. The Ukraine was split into two hostile parts; Muscovy retained the left bank of the Dnieper, while the Poles held the right bank. The King of Poland occupied practically the whole of Little Russia. Both sides were quite exhausted by the protracted struggle. Muscovy was unable to pay her soldiers, and the use of copper coins with the same values as silver coins caused a riot in 1662. Under the leadership of Lyubomirsky, Greater Poland rebelled against the King. It seemed as if both Muscovy and Poland were prepared to fight to the last drop of blood. However, a mutual enemy, Hetman Doroshenko, came to their assistance. In 1666 Hetman Doroshenko accepted the suzerainty of the Turkish Sultan for himself and the Polish-held right bank of the Dnieper.

Faced by a common and frightening enemy, Poland and

[1] For a description of Khmelnitsky's successors and their policies, ibid. pp. 45–64.

[2] Colonel Paul Teteri had represented Khmelnitsky in Moscow.

Muscovy signed the Peace of Andrusovo in 1667, and the war came to an end.[1] Muscovy retained the Provinces of Smolensk and Seversk, as well as eastern Ukraine, which included Kiev, and acquired a frontier which stretched along the Dnieper as far as the rapids at Zaporozhie; beyond that there was a no-man's land, owing allegiance to both Poland and Muscovy.

In this way the new dynasty atoned for the errors it had committed at Stolbovo, Dulino and in Poland. The Peace of Andrusovo completely changed the direction of Muscovite foreign policy. The cautious and shortsighted Morozov was replaced by the capable Ordin-Nashchokin who immediately started to elaborate a new policy. Poland ceased to be dangerous, and for a century there was to be peace between them. The Little Russian question had diverted attention from other related problems, such as Sweden and Turkey. A war with one or both of them necessitated an alliance with Poland, who was herself threatened by both countries; indeed, Poland was strongly in favour of such an alliance, and Ordin-Nashchokin based his policies on this idea.[2]

Before the Treaty of Andrusovo, he had written a report for Tsar Alexis giving three reasons why such an alliance was necessary. First, because this alliance would give the Orthodox population of Poland a measure of protection; second, because it would prevent the Cossacks from waging war on Great Russia at the instigation of the Khan and Sweden; and third, because it would enable Moldavia and Wallachia, at present separated from Orthodox Russia by hostile Poland, to break away from Turkey and become reattached to Russia. In this way, he argued, an nitegrated Orthodox Christian nation would come into being and stretch from the Danube to the Dnieper, to include the peoples of Podolia, Volynia, Great and Little Russia, and

[1] For the diplomatic and military background leading to the Peace of Andrusovo, as well as its terms, see Bickford O'Brien, *Muscovy and the Ukraine*, pp. 110–19.

[2] Ordin-Nashchokin was handsomely rewarded by Tsar Alexis for his services. He was awarded the title of Privy and Court Boyar, appointed Keeper of the State Great Seals, and head of the Department of Foreign Affairs. Moreoever, he was given properties and estates in keeping with his new status.

Chervonny Rus.[1] This particular concept should have appealed strongly to Tsar Alexis, since he had long been interested in the Turkish Christians.

In 1656, after the Easter services, Tsar Alexis had asked the Greek merchants who were staying in Moscow whether they wished him to liberate them from Turkish slavery. 'When you return to your country,' he said, 'ask your bishops, priests and monks to pray for me, and by their prayers my sword will cut the throats of my enemies.' Tsar Alexis then turned to his boyars, and with tears in his eyes said that his heart was grieved by the enslavement of these poor people by the infidels, and that they would have to answer before God at the day of judgement if he neglected to use his power to free them, and he took it upon himself to sacrifice his army, his treasury and even his own blood for them. This, at any rate, is how the Greek merchants told it. In 1672, prior to the Sultan's invasion of Poland, Tsar Alexis had undertaken by treaty to go to the assistance of Poland in the event of a Turkish attack, and to dissuade the Sultan and Crimean Khan from going to war with Poland.

The two new allies did not share the same political views. Poland was primarily concerned with external security, while Muscovy had also to worry about the Uniates, and the problems arising from the Turkish Christians and the Russian Mohammedans.

Religion was already a problem in sixteenth-century Eastern Europe. Tsar Ivan had defeated the two Mohammedan states of Kazan and Astrakhan. The subjugated Mohammedans had turned to their spiritual leader and successor to the Caliphs, the Sultan, praying him to free them from the Christian yoke. On the other hand there lived in the Balkan peninsula as subjects of the Turkish Sultan a vast Orthodox population. They, in turn, prayed that the Sovereign of Muscovy, Protector of the Orthodox East, might deliver the Turkish Christians from the Mohammedan yoke. The idea of a war with Turkey, assisted by Muscovy, spread quickly among the Balkan Christians.

[1] Ordin-Nashchokin's views on foreign policy are discussed in *A History of Russian Economic Thought*, ed. and trans. John M. Letiche (University of California Press, 1967) pp. 213–15.

THE RISE OF THE ROMANOVS

By agreement, Muscovite envoys were sent to Constantinople to dissuade the Sultan from going to war with the *Retch Pospolita*. They returned with important news; on their way through Moldavia and Wallachia they had heard people say: 'If only God would grant us Christians a small victory over the Turks we would begin to surpass them.' In Constantinople, the Muscovite envoys were told that shortly before their arrival envoys from Kazan and Astrakhan and the Bashkirs had begged the Sultan to taken them under his protection; they had pointed out that the Muscovites, who hated their religion, were killing them and hoped to destroy them. The Sultan replied that they must be patient, and gave them embroidered gowns.

The Little Russian problem, therefore, gave rise to two more. First, the Baltic problem, which was concerned with the acquisition of a coast line, and second, the Eastern problem, which, because of a large Balkan Christian population, was to determine relations with Turkey. The resolution of the second problem had been considered only superficially by Tsar Alexis and Ordin-Nashchokin; Muscovy was powerless to deal directly with Turkey, and had to content itself with fighting the Crimean Khan who stood between them and Turkey.

The Crimea was an irritant to Muscovite diplomats, which affected every international alignment that they devised. At the beginning of Tsar Alexis' reign, Muscovy had failed to deal with Poland. Therefore an offensive alliance against the Crimea was suggested to Poland. Accordingly, the Peace of Andrusovo was converted by the Moscow Agreement of 1686 into a perpetual peace treaty. For the first time, Muscovy joined a European coalition of Poland, the German Empire and the Venetian Republic against Turkey. Muscovy's role was the hardest: to fight the Turks and the Crimeans. Muscovite foreign policy became extremely complex. The government had to re-establish or repair relations with a wide circle of powers whom it needed for protection against hostile neighbours, or because they were a necessary adjunct to Muscovy's European policy.

Even when Muscovy was at her lowest ebb internationally during the Time of Troubles, she never quite lost her diplomatic influence. In fact events in the West were quite favourable to Muscovy. The Thirty Years War was just beginning, relations between states were uncertain, and isolation was greatly feared. For all its political weakness, geography and religion made Muscovy important.

Courmenin,[1] the first French Ambassador to Muscovy, called Tsar Michael the leader of Eastern Europe and the head of the Greek faith for reasons other than mere French courtesy. Muscovy lay behind all countries which stretched from the Baltic to the Adriatic. When international relations became thoroughly confused, and war broke out, every country wished to secure its eastern rear by an alliance, or at least a respite from hostilities with Muscovy. This was the reason why the new dynasty, without any effort, was able to strengthen its international relations.

Muscovy became involved in different European political and economic alliances. England and Holland helped Tsar Michael to become reconciled with his old enemies, Poland and Sweden, because Muscovy was a profitable market for them, as well as providing a convenient road to the East, to Persia and India.[2] The King of France invited Tsar Michael to form an alliance with him to protect French commercial interests in the East, which competed with English and Dutch interests.[3] Even the Sultan invited Tsar Michael to join him against the Poles. Gustavus Adolfus, King of Sweden, who had despoiled Muscovy by the Treaty of Stolbovo, found that Poland and Austria were a common enemy. Gustavus Adolfus therefore suggested an anti-

[1] Louis de Hayes Courmenin came to Russia in 1630; he was able to obtain valuable trade rights. See A. Rambaud, *Recueil des instructions données aux ambassadeurs et ministres de France* (Paris, 1890) pp. 27–31; and Walter Kirchner, *Commercial Relations between Russia and Europe* (Indiana U.P., 1966) pp. 113–114.

[2] For details of Anglo-Russian commercial relations see I. Lubimenko, *Les Relations commerciales et politiques de l'Angleterre avec la Russie avant Pierre le Grand* (Paris, 1933); I. Lubimenko, *Les Marchands Anglais en Russie au XVIIe siècle* (Paris, 1922); M. S. Anderson, *Britain's Discovery of Russia 1553–1815* (Macmillan, 1958) pp. 33–6; S. Yacobson, 'Early Anglo-Russian Relations', *Slavonic Review*, vol. 13, no. 59 (Apr 1935) pp. 597–610.

[3] For details see Kirchner, *Commercial Relations between Russia and Europe*, pp. 90–119 and pp. 120–31.

Catholic alliance to Muscovite diplomats, and tempted them into thinking that they might play an important part, by calling the triumphant Swedish army in Germany an advance guard fighting for Muscovy. Gustavus Adolfus was also the first to appoint a permanent resident in Moscow.

Although Tsar Michael was weaker than Ivan or Fedor, he was far less isolated from Europe; and Tsar Alexis was even less isolated than Tsar Michael. Foreign envoys were becoming common, and Muscovite Ambassadors travelled to European courts, including Spain and Tuscany. It was the first time that Muscovite diplomats travelled to so many different places. Although Muscovy was alternatively losing or gaining territory in the west, her expansion eastwards proceeded steadily. In the sixteenth century Russian colonisers had passed the Urals, in the seventeenth century they had reached Siberia and the Chinese border, and by the middle of the seventeenth century they had increased Russian territory by about 70,000 square miles. Muscovy's successful eastward expansion brought her into conflict with China.[1]

Internationally, Muscovy's relations were confused and complex, and affected her internal development in a number of ways. Frequent wars had shown up the inadequacy of Muscovite institutions, and forced the government to examine foreign models. The increased number of foreign ambassadors gave the Muscovites plenty of opportunities to observe them. A better acquaintance with Western Europe caused the administrative classes to break with prejudice and isolation. War and observation of other institutions made the Muscovites increasingly aware of their own poverty, the deficiencies of their armies, the low productivity of their people, and the lack of profitable occupations for them. Every new war, every fresh defeat created new

[1] Russia's eastward expansion was led by individuals who forced the central government to follow. See *Russia's Eastward Expansion*, ed. G. A. Lensen (Prentice Hall, 1964); A. Lobanov-Rostovsky, *Russia and Asia* (Ann Arbor, 1951) pp. 33–69; George V. Lantzeff, 'Russian Eastward Expansion Before the Mongol Invasion', *The American Slavic and East European Review*, vol. 6, (Dec 1947) pp. 1–10.

problems for the government, and new burdens for the people. Muscovy's foreign policy was exhausting the country.

The extent of the people's effort can be shown simply by listing the wars which occurred under the first three Tsars of the new dynasty. Under Tsar Michael there were two wars with Poland and one with Sweden: all three were unsuccessful. His successors waged two wars with Poland over Little Russia, and one with Sweden: two ended in disaster. Under Tsar Fedor there was a war with Turkey which had started under his father in 1673, and which ended with the senseless armistice of Bakhshisarai in 1681, by which the Ukraine west of the Dnieper was abandoned to the Turks.[1]

Thirty, out of approximately seventy years, from 1613 to 1682, were devoted to war, which were sometimes fought simultaneously with several opponents.

[1] Russia retained the territory east of the Dnieper, and the city of Kiev on the west bank of the Dnieper. But payment of an annual tribute to the Crimean Khan, a vassal of the Sublime Porte, was resumed. In the meantime the Ukraine had become a shambles. This period of her history is known as 'the ruin' (*ruina*). See Michael Florinsky, *Russia* (Macmillan, New York, 1953) pp. 263–5; also C. Bickford O'Brien, 'Russia and Turkey 1677–1681. The Treaty of Bakhshisarai', *Russian Review*, vol. 13, no. 4 (Oct 1953) pp. 259–68.

Chapter Seven

★

WHAT WAS happening internally in Muscovy? The immediate consequences of the Time of Troubles, Muscovy's foreign policy, and the serious external problems facing the new dynasty, which lacked the intellectual or material capacity to deal with them, have been discussed. How was a solution to be found?

It is necessary first of all to mention the outstanding features of Russian life of the period. These features are confused, and full of internal inconsistencies. However, they all had a common root: the deep rift caused by the Time of Troubles in the people's minds and attitudes, which has been discussed earlier. The ancient customs upon which the state had relied under the old dynasty had been severely shaken, and the traditions which had guided them had been broken. When men cease to follow custom and break with tradition they are forced to think, and act experimentally. The Muscovites in government during the seventeenth century were noted for their lack of self-confidence. The wealth of new ideas which came about as a result of painful experience and thought was accompanied by uncertain political activity and divergent purpose, a sign of inexperience. They realised that their wealth was limited, that there was a big gap between available resources and what was required. First, they tried to develop new assets from existing resources, and overburdened the people in so doing; and, second, they improved and recreated the system they had inherited from their ancestors.

When finally it was obvious that the country was exhausted, the Muscovites turned elsewhere and enlisted foreign assistance. Once again, however, their own timidity overcame them, and they began to wonder whether they had deviated too far in adopting foreign help, and could in fact do without it. These two continuously interchanging trends continued into the seventeenth century until a clash occurred, and caused a series of political and religious upheavals. During the eighteenth century both trends were combined in the reforms of Peter the Great, and were directed to a common goal. In brief, this was how Muscovy developed internally from the end of the Time of Troubles to the beginning of the eighteenth century. But how did it work in detail?

However hard the new dynasty tried to imitate the old order in an attempt to divert attention from the fact that it was of recent creation, and therefore legally suspect, it could not dispense with innovations. The Time of Troubles had destroyed so many of the old customs that any restoration became of itself an innovation. Indeed, innovations were introduced more or less continuously from 1613 to the end of the seventeenth century, and prepared the way for the reforms of Peter the Great. The duality in policy can be illustrated by two fundamental and conflicting experiments.

Some reforms were carried out without any foreign assistance, and were based upon purely Muscovite knowledge and experience. Any development of national wealth was achieved by a curtailment of freedom and a restriction of private interests, so that any improvement in one direction was accompanied by heavy sacrifices of welfare and liberty in another. Human affairs generally progress according to an established pattern influenced more by circumstance than by men. From their inception the government was instinctively aware that the reforms would be unsuccessful, and as this awareness became more pronounced, so the desire grew to imitate or use foreign techniques.

Reforms which were introduced to maintain or restore a system destroyed by the Time of Troubles were remarkable for their typical Muscovite caution and deficiencies, and absence of any new principles. The general aim of policy was to revise, and not revolutionise the structure of government, to repair it without fundamentally reconstructing it. Above all, some order had to be introduced into relationships between people which the Time of

Troubles had thrown into complete confusion; people had to be circumscribed precisely. Tsar Michael's administration had to face a multiplicity of problems since it had almost to create a completely new structure of government, the old mechanism having been destroyed by the Time of Troubles. The author of a Pskov chronicle from the Time of Troubles wrote that under Tsar Michael 'the state had to be built anew'.

Tsar Michael's reign was marked by a period of intense legislative activity dealing with a wide range of problems. As a result, Tsar Alexis inherited a great many new laws which he felt should be codified. It was an accepted principle of Muscovite legislation that new laws were promulgated in response to the judicial and administrative requirements of Muscovite government departments, who were responsible for their revision and implementation. New laws were added to the Statute book in accordance with one of the articles of the Code of 1150.[1] As a result, the original Code began to look like a tree trunk with branches growing into all departments of state: the supplements to the original Code were known as departmental 'legal registers'. Finally, the individual legal registers had to be combined and incorporated into one Code, in order to avoid repetition of a typical instance which occurred under Ivan the Terrible. A certain Adashev had raised a legal problem in the Boyar Duma which had emanated from his Office of Petitions; an identical problem had already been raised by the Treasury and had been solved by the Boyar Duma. However, the Boyar Duma had apparently forgotten its recent decision, and ordered the Treasury Secretary to insert the new law in their legal register, from which there resulted a duplication. It was quite common for one government department to look at the legal registers of other departments for a law which, in fact, was written in their own legal register. It is easy to imagine the muddle a stupid Secretary could make, or the advantage to be derived by an intelligent one. The necessity for codification was strengthened by departmental abuse, which indeed produced

[1] A brief analysis of Muscovite law can be found in Horace Dewey, 'The 1550 Sudebnik as an Instrument of Reform', *Jahrbücher für Geschichte Osteuropas*, X 161–80.

the necessary impetus, and in part determined its form. Certain other assumptions can be made with regard to this desired reform. It is clear that the unusual circumstances which existed after the Time of Troubles created new problems and challenges. It was the requirements of state and not any new political concept arising from the Time of Troubles which produced the required legislative initiative, notwithstanding the new dynasty's desire to perpetuate ancient customs.

Until the seventeenth century, Muscovite legislation was a haphazard affair, designed only to deal with current problems arising from administrative practice independent of the structure of government. Custom, known and understood by all, was a substitute for law. As soon as tradition was dispensed with, custom no longer served, and it became apparent that precise legislation was desirable. Hence, under the new dynasty, legislation became more organic, and was less the result of *ad hoc* administrative decisions. In fact, it came nearer to becoming the basis of a system of government, and though it failed, it was an attempt to clarify underlying principles.

It is difficult to establish the connection between the *Ulozhenie* and the rising of 1648, which occurred one and a half months before Tsar Alexis and the Boyar Duma met to codify the laws.[1] This revolt revealed the new dynasty's position. The first two Tsars were not universally respected, and in spite of their elective origins, soon adopted the habits of the old dynasty. They regarded the country as their own patrimony, neglected it, and, in general, imitated all the old dynasty's shortcomings. Perhaps there was nothing else to imitate!

The court consisted of the dregs of the remaining boyars and some newcomers who were no better, who both wanted to become the ruling class. The most influential among them were the Tsar and Tsaritsa's family and relatives. For a long time the throne was surrounded by favourites: the Saltykovs; Prince Repnin and again the Saltykovs under Tsar Michael; Morozov, Miloslavsky, Nikon and Khitrovo under Tsar Alexis; and

[1] For the background see Leo Loewenson, 'The Moscow rising of 1648', *Slavonic and East European Review*, XXVIII 146–56.

Yazikov and Likhachev under Tsar Fedor. Even Patriarch Philaret who rejoiced in the title of Second Great Sovereign was transformed from an eminent boyar into a timeserver, who appointed to the Patriarchy a man who might have been a nobleman's son, but was more properly Philaret's lackey.

The first three Tsars of the new dynasty were all under age: the first two were sixteen years old, and the third was fourteen. From the start the ruling classes took advantage of their youth and their lack of character; developed an independence in governing, and a degree of speculation that even the needy officials under Ivan the Terrible would have envied; and they had kept one-half of all revenues for themselves, or so it was said. They were in a privileged position, and since Tsar Michael had given an undertaking that the nobility could not suffer the death penalty, there was nothing to inhibit them. The worst that could happen was exile; under Tsar Alexis a nobleman could be dismissed or lose favour, whereas for the same offence a secretary, clerk or ordinary man could lose a hand or a foot. This tacit understanding between Tsar and boyar placed the new dynasty in a false position, and created the semblance of a Tsar–boyar stand against the people.

Kotoshikhin remarked that although Tsar Michael 'signed as Autocrat he could do nothing without the Boyars' consent'. Tatishchev added to this that the Tsar was glad to be at peace, or in other words that he was content that the Boyars should govern. Nevertheless, the people instinctively felt that something was wrong, and the era of the new dynasty became an era of popular revolt. Tsar Alexis' reign was particularly turbulent. At the same time, Muscovite society created a type of 'strong man' or 'timeserver', as he was called. He was a privileged landowner, lay or cleric, or a favoured courtier, who believed himself to be immune from punishment, and sufficiently unscrupulous to take advantage of his position and the absence of justice 'to oppress and offend' those less fortunate. This species of man was a typical product of the new dynasty's domestic policy, which encouraged Muscovite governing circles to believe that the Tsar was their pawn and could not manage without them. The people hated these favourites.

The revolt in Moscow of June 1648, which was repeated in other towns, clearly expressed this hatred. The people of Moscow had been particularly badly treated by powerful temporal and clerical interests, including the Patriarch, the bishops and the monks. Urban common land was expropriated to provide for settlements, country houses and kitchen gardens; roads leading from the cities to the forests were ploughed up so that the ordinary citizen had nowhere for his cattle to graze, nor any place to cut firewood, a right which they had been guaranteed from time immemorial under earlier Tsars. The June revolt was an insurrection of the ' "black" taxed common people' against the 'powerful' magnates, when 'the mob attacked the boyars' and plundered their establishments together with those belonging to noblemen and officials, and killed the worst of their administrators. The effect was instantaneous: the court was terrified; its members hastily distributed bribes among the soldiers and the mob; the Tsar ordered the Streltsy to be plied with drink; for several days in succession the Tsar's father-in-law entertained a select number of Moscow taxpayers in his own residence; during the procession of the Cross the Tsar himself delivered a self-justifying and tearful speech to the populace, 'begging' the mob to spare his brother-in-law and favourite Morozov. Promises there were a-plenty!

The authorities were frightened that the rural areas would also revolt; to counter this rumours were spread that the Tsar had become merciful, that he had banished 'the strong men', and had put some of them to death with staves and stones.

Certainly, Moscow had never known such turbulence under the old dynasty, nor such popular bitterness against the ruling classes; nor, indeed, had the ruling classes changed so quickly from contempt of, to ingratiation with 'the mob'. Furthermore, lewd comments about the Tsar himself, a common occurrence after the revolt, had never before been uttered: 'The Tsar is a fool, he sees everything through the eyes of Morozov and Miloslavsky; they rule everyone, and the Tsar knows this but keeps silent; the devil has taken his senses.'

However, the Moscow revolt of June 1648, which subsequently erupted in other towns, was not the only reason why the

Ulozhenie was thought necessary. The only difference the revolt made was that provincial representatives were invited to participate in the discussions. The government considered that summoning the provincial council on 1 September to hear and sign the Code, would appease the nation. Patriarch Nikon can be believed when he wrote, as if it was universally known, that this council was not summoned voluntarily, but 'from fear that all taxed people would rise, and not for a better reason'. While, therefore, the revolts were not primarily responsible for codification, they did make some contribution which the government was afraid to negate.

The initiative and idea that it would be desirable to have an *Ulozhenie*, a Code, came from the Tsar and his confidential council, which consisted of the Holy Council and the Boyar Duma. Proclamations distributed in the provinces during the summer of 1648 declared that in response to requests made by the boyars, court officials, and men of all ranks, the Tsar and the Patriarch had given orders to compile a Code. It is difficult to know how, and when, a petition from all ranks could have been presented, or whether indeed it ever had been.

It had been customary for Muscovite governments to speak 'in the name of all the land', a custom which was abandoned with the extinction of the old dynasty. The new Tsars substituted the phrase 'a petition from people of all ranks', which became a stereotype to justify every act of government. The phrase itself was never properly defined. All that was necessary was for a haphazardly-constituted group of men of different ranks to petition the throne for a decree to be drawn up 'according to a petition from people of all ranks'. The official petition, reflecting the will of the people, became *sui generis* a political fiction retained until the early twentieth century for certain well-known cases, a survival from the past whose conditional value was clearly understood! On 14 July 1648, the Sovereign together with the Holy Council and Boyar Duma ordered 'articles suitable for government and nation' to be selected and collated from the Acts of the Apostles and the writings of the Holy Fathers, from the laws of the Greek Emperors, from the decrees of previous Russian

Sovereigns, as well as from the old charters. The decrees and old charters were to be 'compared' with the old codes of law, and new articles were to be written to cover any omission.[1] All this was to be done in 'general council'.

The composition of the draft *Ulozhenie* was entrusted to a special codification committee of five, consisting of the boyars,

[1] The preamble states:

In the year 7156 [1648], the sixteenth day of July, the Sovereign Tsar and Grand Prince, Aleksei Mikhailovich, autocrat of all Russia, being in the twentieth year of his age and in the third year of ruling his God-protected country conferred with his Father and Interceder before God, Most Holy Joseph, Patriarch of Moscow and all Russia, as well as with the metropolitans, archbishops, bishops, and the whole Holy Sobor, and discussed with His Majesty's boyars, *okolnichi*, and [other] Duma members as to the following: to copy the articles written in the rules of the Holy Apostles and Holy Fathers or in the civil statutes of the Greek Emperors which are suitable for the affairs of the state and the country; also to collect the edicts and boyars' decisions concerning various affairs of the state and the country, which were issued by the former Great Sovereign Tsars . . .; and to collate such edicts and boyars' decisions with the old judicial codes. And where some articles [situations] were not provided for in the judicial codes of the former sovereigns or in the boyars' decisions rendered in the past years, the General Council to write and formulate such articles in accordance with His Majesty's order, so that citizens of the Moscow state of all ranks, from the highest to the lowest, have equal [*rovna*] justice and trials in all cases. His Majesty the Tsar and Grand Prince of all Russia, Aleksei Mikhailovich, commanded the boyars Prince Nikita Ivanovich Odoevski [and] Prince Semen Vasilievich Prozorovskoi, *okolnich* Prince Fedor Fedorovich Volkonskoi, and *diaki* Gavrila Leontiev and Fedor Griboedov, to collect all this and prepare a report.

For the purpose of accomplishing this great undertaking of the Sovereign and the country, the Sovereign conferred with his Father and Interceder before God, Most Holy Joseph, Patriarch of Moscow and all Russia, and the boyars resolved to select from among the Moscow gentry . . . two men from each rank, and to take two men from among the gentry, and junior boyars [boyars' sons] of each big town except Novgorod [and] from among the citizens of Novgorod one man from each section, one man from each smaller town, three men from among the great merchants, two men from the merchants' guild and two men from the drapers' guild, one man from the artisans' guild [lit: black hundred], one from each merchant settlement – all of them good and wise men, in order that this great undertaking of the Sovereign and the country be confirmed. . . .

Quoted in Thornton Anderson, *Russian Political Thought* (Cornell U.P., 1967) pp. 106–7.

Princes Odoevsky and Prozorsky, the courtier Prince Volkonsky, and two secretaries, Leontiev and Griboedov. None of them was influential or distinguished in court or official circles. The Tsar himself was as contemptuous of Odoevsky as was the rest of Moscow. The only man to leave a mark was Griboedov, who wrote the first-ever history textbook for the Tsar's children, in which he traced the origin of the new dynasty, through the Tsaritsa Anastasia from the son of a fictitious 'Sovereign of Prussia', a Romanov who was descended from the Roman Emperor Augustus.

The three most important members of the commission were also members of the Boyar Duma, with the result that this 'department of Prince Odoevsky and his colleagues', as it was called in the documents, was in effect a sub-committee of the Boyar Duma. The commission selected articles from the indicated sources, and drew up new ones; all were contained in a report presented to the Tsar and Boyar Duma for revision. Meanwhile, the elected representatives of all ranks, officials and urban commercial classes were summoned to Moscow by 1 September. Rural or district representatives as a separate group were not invited. On 3 October the Tsar, clergy, and Boyar Duma heard the commission's draft Code, which at the same time was being read to the elected representatives from Moscow and other towns who had been summoned to 'this general council', so that 'the whole of the Code might be fixed immutably'. The Tsar then ordered the senior clergy, the Boyar Duma and the elected representatives to sign the Code; it was printed in 1649 together with all the signatures, and distributed among all the departments of state and governors' offices in all the towns, so that 'all affairs might be carried out in accordance with the Code'.[1]

This was the sequence of events as set out in the official preface

[1] No complete translation exists in English. However for the table of contents and chapter XI see first, *Readings in Russian Civilization* (University of Chicago Press, 1964) I 173–9; second, R. E. F. Smith, *The Enserfment of Russian Peasantry* (Cambridge U.P., 1968) pp. 138–52; and third, for chapters I, II, IV, V and VI, *Medieval Russia*, ed. Basil Dmytryshyn (Holt, Rinehart, Winston Inc., 1967) pp. 261–8.

to the Code. The commission was faced with two fundamental problems. First, it had to collate, analyse and elaborate existing laws, which differed in period, purport, and which were scattered throughout different government departments, and codify them. Second, it was faced with the complicated task of creating a consistent body of law to cover situations for which no provision had been made. Moreover, the commission could not rely on its own judicial vision or sense of equity to cover all contingencies. Consequently, it became necessary to enquire into the needs and attitudes of society, its views on equity, as well as the judicial and administrative practice of institutions. At any rate, this is how an investigation would proceed in modern times.

The elected representatives were able to advise the Commission on the first problem. But on the second, the Commission had to review the administrative procedures of the departments in order to find the precedents or 'exemplary cases', as they were called, and determine how provincial governors, centralised institutions, the Tsar and Boyar Duma resolved problems not covered by law. This was an extensive and lengthy undertaking which was never given effect. The government decided to codify the law by accelerating and simplifying the whole procedure. The *Ulozhenie* consisted of 967 articles divided into twenty-five chapters.

In two and a half months, by 3 October 1648, the first twelve chapters, nearly half the work, was ready for consideration by the Tsar and Boyar Duma. The remaining thirteen chapters were written, considered and ratified by the Boyar Duma by the end of January 1649. The work of the commission and council was finished, and the *Ulozhenie* was ready in manuscript; it had taken just over six months to collate this voluminous work. The impetus to a speedy conclusion was given by news of revolts following the Moscow June revolt, in Solvychegodsk, Kozlov, Talitsk, Ustyug and elsewhere; and in January 1649 the Code was being finished against a background of rumours of a further upheaval in the capital. The commission was in a hurry to finish its work so that the elected representatives might return to their towns with the news that the government of Muscovy was pursuing a new policy, and that the *Ulozhenie* promised 'equal' justice to all.

Indeed, the *Ulozhenie* bore all the signs of having been drawn up carelessly and hastily. The commission ignored the mass of departmental documents, and concentrated on the basic sources which had been listed in its brief of 16 July. These were the *Kormchaya*, especially the second part, which included the codes and laws of the Greek Emperors, Muscovite laws, the Tsar's Sudebnik, with its supplementary decrees, and departmental legal registers.

The *Ulozhenie* relied heavily on the departmental legal registers, which were incorporated verbatim or paraphrased into whole chapters. For instance, two chapters on *pomestie* and *votchina* estate holdings were taken from the Estate Department's legal register; a chapter 'On the trial of Kholops' was taken from the Kholop Department's legal register; and a chapter 'On Brigandage and Theft' was taken from the Crime Department's legal register.

The commission also referred to some secondary sources, in particular to the Lithuanian Statute of 1588, which is repeatedly mentioned in that part of the original *Ulozhenie* which is extant. The authors of the *Ulozhenie* organised the early chapters on similar lines: subject matter, order of articles, selection of cases and relationships which required legal definition, and legal problems. However, answers to problems were derived from Russian law, jurisprudence, and legal situations where these were identical with the Lithuanian Statute. Everything that was superfluous or alien to Muscovite law and its legal system was eliminated; everything that was used was rephrased. Therefore, the Lithuanian Statute could not be described as the basic source for the *Ulozhenie*, although it served as a legal guide for its authors, who used it as a framework for their work.[1]

The commission was able to draw on important live evidence, as distinct from archival material: namely, the elected council representatives who had been summoned to consider and sign the *Ulozhenie*. This, as has just been mentioned, was initiated by the Tsar and Boyar Duma, while the work itself was undertaken by a commission from the Duma together with the cooperation

[1] The *Ulozhenie* was none the less vastly inferior to the Lithuanian Statute of 1588.

of government departments, who provided documents and information. It was subsequently examined, revised and approved by the Boyar Duma, read to the elected council representatives, attested and finally, signed.

The elected council representatives were not just passive listeners during the reading of the *Ulozhenie* which had been prepared without their help. There is no evidence that in fact discussions took place during the reading, nor were the representatives required to assent or dissent to individual articles. Yet, they did participate in many ways. The petition of 16 July did not contemplate a new Code. The commission's brief was to collect and co-ordinate existing legislation, and 'make decrees, whether Sovereigns' or boyars', consistent with the old codes'. New articles were only drawn up to fill omissions in the existing laws. Indeed, the commission was charged to work 'in general council', together with the elected council representatives who had been summoned to Moscow that 'they might work for the Sovereign and State together with His boyars', Prince Odoevsky and his colleagues or 'be in his Department'. Therefore, these representatives were either co-opted onto the codification commission, or were simply attached to it. As they gained experience, the elected representatives pointed out required changes or amplifications, and stressed their own requirements, which the commission would present to the Boyar Duma in the form of petitions. The Duma gave its verdict, which was communicated to the elected representatives in the form of a law, and subsequently incorporated into the *Ulozhenie*. This was the extent of the elected representatives' participation in the framing of the *Ulozhenie*.

It is difficult to determine the precise procedure or whether in fact meetings were attended by all 290 elected representatives, or by smaller groups. It is known, however, that on 30 October 1648, representatives of the service and urban taxed merchant classes presented separate petitions asking for an alteration in urban taxes of suburban settlements, town houses and urban trading establishments belonging to non-taxpaying owners. The commission combined both and presented one common petition 'from all the land' to the Boyar Duma. Petitions, reports, notes and amendments, as well as Boyar decrees were worked on by the Boyar Duma in order to determine the structure and situation of urban taxpayers, and their relationship with others who worked in towns. Chapter XIX of the *Ulozhenie*, which was concerned with urban taxpayers, was compiled from these findings.

Thus, the elected representatives participated in the work of codification in two ways. First, by advising the members of the codification committee. Second, by presenting petitions through the commission to the Boyar Duma. There was, moreover, a third way which was most important, and which brought the elected representatives in direct contact not with the commission, but with the Boyar Duma itself. This happened on the occasions when Tsar and Boyar Duma appeared before them, and all three would decide a particular issue. The *Ulozhenie* refers to one such case, although there were others. The elected representatives presented a petition 'from all the land' that land which had passed into the hands of the clergy contrary to the law of 1580,[1] should be restored to their former owners. An article (42) was, as a result, included in chapter XVII of the *Ulozhenie* which was concerned with *votchina* estates, and stated that, on the advice of the Holy Council, the Sovereign had discussed this problem with the Boyar Duma and the representatives of the service class, and that 'it was agreed in council' to forbid the alienation of *votchina* estates to the Church. In this instance, the elected representatives directly influenced legislation, but it must be pointed out that only the service class was involved, in spite of the phrase 'of all the land', since they were immediately concerned as holders of *votchina* estates. It would appear that the elected representatives showed greater political understanding than the representatives of supreme power, in that they were concerned for the good of the whole country, rather than for the welfare of one class.

[1] Determined efforts to control the monastic acquisition of land were not made until the 1570s. In 1580 a Church Council reaffirmed a decree of 1573 which stated that property could only be given to monasteries that had little land and then only with the Tsar's approval. This decree prohibited any church dignitary or institution from buying land or giving mortgages on real property. See Jerome Blum, *Lord and Peasant in Russia* (Princeton U.P., 1961) p. 197.

There is documentary evidence of two other petitions, not directly mentioned in the *Ulozhenie*, which were drawn up with the help of the elected representatives. They submitted a petition to the Sovereign and Boyar Duma, and together instructed the committee to repeal the time limit (*urochnyia leta*)[1] beyond which legal action could not be taken for the return of runaway peasants; indeed, this issue was covered in the first section of chapter XI of the *Ulozhenie* which dealt with the peasants.

Of even greater significance was chapter VIII 'On the redemption of prisoners', which created a general household tax to pay the ransoms of prisoners of war, as well as a ransom scale. This particular chapter was taken from a decree issued by the Sovereign and Boyar Duma together 'with representatives from all ranks'. In this instance all elective participants wielded legislative power.

One particular example clearly illustrates the feelings of the elected representatives about the work of codification, as well as those of the government about provincial petitions. A deputy of the Kursk nobility, Malishev, asked the Tsar for a safe conduct before returning home, to protect him from, of all people, those who had elected him! There were two reasons for his anxiety. First, because he had not discussed in council all his electorate's needs; and, second, because he was so pious that he had presented a petition to the Tsar 'concerned with evil', attacking his constituents for their laxity in observing the Sabbath and Holy days. In his petition Malishev exonerated himself from the first charge that 'he did not fulfil all their *wishes* in council'; however, in the other matter he blamed the government and Tsar saying that

[1] The abolition of the time limit for recovery was one of the two major innovations contained in chapter XI. The other was the ending of freedom of movement for all the members of a peasant family. An ukase of 24 November 1597 allowed a time limit of five years. In 1607 during the Time of Troubles, Tsar Vasili Shuisky extended the period of recovery to fifteen years. However this was ineffective, and at the end of the Time of Troubles a five-year term was restored. Due to pressure from landlords this was extended in 1614 to nine years; in 1642 to ten years for runaways, and to fifteen years for peasants who had been taken away illegally by other landlords. Ibid. pp. 255-6 and 263-4. Also Smith, *The Enserfment of Russian Peasantry*, pp. 98-104.

though the *Ulozhenie* specified the time that could be spent on work and trade during Holy days (chapter x, article 25) it did not deal with prohibitions or penalties for misbehaviour on these occasions. The Tsar agreed to the indefatigable moralist's request, and ordered a statement to be issued concerning proper behaviour during Holy days, but no mention of this was made in the *Ulozhenie*.

It is now possible to establish how the *Ulozhenie* was actually compiled. It went through a complicated process of *codification, debate, revision, legislative decision* and *ratification by signature,* which the warrant of 16 July calls 'the strengthening by hand'. The work was distributed between the Boyar Duma and the Holy Council, headed by the Tsar, the five members of Prince Odoevsky's commission, and the elected representatives who were attached to it, and not to the Boyar Duma. All these constituted the Council of 1648. Prince Odoevsky's commission was responsible for codification, which was achieved by selecting and coordinating laws from specific sources, as well as revising petitions presented by the elected representatives.

The elected representatives acted in an advisory capacity by presenting petitions which were debated; in one instance a critical petition led to the abolition of a royal edict.

Mention has been made of the petition demanding the imposition of taxes on hitherto exempt urban properties. A decree was therefore published making it mandatory for details of these properties to be sent to the Tsar, as well as the origins of their owners, together with the dates on which the properties were acquired. The investigation was not to go further back than 1613. The elected representatives who were afraid that the Muscovite departments would procrastinate, presented a new petition suggesting that details of properties should be forwarded 'ignoring the dates of acquisition and origin of their owners'. The petition was presented to the Tsar, and accepted on the same day.

The Boyar Duma and the Sovereign were responsible for revision and legislation. Revision consisted in surveying existing laws collated in draft form by the commission. The warrant of 16 July had apparently somehow suspended all laws and given them the status of temporary rules, pending fresh legislative ratification. Although they lost the force of law these old laws provided the legislators with a useful source of jurisprudence. The Boyar Duma amended the text, scrutinised the content, altered or abolished existing legal norms, and more often than not supplemented a draft with an existing law which the commission had ignored, or a new statute to provide for an unknown contingency. Revision and editing was carried on simultaneously. One example will suffice.

The first part of chapter XVII deals with *votchina* estates. The commission inserted certain decrees dating from Tsar Michael and the Patriarch Philaret referring to the system of *votchina* inheritance or acquisition. The Boyar Duma approved the draft articles, but stipulated the circumstances in which mothers and childless widows could enjoy security of property acquired through service.

The Boyar Duma alone was responsible for revision; legislative authority was shared between all members of the Council. Decrees emanated sometimes solely from Sovereign and Boyar Duma, sometimes in concert with the Holy Council, and occasionally with some selected representatives from certain ranks. Rarely did legislation emanate from the council of elected representatives from all ranks. Originally it had been intended that 'the *Ulozhenie* be made fixed and unchangeable', but because it was drawn up in sessions it lacked stability and permanence.

The Council's more important responsibility, for which it had been after all convened, was to ratify the *Ulozhenie* with the signatures of both *ex-officio* members and elected representatives. This act must have signified that the ruling classes and the elected representatives were satisfied that the *Ulozhenie* solved their problems, and that 'all things were to be decided according to this *Ulozhenie*'. Patriarch Nikon was wrong to refer to the *Ulozhenie* as 'a cursed book, the devil's law'. Why was he silent in 1649 when he signed this accursed document in his capacity of Archimandrite of the Novospassky Monastery?

The *Ulozhenie* was intended to become the definite work of Muscovite jurisprudence and a compendium of the mass of laws which had accumulated in Muscovite government departments by the middle of the seventeenth century. Glimpses of this intention can be found in the *Ulozhenie*, even though it was never realised. Technically, and as an example, it was inferior to the old Sudebniks. Subject matter was organised as if the state had a vertical structure starting at the top with Church, Sovereign and Court and descending to Cossacks and Taverns, which were dealt with in the last two chapters. It is not difficult to arrange the chapters into the following sections: state law, legal organisation and judicial procedure, property and criminal law. The codifiers followed no systematic system; superficial and inconsistent, they adapted articles from a multiplicity of sources so that the *Ulozhenie* contains internal contradictions, and even articles which are unrelated to the subject matter. If the *Ulozhenie* survived until 1833 it should not be interpreted as proof of its merits, but as an indication that Russia could do without a respectable collection of laws.

From a legislative point of view, however, it was an improvement over Sudebniks,[1] which had been no more than practical reference books for judges and administrators. The *Ulozhenie* was able to indicate ways and means of re-establishing a law which had been broken, without altering the law itself. The *Ulozhenie* was mostly concerned with formal law. Chapter x, which is devoted to 'Justice', is the longest, and contains almost one-third of all the articles in the *Ulozhenie*. There are important, but understandable, omissions in substantive law. There were no legal principles because at that time no such concept existed, and men were content to abide by the will of the Tsar and circumstance. A systematic definition of family law did not exist, and in any event it was closely linked to customary and canon law. Custom was ignored because it was shadowy and inert, and the clergy were left alone because they were sensitive and jealous of their spiritual monopoly.

Yet the *Ulozhenie* covered a wider legislative field than the old Sudebniks. It tried to penetrate the structure of society, and define

[1] See for instance, Horace W. Dewey, 'The 1497 Sudebnik – Muscovite Russia's First National Law Code', *The American Slavic and East European Review*, vol. 15, no. 3 (Oct 1956) pp. 325–38.

the position and relationship between the different classes; it took account of men of service and service landowners, peasants, urban taxpayers, bondsmen, Streltsy and Cossacks. Naturally, the *Ulozhenie* was mainly concerned with the nobility, the ruling military official landowning class, and indeed more than half the articles of the *Ulozhenie* are directly or indirectly concerned with their interests and relationships. Here, as elsewhere, the *Ulozhenie* tried to be realistic.

For all its conservative character, the *Ulozhenie* did attempt to introduce two liberal ideas which indicated the way society was to develop. The warrant of 16 July clearly postulated one liberal thought. The codification commission was charged with drafting a code so that 'to all the people of all ranks from the greatest to the least law and justice shall be equal in all affairs of trial and jurisdiction'. This did not imply that some were more equal than others before the law. It meant that there was to be equality of 'trial and jurisdiction' with no exceptions; and it ignored official differences or class exemptions and immunities which had been a feature of the previous Muscovite legal structure. Boyar and commoner were to be tried by identical jurisdictions and legal procedures even though the sentences might differ. All people, even foreigners, were to be tried 'without fear of powerful men, while the just are to be delivered from the unjust'. With these words an attempt is made in chapter x to provide for equality of trial and justice. This particular approach stemmed from the determination of the commission to abolish privileges which were detrimental to both state and treasury.

Yet another liberal idea contained in the warrant of 16 July was outlined in the chapters dealing with structure of society. It formulated an entirely new approach to the relationship between a free man and the state. The significance of this idea can only be attained if modern ideas of freedom are abandoned. At the present time personal freedom and independence is accepted as an inviolable right protected by law; it is also a legal obligation. No longer can a man contract to become a bondsman: the courts would not tolerate it. In the seventeenth century Russia was a slave-owning society governed by the *Krepostnoe pravo*, serf law,

THE RISE OF THE ROMANOVS

which provided for degrees of un-freedom. A further degree of un-freedom was about to come into existence – peasant enserfment (*krepostnoe krestyanskaya nevolya*).

An individual had the right to give up his freedom, either temporarily or permanently, without the concomitant right of abrogation; indeed, different categories of medieval bondage were based on this very condition. Until the *Ulozhenie* personal dependence apart from bondage existed, which came about because an individual mortgaged himself (*zaklad*). This could be achieved by a peasant mortgaging himself and his labour as security for a loan, or in return for services rendered, as for example, exemption from taxes or legal immunities. But the peasant retained the right to cancel the mortgage and his bond once he had fulfilled all his obligations. These people were known in the appanage period as *zakladniye*, and in the Muscovite period as *zakladchiki*.

For a poor man in medieval Russia, this system of mortgaging himself was a most profitable investment. Although it differed from slavery, the indenture system gradually assumed the right to tax exemptions and freedom from state obligations which had been the prerogative of slaves. Legal steps were taken against both indentured peasants and their masters. Taxes were re-imposed on the indentured peasants, and the *Ulozhenie* (chapter xix, article 13) threatened those who made a habit of mortgaging themselves 'with serious punishment', which meant the knout and exile to Siberia beyond the Lena; those who accepted mortgages were threatened 'with great disgrace' and confiscation of lands inhabited by the peasants.

Nevertheless for the poor, slavery, and especially the indenture system, was a way out of serious economic difficulties. Individual freedom was a cheap commodity, and in the absence of equity a powerful protector was a considerable asset. The abolition of the indenture system was a heavy blow to the peasants, and in 1649 in Moscow they rebelled, heaping abuses on the Tsar.[1] The official

[1] Baron Sigismund von Herberstein who visited Russia in 1517 and 1526 as Ambassador of the Holy Roman Empire was puzzled by this attitude. 'This people enjoy slavery more than freedom; for persons on the point of death

attitude is comprehensible: a freeman, whether in service or taxed, who became a slave or was indentured was lost to the state. The *Ulozhenie*, by restricting or forbidding these practices, was giving effect to a proposition that a freeman could not voluntarily escape taxation or state service by giving up his freedom. An individual could only belong to, and serve, the state; he could not become somebody else's private property. 'Christians are forbidden to sell themselves to other men' (chapter xx, article 97).

Personal freedom became an obligation enforced by the knout. However, an obligation to enjoy a right ceases to be one, and becomes a burden. In the modern world this right is no longer considered a burden, since the state, by forbidding slavery or semi-slavery, protects the individual, and present-day social morality applauds the state for this particular prohibition which is better cherished than any right.

In seventeenth-century Russia, however, this general prohibition was supported by neither public morality nor social conscience. What today is priceless, was valueless to the seventeenth-century Russian commoner. The government was interested in the soldier and in the taxpayer, and knew and cared nothing for the individual or citizen. The *Ulozhenie* did not abolish personal bondage in the name of freedom; it transformed personal freedom into bondage in the interests of the state.

The prohibition against indentures was revealing in another way. It was an attempt, exposed in the *Ulozhenie*, to organise social groups by assigning people to sealed corporate cells, in order to satisfy the requirements of state for labour as well as private interests. The indentured peasants became aware of obligations, which were common to other classes earlier. Those obligations

---

very often manumit some of their serfs, but they immediately sell themselves for money to other families. If the father should sell the son, which is the custom, and he by any means become free, or be manumitted, the father can sell him again and again, by right of his paternal authority.' Sigismund von Herberstein, *Notes upon Russia: Being a Translation of the Earliest Account of that Country, Entitled Rerum Moscoviticarum Commentarii*, trans. and ed. R. H. Major, (Hakluyt Society, 1851) I 95.

were part of a national sacrifice which stemmed from the country's situation. This aspect will be looked at in a later chapter when the structure of the administration and social classes after the Time of Troubles is discussed.

The *Ulozhenie* represented the culmination of legislative activities of a previous age, and served as a transitional setting for future legislation. Its defects became apparent shortly after its implementation. Additions and amendments were made by 'newly created articles', which were a continuation of the *Ulozhenie* itself. Examples of these are the articles of 1669 on *theft*, *brigandry* and *murder*, and the articles of 1676–7 on *pomestie* and *votchina* estates.

The detailed, partial revision of individual articles in the *Ulozhenie* which consisted of either abolishing or restoring its different sections is indicative of a particular moment in the history of the state of Muscovy. It was a time when its leaders began to question the merits of legal norms and administrative procedures which previously had been acceptable. Confused and perplexed they felt the need for something new, something that was not 'home grown', but was European.

Chapter Eight

★

THE *Ulozhenie* of 1649 saw the termination of a continuing process in Muscovite domestic affairs which had started with, and been influenced by, the Time of Troubles. It gave legal recognition to Muscovy's situation in the middle of the seventeenth century. Under the new dynasty, new ideas and new people appeared in government; supreme power was reorganised and the Zemsky Sobor was reconstructed. These innovations came about directly, or indirectly, as a result of the chaos left by the Time of Troubles, which sapped the nation's strength, and undermined its foreign policy. The new dynasty had to find a solution to these problems. The examination in the previous chapter of important seventeenth-century legislation showed the direction towards which the government was moving, and the means adopted to extricate itself from its difficulties. The government abolished legal privileges and tax exemptions, banned the spread of indentures entered into to escape burdens imposed by the state, and simultaneously tried to pre-empt for itself the nation's resources. Everything which could be used was salvaged from the wreck: money, which it lacked, a scattered population, taxpayers and soldiers, and members of a national assembly whose advice was required, and finally the laws.

With all these problems the administration of Muscovy wanted above all to strengthen itself, and felt it imperative to acquire a unity of purpose, and an energetic execution of policies. This was its object, when after the Time of Troubles, it tried to create a centralised administration encompassing local and central government. Centralisation at this time did not mean that all local administrations were subordinated to a single central administration. It meant that one department covered a wide range of interests. The analogy is with a village shop which displays those goods in greatest demand, instead of by type. The people agreed with the government's approach, and preferred to deal with one department; they even complained that dealing with a number of departments was tedious, and that they would prefer to deal with only one department so that 'there should be no pointless offence or loss'.

Tsar Michael implemented this practical suggestion when he reorganised local government. Local government under the old dynasty had been completely disorganised. Ivan the Terrible had reformed local government by dividing the districts into several administrations, and a multitude of rural and urban communities inhabited by taxpayers and men of service. Every community acted independently and had its own elected government. There was no contact between the communities other than for the rare election of a police and judicial officer (*gubnoe starosta*) by all classes who lived in the communities and districts. Consequently the only direct contact with the central administration was through elected officials. Only when a powerful military authority was required in the border towns were governors introduced; from the beginning of the sixteenth century they were responsible for everything except spiritual affairs.[1]

A diffused electoral system of local government could only be effective in peace-time, and with the end of the old dynasty there was no peace. During the Time of Troubles every district, including those in the interior, was in danger of hostile attack; hence governors were appointed in the interior. A document compiled about 1628 has survived which lists thirty-two towns which previously had no governors, who began to make an appearance 'after the coming of the unfrocked monk', i.e. after the coronation of the First Pretender in 1605. They were mainly central Russian towns, such as Vladimir, Pereyaslav, Rostov and

[1] A description of the administration of a frontier area can be found in Alton S. Donnelly, *The Russian Conquest of Bashkiria 1552–1740* (Yale U.P., 1968) pp. 12–23.

Belozersk. Previously there had existed a number of elected judges, police, judicial and urban officials, but from this list it is clear that under Tsar Michael governors became quite common. Every district and its inhabitants came directly under the governor's authority: he was responsible for finance, law, the police and the army in the towns and rural communities.

It might be supposed that the introduction of governors effected an improvement in local government. All classes were united under one authority, as were the districts, who represented the central power. The governor was an appointed and not an elected official. This was a departure from the territorial system introduced by Ivan the Terrible on which local government had been based. But it was not a return to the old system of lieutenancies: the governor was appointed to govern for the Tsar's benefit, not his own. Hence the old system, where the holder of the post retained for his own use part or all of the revenues that accrued to the post, was no longer relevant.

Governors were convenient to the central government; it was easier to deal with one man who was their nominee, than with a number of elected officials. The local population considered that rule by governor was a retrograde step, since the governors of the seventeenth century were the sons or grandsons of the lieutenants of the sixteenth century, and while institutions can change in one or two generations, habit and custom do not. It is true that the governors were not quite as rapacious as the lieutenants, but they were not forbidden to accept voluntary offerings 'for the sake of respect', with the inevitable result. Applicants for the position of governor sometimes openly asked to be sent as governor to such and such a town 'to be sustained'. Governorships deteriorated into a continuation of the system of lieutenancies, in spite of stated ideas to the contrary. Originally, lieutenants were supposed to receive an administrative salary in return for military service; however, this was transformed into an administrative service where payment was made for military duties, because the lieutenant both governed and judged. The authorities had not intended to pay governors a salary. In practice they received untaxed emoluments with an explanation that they were rendering an administrative service. Abuses were encouraged because nowhere was the governor's authority defined; his detailed instructions told him in the last resort to act as seemed most expedient, depending on circumstances, and as righteously as God himself. It is therefore understandable that the provincial communities of the seventeenth century recalled with regret the days before the existence of governors. The combination of a mass of regulations with the exercise of untrammelled power resulting in an imprecise definition of rights and obligations led to abuse and contempt, and to the governor alternating between excesses of power and inactivity.

A governor administered justice and local policy in a *syezhaya* or *prikaznaya izba*, which would correspond to a present-day local government office. He was assisted by another representative of the central government, a police and judicial official (*gubnoe starosta*) whose office was the *gubnaya izba*. In some districts there were two or more such officials. This type of superior judicial police authority, which first appeared in the sixteenth century, had mixed antecedents: it was based in the provinces but enjoyed plenary powers; the office-holder was elected at a local all-class meeting, but dealt with general matters of state, such as criminal offences, and not with local affairs.

During the seventeenth century his powers were extended. His jurisdiction covered not only murder and theft, but homicide, arson, lapses from Orthodoxy, disrespect of parental authority, etc. The trend in government policy was towards an increase in powers derived from the central government to the detriment of local authority. The functions of the police and judicial official began to approximate those of the governor. This was not deliberate policy but how the system evolved. This can be deduced from the fluctuations in the relative positions of both offices. At times the position of police and judicial official was abolished, and then restored; in certain areas the governor dealt with local affairs, and in others the police and judicial official dealt with gubernatorial affairs. At the request of its inhabitants a town could come under the jurisdiction of the official instead of the governor; if he proved unsuitable the governor was reinstated.

At times the official was independent of, at others subordinate to, the governor.

What became of the purely provincial system of self-government which at one time had been responsible for the taxpayers? It did not disappear completely with the introduction of governors; it was restricted and subordinated to the governor, and its activities curtailed. Judicial authority was transferred to the governor, and the boards of justice, which consisted of selected mayors and assessors, were disbanded. Locally elected boards of justice only survived in what are known today as Archangel, Olonets, Vyatka and Perm, as well as on Court lands and in the purely peasant districts.

Tax collection and local finance were the responsibility of the locally elected representatives. Indirect custom and excise taxes remained the responsibility of mayors and their assessors. Direct taxes, urban and rural finance came within the competence of elders and their assessors. Local finance meant the collection of taxes for local needs, the administration of common land, the selection of officials for specified local government posts and the appointment of parish priests and clergy.

Local officials carried on business in local offices (*zemskaya izba*) which were always situated inside the town boundary, behind the walls of the citadel, which also contained other administrative offices. Local offices were supervised by councillors who were elected by the urban and rural population of the district. The introduction of governors into the local government resulted in the imposition of new burdens on the local populace, who now had to maintain the governor, his secretaries and their assistants. This added expense was a serious drain on the local exchequer. Local officials were in charge of the expense book, in which all local expenses were entered for subsequent audit by the assessors.

These accounts clearly show what 'feeding' a governor meant in the seventeenth century. Every item of expenditure incurred by governor and staff was entered daily. The governor's household and office had to be supplied with meat, fish, pies, candles, paper and ink. Festivals and birthdays were the occasion for gifts, small white loaves, or money 'in paper'. Similar gifts would have to be given to the governor's wife, his children, staff, servants, hangers-on and even to the holy fool who lived on the premises. These accounts show the effect of administration through governors.

The elected officials and assessors were the obedient servants of the central administration. They carried out the administration's unpopular policies with which the governor, his secretary and assistants did not care to be associated. The local administration was supervised and directed by the governor, and its officials were forever running errands for him. Only occasionally did a local official dare to act in the interests of his community, and disobey an instruction, by going to the governor's house to 'revile him', to use a phrase current among the local opposition. This sort of relationship between the central administration and local government produced excessive abuses. The 'feeding' of a governor often ruined a provincial community. While avoiding radical measures the government tried to eradicate and mitigate against this evil in different ways. Local communities were allowed to choose their governor and other government officials, and the business of the governor was handed over to the elected police and judicial official. The *Ulozhenie* and different decrees all threatened severe penalties for cases of injustice. Those who had been wronged by their own governor were allowed to complain to a neighbouring governor.

Tsar Alexis did not allow noblemen to become governors in the areas where they owned estates. Tsar Michael and his successors categorically prohibited any monetary 'feeding' or payments in kind, and threatened to impose a fine double their value. Centralisation of local government did irreparable harm to local institutions, altered their character, deprived them of all independence, and did nothing to lessen their responsibilities and obligations. Society had made yet another sacrifice for the state.

Centralisation of local government was not confined within the boundaries of a district. Another move in this direction occurred under Tsar Michael. For the better defence of the border areas during the wars with Poland and Sweden, the government consolidated the western, southern and south-western

extremities of the country into powerful military districts
(*razyryady*). District governors were subordinated to superior
governors who represented the highest military and civilian
administration, and were at the head of the district corps of
soldiers.

Military districts appear at the beginning of Tsar Michael's
reign; Ryazan and the Ukraine are mentioned and they included
Tula, Mtsensk and Novosil. Military districts of Novgorod and
Sevsk or Seversk, Belgorod, Tambov and Kazan were created in
the reign of Tsar Alexis. It was suggested during the reign of
Tsar Fedor that districts in the interior should be turned into
military districts, which is what happened in Moscow, Vladimir
and Smolensk. These military districts became the basis of the
division of Russia into Provinces under Peter the Great.

To a lesser extent departments (*prikazy*) in Moscow were also
affected by the policy of centralisation, even though there was
greater necessity for it here than in the regions. The structure of
government departments in Moscow remained the same throughout the sixteenth and seventeenth centuries. As government
became more complex and demanding, so the number of departments increased to fifty. They were set up without a definite
plan, and were no more than a conglomeration of large and small
departments, ministries, offices and temporary commissions.
Their number and overlapping jurisdictions increased the problems of control and direction. Sometimes even the government
did not know where to refer a particular problem; with the result
that a new department was created!

It became imperative to bring some cohesion into the unco-
ordinated machinery of central government. This was done in
two ways: several interrelated departments were grouped together under one official, while others were merged in a single
department. Tsar Alexis' father-in-law, Prince Ivan Miloslavsky,
became head of the Department of the Great Treasury, one of the
divisions of the Ministry of Finance. He was also head of those
departments which were responsible for the new type of military
forces created during the sixteenth and seventeenth centuries such
as the Streltsy, Cavalry and Foreigners, as well as the non-

combatant Apothecaries which included foreign doctors. Nine other departments were subordinated to the Foreign Affairs department which were responsible for the newly-acquired territories including Little Russia, Smolensk, and Lithuania, as well as for Prisoner Exchange. These departments were probably housed with the Foreign Affairs department in the long row of government offices which stretched from the Cathedral of the Archangel along the edge of the Kremlin to the Spassky Gate. This merger of small government departments into several large departments was the precursor of Peter the Great's Colleges. Two new departments, intended to supervise the rest, were created by Tsar Alexis.

The first, the Department of Accounts was supposed to check the income and expenditure as shown in the ledgers of all central and provincial institutions. It appropriated any surplus that remained after current expenditure, and consulted other departments in order to determine the allocation of grants to be made to Ambassadors or regimental commanders; and summoned the urban assessors to present their accounts of local income and expenditure for audit. It was responsible for all state finance and grew from an accounts department which had been created in 1621.

The other new creation was a Department of Secret Affairs. Its title was more sinister than its function. It had nothing to do with secret police, but managed the Tsar's field sports. Tsar Alexis was a passionate falconer, and this department was in charge of two hundred falconers and gerfalconers, more than 3,000 falcons, gerfalcons, hawks and as many as 100,000 dovecots for feeding and training purposes. This kindly but parsimonious Tsar made this department responsible for a range of personal household, as well as general state, business. His personal, as well as diplomatic and military, correspondence was conducted by this Department, which was put in charge of the Tsar's numerous properties, the Imperial salt and fishing industries, the business of his well-loved Sava Storozhesky Monastery, and distributed the Tsar's alms. When Tsar Alexis wanted to intervene directly in government, initiate new measures, such as mining or granite quarrying, he issued personal directives through the Department of Secret Affairs. It therefore became his Privy Chancellory, and was the government's own particular instrument for surveillance, acting apart from the Boyar Duma which was responsible for general control. Kotoshikhin described one aspect of this surveillance. The Department's staff consisted of a secretary and ten under-secretaries; members of the Boyar Duma were not allowed to interfere with them. The Tsar attached the under-secretaries to embassies travelling abroad, and to governors on tour, in order to see how they behaved, and to listen to what they said, and 'these under-secretaries', wrote Kotoshikhin, 'watch over ambassadors and governors and report to the Tsar on their return. Naturally the noble ambassadors and governors knew why these insignificant supernumararies had been attached to their retinues, and cajoled them in excess of their station.' As an instrument of secret administrative supervision, and a precursor of Peter the Great's fiscals, the Department of Secret Affairs was not a resounding success. It was inept. Kotoshikhin said that Tsar Alexis had created it 'to fulfil the Sovereign's ideas and actions according to his desires, without any interference from the boyars and members of the Boyar Duma'. In this way, the Tsar acted quite independently from his closest collaborators, whom he had appointed, and with whom he to all appearances lived 'in counsel'. Although Tsar Alexis' appanage atavistic impulses were fraudulent, since his ancestors had never been appanage Princes, he perpetrated ancient desires of the *Oprichnina*. The Department of Secret Affairs was closed on his death.

As centralisation in government developed, so was an attempt made to confine society within rigid groups. The old dynasty had left society as fragmented as it had government. Society was divided into a number of categories which, excluding the clergy, can be divided into four classes: 1. men of service; 2. urban taxpayers; 3. rural taxpayers; and 4. bondsmen (*kholops*). Depending on their affiliations the distinction between the classes was expressed by the type of obligation which in turn depended on an individual's proprietorial assets; as far as men of service were concerned, on their origins, and all classes were distinguished by the incidence of similar obligations. The duty of landed men of service consisted of inherited military service which was allied to court and administrative duties. This class was subdivided into members of the Boyar Duma, metropolitan and urban men of service, and which category they belonged to depended on the importance and responsibilities of a position, family background and proprietorial position.

Taxed urban commercial classes were assessed 'according to their cattle and trade', in other words on stock and type of business. They were subdivided into three groups, 'the wealthiest, the average and the youngest', and the determining factor in these sub-divisions was total wealth and concomitant urban obligations. The rural population, and peasants whose tax incidence depended on the size of their holdings, were divided into similar property-tax categories. Bondsmen (*kholops*) who had no legal right to own land did not perform state services, nor pay state taxes. Their obligations were to private individuals. There was nothing rigid about these categories and classes. Men could move from one to the other; a free man could change his status of his own volition, or at the Tsar's request; a bondsman could do the same at his master's will or by legal process. A freeman could change occupation or combine two; a man of service could trade, and a peasant could become bonded or trade.

This mobility produced several intermediate and transitional layers in a heterogeneous social structure. Between the men of service and the bonded there existed a kaleidoscope of children of boyars, whether landed or landless, who served in the army from their own or families' estates, or who became serfs in the household of boyars and other high-ranking officials, and thus created a new category of *boyar serving people*.

Between the men of service and the urban taxpaying population there existed the lesser men of service, who served not because of their origins, but because they were state employees. They were state blacksmiths, carpenters, saddlers, gunners and bombardiers attached to forts and their artillery detachments. They were in a similar position to the service class who had military obligations, but they were also close to the urban taxpaying population, from whom they had come. Although they engaged in trade they did not pay urban taxes.

Indentured peasants hovered around the privileged lay and clerical landowners. Between the bondsmen and the class of free men there existed a large hybrid group of vagrants. These were the non-taxpaying relatives of taxed householders, their single sons, brothers, nephews, and general hangers-on who had no home of their own and who worked in other people's houses. Included amongst them were the children of the clergy who had no parishes; boyars' children who had incurred debts, and given up their posts without becoming attached to another household; peasants who had abandoned their holdings and settled nowhere; and finally, bondsmen who had been freed and had not reverted to bondage. Those of them who lived in villages were landless and paid no land tax, and they attracted no urban obligations if they engaged in trade.

The variety of categories and the existence of intermediate groups of vagrants gave society a motley and disorderly appearance. Society's diversity was maintained by the mobility of labour and its choice of occupation. This freedom created difficulties in government, and vitiated its attempt as expressed in the *Ulozhenie* to make everybody work for the benefit of the country and in the interest of the Treasury. The position of the indentured peasants and free men was especially inconvenient because it led to a shortage of soldiers and state revenue. Taking advantage of their right to give up personal freedom, and therefore the attaching state obligations, both classes promised to become social asylums for men of service and taxpayers who wished neither to serve nor pay taxes.

With the accession of Tsar Michael legislation was introduced to counter this trend. All intermediate groups were amalgamated, into large, closed classes, and identical obligations were imposed on them; mobility was only permitted within the confines of these classes. Men were put into a class which was most appropriate to their occupation.

Social reconstruction was carried out in two ways. First, by the hereditary attachment of people to the positions they occupied; second, by abrogating the right of free people to renounce their freedom. The social structure was therefore simplified and ossified.

Taxation and service based on changing land holdings and positions were changed to fixed assessments based on birth. Thus circumscribed, each class became more self-contained and isolated from the others. For the first time in Russian history there were circumscribed classes with known duties who acquired proper *class* characteristics; the process which created them can be called 'fixity of status'. The cost of this process was loss of freedom, and its results must be set off against the other sacrifices made by the people for the state.

The first to be circumscribed and isolated were those classes with service obligations, in particular the military. The Sudebnik of 1550[1] had only allowed the children of retired boyars to become slaves; those in service and their sons who had not started to serve were forbidden to be slaves. Sons of boyars were the lowest and most impecunious group of men of service, and contained many who aspired to the rank of boyar. A law of 1588 stipulated that only the grandchildren of boyars who were fifteen years old and had reached the age of service but had not yet started to perform, could become bondsmen; others younger or older who had registered for service could not. These restrictions were often violated because service was so burdensome. Under Tsar Michael the nobility and boyars' children frequently railed against their brothers', children's, and nephews' mass flights to slavery. An ukase of 9 March 1642 ordered all noble-bondsmen who owned estates, whether inherited or in service tenure, and who had registered for service to be removed from boyars' households and returned to their posts; no more noble or boyar children were ever to be bonded again. The same prohibition was included in the *Ulozhenie*. Thus, military service became a hereditary and unavoidable obligation of the class of men of service.

At the same time their special class rights as landowners were defined. Legally, the right to own land had been enjoyed by the boyars and monks of similar social standing; their numbers had been increased by men of service who had inherited or held estates in service tenure. The ukase of 1642 returned the former to

[1] See Horace W. Dewey, 'The 1550 Sudebnik as an Instrument of Reform', *Jahrbücher Für Geschichte Osteuropas*, n. s., vol. 10, no. 2 (Jul 1962) pp. 161–80.

the state and forbade the acquisition of inherited estates by boyars, monks or men of service. Individual ownership of land inherited or held in service tenure became the privilege of the service class, in the same way that their particular responsibility was military service. In this way the men of service were united into one class, and were detached from the other classes.

The urban taxpayers were treated in the same way. In the sixteenth century the increase in the number of landowning men of service impeded the growth of towns. The Time of Troubles had ruined and forced urban taxpayers to flee. Towns which had started to recover were threatened again by complications which ensued at the accession of the new dynasty. To ensure prompt payment of taxes urban associations were forced to give a joint and several guarantee of payment. It was therefore necessary for them to have a reasonably permanent and full membership as well as a guaranteed market for their labour and goods. The incidence of taxation forced the weaker members to leave the town, selling or mortgaging their property to non-taxpayers or 'white people'.

On the other hand there was an influx into the towns of Streltsy, peasants from outlying villages, church servants and priests' sons, who engaged in trade and commerce without paying taxes, to the detriment of the remaining taxpayers. Even priests and deacons began to open shops, in direct contravention of Church regulations. Urban tax evasion was powerfully encouraged from above; whenever there was a weak ruler, the upper classes took advantage of the situation and speculated to the detriment of free labour. For instance, under Tsar Fedor there were many complaints about the increase of bondage by contract; but Boris Godunov and his supporters were actively involved in this traffic. The same thing happened to indentured peasants under Tsar Michael. Mention has already been made of the fact that private dependence was not the same thing as enserfment in that it could be terminated by the indentured peasant. It was mostly urban taxpayers, traders, and citizens who entered into this relationship generally with 'powerful people' like boyars, patriarchs, bishops and monasteries.

All this was detrimental to the urban taxpayer. Settlements which were inhabited by treasury-paid employees, the Streltsy, gunners and artificers, surrounded the principal towns of Muscovy, and these men of service competed in industry and trade with the urban taxpayers, without sharing their obligations. Indentured peasants were even more dangerous since 'powerful men' took them on in large numbers, and settled them in entire communities in the towns, both in their private holdings and on town common land. In 1648 in a settlement in Nizhni-Novgorod owned by the Patriarch, there were more than 600 newly-arrived merchants and artisans 'who had assembled thither from different towns and settled there for their own trade and profit'. This was the complaint registered with the council assembled to discuss the *Ulozhenie* by the urban taxpayers' representatives.

This was a new and illegal development in indentures. In its simplest form an indenture was entered into as security for a loan, on condition that the man worked on the lender's land or in his house. Urban taxpayers were becoming indentured with no deposit or a fictitious deposit, and generally to privileged clerical and lay landowners. No household work was performed; instead they settled on tax-exempt land in individual households or in whole settlements, wilfully avoiding any payment of urban taxes, and 'engaged in all kinds of trade and commerce'. These were capitalists and not poor domestics working out a loan.

These activities were, of course, quite illegal. The Sudebnik of 1550 had forbidden urban merchant taxpayers to live on tax-free urban church property in order to take advantage of their tax-exempt privilege. Under Tsar Michael there was a clear legal distinction between 'black' taxed urban land and 'white' tax-exempt land. Tax-exempt urban dwellers were not allowed to avoid the taxes levied on urban property or land they had acquired; similarly taxpayers were not allowed to enjoy tax exemptions when settling on untaxed land.

This was a flagrant abuse of the whole system: indentured labourers were not bondsmen who were not subject to tax, and in fact they took advantage of certain privileges without any of the obligations these carried. Complaints were frequent during the reign of Tsar Michael. The new dynasty, which was short-sighted and only reacted to force or threats, satisfied individual complainants but never introduced any general law. In 1643 the taxpaying towns of Tobolsk region complained about the increase in indentured men at the local monastery who were competing with the town merchants and forcing them out of business. The petition drew the government's attention to the fact that these people fulfilled no state service nor paid any taxes. The Tsar ordered the indentured men to move into the town and pay the same taxes as the rest of the taxpayers.

There were four reasons for the fundamental reorganisation in the structure of urban taxpayers. First, the insistent petitions against indentures before and during the council meeting of 1648. Second, the unforgettable memory of the June revolt in Moscow. Third, the government's fear of a decrease in revenue. Fourth, and finally, the government's desire to acquire thousands of new taxpayers. The measures that were adopted were embodied in chapter XIX of the *Ulozhenie* which dealt with urban taxpayers. All privately-owned settlements, which had been bought or seized, and which were on taxed urban land, were confiscated by the Sovereign without compensation and given to the towns and henceforth were subject to tax; 'settlements may not be built on state land and may not buy town land'. Every contract of indenture was declared invalid. Suburban *votchina* and *pomestie* estates which adjoined towns 'house to house' were included in the town, and exchanged for treasury-owned villages elsewhere.

Indentures were declared illegal and carried a heavy fine. Urban dwellers were confined to their towns and burdened with taxes. An ukase of 8 February 1658 threatened whomsoever moved from one town to another, or even married an outsider, with the death penalty. In this way, the payment of urban taxes on trade and commerce became the obligation of the urban classes, and the right to trade and manufacture became their privilege. Peasants were allowed to sell 'all sorts of goods' in the market place direct from their carts, but they were not allowed to own shops in the commercial quarter.

Chapter Nine

★

AT THE same time as the men of service and urban taxpayers were being organised into separate classes, changes were taking place in the position of the rural agricultural population. Peasants who lived on privately-owned land formed the vast majority of the rural population, and were the most seriously affected.[1] Not only did they become completely segregated from the rest of society but also from the remainder of the rural population, the taxpaying, Treasury, and domestic peasants. This change was the enserfment of the seignorial peasants.

In the seventeenth century Treasury and court peasants were attached to the land or to rural associations. Their position was unclear because of the clash of sectional interests. However, all the economic conditions for the enserfment of seignorial peasants existed at the beginning of the seventeenth century, and it only remained to find a legal precept to convert their virtual lack of freedom into legalised serfdom. Three considerations, political, legal and economic, affected the position of seignorial peasants as a class in the sixteenth century: land tax, freedom of movement, and the need to borrow. Each consideration was hostile to the other two, and the conflict of interests acted as a deterrent to any final, legal decision being taken. It was the economic consideration which caused the most serious problems. For a number of reasons, in the second half of the sixteenth century, there was a great increase in the number of peasants needing loans, which

[1] By the 1680s they occupied 90 per cent of the estimated 800,000 homesteads of the realm. See Jerome Blum, *Lord and Peasant in Russia* (Princeton U.P., 1961) p. 268.

created conditions of debt servitude, and conflicted with their freedom of movement, which became invalid. Freedom of movement was not legally forbidden but became a judicial fiction.

The land tax was also an obstacle to freedom, since bonded serfs were exempted from paying it, and early seventeenth-century legislation tried to prevent the transformation from peasant to bondsman by creating 'peasants in perpetuity', which made it impossible for a peasant to avoid taxation.

A combination of these three conditions on which medieval Russian personal bondage had been based produced a legal precept which created the enserfment of seignorial peasants. Medieval Russian law defined bondage as an action, whether symbolic or written, which confirmed an individual's authority over a given article. This authority conferred on its possessor a bonded right over the particular article, which in medieval Russia could be a person who was called either a *kholop* or a *rab*. In medieval Russian legal parlance, a bonded man was called a *kholop* and a bonded woman, a *rab*. The expressions *rab* or *kholop* were not used in medieval documents, and are only found in ecclesiastical records. Bondage was the oldest type of unfreedom in Russia, and had existed for many centuries prior to the establishment of peasant enserfment.

The only type of bondage that existed until the end of the fifteenth century was complete bondage, which occurred in the following ways. First, by becoming a prisoner of war; second, by being sold into bondage, either voluntarily, or by parental desire; third, by way of punishment for certain offences at the discretion of the state; fourth, by being born to a bonded person; fifth, by a merchant deliberately going into insolvency; sixth, by the voluntary entry of a freeman into the household service of another without a contract guaranteeing his freedom; and, seventh, through marriage to a bonded woman without a similar contract.

A full bondsman was not freed by his master's death, and was passed on to his heirs. *Rights over a full bondsman as well as his status were hereditary*. The most important legal difference between bondage and other degrees of personal unfreedom was its permanence over which a bondsman had no control; he could only be freed by his master's will.

Muscovy developed different types of conditional bondage. Towards the end of the fifteenth century and beginning of the sixteenth century there developed what was called *dokladnoe*, or deeded bondage. This arose out of the personal servitude of clerks, bailiffs and stewards, and was so called because the deed of bondage for this type of servitude, had to be confirmed by a regional governor. A 'deeded' bondsman differed from a complete bondsman in that his terms could be changed, and could sometimes be terminated on his master's death. At others he could be passed on to his master's heir, but no further.

A type of temporary bondage or indenture already discussed, existed at varying times on different conditions. Originally, and in its simplest form, it was a personal contract or hire agreement, where an obligation existed to work off a debt and live in the mortgagee's household. *Zakup* indentures dating from the era of the *Russkaya Pravda*, the *zakladen* of the appanage period, and the indentures of the seventeenth century were not bondsmen, because they all had the right to terminate their bondage. The debt could be written off in two ways, it could either be repaid, or worked off by a terminal date fixed contractually. 'They must serve their terms and thence go forth having earned their roubles; but if they do not work off their term then they must return all the money they had borrowed.' This is how a fifteenth-century decree explains the promise to serve.

There were also indentured peasants who worked only to pay off the interest on a borrowed sum, and not the principal, had to be paid back at the end of the agreed term. The document in medieval Russia, by which the peasant acknowledged his indebtedness was known as *kabala*,[1] a word derived from the Hebrew. A personal dependence created by the obligation to meet the interest payments was incorporated in a deed which was

[1] In Hebrew the word *kabala* means receipt, and in the context discussed above denotes a contract in law. Its use in the sense of an acknowledgement of debt had been brought to Russia by the Mongols. Ibid., p. 243.

distinguished from the loan contract by an obligation to work for the creditor, and in the sixteenth century was called a 'deed of service' or 'deed of service for interest'. From the end of the fifteenth century documents increasingly refer to contract (*kabala*) people; however, for a long time there was no evidence that they became contracted bondsmen.[1] The loan contract with its security of personal dependence allowed a debtor to repay the loan interest-free.

'Service for interest' acquired a special meaning and name, *sluzhilyi*. It compelled the debtor to work in the creditor's household against which only the interest payments could be set-off; but he still had to repay the capital within the stated period. These were the characteristics of the 'contracted people' as described in documents up to the middle of the sixteenth century. The Sudebnik of 1550 recognised only this type of 'service by deed' and fixed at fifteen roubles the maximum that could be borrowed.

A decree of 1560 states clearly that these debtors could be sued for debt recovery, this being evidence that they had not been reduced to servitude[2] but could redeem themselves if the occasion arose. The same decree also states that those debtors who were in arrears with their repayments asked to have them commuted by becoming fully bonded or indentured. However, this practice was illegal; the law stated that defaulters were as before, to be handed over to their creditors until they had either paid or worked off the debt. This prohibition, the willingness to enter into full bondage, as well as the English Ambassador, Fletcher's, statement that he had been told in Moscow in 1588 that it was legal for a creditor to sell a debtor's wife and children who were

---

[1] Though the *kabala* was known in the fifteenth century it apparently had not yet become of sufficient importance to warrant legislative attention. The Law Code of Ivan III of 1497 contained no reference to it. Half a century later the Sudebnik of Ivan the Terrible dealt with peasant borrowing at length. This Code ordered that only free men could enter into *kabala* contracts, loans made to bondsmen being declared forfeit. Ibid. pp. 244–6.

[2] The earliest extant obligation to serve as a result of enserfment through debt has been reproduced in R. E. F. Smith, *The Enserfment of Russian Peasantry* (Cambridge U.P., 1968) pp. 85–6.

his temporary or permanent surety, was indicative of conflicting trends.[1] On the one hand, there were the debtors who tended towards the acceptance of complete servitude, and, on the other, there was the law, which encouraged temporary, unbonded servitude. During this conflict the indenture system conditional upon repayment of interest was transformed not into full bondage, but into bondage by deed. However, their wretched condition meant that they were in servitude for life, the time it would take for them to repay the debt. In this way 'service for interest' became the accepted form of loan repayment, and personal contracts for loan repayments became individual hire contracts with wages paid in advance. The combination of 'service for interest' and elimination of the debt, together with the personal nature of the contractual situation were incorporated into the legal basis for servitude and 'service by deed', as well as defining the parameters of dependence by contract.

As a personal obligation between the parties 'service for interest' lost its validity on the death of either creditor or debtor. In the seventeenth century, there existed contracts in which the debtor commits himself to 'serving my master in his household until my death'. This occurrence would have invalidated the personal relationship in the event that the creditor predeceased the debtor, since he would have had to serve the wife and children of the deceased as a hereditary chattel.

There were two types of household servants whose limitation of service was the death of their master. A decree of 1556 stipulated that a legally-bonded prisoner of war served 'until his master's death'. The other concerned those who entered household service

[1] Giles Fletcher was appointed ambassador to Muscovy on 6 June 1588 to negotiate the restoration of trade between England and Muscovy. Three new editions of his *Of the Rus Commonwealth* (1591) have been published. These are 1. *Of the Russ Commonwealth*, ed. Albert J. Schmidt (Cornell U.P., 1966). The statements mentioned above can be found in this edition on page 72. 2. *Of the Russe Commonwealth*, introduction by Richard Pipes (Harvard U.P., 1966). This is a facsimile edition with variants. 3. *The English Works of Giles Fletcher, the Elder*, ed. Lloyd E. Berry (University of Wisconsin Press, 1964). This edition was prepared mainly for the specialist in Tudor literature rather than for the historian of Russia.

with the same termination condition, but without there being
any question of loan or contract. A quasi-service contract dating
from 1596 shows a free man pledging himself to serve 'for as long
as my master shall live' without any loan or interest considerations; after the master's death the servant with his wife and
children was to be freed, and was to receive 'whatever substance
he held and was not to be handed down to the deceased's heirs'.

There are three separate situations which illustrate the personal
character of service contracts: servitude for life, its inalienability,
and a right to acquire property. These characteristics, which also
formed part of the legal basis of service by contract, were now
established by agreement; at any rate until 1597 there were no
decrees explicitly legalising these conditions for service by
contract or for prisoners of war. The inception of service by
contract for life was converted into bonded servitude: the debtor
renounced his right of redemption, and his bondage could only
be terminated by the death or with the concurrence of the
creditor. A decree as early as 1555 equates service by contract
with *bondage*, an act of enserfment, on a par with complete and
indentured servitude. A testament of 1571 used the expression
contractual *kholops* and *rabs* instead of the hitherto more usual
contractual people or simply the *contracted*. About this time another
type of service contract appeared which lasted for over a century.
A single or married freeman with children would borrow a
certain sum precisely for one year, from a particular individual,
generally a man of service, and undertook to 'serve in the household every day of the year for interest and accumulate money
against the dead line and the interest'. This stereotyped declaration
indicates that the subject of a contractually agreed fixed term was a
person, not a thing; and one which provided for the possibility of
delay in repayment. The conditions, and often the expressions
used in contracts of indenture, were similar to those used in
'service for interest' contracts. In 1636, for instance, a man gave
his son to his creditor, 'to serve for one year' in payment of
interest on a debt; in the event that the money was not repaid
within the agreed period, the son was to be turned over permanently to the creditor for household service.

This was the situation of those in servitude by contract as described in a decree issued by the Bondage Department on 25 April 1597. This decree was intended to regulate the ownership of bondsmen, and provide for its permanent observance. No new principle was introduced into the legal structure of contractual servitude; the new decree merely strengthened and defined the intricate and complicated relationships. Only 'contracts covering service for interest' became legal, and they had to be entered in the contract registers of the Court of Bondsmen, in Moscow or at its provincial offices. It required everybody else who had been bonded by contract, together with those wives and children who were named in the contract document, to remain bonded until their masters' death. Early repayment was forbidden and the masters were not allowed to accept any money; petitions by bondsmen concerning redemption were not allowed to be heard in court, and they were to remain in servitude until their masters' death; moreover, a bondsman's children who had been entered into the contract, or who had been born during his servitude, were bound to their father's master until his death. This decree contains certain new ideas which concealed the intentions of the ruling classes which were detrimental to free labour.

There existed alongside the contractually enserfed a category of free servants, or voluntary servants, as they were called in the documents, who served without any formal agreement. They sometimes engaged themselves for up to a period of ten years, without contract. They maintained their right to leave their master at will, a right recognised by the decree of 1555. The Law of April 1597 reduced the period of this engagement to six months; if he stayed beyond this period he was bound to enter into a contract of dependence on his master who 'fed and dressed him and supplied him with books'. Karamzin quite properly called this 'a law unworthy of the name, with its open injustice, and so singularly in favour of the important nobility'. However, there were numerous legislative modifications. The Boyar Tsar Vasili Shuisky reverted to the decree of 1555; the Boyar Duma restored the six-month period; and the *Ulozhenie* cut it back to three months.

A precept contained in the law of 1597 clearly indicated in whose interests the government was acting in the reign of the weak Tsar Fedor. A law of 1560 opposed any extension of complete servitude and forbade insolvent bondsmen from selling themselves into complete servitude to their creditors. None the less, the law of 1597 allowed runaway bondsmen who had been caught by their masters to be transferred at their pleasure into a harsher degree of servitude. Thus, on the whole, the law of April 1597 intensified, rather than diminished, servitude.

The monk, Abraham Palitsyn, helpfully explains the reasons for this legalistic activity. He saw that under Tsar Fedor, the leading noblemen, the magnates, and especially the relatives and supporters of Boris Godunov, who was all-powerful, were overcome with a desire to enslave whoever they came across.

They enticed people into servitude in a number of ways: they coaxed, made gifts, extorted 'signed contracts of service' by force and torture. They invited people into their houses 'to drink some wine'; after three or four glasses a careless guest would find himself enserfed; after three or four glasses he was convinced that he was a bondsman! After Tsar Fedor's death Boris Godunov ascended the throne and there started terrible years of famine. The masters saw that they could not feed their numerous slaves; some were freed, others were sent away without their deeds of release, while others simply fled. In this way all this human wealth, so wickedly acquired, was dispersed like dust; and during the Time of Troubles many of these abandoned bondsmen turned on their masters.

The history of servitude by contract has been discussed in such detail in order to explain its influence on the fate of the seignorial peasants. The connection between bondsmen and peasants enjoying such different social standing is not immediately apparent. One was untaxed, the other was taxed; one worked in the household, the other on the land. The connection between the two was the master. He was the focal point of both their legal and economic relations, and was responsible for both.

No precise definition was given on the accession of the new dynasty of the relationship between the peasant and the land and the landowner. The law of 1607 issued by Tsar Vasili Shuisky which bound peasants to their masters on the basis of the cadastral registers fell into desuetude during the Time of Troubles.[1] The settlements reverted to the system that existed at the beginning of the seventeenth century. Peasant contracts were voluntary agreements: the peasant undertook 'to work according to my amicable agreement'.

When property changed hands those peasants who were not tied by length of residence or loan obligations were free to go where they wished; the new owner had no interest in them or in their stock, he 'let them go completely' as the old documents put it. Peasants of long standing who had been born on their own land or had grown up under the same landlord, and peasant dwellers of long standing who had remained for at least ten years stayed where they were. Recent arrivals who had settled with the help of a loan could be transferred to another property. The peasant continued to work off the interest on the loan through his own labour (*barshchina*).[2] The system of working off the interest on a loan produced an affinity between peasant debtors and the contractually enserfed. Both gave of their labour, although the first worked in the fields, and the second indoors, 'he entered the household and carried out menial tasks'. The similarity in their economic position led to legal similarities.

The legal implications that contractual obligations affected a man's activities as well as his person were understood by the landowners and influenced their attitude towards the peasants. The propagation of this particular appreciation of the peasant situation was given further impetus by those in servitude; peasants became enserfed, and those in servitude became peasants. The peasant–husbandman was joined in the fields by the household worker. The Time of Troubles had swept through the country like a hurricane denuding central Russia of most of its peasants. There was such an acute shortage of agricultural labour that land-owners were forced to use bonded labour. Household bondsmen

[1] See Smith, *The Enserfment of Russian Peasantry*, pp. 103–7.
[2] A detailed discussion of *barshchina* and what it entailed can be found in Blum, *Lord and Peasant in Russia*, pp. 224–8.

were settled on the land, granted loans, and provided with houses, farm implements and plots of land. The landowners drew up special agreements to cover these arrangements; they were called 'loan contracts' as were the agreements entered into by peasants.

This was how an agricultural class was created from bondsmen; they came to be known as 'backyard people', *zadvornye*, because they settled in special dwellings 'away from the owner's house'. This class already existed in the second half of the sixteenth century; the term *zadvornye* or *zadvornye dronshki* was used in documents from 1570 to 1580, and referred to those 'who lived behind the large manor houses'. Their numbers increased considerably during the seventeenth century.[1] They were rarely referred to in the land registers of the first half of the seventeenth century, but in the second half they constituted the largest section of the agricultural population of most localities. In the cadastral register made in 1630 for the district of Beleev about nine per cent of all homesteads belonged to bondsmen of all conditions, of which the *zadvornye* only formed a small proportion; in 1678 the *zadvornye* homesteads alone came to twelve per cent. In time a group known as the *delovye lyudi* or 'men of all work' was included in the same class as the *zadvornye*. Although the *delovye lyudi* were described in the cadastres as living in the landowners' households, they enjoyed the same economic and legal status as the *zadvornye*.

The *zadvornye* were created from all manner of bondsmen, but predominantly from the bonded-by-contract. Their situation was analogous to bonded agricultural labourers or bonded homesteaders, and all were subject to certain legal responsibilities: a law of 1624 provided that the *zadvornye* and not his master was responsible for any illegality. Evidently, the *zadvornye*'s holding was considered as his own, even if this were not strictly true A

[1] The main reason why there was an apparent increase in the *zadvornye lyudi* in the seventeenth century was that landowners would have preferred people who owed obligations only to them and for whom they had no tax responsibility, while peasants who had lost their liberty anyway through enserfment, would have welcomed a situation in which they did not have to pay taxes. Ibid. p. 273.

zadvornye was bonded in a special way: he entered into a loan contract either when he gave up his freedom and settled near the manor house, or when he transferred from household service. In this way the *zadvornye* agreement created a special type of servitude, becoming a transition from household service to peasant farming.

In a document dating from 1628 a landowner wrote that he had settled a wasteland 'with bonded domestics and old people and transformed them into peasants and given them a loan'. However, this did not signify that he had transformed his bondsmen into real peasants: such a transformation would have created a freeman and turned a non-taxpayer into a taxpaying agricultural labourer. Neither would have benefited the landowner. There was nothing unusual in settling bondsmen on the land; they were an integral part of the rural scene. But the expression 'to transform bondsmen into peasants' had not been used before and had never appeared in a legal document; it is a good indication of the extent to which a peasant who had signed a loan agreement resembled a bondsman. Contracts between peasants and landowners of this era begin to provide for conditions of servitude. In a loan agreement of 1628 a freeman contracted to 'live with his master as a peasant for the rest of his life, and not to depart from this condition'. The phrase 'not to depart' had many meanings. Formerly, a peasant who settled on land, with the assistance of a loan, agreed contractually that if he left without fulfilling all his obligations he was to repay the loan and some extra as compensation to the landowner 'for damages, and for having procrastinated', in other words to cover any financial loss and the cost of legal proceedings but not more. Now, however, a new condition was created: the landowner 'my master is free to take me back from wherever I may be', and 'henceforth I shall live on this plot as peasant and taxpayer', because 'once a peasant, always a peasant, and for the loan granted me I shall be a peasant for ever and not run away'. All these expressions had but one meaning: the peasant renounced the right to leave of his own volition; the right to terminate the contract when all the conditions precedent had been fulfilled was converted into the payment of penalties for desertion; his freedom of movement could not be restored nor could his contract be annulled. The inability to move freely very quickly became a general and final condition in all loan agreements, and created *peasant serfdom,* or 'a peasant in perpetuity' as it was called in the seventeenth century. For the first time these conditions transformed peasant loan contracts into acts of enserfment, and confirmed that personal peasant dependence carried with it no right of termination.

That the enserfment of peasants and the transformation of bondsmen 'into peasants' occurred during the third decade of the seventeenth century was not a coincidence. Both were intimately linked to the fundamental changes that took place in agriculture, and in the national economy. During the Time of Troubles the dispersion of large numbers of urban and rural taxpayers had disorganised the rural communes which previously had given a joint and several guarantee to ensure their members' regular tax payments.

One of the new administration's responsibilities was to re-establish the rural commune. The Zemsky Sobor of 1619 decided to take a census of all taxpayers; fugitives were to be returned to their former places of residence, and indentured peasants were to become taxpayers. This particular census failed through the incompetence of its executors, the clerks and inspectors. Their failure, coupled with the spectacular fire of Moscow in 1626 which destroyed all the metropolitan departmental land registers, impelled the government in 1627-8 to undertake a new, and better-conceived general census.[1] The census had both a supervisory and a fiscal objective. It intended to find out how many taxpayers existed, and establish their legal residence from which they were not allowed to move. The information gained from this census was used from 1649 on to deal with the peasants in exactly the same way.

[1] The oldest surviving cadastral registers are those made for Novgorod towards the end of the fifteenth century at the order of Ivan III. In the sixteenth and seventeenth centuries three cadastral surveys were carried out for the whole realm, the last one being completed in 1630. For the methods used by the officials, ibid. pp. 231-5.

The census was also used to examine the actual relationship between peasant and landowner in an attempt to avoid future conflict and disputes. However, no new legal precepts were introduced as a result, nor was any attempt made to create a new type of relationship where none had existed previously. It was deemed preferable to leave this to the voluntary, mutual consent of both parties. Never the less, 'the cadastral surveys', registers drawn up on the basis of domicile, influenced, regulated, and indirectly encouraged these agreements. For example, if an itinerant, free agricultural labourer was inscribed by a census clerk on a particular estate, where he had taken temporary 'peasant refuge', he was registered as belonging to it, and was obliged willy-nilly to join other peasants who had settled voluntarily. As a result, the free agricultural labourer became attached to the landowner in two ways: by entry in the cadastral register, and contractually.

Attention must now be given to agreements which refer to the conditions of contract. Some labourers, before becoming peasants by contract, lived 'freely' for several years without formally concluding an agreement. Others agreed to settle without any loan considerations, and concurred contractually to live as peasants on their master's land until his death; 'when, by the grace of God he was no longer living', they were to be free to leave, and go where they liked. This condition was basic to service contracts. Another, in the loan agreement of 1628 referred to above, undertook 'to live as a peasant until his own death and not to contract out'. It was more usual for peasants to exchange their freedom for a loan which they undertook to repay 'in full' at due date, or in instalments 'little by little'. Most contracts, however, had nothing to say on this point, and provided for the repayment of the loan only in the event that the debtor either failed to fulfil his obligations, or simply absconded.

In spite of the varied, confused, and inconsistent conditions of peasant contracts, it is possible to discern the basic elements which went into the making of peasant enserfment. These were: 1. police registration and attachment to their place of domicile; 2. loan indebtedness; 3. the effects of bondage by contract; and

4. voluntary agreements. The first two were basic to enserfment, and provided the landowners with the opportunity of wielding power over their peasants; the last two were concerned with the detail of service conditions and provided the landowners with the opportunity of acquiring the requisite authority. Peasant contracts even indicate the moment of transition from freedom to serfdom: the census of 1627. Indeed, the earliest known contract involving the obligations of a serf dates from 1629. In this particular instance a group of 'long-established' peasants entered into new contracts with their landowner, and undertook 'not to go away, or flee, but to remain attached to him in serfdom'. As 'long-established' peasants they had a precise and established relationship with the landowner; however, it is possible that, even ignoring the time element, they were unable to leave their land, and were unable to discharge the debts entered into at one time or another. In other agreements the peasants specifically undertook to remain 'bonded' to their own landowner 'as before'. Therefore, the new conditions of serfdom were only a legal confirmation of an existing situation.

The registration for tax and domiciliary purposes raised the question of attaching a peasant to the landowner on whose land he was registered. No legal precepts existed for this purpose. They were adapted from a variety of sources, including service contracts and loan agreements, and combined with the different regional conditions governing peasant taxpayers and household service. This multiplicity of heterogeneous legal relationships was brought about by the abrupt changes in agriculture and land tenure after the Time of Troubles.

Previously the subject of contracts between peasant-tenant and landowner had been land; and its conditions of tenure were such that the peasant either supplied the landowner with produce from the land, or its equivalent monetary quit rent. A loan had always taken the peasant's own labour into account as payment in excess of the actual sum due; sometimes even his property and inventory which had been acquired with the loan were attached.

After the Time of Troubles a radical change occurred: land

which had been abandoned fell in price, but the price of peasant labour and the rate of interest increased. The peasant needed a loan more than land, and the landowner required labourers rather than tenants. Both these requirements explain a contract dated 1647, by which time serfdom had not only become fully established, but had also become hereditary. In this contract the peasant no longer gave an undertaking not to run away; it was the landowner who had to agree not to evict the peasant from his holding which he had held for some time. In the event that this did occur, the peasant was free to 'leave the landowner and go to the four corners of the land'.

In time, and influenced by the general census of 1627, these requirements converted peasant contracts from agreements on the use of manorial land into transactions relating to compulsory peasant labour. Indeed, the right to such labour gave the landowner his authority over the person of the peasant, and his freedom. Moreover, the census itself had been undertaken because of Treasury requirements, and resulted in the incidence of tax being transferred from land to labourer. The new combination of economic relations threw the previous legal arrangements into confusion: bondsmen became peasants, and vice-versa; household workers became agricultural labourers, and agricultural labourers performed household duties. Peasant serfdom emerged from this confusion.

On the face of it, it would appear that the law and the landowners' interests were identical as far as the peasant was concerned. This, in fact, would only be a superficial assessment, since their interests diverged. The State needed punctual taxpayers, who could always be traced through the census register to a known holding, and whose taxpaying capacity was not inhibited as a result of private obligations. The landowner needed agricultural bondsmen who would work efficiently 'on the estate, ploughing, reaping, and in the house', could pay his quit rent and above all, who could if necessary be sold, mortgaged or bequeathed apart from the land.

The government of the first Tsar of the new dynasty, which owed its election to the support of the supreme ecclesiastical hierarchy and the nobility, was so fundamentally obliged to the boyars that, in so far as the peasants were concerned, it had to settle accounts with the powerful boyar and ecclesiastical land-owners, as well as with the lesser nobility. Taking full advantage of the difficult situation in which the taxpaying population found itself after the Time of Troubles, these powerful landowners, boyars, prelates, and the monasteries, deprived the Treasury of taxpayers by offering their powerful protection to taxpayers and peasants who wished to become tax-exempt indentured labourers.[1]

The Zemsky Sobor had already resolved on 3 July 1619, that 'indentured people were to return to their previous situations'; in other words, that they were to pay taxes and return to their former domiciles. For thirty years, however, powerful lay and clerical interests opposed this resolution and it was only in 1649 that the elected noble and urban representatives inserted definitive articles into the *Ulozhenie* providing for confiscation of boyar and church estates which had been settled with indentured labour.[2]

Many other problems affecting the peasants had still to be resolved legally; but nothing was done to expedite this. Tsar Michael, an insignificant ruler, was surrounded by inept states-men; the government itself always lagged behind, never catching up with events, which tied knots future generations were unable to unravel.

With the appearance of serf obligations in peasant contracts it became imperative to differentiate in law between private and state interests. The census lists fixed the peasant's status, assessed him as a taxpayer according to his domicile, whereas the loan contract, a personal agreement, tied him to a landowner. This conflict of interests produced anomalies in the documents dealing with serfdom. In most cases the peasant gave a vague undertaking 'by this contract to remain with my master in serfdom'. But it

[1] Church institutions and prelates gained in strength and wealth during the sixteenth and seventeenth centuries. Both Clement Adams and Giles Fletcher claimed that one-third of all landed property belonged to monasteries. Ibid. pp. 188–98.
[2] See Smith, *The Enserfment of Russian Peasantry*, pp. 141–2.

was also fairly common for a peasant to be tied to an individual as a result of the system of land tenure and without specifying a particular holding. In such a case, the peasant was obliged to live in a particular village or 'wherever the master indicates'; or he could bargain for a particular holding which 'he, my master, shall grant me according to my strength, and where I may prosper'. It was less common for a peasant to be tied to his master 'through this taxed plot of land and by this deed', thus combining both aspects of serfdom, and undertaking to remain on a given plot of taxable land and live 'on it for ever, never to leave'. Finally, and even more rarely, and then only towards the end of the seventeenth century, can an example be found of a peasant being attached to a particular place without being attached to a particular individual. A loan agreement of 1688 which stipulated the usual obligation of a peasant to live in a certain village, added a further condition that he was to live 'in that village irrespective of its owner'.

There were no legal restrictions on either the term or the conditions of peasant enserfment, as it was considered preferable to leave these to voluntary agreements. As has already been mentioned, loan agreements also contained only vague conditions of service. Peasant contracts from the Zaleesky district concluded between 1646 and 1652 defined the peasants' labour obligations very precisely. A landless peasant (*bobil*) contracted to work for a boyar 'one day a week on foot', a peasant agreed 'to work one or two days with a horse'; either might work one day during one week, or two days the next. However, these were regional variations which had nothing to do with the more generally accepted legal practice. The general, stereotyped conditions of contract contain an obscure obligation by the peasant 'to do any work indicated by the landowner, to pay such tithe as he requires, as is determined by my plot, even as my neighbours do', or 'to obey the landowner in all things, to plough for him and do his household work'.

This unregulated struggle between private interests produced no decision on one particularly important national problem: to what extent was a landowner entitled to exploit the labour of his serfs. This was either an oversight, or a half-hearted compromise with the nobility by the administration; being the stronger party the nobility did not hesitate to take advantage of their position.

The government made another concession to the nobility in their dealings with the peasants by abolishing the 'fixed years', the time limit during which action might be taken against runaway peasants. From the beginning of the sixteenth century the time limit had been fixed at five years, but this had been altered to fifteen years in 1607. After the Time of Troubles it was once again reduced to five years, which was long enough for a runaway to remain untraced by a landowner. In 1641 the nobility asked the Tsar 'to abolish the time limit'; instead, the time during which a runaway could legally be prosecuted was increased to ten years, and to fifteen years for abducted peasants. In 1645, in response to continued agitation by the nobility, the government reconfirmed the decree of 1641. When a new census was taken in 1646, the government capitulated to the nobility, and promised 'that all peasants with land, peasants without land, and their households, together with their children, brothers and nephews shall be registered in the census registers, and bonded without the application of any time limits'. This promise was given effect in the *Ulozhenie* of 1649, which legalised the return of runaway peasants who were named in the census registers of the 1620s and 1646–9 'without any time limit'.[1]

The abolition of the time limit in itself did not change the legal character of peasant enserfment as a civil obligation; a breach of peasant contract exposed the offender to a civil suit to which no statute of limitation applied, as indeed was the case of those in servitude. Furthermore, this applied not only to individuals, but to households and families. The requirements that a peasant remain domiciled in the location written into the census register applied equally to his descendants and relatives; moreover, they were all bound to the landowner who now had the power to compel them to return, irrespective of the length of time they had been gone, as though they were truly in servitude. Personal peasant enserfment had become hereditary.

[1] Ibid. pp. 141–2 and 144–5.

Possibly, this extension to the enserfment of peasants only confirmed a situation which had existed for some time.

It had been common for a peasant's son inheriting his father's homestead and stock not to enter into a new agreement with the landowner. Only when an unmarried daughter came into this inheritance was a new agreement made with her betrothed who entered into her homestead 'and took possession of her father's living'. The ordinance of 1646 also influenced peasant contracts: henceforth obligations incurred by the contracting peasants were extended to their families. One particular agreement shows how an unmarried, free peasant mortgaged himself to the Kirilov Monastery in order to acquire land, and agreed to extend his obligations to his future wife and children 'whom God might give him after marriage'.

This hereditary feature of peasant serfdom raised the question of the relationship between the state and the serf owners. In the interests of the Treasury early sixteenth-century legislation had already made the peasants pay taxes on land, and had restricted their freedom of movement. Similar provisions were enacted to cover other classes at the beginning of the seventeenth century, when an attempt was made to organise the population into classes carrying the same type of obligations. The situation of the seignorial peasants was further complicated by the fact that, between the Treasury, for whose benefit this reorganisation was taking place, and the peasant, was the landowner with his own interests. As long as Treasury interests were not adversely affected, there was no legal interference with private arrangements between peasant and landowner, and this is the reason for the appearance of serf obligations in contracts. However, these had been private transactions between peasant and landowner. Subsequently, all peasants and their families became attached to the person of the landowner in perpetuity. Personal peasant enserfment *by contract*, by loan deed, was transformed into perpetual enserfment *by law*, by registration. A new obligation to the state emerged from the peasants' private, civil obligations. Hitherto legal precepts had developed, and been generalised from the relationships arising from transactions between peasants and landowners. The census registers of 1646 suggested legal precepts designed to create new economic and legal relationships. The *Ulozhenie* of 1649 was supposed to guide and watch over these relationships.

The *Ulozhenie* dealt with enserfed peasants in a superficial and hypocritical manner. Article 3, chapter XI states '. . . the present Sovereign decrees there shall be no legal prohibition to a man taking peasants unto himself'; whereas the decree of 1641 clearly states 'that no man shall take unto himself landed or landless peasants of another'. Chapter XI was almost completely devoted to runaway peasants, yet it neither defined peasant serfdom, nor limited the landowners' authority. The chapter consisted of a miscellany of former statutes to which no references were made. These statutes are of great assistance in any description of peasant serfdom, and are a necessary supplement to the *Ulozhenie* with all its shortcomings.

The decree of 1641 distinguishes three basic elements in the structure of peasant serfdom: *peasantry, peasant property*, and *peasant ownership*.[1] Since peasant ownership meant the right of an owner to the labour of an enserfed peasant, and peasant property meant movables and stock, 'agricultural and household belongings', it must follow that by peasantry meant the belonging of a peasant to his owner. Or put in another way, the landowner had an absolute right over the peasant irrespective of the peasant's situation or the use to which his labour was put. This right was confirmed by cadastral surveys, census registers, and other 'bondage instruments' by which a peasant or his father was registered with a landowner. Whether these three elements were harmful or not depended on the extent to which there existed a precise legal definition of the conditions of peasant enserfment. According to the *Ulozhenie* an enserfed peasant was hereditarily, and in perpetuity, tied to the physical or legal *personality* to whom he had been assigned in the cadastral or other registers. Moreover, he was tied to the landowner through *the land* on an estate to which he had been committed at registration. Not one of these conditions was described sequentially in the *Ulozhenie*.

[1] For the appropriate documents, ibid. pp. 115–17 and 119–23.

Landowners were forbidden to transfer peasants from *pomestie* to *votchina* estates.[1] This was considered detrimental to the national interest since *pomestie* estates were considered part of the public domain. They were not allowed to enter into service contracts with their peasants, nor were they allowed to free *pomestie* peasants, because in both cases this would remove any tax-paying liability, thereby depriving the Treasury of revenue. At the same time, however, landowners were allowed to free their *votchina* peasants (chapter XI, article 30; chapter XV, article 3; chapter XX, article 113). Moreover, the *Ulozhenie*, either implicitly or explicitly, tolerated the actions of landowners in removing peasants from their holdings alienating them from both land and stock, and tacitly approved of their transference from one owner to another at the landowner's whim. The nobleman who, after the census registration, sold his estate together with peasants who had run away, and who were bound to be returned, was obliged to replace them with 'similar peasants' from other properties who had no redress against their owner's trickery. Chapter XI, article 7, and chapter XXI, article 71, states that a landowner who unintentionally killed another man's peasant was required to replace him with another from 'his best peasants together with his family' who were to be transferred to the dead man's owner.

The law only protected the interests of the Treasury and the landowner. The landowner's authority was only curbed when it clashed with the interests of the Treasury. The peasants' personal rights were ignored, and their individuality was submerged in the sophistry of the landowner's interests; they became simple financial counter-weights in an attempt to restore the nobility's shaken equilibrium. With this in mind, peasant families were even separated; a fugitive female serf who married either a peasant or a bonded man belonging to another owner had to be returned together with her husband to her previous owner, while his children from any previous marriage remained with his owner. The dispersal of whole families, against all the teachings of the Church

[1] This law was apparently disregarded by the landowners, for the prohibition had to be repeated on at least six occasions in the second half of the seventeenth century. Blum, *Lord and Peasant in Russia*, p. 265.

was legally permissible and applied equally to those in servitude (chapter XI, article 13).

A disastrous omission in the *Ulozhenie* which had serious consequences was that it did not provide a legal definition as to what constituted a peasant's personal stock. Neither the authors of the *Ulozhenie*, nor the elected representatives (none of whom were seignorial peasants) who were supposed to comment upon it, thought it necessary to establish how much of a peasant's stock belonged to him, and how much to the landowner. Chapter XXI, article 71 states that if a free man unintentionally murdered a peasant belonging to somebody else he was liable to pay the dead man's 'contractual dues' as confirmed in the loan document. From this it would seem that a peasant was legally entitled to enter into obligations based upon the possession of property. If, however, a peasant married a runaway peasant woman he was handed over together with his wife to her owner; but his possessions remained with his previous owner (chapter XI, article 12). It would appear that the stock was not his, as it would have been had he been a freeman, and that by marrying a runaway peasant woman he had forfeited his possessions, even though the marriage took place with the consent and at the instigation of his master.

These practices which revealed themselves in private agreements explain the existing legal contradictions. From the private agreements it is possible to deduce the composition, and sometimes the legal significance, of a peasant's possessions. His possessions consisted of agricultural implements, money, livestock, seed grain, milled grain, 'all clothes and all household goods'. The documents indicate that a peasant's possessions were passed on to his sons, wife, daughters as an inheritance, or to a son-in-law by way of dowry; but in all cases this had to be done with the agreement or at the instigation of the landowner.

It often happened that a free, single man would go empty-handed 'with only a soul to his body' into an enserfed peasant's household 'for a term of years and for a living', and would marry his daughter. As a result the bridegroom would bind himself to his father-in-law for a period of eight to ten years during which he agreed to live under the same roof. At the end of the agreed period, he was allowed to set up his own establishment and take from his father-in-law, or in the event of his death, from his brother-in-law, half or a third of everything, 'not only possessions, but what lies in the byres, in the land, in the ploughed fields and in the kitchen gardens'.

Peasants married to orphaned daughters and widows entered their homes for similar reasons, and succeeded to the possessions of the deceased father or husband. These possessions 'were held' by the recently married newcomers; however, the newcomers were indebted to the landowner for both their wives and their possessions, and they contracted themselves 'into the peasantry', thereby becoming his serfs. The double ownership of a single property stemmed from the dual origin of the peasants' possessions, which were acquired by the labour of a peasant with the assistance of a loan from his master. Mention has already been made that the *Ulozhenie* stated that the husband of a runaway peasant girl lost all his possessions when he was handed over to his wife's owner. Contract documents dating from the 1630s produce some even more striking examples which had not been foreseen in the *Ulozhenie*. A runaway peasant was returned together with his wife whom he had married whilst in flight, to his master; but the property inherited by the wife from her father or first husband was retained by the wife's owner, even though the marriage had taken place with his permission. The owners considered that they were legally entitled to keep their peasants' possessions by agreement with a third party. In 1640 a freeman, on marrying the foster daughter of a peasant, mortgaged himself to the owner in accordance with service contract law until the owner's death, on condition that, having served his time in his 'father-in-law's' dwelling, he would be free to take half his or his son's possessions and could, together with his wife, 'go away in freedom'. This was clearly detrimental both to the peasant household and the peasant community.

What has emerged from these illustrations is that a peasant's possessions belonged both to him and to the landowner, the distinction being that the peasant could possess, but only the landowner had the right to own. The system was somewhat similar to the *peculum*[1] in Roman Law or to the *otantsa* of medieval Russian law. In so far as property rights were concerned, the enserfed peasant of the era of the *Ulozhenie* reverted to the status of the agricultural labourer of the *Russkaya Pravda*.

These possessions, or *sobini* as they were called in the seventeenth century, could also belong to bondsmen who used them as security in property transactions even with their own masters. One service contract dating from 1596 shows that a bondsman in binding himself to his master 'for his lifetime' extracted an undertaking from the master that on his death, he would free the bondsman and allow him to take away 'the possessions he had accumulated'. The bondsman had no legal right to any possessions, and could only rely on his master's integrity in fulfilling this obligation. The *Ulozhenie* made no distinction between the possessions of bondsmen and serfs; otherwise how could chapter x, article 262 have made the debts of insolvent noblemen and boyars' children the responsibility of their bondsmen and serfs. This approach explains the existence of 'contractual debts' to which the *Ulozhenie* refers: a serf was allowed to use his possessions as security for an obligation into which he had entered; if he failed to fulfil it his possessions could be distrained upon, as could those belonging to the 'backyard bondsmen'.

It is worth noticing that peasant possessions were acquiring the same characteristics as bondsmen's possessions at the same time that loan documents started to contain references to the obligations of serfs. Already in 1627-8 landowners were complaining that peasants were escaping with '*their* property', such as horses, worth so much. Serfdom had not yet become a state institution, although landowners by referring to the peasants' possessions as their property were instituting searches for their own property which the runaway peasants had stolen. The word *snos*, was bondsmen's jargon and referred to the clothes worn or stolen by a fugitive which belonged to his master.

---

[1] *Peculum* is defined as such private property as might be held by a slave, wife or son who was under the *patria potestas*, separate from the property of the father or master, and at the personal disposal of the owner. Black's Law Dictionary, 4th ed. (1951) p. 1287.

From the inception of serfdom the peasants were aware that they were becoming taxpaying bondsmen. The realisation that the peasants' possessions were the masters' property and that the peasants were unable to share it legally was not a result, but one of the fundamental causes, of the enserfment of the seignorial peasants, a situation brought about by the long-standing indebtedness of the peasants to their masters.

Registration, together with a loan contract as a legal weapon, resulted in hereditary enserfment; the economic justification of the landowners' right of ownership to their peasants' possessions and stock was the loan; and the labour obligations owed by the peasants in exchange for land was the basis of the landowners' discretionary power to dispose of that labour; these were the three knots drawn together in a noose which became known as peasant serfdom. As it tightened the noose, the law was not guided by a sense of justice, nor indeed by any consideration for the public weal. It was concerned with what was possible, and as a result propounded no eternal truths; what emerged was a conditional situation. Indeed, this was precisely the point of view expressed by Pososhkov in his *On Poverty and Wealth* under Peter the Great. He wrote that the landowners only owned the peasant temporarily since the 'true lord of the peasant is the Tsar'.[1] Consequently serfs fell into the same category as estates held in service tenure, namely state property held temporarily by private individuals or institutions. But how could the government, even temporarily, be so complacent about subordinating the vast proportion of the labour force on which it relied, to private interests? The reason for this was that the myopic government was influenced by a situation which in part had been created by legislation, and in part by *de facto* relationships which had existed in the past. Since early times many landowners had jurisdictional rights over their peasants in respect of all offences, other than sacrilege, murder and the possession of stolen goods.

In the sixteenth century already a landowner was an intermediary between his peasants and the Treasury, and even paid

[1] For the significance of this statement by Pososhkov see V. Klyuchevsky, *Peter the Great*, trans. Liliana Archibald (Macmillan, 1957) pp. 125-6.

their taxes, and during the seventeenth century this practice became general. After the census of the 1620s the landowner was endowed also with police powers over all peasants on his register. On the other hand the economic measures affecting the seignorial peasants, such as loans, exemptions, labour dues and tithes, became so entangled with the economy of the landowners that neither could distinguish one from the other. In disputes, particularly over land, between seignorial peasants and others the landowner naturally sided with his own peasants. Chapter XIII, article 7 of the *Ulozhenie* merely reiterated a generally-held, old and customary contemporary belief that 'the nobility and boyars' children must inquire into, and be held responsible for all the affairs of their peasants; other than theft, robbery, the possession of stolen goods, and murder'. This meant that where they had the jurisdiction, the landowners were both interested parties and judges in cases between their own peasants and other people. The legal and administrative functions of a government official were carried out by the landowner who ran the estate court, enjoyed supervisory police powers, and was entitled to interfere in his peasants' affairs; he fulfilled these functions not as of right, but as part of his obligations. Yet another responsibility which was designed to protect the Treasury's interest was imposed on the landowner in an attempt to remedy administrative weaknesses.

Serfdom was tolerated on condition that a taxpaying peasant who became a serf remained a taxpayer. Having jurisdiction over the peasants resulted in the landowners becoming responsible for the collection and prompt payment of state taxes. At no cost to the government the landowner became an inspector of peasant labour responsible for collecting state revenue from his peasants. A landowner was held responsible for paying taxes on behalf of those peasants who had run away until such time as a new register was drawn up. The *Ulozhenie* had already accepted that 'the State shall levy a percentage of all incomes derived from the peasants belonging to *votchina* and *pomestie* estate owners'; a general tax of 'ten roubles a year' was paid for each runaway peasant (chapter XI, articles 6 and 21).

Legislative recognition that landowners were responsible for paying their peasants' taxes completed the legal structure of peasant servitude. The interests of the Treasury were merged with those of the landowners, although these were essentially different. Throughout the land, private landowners became fiscal police agents of the state Treasury, and instead of being its rivals, became its agents. Reconciliation of this sort could only be achieved at the peasants' expense. Peasant servitude, as confirmed by the *Ulozhenie* of 1649, differed markedly from bondage even though it showed signs of being based on similar precepts. There was a fine distinction based on law and custom:

1. A serf paid state taxes and retained the appearance of a civil personality;

2. a serf owner was obliged to provide him with a plot of land and farming implements;

3. a serf could not be dispossessed of his land by becoming a household serf; if freed he could own land;

4. he could not have his possessions, even though he did not own them outright, taken away from him 'by force', to use Kotoshikhin's expression;

5. he could complain against his master's exactions 'through violence and pillage', and could sue for compensation through the court.

Badly conceived legislation helped to blur these distinctions, and impelled serfdom towards bondage. This chapter has been devoted to an exposition of the origins and structure of serfdom; it will subsequently be necessary to examine the economic effects of serfdom.

In conclusion, it is only necessary to assert that the establishment of serfdom, with its superficial appearance of order and even prosperity, created distortions in the labour force which resulted in a reduction in the general standard of living and led to a succession of disturbances.

Chapter Ten

★

THE DIVISION of Russian society into self-contained, separate classes resulted in another political and institutional sacrifice: *the Zemsky Sobor was no longer summoned*.[1]

The most sinister effect of this division was serfdom, which had been created from bondage and degrees of peasant-unfreedom. Its moral influence was more far-reaching than its legal consequences. It considerably lowered the level of Russian civilisation, which in any event had never stood particularly high. All classes to some degree participated directly or indirectly in the evil of serfdom: from the privileged lay and clerical non-taxpaying groups, who benefited from loan service contracts entered into by peasants and bondsmen, to boyars' bondsmen who became indentured for specific time periods.

Serfdom was especially detrimental to the landowners' social position and political education. Legally permissible and enforceable serfdom forced owners of 'souls' into complete dependence on the powers which upheld it, and into opposition against any measures which threatened it. Simultaneously, they devoted most of their energies and attention to petty disputes between themselves and their serfs, and amongst each other. Eventually these disputes created a social cleavage which for a long time hampered the natural development of the country's labour force; moreover, the landowning nobility, as the ruling class, were responsible, as a result, for distortions in Russian cultural developments. The consequences of serfdom were already obvious in the seventeenth century.

[1] Zemsky Sobors were never abolished by law; they simply ceased to exist.

The Bondage Department was inundated with landowners' testimonies concerning runaways, their enticement by other landowners, theft, arson, murder and other crimes. A landowner had to deposit this evidence in order to exculpate himself from any responsibility for a runaway peasant who had damaged or stolen property in his flight. There was an epidemic of runaways, including ordinary serfs and their overseers who had served their masters for twenty-five years, and would have become clerks. They took with them goods, clothes, cattle, and property which clearly belonged to their masters worth the equivalent of two or three thousand (late nineteenth-century) roubles. They even absconded with strong-boxes containing their deeds of enserfment, thereby destroying any evidence against them so that they could use a different name in a new locality. However, the landowners were nothing if not inventive; they pursued the runaways with dogs who would recognise them and reveal their identity. Peasants fled either singly or in groups of five or six. A minor official, whose business took him from Suzdal to Moscow, had a serf who, together with his family, tried to set fire to the master's house, still occupied by the master's wife and children; the serfs then fled taking with them some of their master's property. The official, who was at this time in Moscow, 'set off from thence in pursuit' of the fugitives; no sooner had he left Moscow than a serf whom he had left behind fled 'taking the rest of his master's property'. These events took place in Moscow and in Suzdal within a period of eight days.

Social status and relationships as such, had nothing in common with serfdom, yet even they were affected and transformed as a result. In 1628 an indentured man called Vaska ran away together with his wife from an official; eight years later he returned as the priest Vasili, having been ordained by the Metropolitan of Kazan and Sviatka. The priest's capacity is not known, although he proved acceptable to his erstwhile master, and in the same year 'this same man, the priest Vasili together with his wife ran away again, taking twenty-eight roubles belonging to the official'.

The *Ulozhenie* later stipulated that ordained priests who had originally been serfs were to be sent to the ecclesiastical authorities to be dealt with 'according to the rules of the Holy Apostle and the Holy Father' (chapter xx, article 67).

Conditions of serfdom affected the most elementary aspects of education. A boy could be contractually enserfed for a certain number of years to a teacher who was supposed to teach him to read; if the boy was disobedient the teacher was entitled to chastise him 'with all manner of punishment'. In 1624 a woman living in the Moscow Orphanage gave her son to a priest attached to a Moscow Nunnery, and together with the boy's grandmother who belonged to the Nunnery, guaranteed his good behaviour; in exchange the boy was to 'do all the household duties'. Father Khariton taught him to read and write in four years; however, the contract of enserfment was valid for twenty years. Seeing that Father Khariton 'had made a man of the boy', and had taught him to read and write, the mother and grandmother decided to save him from the subsequent sixteen years of enserfment. They conferred with other people, and abducted the boy; then to divert suspicion from themselves, they 'sued' the priest. The outcome of this story is unknown.

The treatment of runaways, as related in official documents, makes it difficult to remember that this was a Christian society which was endowed with the relevant ecclesiastical and police powers. In one case a household serf deserted, leaving his wife and children behind him; he wandered from one estate to another, using a variety of aliases, pretending that he was a freeman and a bachelor. He married another household serf on another estate, and entered into a service contract which was registered with the Department of Bondage. His new wife 'fell out of love with him'; he left her and 'having realised his sin' returned to his previous master 'to steal away with his former wife and daughters'. He was unsuccessful. This particular case was mentioned in a document dated 1627, but similar cases were so common that they were later referred to in the *Ulozhenie* (chapter xx, article 84).

The enserfment of peasants dealt a political and moral blow to national representation. The Zemsky Sobor was just becoming an elective, national representative assembly when practically all rural landowners became detached from its structure. The Zemsky

Sobor no longer had a broad-based territorial affiliation, and represented only the narrow vested interests of the men of service and the urban taxpayers. As such, their opinions were neither respected by the Tsar, nor trusted by those in inferior positions. The petty aspects of serfdom as discussed above are symptomatic of the interests and attitudes a serf-owner displayed in a representative assembly. The landed ruling class, privileged, and therefore alienated from the rest of society, was consumed with the sordid details of serf ownership, and corrupted through the availability of unpaid labour; disinterested in agriculture, the ruling class devoted little time to social activities. An estate-owner who oppressed the local village, and was estranged from the town was incapable of persuading the central Chancellory that the rural council should represent independent rural demands and opinion.

The 'Zemsky Sobor', the 'Zemsky Soviet', or the 'Assembly of All the Land' of seventeenth-century Muscovy consisted of 'men of all ranks' or 'every kind of person from every town of Russia', to quote Sobor documents. In the sixteenth and seventeenth centuries it was possible to distinguish two unequal divisions within the Sobor; the elected representatives, and those who were appointed, and formed the official party. The latter consisted of two superior institutions, whose members appeared in full strength at Sobor meetings, together with some departmental officials. These institutions were: 1. the Boyar Duma together with departmental clerks, and 2. the Holy Council, consisting of the Patriarch, metropolitans, bishops, and augmented by archimandrites, abbots and archpriests who attended by invitation.

The elective composition of the Sobor was complex, due to the variety and fragmentation of the electoral 'estates'. There were the high-ranking metropolitan men of service, the *stolniks*, *stryapchie* and *zhiltsy*, the metropolitan nobility, and commercial sectional interests from the different guilds. All these groups were represented at the Sobor. Then there was the urban provincial nobility, which was subdivided into high-ranking men of service, the nobility, and boyars' sons.

Only in Novgorod and Ryazan were the electoral boundaries

based on units smaller than the district: in Novgorod the unit was 'a fifth' and in Ryazan it was 'an eighth'.

Men of service, not of noble birth, as well as foreigners in Russian service were also represented at the Sobor, as were those who served in the Streltsy, the Department of the Streltsy, the artillery or with the Cossacks, wherever they might be.

The representation of taxpayers was organised in a simpler manner, with a strictly territorial affiliation, either through local rural associations or through urban provincial associations. The suburbs of Moscow were divided into 'black hundreds and settlements', and in the first half of the eighteenth century there were thirty-three of them. The Sobor contained representatives from the 'black hundreds' of Dimitrov, Pokrov, Sreten, and from the 'half-hundreds' of Ogorodnaya, Sadovaya, Ordinskaya and Kuznetskaya. Towards the end of the nineteenth century streets in Moscow still carried these names, thereby indicating the territorial and commercial importance of these areas. Provincial 'urban' boroughs were in themselves electoral circumscriptions.

Sobor representatives were elected from the higher nobility and metropolitan commercial classes according to *rank*; from the urban nobility according to their class *associations*; from the other men of service according to their organisational *unit*; and from all urban and rural taxpayers according to their *communities*.

Besides the classes mentioned above, the Sobor of 1613 was attended by elected representatives from the urban clergy and the rural population. How they were elected is unknown.

The archpriest of the town of Zaraisk signed the charter electing Tsar Michael 'for himself and for the elected urban and rural priests'. Whether they received their mandate from a general assembly of the Zaraisk clergy or in another way is not clear. It is even harder to explain the rural population's system of representation. The districts of the southern and south-eastern Steppes were inhabited by considerable numbers of men of service, and in particular, the Cossacks. However, they were included with the urban, and not with the rural population; they signed the charter of 1613 with the other men of service, but used the nomenclature of Cossack. It can only be supposed that the expression 'people from the districts' referred to peasants; and that probably this is why their signatures as non-service taxpayers appeared alongside the signatures of urban taxpayers. The existence of taxpaying peasants can be found in such districts as Kolomna and Tula, even though by the beginning of the sixteenth century they were no longer listed in the census registers. It can therefore be assumed that seignorial peasants were included among the 'people of the districts' who signed the charter; and that in 1613 they were still considered to be free men belonging only to the ruler.

In the 'maritime' towns of the North, where land tenure conditional on service hardly existed, the district peasants were amalgamated with the urban taxpayers into one association, which was responsible for everything affecting agriculture and the payment of taxes; they formed one district commune which sent representatives to the town council for joint consultation. This was the procedure followed for the election of representatives who were sent to the Sobor, and indeed, this was the reason why district peasants were able to appear at all. Whether in 1613 this situation obtained in the southern towns, or whether the district peasants were represented apart from the urban population is difficult to know. Certainly, elected representatives from the clergy and the rural population are absent from future Zemsky Sobors, which ceased, therefore, to be truly representative of the whole community.

The number of representatives varied from one electoral circumscription to another, and was of no particular significance. The writ of summons for the Sobor of 1619 called for one representative from the clergy, two from the nobility and the sons of boyars, two from the urban population. The writ of summons for the Sobor of 1625 called for between five and twenty representatives from the larger electoral circumscriptions but only between two and five from the smaller ones. The writ of summons for the Sobor of 1648 called for two representatives from the metropolitan men of service, two from the provincial association of noblemen from the 'large towns', one from the 'smaller towns', and one each from the urban districts, the 'black hundreds' of Moscow, and its suburbs, two from the 'important hundreds', and three from the merchant guilds.

Complete and uniform representation was never attempted, and could not have been achieved. Among 192 elected representatives at the Sobor of 1642, there were 44 metropolitan men of service (10 courtiers, 22 metropolitan noblemen and 12 courtiers who slept at court); at the Sobor of 1648 there were 290 elected representatives of whom only 8 were metropolitan men of service. From these Sobors whose composition is known, it is clear that large numbers of associations of noblemen and urban taxpayers were absent. Local gatherings of noblemen were badly attended, and 'the choice was poor' from the urban taxpayers. A governor wrote in this connection that 'there are few taxpayers living in the towns; they are going about Your business, Sovereign, collecting excise and other taxes'.

The composition of the Sobors was varied and lacked a permanent organisation. No one Sobor resembled another, and it is difficult to find even one which was attended by representatives of all classes from all districts and all electoral circumscriptions. The 1648 Sobor was attended by elected representatives from the nobility and urban taxpayers of 117 provincial towns; the 1642 Sobor had only been attended by the nobility from 42 towns. If writs of summons were issued hurriedly it was considered sufficient only for delegates from the provincial nobility who were on duty in the capital to attend; at other times the Sobor was attended only by the metropolitan nobility. On 28 January 1634 the Tsar ordered a Sobor to be summoned for the following day to discuss new taxes for military purposes. The meeting was attended by the metropolitan nobility, and those 'provincial noblemen who happened to be in Moscow'.

Town governors summoned assemblies and meetings, and supervised the elections of Sobor representatives. The ukases stated that 'the best men who were good, intelligent, and steadfast', were to be elected; by this was meant men of substance who were industrious and clever. As a result attempts were made to elect representatives from the 'best' estates; for instance, the provincial nobility selected their representatives from those who enjoyed the highest urban rank, which was called *vibor*. Literacy was not an indispensable condition for election. There were 292 representatives at the 1648 Sobor, nothing is known about 18 of them, but of the remaining 274, 141, or more than half, were illiterate.

The electoral protocol, signed by the electors, was given to the governor as proof that those who had been elected 'were suitable to carry out the Sovereign's and the country's affairs'. The governor then sent the representatives, together with their writ of summons, to the Department of Elections which verified the validity of their election. A governor once wrote to Moscow saying that he had carried out the Tsar's ukase, and had sent two of the best noblemen of the district to the Sobor of 1651. However, as far as the best urban taxpayers' representatives were concerned, the governor believed that there were only three competent men available in his town; the rest were drifters, poor and quite unsuitable; he had therefore nominated the son of a boyar, an artilleryman, to represent the urban taxpayers at the Sobor. The clerk of the Department of Elections, a jealous guardian of free provincial elections, noted on the writ of summons 'it is ordered that the nobility choose a good man from among themselves, and it is not for the governor to elect him; he shall be blamed for this, for he has been stupid, and has sent the son of a boyar, an artilleryman, instead of urban taxpayers'.

It is not clear whether the representatives were given written instructions by those who had elected them. In 1613 the provisional Muscovite government sent writs to the towns summoning representatives to come to elect a Tsar, stipulating that they were to act in accordance with the wishes of their electors; and that during the election they were to act 'in accordance with their mandate'. This was an extremely important event, which required unity of opinion, and an independent mandate from the people. It was for this reason that in 1612, when Prince Pozharsky together with Minin went to the relief of Moscow, they summoned a Zemsky Sobor, and issued a writ stating that the towns were to send delegates 'with written and signed instructions'. By this they meant that the electors were to give written and signed instructions that their leaders were to unite against the enemy, and elect a Tsar. However, these written instructions were never mentioned in Sobor documentation, nor indeed were they ever referred to by the deputies.

The deputies were allowed a certain latitude, and at the Sobor of 1648 a nobleman from Kursk even criticised his own electorate. In a report to the Tsar 'he spoke evilly of the whole town', and accused them of shameful behaviour on Holy days. This display of righteous indignation went far beyond the deputy's brief, and there was an immediate reaction from his electors who threatened him 'with all manner of harm'. Even in the absence of formal instructions the deputies were supposed to act in the interests of their electors, and to intercede 'in all their brethrens' needs'. This anecdote about the nobleman from Kursk indicates that the electors felt that they were entitled to call their representative to account, if laws dealing with particular points raised in their petitions were not forthcoming. Moreover, the government shared this attitude. In 1619 the government summoned representatives from the clergy, nobility, and urban taxpayers 'who could recount the offences, the deeds of violence and destruction' so that the Tsar 'might know how the people were being oppressed, their needs, and what they lacked', and having heard their petitions he 'could consider them and improve their condition'. The elected petitioner of the seventeenth century replaced the government agent of the sixteenth century, and the petition in Sobor became a customary means of national expression; it represented a high-level legislative link between the supreme power and the people. The influence this system exerted over the drafting of the *Ulozhenie* of 1649 has been discussed elsewhere.

The elected representatives were incapable of making peremptory demands, forcing through any legislation, or imposing their will on the Tsar.

Questions raised in the Sobor could only be decided upon after a mutual exchange of views, which affected the way in which the questions were put. The Sobor of 1613 which met to elect a Tsar was quite exceptional. Sobors were convened every time by a ukase issued by the Tsar. Only on one occasion did the Holy

Council show initiative. This occurred when the father of Tsar Michael returned from captivity in 1619, and was ordained as Patriarch. Together with the ecclesiastical dignitaries, he approached the Tsar to discuss the structural defects of the State of Muscovy. The Tsar, his father, the Holy Council, the boyars and 'all the people' made a Council to discuss reform and reorganisation.

However, this occurrence is explained by the fact that in this instance the Patriarch was not only head of the Holy Council, but was also Michael's co-ruler. Generally, the Tsar ordered a 'Council to gather' to discuss a particular issue (in either the Granovitaya Palata or the Stolovnaya Izba) and opened it formally either 'by speaking himself' or by ordering a clerk to read 'his speech to Council' in his presence, which outlined the subject to be discussed. Thus, at the Sobor of 1634 the Tsar stated that a new, extraordinary tax was required to pay for continuing the war with Poland, and that unless it was raised the Sovereign's Treasury 'would no longer exist'. The Tsar's speech ended with a declaration to the Sobor 'that the Sovereign will bear your aid in mind, and will not forget it; and now deigns to bless you in all measures which might be taken'. There were no provincial urban taxpayers' representatives present. However, the Sobor members responded by declaring 'that money will be given according to each man's wealth, and every man will give what he can'; and that was that. It seems that this question was resolved in one day, at one meeting and during one sitting. Six days later, the Tsar appointed a commission consisting of a boyar, a courtier, the archimandrite of Chudovo, and two secretaries to collect the new taxes. None the less, at a Sobor meeting of 1642, a similar question was put through a complicated procedural process which might have been used at other Sobor meetings; in any event, the minutes which are extant are so highly compressed that no reliance can be placed on them for a detailed description of what actually happened.

In 1637 the Don Cossacks took Azov, repulsed the Turkish assaults, and presented the captured fortress to the Tsar. At a Sobor meeting, attended by the Tsar, the ecclesiastical authorities and the Boyar Duma, the clerk of the Boyar Duma read the Tsar's decree summoning a Sobor; subsequently, in the presence only of the Boyar Duma, he read a letter in which the Tsar raised two questions. Should Muscovy go to war with Turkey and the Crimea over Azov? If the answer was in the affirmative where were the large sums of money to come from? The letter charged the boyars 'to ponder deeply on these questions, and to put their thoughts in writing to the Tsar, so that he might know everything to do with this business'. Following this, the Tsar's letter was 'distributed to the elected representatives of all ranks, so that each man could deliver his views in the presence of the boyars'. The ecclesiastical authorities were instructed separately, and were told to give the Tsar their individual opinions in writing. The clerk was told to inform the other ranks of this problem, and seek their views.

The other ranks were questioned 'separately' at other Sobor meetings; their replies were contained in written 'statements' or 'memorials'. The procedure for 'questioning the other ranks separately' was one way in which votes were taken. Another way is illustrated by what happened at the Sobor of 1621. The Tsar and Patriarch proposed that war be declared against Poland; the other ranks responded with a petition signifying their concurrence. So far as can be judged from the documents, the difference between the reply by 'memorial' and a petition responding to a proposal was that a 'memorial' was a response to a specific question where the ultimate decision was left to the Tsar, whereas a petition contained a specific answer. However, the system was further complicated since somehow the other ranks were able to state their opinions both in 'memorials' and petitions.

At the Sobor of 1642 the elected representatives of the service classes were divided into three groups. 1. the courtiers (*stolniki*); 2. the metropolitan nobility, which included the Streltsy and the *zhiltsy*; and 3. all the urban nobility. A special clerk, whose brief was to guide and edit all written opinions, was attached to each group. No clerk was attached to the metropolitan commercial classes, and the urban taxpayers from the districts were absent from this particular Sobor meeting. However, opinions were not necessarily submitted in accordance with this grouping. In all, eleven written 'speeches' were submitted from the ecclesiastical authorities, the courtiers, the metropolitan nobility, from two noblemen who submitted a minority decision, the Moscow Streltsy (none from the *zhiltsy*), from the urban nobility from Vladimir, and three other towns of the central regions around Moscow; as well as from 16 other central and western towns, from 23 southern towns, from the trading and cloth guilds, and finally from the Moscow 'black hundreds and settlements'. These submissions appear in the Sobor documents immediately following the list of 192 delegates who attended. From other reports it is possible to deduce that noblemen from 43, instead of from 42, district towns that were mentioned, attended. The reason for this was that noblemen from eight of the towns that were listed did not make any submissions, whereas noblemen from nine towns not on the list, did. How this happened is not clear. It must, however, be remembered that the elected urban nobility were assisted with their submissions by those of their colleagues who happened to be in Moscow on business. For instance, although only one representative from the town of Lukh was listed, the submission speaks of 'the people from Lukh who are in Moscow'. Some noblemen whose names appear on the registers were not summoned to the Sobor, while those who happened to be in Moscow on business at the time were elected in their place.

The ukase summoning the Sobor is dated 3 January, and already on 8 January the representatives were submitting their reports. This haste explains the absence of the urban taxpayers from the Sobor. The submissions resembled one another, and ideas, expressions and whole paragraphs were plagiarised from previous submissions. The documents themselves indicate the procedure in 'debates'. Somewhere, somehow, the delegates grouped themselves together to discuss and exchange ideas; they then expanded and changed their submissions. For instance, a submission from 23 towns was similar to another from 16 towns, while an opinion from the 'black hundreds' and the settlements was culled from a submission presented by the guilds and both 'major hundreds', although it was somewhat altered to present a particular class interest. In a real sense there were no debates during the general Sobor meetings, nor did any general decree emanate from them. The question as to whether to go to war with Turkey and the Crimea over Azov was decided by the Tsar and the boyars, who agreed that they would not go to war nor accept Azov from the Cossacks; they were probably influenced by the views expressed in the submissions, but in any event there was no money, and no possibility of raising it.

Not all Sobors proceeded in the same manner as the Sobors of 1642, but its detailed protocol helps to clarify the political significance of the seventeenth-century Sobors. As during the sixteenth century they were summoned to discuss specific issues of importance, such as the structure of government and foreign policy, war and associated taxes to pay for it. The changes that occurred were not in the Sobor's powers, but in the structure and nature of the Sobor's representatives. Whereas previously the government dealt with its official agents, it now had to deal with elected men who were concerned with the needs and deficiencies of their electors.

The Sobor's political importance depended entirely on the extent to which the Boyar Duma and the Tsar participated in its activities. A dual mechanism existed: the Boyar Duma acted either together with, or separate from, the elected representatives. In the first instance the Tsar and boyars withdrew after the reading of the government's proposals, and took no further part in the Sobor's proceedings. However, the proceedings were confined to discussions between different groupings and the submission of their views; no final general Sobor meetings took place, nor were decisions drawn up. As a result, the Sobor only played a consultative and advisory role. Ultimate decisions were the prerogative of the Tsar and the boyars who considered the viewpoints expressed by the elected representatives when framing legislation.

In fact, this was the procedure adopted by both the Sobors of 1642 and 1648. The draft *Ulozhenie* was read to the elected representatives, presided over by a nominated boyar and two colleagues, thereby forming a type of presidium; simultaneously, reports on the draft were being considered by the Tsar and the boyars, who sat in another chamber. This separation of functions did not mean that the Boyar Duma and the Sobor resembled an upper and lower chamber. The Boyar Duma with the Tsar was not merely one of the legislature's organs: it was the supreme government which incorporated within itself the entire legislative power. Having listened to the reading of the draft articles, the Boyar Duma amended and ratified them; in this way it created laws. The Sobor did not work alongside the Boyar Duma, but was attached to its codification committee. During the hearings the delegates could petition the Tsar either to alter or amplify the articles; the petitions were transmitted to the Tsar and the boyars through the codification committee; these petitions 'from all the ranks of the people' were considered, and subsequently new laws were promulgated.

At other times the Sobor delegates were more directly involved in the legislative process. This occurred when the Boyar Duma led by the Tsar became part of the structure of the Sobor, as though fused into one legislative body. The boyars stated their opinions as did the delegates, and a general decree in Sobor was framed which acquired the force of law. However, the Boyar Duma, in this situation, became the executive body responsible for giving the law effect.

The Sobors of 1618, 1619, 1621, 1632 and 1634 under Tsar Michael, followed the procedure adopted by the Sobor of 1613, and was particularly obvious in the Sobor of 1621. Turkey, the Crimea and Sweden had invited Muscovy to join a coalition against Poland. This seemed like a good opportunity to settle accounts with the Poles for their interference in the Time of Troubles. During this Sobor, which had been summoned to consider this proposition, the ecclesiastical authorities undertook to pray 'for victory over all our enemies'; the boyars and men of service agreed to fight valiantly against the King of Poland, and the commercial delegates said that they would provide money according to their means. A general Sobor decree was issued which stated that Muscovy would join an alliance of the King of Sweden, the Turkish Sultan and the Crimean Khan against the Polish

King. The nobility and sons of boyars petitioned the Tsar to enrol able-bodied men on a territorial basis so that 'no man could default'. The ukase which provided for the enrolment of the nobility, and which ordered the distribution throughout the towns of the Sobor's decision, as well as the order to the men of service to prepare themselves for the campaign by 'feeding the horses and laying in stores' was issued in the name of the Boyar Duma alone.

This was the extent of legislative influence enjoyed by the Zemsky Sobor during the last years of Tsar Michael's reign, until the Sobor of 1642. It played a similar role at the Sobor of 1653, which had been summoned to consider the Little Russia affair. On this occasion the boyars were on equal terms with the delegates, who, as in 1642, 'were questioned in groups according to rank'. None the less, the decision to give Bogdan Khmelnitsky Muscovite nationality was made by the Tsar together with the whole Sobor, and not just by decree emanating from the boyars alone. Even the consultative deliberations of the 1648 Sobor were interspersed with legislative activity. Thus, the Sobor 'laid down' that Church institutions were forbidden to acquire or accept as security the *votchina* estates of men of service (chapter XVII, article 42).

The duality of function, at times consultative, at others legislative, reveals the political instability of Sobor representation. Its legislative authority was not derived from any law, and it did not reflect the will of the people; the Sobor had no political power, and was only the instrument through which power was exercised. As such it, and not the supreme authority, could be held responsible for failure. In short, the Zemsky Sobor did not wield power as of right, but merely as a concession, and this explains its incongruities.

There were elections, electors and elected representatives; the government asked questions and the delegates responded; there were meetings, memorials and statements. The representational apparatus existed. No precise, political delimitation of Sobor activity existed nor was there even a fixed procedure. Sobors were not called at predetermined dates, nor was their structure or competence uniform through time. Moreover, their relationship to the government was also variable, and their authority had no legislative basis. These are times when positive action might have been taken to establish a properly-organised and legally-based institution, but no action was ever taken.

In western Europe a government's desire for revenue was a powerful impulse in the creation of a nationally representative institution, and led to a government seeking help from the ruling classes. However, considerations were extracted for the required assistance; concessions were extorted, and subventions led to rights and guarantees. There were frequent opportunities for this to have occurred in seventeenth-century Russia. Only three of the seventeenth-century Sobors were not concerned with finance. These were the 1618 Sobor which was summoned while Vladislav, the King of Poland's son, was approaching Moscow; the 1648 Sobor which drew up the *Ulozhenie*, and the 1650 Sobor when the government wished to exert some moral influence on the rebels at Pskov. It was the Treasury's chronic shortage of funds which served to remind successive governments of the existence of the Zemsky Sobor: until such time as an equilibrium between revenue and expenditure was restored after the Time of Troubles, the government had to rely on levying extraordinary taxes, forced loans or non-returnable levies from the capitalists 'for assistance' without which the Treasury 'could not exist'.

This was only made possible by the approval of the country. In 1616 the immensely wealthy Stroganovs[1] were forced to pay over 16,000 roubles in taxes, and 40,000 roubles in advance to cover their future tax payments. This weighty assessment was ratified by a general Sobor decree. It was difficult to disobey 'an agreement of the elected men from all towns and the superior powers'. Non-taxpayers were expected to make voluntary

[1] Brief details of the Stroganov family can be found in William L. Blackwell, *The Beginnings of Russian Industrialization 1800–1860* (Princeton U.P., 1968) pp. 13–14; Peter I. Lyashchenko, *History of the National Economy of Russia* (Macmillan, 1949) pp. 211–13, 225; A. Lobanov-Rostovsky, *Russia and Asia* (Ann Arbor, 1951) pp. 39–43.

contributions. At the beginning of the war with Poland in 1632, the Sobor asked the non-taxpayers to collect 'whatever they could give' to pay the soldiers' wages, and the ecclesiastical authorities announced how much they would contribute from their domestic and private funds, while the boyars and men of service undertook to list how much each of them would give. Voluntary donations were transformed by the general Sobor decree into compulsory self-assessments. Thus the Sobor provided the Treasury with indispensable revenue which could not have been obtained otherwise. In this situation the Treasury was entirely dependent upon the Sobor. Although the delegates grumbled, they paid without even demanding, let alone asking, for concessions. They were satisfied with the gracious but vague promise 'that the Tsar will remember your help, and will never forget; he blesses you in all your ventures'.

It is obvious that the idea of equal representation underwritten by political guarantees had occurred to neither government nor society. The Sobor was considered as a government instrument; the obligation to advise when asked to so do was not a political right, but a duty which was no different from the duty of paying taxes. This explains the indifference with which national representation was treated.

The urban delegates attended the Sobor in the same spirit that they fulfilled their military obligations. The electors attended the urban electoral meetings so reluctantly that the governors were often obliged to issue two summonses.

The Sobor failed to find encouragement in contemporary political ideas, in the structure of government as then constituted, or from within itself. When, after the Time of Troubles, solutions had to be found to difficult problems, no one person, political party or group of officials was called upon. Instead, the assistance of the collective intelligence of the country was sought. The ideas of different groups generally acceptable to all were incorporated into one national decree. Given that the Sobor had an important part to play in central government, it might have assumed that local government would have supported and strengthened it, since national representation without any local affiliation is a ridiculous concept. Moreover, a free delegate and an unfree elector is a contradiction in terms.

The most fruitful era of the Zemsky Sobors coincided with a decline in provincial institutions, and their complete subordination to central departments. The new dynasty's legislative activities flowed in opposite directions; what one had created was destroyed by the other. While elected representatives from the districts were being summoned to decide on problems of government together with the boyars and the metropolitan nobility, their electors in the districts were being delivered into the power of those very same boyars and noblemen. Central government departments became the last retreat of the territorial principle, while departmental officials were making themselves masters in the provinces. This contradiction occurred elsewhere. No sooner had the Sobor representing all ranks started to function, and establish the new dynasty, than nearly all the rural population (85 per cent and 95 per cent of the household peasants are included) lost their freedom, and their elected representatives ceased to attend the Sobor meetings, which as a result, lost any semblance of complete national representation. Finally, as classes were segregated one from the other their structure disintegrated and relationships were fundamentally changed.

Many different opinions were expressed at the Sobor of 1642. The Holy Council replied formally to the question whether Muscovy should go to war with Poland: 'this was a matter for his Tsarish majesty and his boyars to consider; it was not a matter for the servants of God'. Never the less, they promised to contribute what they could to the army, in the event of war. The courtiers and metropolitan nobility, the *élite* among the noblemen and the future guardsmen, replied tersely that it was for the Tsar to decide on war, to gather an army, and equip it. It was up to the Tsar also to order the Cossacks to hold Azov having sent some volunteers to help them. Two noblemen, Beklemishev and Zheliabuzhshky, dissociated themselves from their colleagues' reply, and prepared a closely reasoned memorandum in which they advocated that the offer of Azov should be accepted, and that taxes should be levied on all classes, including the monasteries, to pay for the impending war.

The representatives of the lowest classes were the most vociferous at this Sobor. Urban noblemen representing thirty-nine
central and southern districts presented two memoranda, which
were a proper political critique of the existing system, and set out
a complete programme of reform. They were bitter about the
existing chaos, the inequitable distributions of state obligations,
and the privileged position of the metropolitan nobility, especially
those in service at Court. The urban nobility were envious of the
Moscow clerks or secretaries who had enriched themselves
'through venal practices', and had built themselves splendid
marble mansions which even noblemen of previous times could
not have afforded. The urban nobility demanded that landowners'
service obligations be assessed not according to the size of their
landholding, but according to the number of peasant homes on
their estates. Furthermore, they suggested that an exact count of
peasants living on these estates should be made, that an investigation be made into the landholdings of the clergy, and that 'the
household treasures' amassed by the Patriarch, the bishops and
the monasteries should be taken over by the state.

The nobility were prepared to fight the enemy 'with their lives
and hearts', but wanted the army to be recruited from all ranks
except 'their own bondsmen and peasants'. They capped these
criticisms and proposals by criticising the government: 'We are
more ruined by Muscovite malfeasance, injustices and bad judges
than by Turkish and Crimean heathens.'

The wealthier metropolitan merchants and the commercial
classes from the black 'hundreds and settlements' were, like the
urban nobility, prepared to accept the offer of Azov; they were
not afraid of war, and were ready to make financial sacrifices.
However, they were more humble in their approach, more
pessimistic, and less designing; but they were bitter over their
impoverishment from heavy taxation, their services to the
Treasury, and their ill-treatment by the governors, and asked the
Tsar 'to look into their poverty', and gloomily recalled the end
of local government.

The tone of the Sobor reports of 1642 was fairly expressive.
In answer to the Tsar's question of how something was to be

achieved, some replied drily 'as you desire'; others, loyally good-natured said: 'You, our Tsar, are free to obtain men and money from whoever you wish, and your boyars, as your agents, will see to it.' At the same time, however, they intimated to the Tsar they had elected, that his was a bad administration, that his institutions were inefficient, that the services and taxes imposed were beyond the people's means, and that his administrators, the governors, judges and clerks, were corrupt; their depredations were worse than the Tatars, they were ruining the country, while the ecclesiastical authorities were only interested in amassing wealth. 'These are the thoughts and statements of we, the slaves.'

Dissatisfaction with the government was exacerbated by internal class discontent with their respective situations, and over the inequitable distribution of taxation. The upper classes tried to impose new burdens on the lower classes; the commercial classes envied the numerous estates belonging to the men of service, while the latter envied the immense wealth of the merchants; the metropolitan nobility upbraided the provincial nobility for the easy conditions of service they enjoyed; and the provincial nobility were jealous of the lucrative positions and great wealth of the metropolitan nobility. The provincial nobility did not forget to mention the great wealth of the Church that did not benefit the state, nor the sanctity of the Church's bondsmen and peasants. The impression gained from these reports presented by the delegates of the service classes at the Sobor, is that they had nothing to do with each other, that they had nothing in common, and that their interests were completely different. Each class was only concerned with its own interests, its own needs, and the inequitable privileges enjoyed by the others. The political segregation of one class from the other led to mutual estrangement, and put an end to any hope of united action being taken at Sobor meetings.

Although a Zemsky Sobor lost its attraction for the ruling and privileged classes, it did not do so among the small groups of taxpayers who escaped enserfment. Pronouncements of the leading Moscow merchants, black hundreds and settlements, who were the government's administrative executives, show that they were superior to the 'white' or tax-exempt groups. They were ready to serve their Sovereign 'with their lives', and declared that the question as to whether or not Azov should be accepted was not one which affected only one class. 'It affected the whole country and all Orthodox Christians,' and that therefore, the burden should be distributed equitably, and no exceptions should be made. No such opinion was held by the nobility, who did nothing but wrangle with one another: they were concerned lest one of their number have so much as one crumb more than the rest, and they were forever trying to shift new obligations on to others.

The commercial classes fully appreciated the reasons for their attendance at Sobor meetings; they had a basic understanding of where the country's interests lay, and were sympathetic to the spirit of territorial representation. The delegates from the 'black hundreds' who represented the lower classes in the seventeenth century, had a lively social conscience, an attribute which was lacking among the upper classes. At a later date, when the Zemsky Sobor had ceased to exist, spokesmen from the lower classes marshalled their arguments even more forcefully in favour of national representation.

The substitution of copper coins for silver in 1656 led to a rise in prices and a great deal of discontent. The crisis involved the whole population, and could have been avoided had there been a measure of cooperation between government and all social classes.[1] However, the government believed that it could get out of its difficulties by consulting only the metropolitan commercial classes. In 1662 Ilya Miloslavsky, the Tsar's father-in-law and an unscrupulous boyar, together with some other boyars, was made responsible for discussing the problem with the commercial classes; his own malfeasances had helped, if anything, to exacerbate the financial problem. The written opinions of the

[1] This debasing of the currency brought about a sharp rise in the cost of living, much hardship for the masses, and large profits for unscrupulous speculators. In 1663 the government was forced to redeem in silver the copper coins at a mere fraction of their face value. See M. Florinsky, *Russia* (Macmillan, 1953) I 275.

trading and cloth guilds, and the Moscow 'black hundreds and settlements' were as sensible at this time as they had been at the 1642 Sobor. They revealed the nation's economic imbalance, the class antagonisms between village and town, and between land-owner and trader. They drew the government's attention to many bitter truths, pointed out its ignorance of what was going on in the country, its inability to enforce law and order, and its indifference to public opinion.

The right to trade and manufacture carried a concomitant legal obligation to pay dues and tolls to the Treasury. The merchants were now complaining that the most lucrative trade, and the largest manufacturing establishments had, *against the law*, fallen into the hands of the *ecclesiastical, military and legal classes*; bishops, monks, priests, men of service, and departmental officials were 'trading, free of tax', in defiance of state regulations and denuding the Treasury of considerable revenue. Moreover, the merchants were forced to sell at high prices in order to counteract the fall in the value of the copper currency, which earned them the hatred of the rest of society, who deemed that they 'had acted without reason'. Having stated their opinions, the Moscow merchants unanimously agreed that they had nothing more to contribute to a solution because 'this affair affects the state, the country, the towns and every rank'. They begged the Tsar to consult 'the best people from every rank in Moscow and in the towns, since without them nothing can be decided'. This request to summon a representative Sobor was an implicit criticism of the government's tendency to replace the advice given by a broadly-based Sobor with discussions only with the leaders of the upper classes. The merchants believed that the government was showing bad judgement by so doing. In fact, the merchants were drawing the government's attention to the identical administrative and social weaknesses they had discussed so heatedly twenty years before at the Sobor of 1642. At that time they had used the Sobor as the proper place to discuss these weaknesses; now they considered it as the proper institution to deal with them, even though the Sobor consisted of the representatives of the very classes that were perpetuating these weaknesses through their mutual antagonism.

None the less, this shows that the merchants of Moscow believed that a Sobor was the only way of reconciling conflicting and divisive social and economic interests.

If territorial representation were ever to be re-established it would have to face a new problem. It had come about originally to restore law and order after the Time of Troubles. Now, however, it had established a system which the authorities it had elected had so signally failed to do; in other words it had to create a society in the same way that previously it had established a government. Was a representative Sobor capable of undertaking this task when the government itself was one of the active ingredients contributing to the problem? Indeed, was a reconciliation possible, given that the ruling and privileged service classes did not require it? After all, they caused the problems, benefited from them, and were quite indifferent to social dissensions so long as 'their serfs and peasants' were unaffected. Were the guilds of Moscow and the merchants too insignificant to redress the social balance?

The establishment of peasant servitude, the political insignificance and absence of social responsibility on the part of the clergy, found the needs and interests of rural taxpayers being represented by weak spokesmen from the urban taxpaying and metropolitan merchant class, who themselves were overburdened with class obligations. As a result they would have been overwhelmed by the service classes and the boyar officials who represented the majority view at Sobor meetings. In fact, the Sobor which the merchant class had wanted to be summoned in 1662 was never convoked; as a consequence, the government had to endure fresh riots in Moscow which were suppressed with typical Muscovite ineptitude.

The duality of the Sobor's character, its political confusion, centralisation of government, the establishment of peasant servitude, class divisions, and the government's inability to solve its problems – all these were factors in the failure of the Zemsky Sobor, and explain why its activities ceased, and why there was a gradual demise in national representation.

There is no need to dwell upon the low standards of political ideas, habits or demands; the political temperature of the times would have put any administration which was concerned with fostering a spirit of freedom into cold storage. This was the background against which the new dynasty introduced its unsuccessful and harmful innovations, and its effect was to alter the composition of the Zemsky Sobor, a process which started at the beginning of the new dynasty's rule. After 1613 Sobors ceased to be attended by elected delegates representing the clergy and the rural population. The Sobor no longer represented the whole of society, and was only attended by the service classes and urban taxpayers. However, even this minimally representative basis was sometimes further eroded, since the government could, at its own discretion, and depending on its needs, summon only metropolitan representatives and provincial noblemen who were in Moscow on state business; it did not even bother with the urban taxpayers.

The Sobor of 1634 which levied extraordinary taxes from 'all the people', as well as 'fifth moneys', which was a tax imposed primarily on urban taxpayers, was not attended by delegates representing these classes.

The Zemsky Sobor was destroyed from below.[1] The lower classes with their strong territorial affiliations had no representation, and delegates from the districts, the clergy, urban and rural taxpayers, and even from certain service groups, ceased to be summoned. Having lost any national significance, the Zemsky Sobor reverted to its sixteenth-century organisation, and became an official assembly of the metropolitan service classes, and the metropolitan merchants who paid taxes and performed state services. The Sobor of 1650 was again not attended by urban taxpayers, and the metropolitan taxpaying merchants were represented by officials, the *starosti* and *sotskie*, as in the sixteenth century. As the territorial basis contracted so did the Sobor disintegrate socially: the government decided it would confer with its nominees. By this is meant that the government allocated a particular departmental or class label to each problem confronting

[1] See J. L. H. Keep, 'The Decline of the Zemsky Sobor', *Slavonic and East European Review*, XXXVI (Dec 1957) 100–22.

it, and summoned either elected or nominated representatives from the class most directly concerned, for discussions. Thus, when in 1617 the English government suggested that the government of Moscow permit English merchants to travel down the Volga to Persia, and allow them commercial privileges and concessions, the Boyar Duma replied 'that nowhere is it said that this can be decided without the advice of the whole country'. Yet 'the advice of the whole country' consisted in seeking the views of the guilds and the metropolitan merchants.

Certain questions raised at general Sobor meetings were discussed only by some delegates. For instance, the government decision, referred to elsewhere, on service patrimonies, was taken by the Sovereign and Boyar Duma in consultation with the clergy and men of service without the participation of any other class. No Zemsky Sobor was convened between 1654 and the death of Tsar Fedor in 1682. Problems of particular importance to the State were decided by the Sovereign together with the Boyar Duma and the Holy Council, but without any assistance from delegates from other classes. In 1672 when the Sultan of Turkey was threatening to invade Muscovy, the raising of special taxes was provided for by a decree drawn up by the Tsar, Boyar Duma and the upper clergy. Yet a Zemsky Sobor was summoned in 1642 for a similar, but less pressing reason. Clearly, the government preferred to consult with various classes, and indeed, this became the only way in which society could participate in affairs of state. Between 1660 and 1682 the government is known to have conferred with the leaders of different classes at least seven times. In 1687 only delegates from the service ranks were invited to attend a conference presided over by the Boyar Prince V. Golitsin to discuss military reforms; only taxpayers' representatives were invited to conferences dealing with finance. The government itself destroyed the Zemsky Sobor, and replaced national representation by conferences with selected people, which of course, committed the government in no way whatever, and transformed general affairs of state into questions appertaining to specific classes.

The history of the Zemsky Sobor in the seventeenth century is the history of its decline. This was because it came into being as a result of the country being temporarily without a Tsar, and a desire to emerge from anarchy; it was retained to satisfy a transient desire of a new government to consolidate its position in the country. The new dynasty and the classes on which it depended, the clergy and the nobility, needed the Zemsky Sobor until such time as the country had recovered from the upheavals caused by the Pretenders. With the restoration of peace, government reliance on the Zemsky Sobor diminished. However, signs of its work survived its passing. Appearing in 1613 as a representative constituent assembly, the Zemsky Sobor created a new dynasty, restored peace, and for two years virtually replaced the government; it was on the way to becoming a permanent institution, and occasionally acted in a legislative capacity, even though there was no legal basis for this activity. It was summoned ten times, sometimes for successive years, under Tsar Michael. Tsar Alexis summoned it only five times during the first eight years of his reign, after which with its structure weakened, it became transformed from a representative assembly first to a two-class, and then to a one-class, assembly, that of the nobility. In the end even this was abandoned by the government which preferred to confer with leading representatives of specific classes. It was never summoned under Tsar Fedor, and in 1682 it was hurriedly summoned with the most haphazard representation to seat both his younger brothers on the throne. It was last summoned by Peter the Great in order to pass judgement on the conspiratorial Tsarevna, Sophia.

The Zemsky Sobor had no real political influence, and as an administrative organisation, was never able to solve the government's problems. Some articles in the *Ulozhenie* were affected by its legislative activities; it survived temporarily in the political consciousness of the metropolitan merchants and then was promptly forgotten. Only in the maritime regions of Northern Russia, where historical memories were particularly long, were recollections of the Zemsky Sobor preserved. An epic tale from these regions tells how Tsar Alexis, who once wrote in jest that he 'always listened to speeches from the ruralities', although he was busy suppressing the Zemsky Sobor, spoke to his subjects from Execution Square in Moscow saying:

> Help your Tsar that he may advise the Duma.
> The Duma must think hard but not too long.

The elective Zemsky Sobor entered the structure of Muscovite government by chance as a fortuitous result of the extinction of the old dynasty, following which it appeared only from time to time. Through the Zemsky Sobor, the country and the nation appeared on the administrative scene for the first time, in the government's absence. The Zemsky Sobor reappeared subsequently when the government needed the nation's help. The Time of Troubles was responsible for gathering together what remained of the nation's strength to restore order from chaos, and it was these enforced pressures which created and maintained the Zemsky Sobor. In Russia popular representation came into being not to impose limitations on authority, but to find and strengthen it. This was the essential difference between Russia and Western Europe.

Having created a Sovereign and given him the necessary support, the Zemsky Sobor became for a time his partner in government, and eventually might have become a permanent collaborator. This never came about because state requirements together with government policies destroyed the unity which disasters had imposed on society. As a result society was divided into self-contained classes which led directly to the enserfment of the peasants by the landowners. This deprived the Sobor of its broadly-based representative characteristics, and turned it into an upper-class institution. Meanwhile, the upper classes were disunited politically as a result of inequalities in privileges and responsibilities, and morally, as a result of internal antagonisms.

On the other hand, neither the experiences of the Time of Troubles, nor the Sobor's tremendous activities under Tsar Michael was sufficient to instil in people a feeling that national representation was a serious political issue, or that the Council should become a permanent institution where national issues could be discussed. Not one class of any influence felt that this was an important issue. With the establishment of peasant servitude, the boyars became absorbed into the nobility, who became in fact the ruling class. The nobility found a more convenient way than through the Sobor of furthering their interests: direct appeals to the Sovereign with collective petitions. The circle of boyars and noblemen who successively put weak Tsars on the throne facilitated this approach. The metropolitan merchants who had taken up the cause of national representation were unable to fight for it alone, and in 1662 their delegates complained that they were able to achieve very little.

It appears, therefore, that two conditions prevented the consolidation of Sobor representation in the seventeenth century. 1. Originally the Zemsky Sobor had supported the new dynasty and was part of the administrative machinery; but the government found it increasingly less useful as the dynasty entrenched itself, and its own resources increased and it was able to rely heavily on its officials. 2. Society was divided by different class responsibilities and privileges, and, lacking any sense of equity, was not in any position to cooperate and transform the Sobor into a permanent legislative institution with proper political guarantees and incorporated into the state system. Therefore, national representation was a victim of increased centralisation in government, and rigidity in the class structure.

Chapter Eleven

★

NATIONAL REPRESENTATION lasted longer than local self-government. The disappearance of one, and the extinction of the other, was the result, albeit not concurrently, of the two fundamental changes in government discussed in the previous chapter. The growth of centralisation muzzled local government institutions, and their increasing impotence coupled with inter-class isolation led to the downfall of the Zemsky Sobor which had been the highest institution in which local interests could participate in the legislative process. Both these fundamental changes stemmed from a common source: the financial requirements of state. It was lack of revenue that influenced the government's administrative and social policies, that impelled it to reorganise the administration and society, and that called for sacrifices to be made at the expense of public welfare and national prosperity.

Almost the weakest part in the economy of Muscovy under the new dynasty was its finances. A substantial increase in revenue was required as a result of the numerous, expensive, and rarely successful wars which were an intolerable drain on the government's available resources; its constant concern was how to bring income and expenditure into balance. In the end the army overwhelmed the Treasury. When the Tsar asked the Sobor to help prolong the war with Poland in 1634, he explained that the Treasury had accumulated a surplus from indirect taxes collected in peace-time, and that this had all been spent on preparations for war; as a result he was unable to maintain his auxiliary forces 'without an increase in Treasury funds', by levying extraordinary taxes. Military setbacks which arose during the conflict with

Poland and Sweden forced the government to adopt foreign models in an attempt to improve the quality of its own armies.[1]

Two documents have survived which describe the reorganisation of the militia of the nobility, as well as the extent to which their cost of upkeep increased over a fifty-year period. The budget estimate for 1631 lists the armed forces directly maintained at Treasury expense; payments were made in cash, in kind and by grants of estates in service tenure. The documents mention that there were 70,000 in the militia consisting of metropolitan and urban noblemen, gunners, Streltsy, Cossacks and foreigners. There were approximately 15,000 easterners in the circumscriptions covered by the old khanates of Kazan and Siberia: men of service from the Murzi, Tatars, Chuvashi, Cheremis, Mordvins and Bashkirs. However they received no money for their services, and were only used 'when general service obtained throughout the country', or, in other words, when there was a general mobilisation. In 1670 Reitenfels[2] admired 60,000 noblemen who were parading past the Tsar, and must have included not only the metropolitan nobility but also the upper ranks of the provincial nobility who were used for long marches, and were attended by their armed dependants. The glitter of weapons and costumes must have blinded the foreigner. They made a better impression in Moscow and on the aesthetically-minded Tsar than on the battle-fields of Lithuania and Little Russia, even though nothing had been denied them.

The military efficiency of this motley collection of noblemen, Cossacks, Tatars, and Chuvashi who were disbanded after each

[1] The first full-time paid infantry, the Streltsy, was mobilised by Ivan the Terrible, who also began large-scale recruitment of foreign mercenaries. In the first three decades of the seventeenth century the total number of traditional, non-noble elements fell from about half to one-quarter of the Russian army. The Russian army started its most dramatic expansion during the war with Poland in 1632–4. It increased from about 100,000 to about 300,000 in the last stages of the victorious campaign against Poland in the 1660s. See James H. Billington, *The Icon and the Axe* (Weidenfeld & Nicholson, 1966) pp. 111–12.

[2] Jacob Reitenfels, a native of Courland, was an envoy from Rome to Moscow from 1670 to 1673. His *De Rebus Moscovitius* was published in 1680. See P. Pierling, S.J., *La Russie et le Saint-Siège*, vol. IV (Paris, 1907) pp. 68–70.

campaign can best be expressed in Kotoshikhin's words; he wrote: 'there is no military instruction, nor is there any military organisation'. Only the Streltsy, who were organised in permanent regiments, had a proper military structure.

The reorganisation of this warlike material consisted of the following: foreign colonels and captains, mostly Germans, were posted to command companies of cavalry, infantry, and dragoons. The companies consisted of the urban nobility and boyars' children, especially those who were landless or only had small or poor estates, as well as of volunteers and recruits from other classes, including peasants and bondsmen. In the outlying districts of Southern Russia whole villages were converted into military settlements. In 1647, for instance, a village of almost 400 peasant homesteads belonging to a monastery in the Lebidian district was enrolled into the dragoons.

According to instructions issued in 1678, all 'poor' noblemen fit to serve were to be conscripted and paid a monthly wage. An ukase of 1680 ordered all fit noblemen from the military districts of Seversky Byelgorod and Tambov to enlist for regimental service. However, these were extreme measures. Normally, these regiments which were organised on foreign lines were reinforced in two ways. Either one dragoon and one infantryman had to be sent from every 100 peasant homesteads, or recruitment could be based on a family unit, in which case a family with two or three single men had to send one man, and with four, two. All were unpaid. These conscript levies supplemented the old system of recruitment.

According to calculations made between 1654 and 1679, conscripts diminished the labour force by at least 70,000 men. The new regiments were taught to drill, and instructed in the use of firearms. The military register for 1681 shows what resulted from the slow military reorganisation. The soldiers listed in this register belonged to nine district corps. Only the Moscow-based corps, consisting of 2,624 men from the metropolitan ranks, together with their 21,830 bondsmen and conscripts, and 5,000 Streltsy were organised on traditional Muscovite lines. The remaining eight district corps together with 16 Streltsy regiments were listed in the register together with 25 foreign cavalry regiments and 38 infantry regiments commanded by foreign colonels. Only three regiments were commanded by Russians who were ranked as generals. The militia of noblemen who numbered 40,000 according to the lists of 1631 were reduced to 13,000 organised in the old way, while the rest were absorbed into 63 reorganised regiments totalling 90,000 men.

In no sense could this be called a regular army since it was not on a permanent footing. At the end of every campaign even the new regiments were disbanded, and the soldiers sent home; only officer cadres remained.

According to figures listed in 1681, excluding 50,000 Little Russians, but including the Cossacks, the army consisted of 164,000 men. A comparison of these figures with those of 1631, but excluding all non-Russian forces, shows that between 1631 and 1681 the Treasury was responsible for two-and-a-half times as many men. Foreign colonels and captains were very highly paid, and if they remained in the service of Muscovy their 'monthly sustenance' was converted into salaries for life; when they died their wives and children received a pension based on half their salaries. Cavalrymen, infantrymen and dragoons recruited mostly from the poorer classes were paid high money wages, received free weapons and ammunition, and on campaigns were fed at Treasury expense. The annual cost of the army (converted into nineteenth-century rouble values) increased from 3 million in 1631 to 10 million in 1680. While the army was two-and-a-half times as large, costs had trebled. Wars were becoming more expensive; the unsuccessful year-and-a-half campaign against Smolensk under Tsar Michael cost at least 7–8 million roubles, while Tsar Alexis' first two campaigns against Poland in 1654–5 which won for Muscovy Smolensk, White Russia, and Lithuania cost 18–20 million roubles. This almost equalled the total annual revenue received by the central finance departments in 1680.

The national budget increased in proportion to military costs. It is worth explaining in general terms the financial system within which the government tried to balance income and expenditure.

Treasury income came from *assessed* and *unassessed* revenues.

Assessed revenue was the name given to a predetermined amount of money which had to be raised (*oklad*) from both direct and indirect taxes. Direct taxes were paid either by whole communities or individuals. The aggregation of these apportioned taxes was called *tiaglo*, and the people who paid them, *tiaglie*. The unit of taxation was land and homesteads, which were also called *tiaglie*, and taxes were apportioned on the basis of the *sokha* contained in the cadastral surveys (*soshnoye pismo*). *Sokha* was a unit of taxation comprising either a definite number of taxable urban dwellings or a specified area of taxable farm land. On good *pomestie* or *votchina* land a *sokha* might consist of 800 quarters in one field; on good monastery land this might be 600 quarters, and on good 'black' or taxed land, 500 quarters. The number of quarters of average and poor land increased proportionally in each *sokha* since the quality of land was determined by the income it produced, rather than by the quality of the soil.

The structure of the urban *sokha* was extremely varied. Towards the end of the sixteenth century a *sokha* in Zaraisk consisted of 80 homes belonging to prosperous people, 100 homes belonging to middle income groups, and 120 squalid homes belonging to the poor.

Assessed revenue can be listed as follows: indirect taxes, of which the most important were those derived from customs and excise and which were the Treasury's most lucrative revenue in the seventeenth century. Custom dues were varied, and were levied both on transport and on the sale of goods. Excise taxes were imposed on alcohol which was a Treasury monopoly. The rate of tax was set by the government. The government farmed out the collection of these taxes to '*trusted men*' or to superintendents who sold the alcohol; these 'trustees' were elected by the local taxpayers from amongst themselves, and any shortfall in revenue had to be made good either by the 'trustees', or by their electors should they have failed to notice and report the theft or negligence of their 'trustee'. Both 'trustees' and superintendents who were discovered by third parties pilfering or embezzling were, according to the law of 1637, liable to be 'punished by death, without mercy'. In other words, the law punished the government's agent for its own negligence and incompetence in imposing both an obligation and the responsibility for fulfilling it, when both functions properly lay within the government's own jurisdiction.

In the middle of the seventeenth century all indirect taxes were combined into one tax. In 1653 the government introduced the so-called 'rouble tax'; it was in effect a sales tax where the vendor paid a 5 per cent tax, calculated on the sale price, and the buyer paid 5 per cent.

Basic direct taxes were called '*dengi dannie*' (given money) and *obrok*, quitrents. The term '*dengi dannie*', or simply '*dan*' applied to a range of direct taxes paid by merchants and the rural population. Their incidence depended on the number of *sokha* allocated to particular urban or rural communities in the cadastral surveys. *Obrok*, or quitrent, had a double meaning. At times it referred to the payment made by an individual to the government either for the right to use government land, whether timber land or pasture, or to engage in trade. Used in this way the term *obrok* referred to revenue raised by fishing, hay-growing land, hunting grounds, as well as from shops, taverns, washhouses and industrial establishments owned by the Treasury. At other times *obrok* meant one general tax imposed on the inhabitants of one area, instead of a variety of taxes and other obligations. *Obrok* for instance was used to denote the one tax that replaced the imposts payable to governors and heads of territorial communes when these posts were abolished by Ivan the Terrible. *Obrok* in the sense of one general tax became part of the tax structure and its incidence was based on the cadastral surveys. The amount and rate of the *dan* and *obrok* as general taxes never changed, whereas the level of other state taxes varied and were regulated by special decrees issued by the Tsar.

Earmarked taxes for specific purposes were included in assessed revenue. They were called *yamskoy*, *polonyanichny* and *streltsy*. *Yamskoy* taxes were earmarked to maintain the postal services which carried envoys, courtiers, the military and officials; posting stations, or *yamy*, were established along the principal routes. This tax was levied on townsmen and peasants alike based on the cadastral surveys, and was paid into a special central department called the Postal Department which was responsible for the post-riders who were paid a salary and allowances in exchange for keeping horses ready at each posting-station.

The *polonyanichny* tax was earmarked to pay ransom on prisoners in the hands of the Tatars and the Turks; it was levied on individual homesteads and not according to the *sokha*. Under Tsar Michael it was levied on special instructions from the government as a temporary measure. However, later on, it became permanent, and the *Ulozhenie* of 1649 stated that it was to be collected annually 'from all people', both taxed and untaxed, albeit at different rates. Urban dwellers and Church peasants paid about 60 kopeks (in nineteenth-century values) on each home-stead, court, 'black' and *pomestie* peasants paid 30 kopeks, and the Streltsy, the Cossacks and the lower ranked men of service paid 1 kopek each. Kotoshikhin stated that approximately 150,000 roubles (2 million in nineteenth-century values) were collected annually in this way, and were paid to the Department of Foreign Affairs who were responsible for ransoming prisoners.

The *Streltsy* tax was earmarked for the upkeep of the Streltsy, a permanent corps created by Ivan the Terrible in the sixteenth century. At the beginning this was an insignificant tax on grain; in the seventeenth century it became a tax in money and on grain, and as the Streltsy grew in number so the tax increased until it became the highest direct tax of all. Kotoshikhin stated that even in peace time during Tsar Alexis' reign, there were more than 20 Streltsy Regiments in Moscow, each with a complement of between 800 and 1,000 men (in 1681 they totalled 22,452), and there were almost the same number in the provinces.

With the exception of the *polonyanichny*, all the above-mentioned taxes were assessed on the basis of the cadastral surveys. Each *sokha* was given a tax assessment, payment of which was apportioned among the taxpayers according to their financial resources; 'they produced the money based on their property, goods, arable land and all possible possessions'. The basis of the *sokha* tax assessment then was the cadastral survey. From time to time the government made inventories of all immovable taxable property by sending assessors to each district to enumerate the tax-able items declared to them verbally or in writing by the inhabi-tants; everything was subsequently verified by the assessors, either through personal inspections, or from previous cadastral surveys.

A cadastral survey described a town and its districts, their population, land, pastoral and timber concessions, trading and manufacturing establishments, as well as the taxes each carried. In listing urban and district settlements, townships, and villages, the cadastral surveys also enumerated the taxed homesteads and taxpayers; details were given of the houseowner together with his children and relatives. Moreover, they recorded the arable, barren, pasture, and forest lands belonging to each settlement. Taxed urban dwellings and rural land were organised into *sokha*; the incidence of tax was then determined by the taxpaying capacity of the inhabitants.

The Moscow archives of the Ministry of Justice contain hundreds of sixteenth and seventeenth-century cadastral surveys, which are fundamental sources for the history of the financial structure and economic life of Muscovy. Similar surveys had been undertaken in early times, but only a few from the end of the fifteenth century have survived, and then only those referring to Great Novgorod. The surveys, which were of great financial and cadastral value, were often used as a basis of settlement in civil actions. Disagreements over land and the rightful ownership of immovable property were settled by reference to the cadastral surveys, which were also used in the selection of unpaid con-scripts. When Philaret, Tsar Michael's father, returned from Poland in 1619, the two Sovereigns summoned a Sobor which was bidden to send writers and assessors to compile lists of all towns, and return their inhabitants to the localities where they previously lived and paid their taxes. This decision necessitated a general census of taxpayers which was started in the 1620s with the object of ascertaining the taxpaying capacity of the people, and organising a tax system. The census registers of the late 1620s used in the *Ulozhenie* was a documentary basis for establishing serf ownership, and other aspects of enserfment. Furthermore, legal action against runaway peasants was determined in accordance with information contained in the census, and it was following this census that conditions of servitude were inserted into peasant loan contracts.

Unassessed revenue consisted mainly of payments made by private persons for services performed by government departments. Examples of these were stamp duties on private transactions, on petitions sent by individuals to administrative and judicial departments, and on legal documents emanating from them.

Given this financial system in the seventeenth century, the Treasury embarked on a programme of innovation which either mitigated against the existing system or completely altered it. First of all, however, the Treasury had to find the scattered tax-payers. The Time of Troubles had relieved a great many tax-payers from their liabilities. With the restoration of order, people resumed their occupations without paying any taxes. A continuous legislative and police struggle was undertaken with these 'defaulters'. After the Sobor of 1619 the government began to prosecute those who mortgaged themselves, but it clearly was unable to deal properly with these people, as witness the pro-ceedings of the Sobor of 1648–9. The *Ulozhenie* stated that rural inhabitants who traded in towns had either to give up their business or pay their share of urban taxes.

Mention has already been made of the fact that the Treasury had to secure for itself a permanent income from indirect and direct taxes, and that in order to achieve this, legal provision was made to organise society into self-contained classes each with concomitant responsibilities; urban dwellers were not allowed to change their residences, and servitude for life by contract was converted into hereditary enserfment. However carefully the government might legislate, there were still many who evaded their taxpaying responsibilities.

Like a fisherman who uses a huge net to catch one fish, the government hoped to enmesh the whole population, the ordinary people as well as the privileged classes, adults as well as children of both sexes, into working for the Treasury's benefit. Con-currently in western Europe political economists believed that direct taxes should be replaced by indirect taxes, and that taxes should be imposed on goods for consumption, rather than on capital and labour. Muscovy tried to carry out similar policies independent of any foreign theories, merely following rather bad domestic practices. Indirect taxation was commoner in Muscovy than direct taxation. However, during the seventeenth century the government rigorously imposed a wide range of indirect taxes in the belief that a taxpayer would prefer to pay a tax on goods rather than direct taxes, since at least he had something other than a tax receipt to show for his money.

It was this type of thinking that produced the idea, commonly attributed to a former guildsman and present secretary, Nazarei Chisty, of substituting the highest taxes by an increased tax on salt. Since salt was a general necessity, the Treasury would benefit, and there could be no defaulters. Until 1646 the tax on salt amounted to 5 kopeks (60 kopeks in nineteenth-century values) on a pood[1] of salt. A law passed in 1646 raised the tax to 20 kopeks on a pood, which came to half a kopek on a pound of salt. A comparison between the purchasing power of the seventeenth-century half-kopek with six nineteenth-century kopeks, using the price of grain as a standard, shows that the Treasury tax alone amounted to six times the nineteenth-century market value of a pound of salt. This law was justified by a number of naïve considerations: that the taxes for the upkeep of the Streltsy and the posting services, which were the heaviest and the most unequally distributed, would be abolished; that everybody would pay a standard tax, that there would be no defaulters, that people would pay their own taxes, and that it would not be necessary to force them or prosecute them, and that even foreigners living in Muscovy, who paid nothing into the Treasury, would pay it. However, these hopes were never realised. Thousands of poods of fish, which was cheap, and on which the people lived during the days of fasting, were left to rot on the banks of the Volga because the fishermen could not afford to salt them. Moreover, greater quantities of cheap salt were sold than before, so that in fact the Treasury suffered a loss.

[1] One pood equals 36·113 lb.

The government decided to abolish the salt tax at the beginning of 1648. It had caused a great deal of resentment which culminated in summer riots. The rioters killed Nazarei Chisty crying out: 'There you are traitor, here's for your salt!' Financial necessity caused a pious government to deal with a national and ecclesiastical prejudice, and create a state tobacco monopoly. Tobacco had hitherto been referred to 'as a poison abominated and reviled by God', and a law of 1634 had threatened anybody selling it with the death penalty.[1] The Treasury now proceeded to sell tobacco almost as if it were gold at 3 to 3½ (nineteenth-century values) roubles an ounce. After the 1648 riots the tobacco monopoly was abolished and the law of 1634 restored. In its ignorance the government indulged in some very foolish decisions.

Another financial venture was even more catastrophic. Muscovite financiers of the seventeenth century were really incredibly inventive! Having decided to replace direct taxes by indirect taxes, they became singularly original in their ideas concerning the currency.

With the successful conclusion in 1656 of the first war with Poland, Muscovy was ready to break off relations with Sweden, but it was found that there was not enough silver in the Moscow Treasury to pay the soldiers. It was said that Fedor Rtishchev, one of the Tsar's intimates, had the idea of issuing copper coins. Muscovy was already quite accustomed to using monetary tokens of nominal value; and the Treasury was used to debasing the coinage. There were no native gold or silver coins of a large denomination in circulation; the *rouble* and the *poltina* (half a rouble) were the units of account. The only small coins in circulation were the *kopeks*, half-kopeks (*dengi*) and the *polushka*,

---

[1] The last chapter of the *Ulozhenie* deals with the sale and use of tobacco. Both the ukase of 1634 and article 11 of chapter xxv prescribed the death penalty. In practice, however, tobacco was made available to Russian soldiers, and enforcement of the ban became increasingly lax. The ban was repealed by Peter the Great in 1697. See Jacob M. Price, 'The Tobacco Adventure to Russia', *Transactions of the American Philosophical Society*, n.s., vol. 51, part 1 (1961) pp. 17–20.

quarter-kopeks, which weighed one-quarter to one-sixth of the weight of a kopek. Buyers at market, afraid of pickpockets, generally kept these small, awkward, oval, and other shaped coins in their mouths, firmly pressed against their cheeks.

Unable to obtain sufficient silver of its own, the Treasury issued its own coins from imported German Joachimsthalers, which the Russians called *efimki*.[1] Naturally, in the process the Treasury looked after its own interests. In the market the *efimok* was worth between 40 and 42 kopeks, but when it was melted down it became worth 64 kopeks, thereby assuring the Treasury a profit of between 52 per cent and 60 per cent in the re-minting process. Re-minting was sometimes limited to placing a seal known as 'the Tsar's seal' on the *efimok* thereby transforming it from a coin worth 40 kopeks to another worth 60 kopeks. Only from the beginning of the first war with Poland were silver roubles and quarters minted with the same nominal value as the stamped *efimok*. Small copper coins were subsequently issued equal in weight and shape to silver coins. At first these metal tokens enjoyed the peoples' confidence, and circulated on equal terms with silver coins. However, this attractive operation fell into the hands of greedy men, and the artisans in the Mint who had been poor suddenly became affluent. They openly squandered their money, built themselves magnificent houses, decked their wives out like boyars' ladies, and bought goods without haggling over the price. Even rich merchants and guildsmen who were supposed to supervise the issue of these coins, bought copper, took it to the Mint with other coins where it was transformed into the new tokens, and took them home. The market was flooded with debased coinage made from coins which had been taken out of circulation. A rate of exchange soon came into existence which rapidly widened. At the beginning there was a difference of four kopeks between the silver and copper coins; at

[1] Joachimsthal is the German name for the Bohemian town of Jachymov, the location of a silver mine, and the place where reichsthalers were first coined. The word *efimki* is evidently a corruption of *iakhimki* – i.e. coins from Jachymov. See *The Travels of Olearius in Seventeenth-century Russia*, trans. and ed. Samuel H. Baron (Stanford U.P., 1967) p. 178, n. 11.

the end of 1660 two copper roubles equalled 1 silver rouble; by 1663 twelve copper, and sometimes fifteen roubles, equalled one silver rouble. Goods increased in price, and life was particularly difficult for the soldiers who were paid in copper coins at half the conversion rate. It was eventually disclosed that officials from different departments had been bribed to conceal the dishonest activities of the financiers and guildsmen. Dishonesty among those in high places was clearly in evidence, since the chief beneficiaries were the Tsar's father-in-law, boyar Ilya Miloslavsky, and the Tsar's uncle by marriage, a nobleman called Matiushkin, who was responsible for the copper coin operation. However, Miloslavsky was considered to be the instigator of the fraud. The Tsar was extremely angry with his father-in-law, relieved his uncle of his position, and ordered that the departmental officials, financiers and guildsmen were to have their hands and feet cut off, and exiled. Other participants in the fraud saw that the nobility had escaped punishment; taking advantage of the general discontent over price increases they decided to turn on the boyars and riot as in 1648. Inflammatory posters all over Moscow accused Ilya Miloslavsky and others of treason. In July 1662, while the Tsar was living in the Moscow suburb of Kolomenskoe, a mob of some 5,000 approached the Tsar who advanced towards them; they demanded that the traitors be brought to trial. Some of them held the Tsar by the buttons of his kaftan, while he was made to take an oath that he would deal with the matter himself, and he was forced to shake hands on it. However, the first mob was joined by a second from Moscow, and both boisterously began to demand that the Tsar hand over the traitors to them; if he did not they would be taken by force. Tsar Alexis called on the Streltsy and his courtiers for assistance, and an indiscriminate slaughter ensued, followed by tortures and executions. Hundreds were drowned in the River Moskva, and whole families were exiled permanently to Siberia. The Tsaritsa was ill for more than a year following the July riots.

A variety of people were involved both in the copper fraud and in the riots: priests, churchmen, monks, guildsmen, urban taxpayers, peasants, and bondsmen; some soldiers and a few officers joined in the riots. Contemporary observers estimated that over 7,000 men were sentenced to death, and that over 15,000 either had their hands and feet cut off, or were exiled, or had their property confiscated. However, there were no more than 200 active conspirators, most of the mob having consisted of curious onlookers who wanted to look upon the Tsar.

The effect of the copper coin affair was seriously to disrupt industry and trade, and the Treasury's attempts to sort itself out of its difficulties merely created greater confusion.

The Moscow merchants clearly stated their opinions as to the reason for a rise in prices at conferences in 1662 with Streshnev and Ilya Miloslavsky. The Treasury had exhausted its stock of imported silver coins, and tried to re-fill its coffers by forcing the merchants to sell furs, hemp, potash and beef suet, intended for export, to the Treasury for copper coins. The Treasury then re-sold these goods to foreigners for *efimki*. At the same time Russian merchants paid in silver for imports, since foreigners would not accept copper coins. However, the merchants were forced to resell these goods internally for copper. In this way silver coins were taken out of circulation, and the merchants were eventually no longer able to buy foreign goods; deprived of silver, bereft of goods, the merchants became 'non-trading'.

This ill-advised experiment had to be abandoned. The issue of copper coins, which was a non-interest-bearing state debt, suggested that they might in fact be exchanged for real money. An ukase of 1663 reintroduced silver coins, and forbade the hoarding or issuing of copper coins. Copper coins were either to be melted down and turned into useful goods, or be returned to the Treasury which according to Kotoshikhin, paid ten silver *dengi* for one copper rouble and according to an ukase of 22 June 1663, two silver *dengi*. The Treasury behaved like a bankrupt paying its creditors one to five kopeks in the rouble. Before and after the July riots, government departments had amassed from their export monopoly nearly $1\frac{1}{2}$ million roubles worth of copper coins (19 million in nineteenth-century values). Undoubtedly this was only a part of the total quantity that had been issued by the Mint; it was rumoured that over a five-year period 20 million roubles in copper coins had been issued (280 million in nineteenth-century values).[1]

Even more serious were three modifications the government introduced into its financial structure. These were: 1. substitution of the basis of assessing direct taxes by a new system of land registration; 2. the allotment of direct taxes by classes; and 3. the inclusion of rural associations within the financial system. The household (*dvor*) was substituted for the *sokha* as the basis for apportioning direct taxes. The substitution from one basis to the other was effected through an intermediate stage known as 'the inhabited quarter of land'. A. S. Lappo-Danilevsky was the first to notice and investigate this intermediate stage in his analysis of direct taxation in seventeenth-century Muscovy. The census registers help to explain the origin of this unit of assessment. The structure of the rural *sokha* varied constantly, and was never a source of payment of any consequence. With changes in agricultural techniques land was left to lie fallow in rotation. No taxes were paid on fallow land, only on land brought into cultivation. The migration of people from central regions to outlying areas, and the decline in cultivated land during the second half of the seventeenth century destroyed the value of tax assessments based on the *sokha*. Abandoned land, 'plots that were left barren', constantly increased at the expense of 'living land', taxable arable land. There was no tax benefit to be derived in this situation, and indeed, the reverse obtained. Agricultural labour became an extremely scarce commodity during the Time of Troubles. One contemporary observer stated that ploughing had come to a standstill almost everywhere, and that the peasants were living somehow on old stocks of grain. As peaceful conditions were restored peasants who had remained where they were, and those who returned observed empty houses, and homesteads surrounded by overgrown arable land.

As conditions improved after the upheavals of the Time of

[1] However, the government's continuing preoccupation is evident from article 73 of the New Commercial Code of 1667 which obliged foreign merchants to pay customs duties in gold *efimki*. See *A History of Russian Economic Thought*, ed. and trans. John M. Letiche (University of California Press, 1964) pp. 222–5.

Troubles, the peasants started to plough their small, previously taxable, plots; and with their surplus labour turned to what was called 'strange ploughing', by which was meant that they ploughed fields abandoned by former neighbours who had been killed, taken prisoner of war, or simply disappeared, and were therefore incapable of producing revenue. The cadastral surveys show that in the sixteenth century in one area the peasants had 4,350 desyatin of land under the plough, the same area in 1616 had only 130 desyatin of taxable land under the plough but 650 desyatin of untaxed land under the plough. An estate in Ryazan in 1595 consisted of 1,275 desyatin under peasant cultivation; in 1616 all that remained were 9 peasant homesteads surrounded by 3 desyatin of taxed land, although the peasants had ploughed 45 desyatin on land belonging to 'abandoned homesteads where their neighbours had disappeared'. Elsewhere, six or seven peasant homesteads working one taxable quarter of land (i.e. 1½ desyatins in 3 fields) and also worked 40–60 desyatin of presently untaxed land belonging to owners who had vanished. Agricultural exploitation of this type together with a decrease in taxed arable land was of no use to the Treasury which wanted to curtail these activities.

Having undertaken a general land census in the 1620s, the government contemporaneously issued ukases attempting to establish as many homesteads as possible to a district who were to pay taxes on their own arable land. But the government hesitated, wavered and continued to correct its own estimates. Initially, it decided that the metropolitan ranks were to pay a favourable tax rate related to an arable quarter of land which supported 12 peasant and 8 cotter homesteads, or 16 peasant homesteads, on the reckoning that one peasant homestead was worth 2 other homesteads. The assessment was subsequently quintupled so that 3 peasant households were assigned to a quarter of land; it was then decreased to five peasant homesteads to a quarter. The assessment on a quarter was calculated on the number of homesteads on it. For instance, if there were 8 peasant homesteads, and one peasant ploughed one-eighth of the quarter, he contributed the equivalent of a quarter of its yield.

As more arable land was brought into the tax structure so its relationship to a *sokha* became less important, and the quarter became a unit of assessment in its own right. Every homestead in a group of eight living on a taxable quarter of land paid one-eighth of its output in taxes, even though a peasant might be capable of ploughing 4-5 taxable quarters.

The tax assessment on the *sokha* was raised as more land was brought within the tax structure and was levied on the group of homesteads contained within the quarter of land. The taxes were apportioned unequally between the homesteads. If, according to the registers one homestead worked a quarter of the land where the total tax due was 2 roubles, it paid 25 kopeks in tax, even though this one homestead might have broken in more land.

There was a difference between the calculated, and the actual payment. A homestead which according to the registers worked three-sixteenths of a desyatin[1] in three fields, but actually ploughed four taxable desyatins, paid at a different rate to the homestead which worked three-sixteenths of a desyatin but ploughed eight desyatins. The proportional tax assessment on arable land devolved upon either the landowner or the peasant commune, and was no longer the responsibility of the census officials or assessors.

From financial necessity, consideration was also given to notions of determining land tax on the basis not only of arable land but also on the labour force and on local agricultural conditions. This was an attempt to tax worked land and the labourer himself with the object of making him work more land, and led to the number of homesteads on each taxable quarter of land being made uniform throughout the districts. Taxation on this double basis of assessment confused both taxpayers and assessors, and increased the technical inconvenience of the cadastral surveys. The difficulty of measuring squares of ploughed land and fitting them into a *sokha*, without including barren and overgrown arable land, as well as the complicated calculation of parts of a *sokha* based on the old Russian method of calculating fractions, was extremely confusing.[2] And when it is remembered that land

[1] One desyatin equals 2·7 acres.
[2] The assessors' knowledge of arithmetic was imperfect, and fractions were a constant problem. Their mathematical learning did not go beyond simple

was graded into good, average and poor, and that it was difficult to verify the statements of the local inhabitants, and the mistakes of clerks, and that endless tricks were used to avoid tax or obtain a reduction, it is self-evident that the possibilities of abuse, misunderstanding and chicanery were manifold.

Taxation based on the homestead was certainly simple, and could have been made uniform. During the Sobor of 1642 the urban nobility urged the government to allow them to collect money for the upkeep of the army according to the number of peasant homesteads, and not according to the census registers. The smaller landowners in particular realised that with the enserfment of the peasants it was they, together with their implements, who should be exploited, and not the land. A general census was therefore taken in 1646, and resulted in attaching peasants to their landowners in perpetuity; the basis for direct taxation became the homestead and not the cadastral surveys. Another census of homesteads was taken in 1678–9. As a result a strange type of tax schedule came into existence, known as the *Perepisnaya Kniga*. It differed from the older type of registers in that, whereas they were concerned with land, timber and hay rights, and trades, in other words with industrial resources on which taxes were assessed, the new tax schedules were concerned with the labour force, and taxes were assessed on homesteads and their inhabitants. Although the tax schedules based the incidence of tax on homestead units the method of estimating and allocating of direct taxes did not change. The government set an average homestead tax rate for every district, and calculated the total amount due based on the number of homesteads. The taxpayers themselves allocated the tax due among individual homesteads inhabited by

---

fractions, and in fact the only ones they seemed to know were 1/2, 1/4, 1/8, 1/16, 1/32, and 1/3, 1/6, 1/12, and 1/24. Nor did they know how to add or subtract fractions with different divisors. This led them to some remarkable arithmetic circumlocutions. If, say, they wanted to express 80 *chetverts* in terms of a *sokha*, they did not enter it as one-tenth of a *sokha*, but instead recorded it as 'one-half of one-half of one-quarter, and one-half of one-half of one-half of one-quarter of a *sokha*, and 5 *chetverts* more'! See Jerome Blum, *Lord and Peasant in Russia* (Princeton U.P., 1961) pp. 231–3.

taxpayers, in exactly the same way that formerly they had apportioned taxes due from homesteads comprising a *sokha* 'according to the means and taxpaying capacity' of the inhabitants of each homestead.

The change in the basis of assessment necessitated the consolidation of all other existing direct taxes into one general tax, since the new tax unit was too small to make a proper assessment possible. Indirect taxes had already been consolidated in 1653, so a precedent did exist. However, there was a difference in that indirect taxes affected the individual as a consumer, whereas direct taxes were forced to take his economic situation into account.

Serfdom had divided the taxpaying population into two sections: the free urban and rural inhabitants whose only obligations were to the state; and the serfs whose obligations were divided between the Treasury and the landowner's estate office. As a result consolidated direct taxes had to be allocated between both groups of taxpayers in proportion to their separate capacities. However, a different solution suggested itself as a result of the extreme difficulties in which the Treasury found itself. The Streltsy tax became an established feature of the tax structure during the seventeenth century, and of all the direct taxes was the one constantly to be raised so that it increased nine times between 1630 and 1663. The steep increases in the rate led to the development of arrears in payment. Other direct taxes were consolidated with the Streltsy tax following the homestead census of 1678. An ukase of 5 September 1679, assessed these taxes based on the homestead unit at varying rates known as the '*roznye stati*'. Payment arrears increased. The government listed them, and in 1687 summoned two elected representatives from each town in order to ask them whether or not they could pay the Streltsy tax at its existing level and if not, why not. The answer to this naïve and stupid question was in the negative, the reason given being that there were serious difficulties over other taxes and obligations. The government then set up a committee of guild representatives who were told to lower the tax rate; the tax was reduced by 31 per cent. The government of Muscovy was unaware of its own incompetence, and unashamed of its ignorance of the state of affairs; indeed it even flaunted its own shortcomings as being natural and proper which would be rectified by the administration in the same way that they would solve the country's financial problems. After all, they said, it was their duty to so do!

The ukase of 1679 combined the postal service tax and the ransom tax into one tax. The Streltsy tax and this single tax were apportioned between the two categories of taxpayers mentioned above. A single Streltsy tax was substituted for the other direct taxes, and imposed upon the urban taxpayers of every town, and upon the 'black' peasants from the northern and north-eastern areas. The rating structure contained 10 variables, and was from 2 roubles to 80 kopeks depending on the capacity of the districts to pay. Seignorial peasants who had to fulfil their responsibilities towards their masters paid a combined post and ransom tax; peasants on church lands paid 10 kopeks on each homestead, while those belonging to the Court and to lay landowners paid 5 kopeks. This was eight or sixteen times less than the lowest rate of Streltsy tax. It is obvious that the Treasury conceded a high proportion of possible revenue to the benefit of landowners. Thus, financial policy was also determined by the general system of class distinction which prevailed in seventeenth-century Muscovy.

The government had displayed great ingenuity in its attempts, albeit unsuccessful, to raise more revenue; it was, however, extremely cautious with what it had. There was a tendency to try to channel revenue into the central Treasury, and to curtail local expenditure. Officials such as local urban officials, secret police officers, posting masters, grain inspectors, and even elders who depended on 'feedings' were considered redundant and their positions abolished. Their functions were entrusted to the local governors. It was argued that since the taxpayers were no longer responsible for 'feeding' they would be in a better position to pay their taxes direct to the Treasury. In order to reduce the cost of collection, the governors and their officials were relieved of all responsibilities for collecting either the new Streltsy tax or customs and excise duties. Instead, responsibility devolved upon the taxpayers' elected representatives, the elders, and 'trusted men' together with assessors, implying a reversion to sixteenth-century local administrative practices. It would be wrong to assume that this meant that local government had been restored. All that happened was that the burden of collection was shifted from government officials to local and unpaid taxpayers' representatives.

The change-over to a system of taxation based on the homestead is doubly important for any review of seventeenth-century Muscovite social structure. It widened the tax base, or to be more precise, it complicated the composition of the taxpaying population, and it provides historians with sufficient information to be able to assess the way in which the labour force was distributed. One result of this tax system was that it enabled the Treasury to create a new and large class of taxpayers.

It was shown in Chapter Nine that although courtyard people were legally bondsmen they enjoyed the same economic situation and contractual relationships with their masters as peasants; they lived in special cots, were granted the use of allotments, and rendered peasant obligations to their masters' advantage. With taxation assessed on homesteads instead of on land, the courtyard people were treated in the same way as peasants and *bobili*. Some of the financial documents investigated by Miliukov[1] indicate that taxation based on homesteads was introduced following the homestead census of 1678. This census was the first step towards the legal integration of bondsmen and seignorial peasants into one class of serfs, which was completed under Peter the Great.

The census registers of 1678 provide total figures of taxed homesteads for the whole country, and these figures were used by Peter the Great's officials in their tax estimates. These figures also help to elucidate the social structure during the last twenty-five years of the seventeenth century on the eve of the Petrine reforms. Although the documents are inconsistent, the most reliable are those with the highest figures; some documents contain

[1] Paul Miliukov, *Gosvdarstvennoe khozyaistvo rossii v pervoi chetverti XVIII stoletiia i reforma Petra Velikogo*, 2nd ed. (St Petersburg, 1905). See Miliukov, Seignobos and Eisenmann, *Histoire de Russie* (Paris, 1932–3) vol. I, where Miliukov's findings are summarised.

figures compiled from incomplete data, and while there were reasons for minimising the number of taxed homesteads there were none for increasing them. On this basis, and according to the census registers of 1678 there were altogether 888,000 taxed urban and rural homesteads. Kotoshikhin, as well as 1686 and 1687 ukases, furnished figures of homesteads tenanted by free urban and rural peasants, Church, Court, and seignorial peasants belonging to boyars, and the upper-class administrative officials. If these are deducted from the total given in the 1678 census registers it is possible to obtain the number of peasant homesteads belonging to the metropolitan and provincial urban men of service, who constituted the nobility in the true sense of the word. The distribution of taxpayers according to categories of land-owners, in round figures, is as follows:

Homesteads belonging to free urban and rural peasants	–	92,000 – 19·4%
Homesteads belonging to the Church, Bishops and Monasteries	–	118,000 – 13·3%
Homesteads belonging to the Court	–	83,000 – 9·3%
Homesteads belonging to Boyars	–	88,000 – 10 %
Homesteads belonging to the nobility	–	507,000 – 57 %
		888,000 – 100 %

This provides some evidence of a curious nature. Only about one-fifth of all rural and urban taxpayers were free independent men. Over half the taxpayers had been handed over to the men of service in exchange for an obligation devolving on the whole class to defend their country from external enemies. Less than one-tenth belonged to the Sovereign's Court, and more than one-tenth belonged to the Church. One-sixth or nearly 20,000 Church peasants, worked for the monasteries, and therefore for prelates who had renounced the world in order to undertake its spiritual direction. Nearly five-sixths of all Church peasants, excluding those belonging to cathedrals and parish churches, worked for monks who had renounced the world in order to pray for its sins. Finally, nearly nine-tenths of the total taxpaying population were in servitude to the Church, the court, or the military men of service. It would be unreasonable to expect any effective political, economic, civil or moral evolution from a country organised in this way.

However much the government imposed on the taxpayers, it was generally incapable of estimating precisely its expected expenditure and balancing it with its income. It would suddenly realise that its preliminary calculations were faulty, and that extraordinary taxes would have to be levied. During the early years of the reign of Tsar Michael, when times were particularly difficult, the government, together with the Zemsky Sobor, was forced to extract compulsory loans from such capitalists as the Stroganovs, or the Troïtsa-Sergeev Monastery. Occasions such as these were, however, rare. Usually the government resorted to voluntary surtaxes and loans on which it paid a rate of interest; and both had a class significance. The government issued a sub-scription list through the Zemsky Sobor inviting the privileged classes, such as the landowners, both spiritual and temporal, as well as the men of service, to pay a voluntary surtax. The money raised in this way was used to pay for extraordinary war expenditure.

At the beginning of the war with Poland in 1632, at the behest of Philaret and Tsar Michael, an assembly of clergy and men of service declared that they were prepared to contribute money, while other ranks promised to provide the government with lists of what their members could afford to pay. A similar procedure occurred in 1634. Voluntary surtaxes were extracted from the free peasants not in the form of a voluntary subscription, but on a scale based on 1 rouble to 25 kopeks a homestead.

Interest-bearing loans were an innovation emanating from the same Sobor that elected the new dynasty and were mandatorily taken up by the commercial classes. In 1614, the year after Tsar Michael's election, the Sobor ordered money to be collected for the army by 'a levy from assessed profits; from whomsoever can give of his substance and his living one hundred roubles there shall be taken one-fifth; and whomsoever can give more or less will give in accordance with the same formula'. This statement contains at least three incompatible bases for taxation. '*Substance and living*' by which was meant stock and working capital, '*assessed profits*' which meant net income as assessed by a taxation committee, and the *possibility* that a conscientious declaration by a taxpayer might reveal his capacity to pay more or less.

The Sobor's intentions were embodied in a proclamation drafted by Muscovite officials in their customary manner which allowed for at least three different interpretations. The Sobor's intentions were comparatively straightforward. Why, however, did it call for 'fifth' money rather than 'fourth' or 'sixth' money? The reason for this was that in the money market the highest legal rate of interest on a loan, and the most usual, was 20 per cent. A borrower could only afford to pay this high interest rate if his profits were greatly in excess of 20 per cent, and meant that the 20 per cent interest rate represented a minimum return in capital which doubled itself in five years. The Sobor also demanded that there should be a moratorium on the first year's interest, so that in fact the investment doubled itself in six and not five years. The essence of this profits tax was not that it creamed off 20 per cent of property values or income deriving from such property, but that it only represented the minimum net annual income derived from commercial transactions or investments in property such as shops and workshops.

Unfortunately the proclamation was so badly drafted that only misunderstandings and even breaches of the peace occurred. In some areas it was believed that this 'fifth money' was a tax on property, and the assessors began to register every property, which was vociferously opposed by the taxpayers. Elsewhere the tax was assessed on the basis of ordinary taxes, such as the Streltsy tax. The tax was best understood where it was regarded as a turnover tax, where the assessors, calculating from the customs returns 'how many roubles worth of what goods had been brought hither and dispatched' took 2 per cent of their value. Similar misunderstandings and disagreements occurred when interest-bearing loans were introduced again due solely to lack of definition of the phrase 'substance and living'. In fact, as Reitenfels who was in Moscow in 1670 clearly saw, this was a tax on income.

These taxes were imposed upon everybody connected with trade and manufacturing, irrespective of whether they were officially taxpayers or not, excluding only the clergy and the non-taxpaying men of service, but including the Streltsy, artillerymen, peasants, *bobili*, and even 'trading bondsmen'.

Fifth money was levied in 1614 and 1615, and twice during Tsar Michael's second Polish war in 1633 and 1634. Having doubled the Streltsy tax in 1637-8 when the country was defending itself from the Crimeans, the government asked the Zemsky Sobor to authorise a collection from Court and seignorial peasants, and an extra 20 roubles (nineteenth-century values) on each homestead belonging to the commercial classes, and 10 roubles (nineteenth-century values) from taxpaying peasants. This extraordinary tax was repealed in 1639. Arrears in payment increased, a certain sign that the taxpayers had reached the limit of their resources. They complained that 'life was exceedingly difficult for them'. Not only were extra taxes imposed; sales of highly profitable commodities, such as flax at Pskov, were mandatorily sold to the Treasury at prices regulated by decree. This explains the bitterness of a Pskovian chronicler who complained 'that the price is fixed, there is no profit in the purchases, and there is much grief and unspoken enmity, and nowhere does anybody dare to buy or sell'.

Extraordinary and heavy taxes were a common feature under Tsars Alexis and Fedor during the prolonged and ruinous wars with Poland, Sweden, Turkey and the Crimea, which entailed heavy sacrifices in men and money. During twenty-six years, between 1654 and 1680, loans at interest rates of 5 per cent and 6·66 per cent were raised once, of 10 per cent five times, and of 20 per cent twice, and this ignores the annual fixed taxes assessed on homesteads. Thus extraordinary taxes and forced loans became a common feature of the whole system of taxation.

How financially successful was the government during the seventeenth century with its weighty, variable and badly regulated tax impositions? Referring to the 1660s, Kotoshikhin wrote that total Treasury annual receipts amounted to 1,311,000 roubles, excluding Siberian fur revenues, for which he lacked the figures, but which he estimated at somewhat more than 600,000 roubles twenty years later. Neuville, the French Agent who arrived in Moscow in 1689, heard that the Treasury's annual revenue did not exceed 7–8 million French livres. In seventeenth-century Muscovy 1 livre was worth one-sixteenth of a rouble, so that the estimates of both Kotoshikhin and Neuville are similar; however, it is very difficult to estimate the income derived from compulsory Treasury commodity sales.

Miliukov discovered a statement of income and expenditure for 1680 which he analysed in his work on the economy of Russia and the Petrine reforms. Total revenue was estimated at $1\frac{1}{2}$ million roubles (20 million in nineteenth-century values). 49 per cent of this came from customs and excise; direct taxes accounted for 44 per cent, of which 16 per cent represented extraordinary taxes. Military expenditure absorbed nearly half of total revenue; and the court absorbed 15 per cent. Social welfare and amenities such as public buildings, and the internal communications system accounted for less than 5 per cent. However, this statement only provides a partial picture of the economy because not all income was paid into the Treasury centrally; some revenue was collected and spent locally. Although the 1680 statement shows a large surplus of income over expenditure, it is more significant in that it shows the difference between estimated and actual revenue. Arrears in tax payments that had accumulated by 1676 exceeded one million roubles, and in 1687 they had to be written off. The country had reached the limit of its taxpaying capacity.

Chapter Twelve

★

WHEN THE government of Muscovy re-established order after the Time of Troubles it ignored the radical break that had been effected with the past, and tried to preserve traditionally accepted principles by introducing partial technical changes which it believed would produce the desired amendments and improvements. In fact, the government's attempts to reform its administrative system, the segregation of classes, and changes introduced in the national economy were not products of a preconceived plan but were timid, inconsistent reactions to given situations, all stemming directly or indirectly from its financial difficulties. All its efforts were concentrated on solving its problems, but all were uniformly unsuccessful. Centralised government was neither cheaper nor more effective than decentralised government since neither was able to lessen the tax burden. The stratification of society merely emphasised the difference in class interests and attitudes, while financial innovations were debilitating financially, and led to bankruptcies, and a chronic accumulation of tax arrears. The people became increasingly aware of their difficulties. The court, the Tsar's advisers, and the country's foreign policy created national discontent.

Under the first three rulers of the new dynasty the government of Muscovy apparently consisted of men who achieved power fortuitously, and then did not know what to do with it. With three or four exceptions, they were excessively ambitious; but they were quite without talent, displayed no skill in governing, and what was worse, lacked a social conscience. It was pure chance that brought these men to power. Bad luck plagued the new dynasty: most of the rulers were, on their accession, still minors. Three of the first five Tsars, Michael, Alexis and Ivan, were only sixteen. Another two were even younger, Fedor was fourteen, and Peter was ten. There was another dynastic peculiarity: the women were strong, lively, even energetic and brave, like Sophia; the men were like the founder of the line, sickly, short-lived and degenerate, like Fedor and Ivan. Even Tsar Alexis who seemed lively and healthy had a weak constitution, and he only lived for forty-six years. It is impossible to know what might have happened had Alexis' younger brother, Dimitri, who resembled his great-grandfather Ivan the Terrible in his rages, survived. If Kotoshikhin can be relied on, some friends of the boy's father poisoned the child with such ingenuity that it was impossible to guess that he had not died a natural death. Peter the Great was exceptional in every way.

Tsar Michael was surrounded by administrators well before he acquired either the ability or the desire to impose his own personality, and it was they who gave the tone, and set the trend to the whole of his reign. This unfortunate situation revealed itself particularly clearly in the conduct of foreign policy, which was directly responsible for the government's financial problems. The territorial losses incurred during the Time of Troubles should have shown the new dynasty that foreign policy was the one area which could have justified its election.

Tsar Michael's diplomacy, particularly after Muscovy's badly planned and incompetently executed Smolensk campaign, was distinguished by the caution usually shown by a defeated power. The buffeting sustained by Muscovy under Tsar Michael was almost forgotten during the reign of Tsar Alexis. Although the people had been involved against their will in the struggle over Little Russia, Muscovites were encouraged by the brilliant campaign of 1645–55 when Smolensk, Little Russia and Lithuania were taken. Imagination unfortunately outran reason, and the Muscovites forgot that victories had been won with the assistance of the Swedes who had attacked Poland from the West, thereby diverting the best Polish troops from the Russian front. Muscovite policy assumed grandiose proportions. Neither men nor money

were spared in the attempt to defeat Poland, to seat the Tsar of
Muscovy on the throne of Poland, to rid Poland of Swedes, to
clear the Crimeans and Turks from Little Russia, and to seize
both banks of the lower Dnieper and the whole of Galicia, which
had been the destination of Sheremetiev's army in 1660. These
complicated schemes so bewildered and weakened the country,
that, after twenty-one years of exhaustive struggles on three
fronts, and a series of unprecedented defeats, Muscovy was
forced to abandon Lithuania, White Russia, the Ukraine west of
the Dnieper, and had to content herself with the provinces of
Smolensk and Seversk, and Little Russia to the east of the Dnieper,
and Kiev to the west. By the Treaty of Bakhshisarai concluded in
1681 with the Crimean Tatars, Muscovy was unable to obtain
relief from the humiliating annual tribute payable to the Khan,
recognition of her suzerainty over Zaporozhie, or even a satisfactory frontier along the Steppe.

Not only were people aware of the heavy sacrifices they had
made, and the misfortunes they had suffered, but they had become
increasingly dissatisfied. This dissatisfaction was expressed by
people accustomed to unrest by the Time of Troubles, and although the upper and lower classes reacted in different ways it
was a feeling shared by all. During the seventeenth century the
masses agitated ceaselessly, and the period was characterised by
its popular risings. Ignoring uprisings that occurred during Tsar
Michael's reign, it is sufficient to enumerate those relating to Tsar
Alexis' reign to judge the extent of discontent. In 1648 there were
disturbances in Moscow, Ustyug, Kozlov, Solvychegodsk,
Tomsk and elsewhere; in 1649 a rising of mortgagees was averted
in Moscow; in 1650 there were riots in Pskov and Novgorod;
in 1662 there were the copper riots in Moscow; in 1670–1 Stenka
Razin's rebellion broke out along the south-eastern regions of the
Volga. Although it originated among the Don Cossacks, the
rebellion spread to the masses who rose against the upper classes.
There was a revolt in 1668–76 of the Solovetsky Monastery
against the revision of Church writings. This turbulence was
symptomatic of the people's attitude towards authority which
was elaborately enveloped in official ceremonials and ecclesiastical

teachings. The masses showed neither respect nor common courtesy towards either the government or the Sovereign.

Upper class discontent was expressed differently. Whereas the lower classes reacted physically, the upper classes were provoked into using their intellectual powers and criticising the internal structure of the country. Detestation of the upper classes provided the lower classes with their impetus to riot; but underlying all upper class criticism was an awareness of the nation's backwardness and impotence. Almost for the first time Russian thinkers adopted a critical approach to the realities of a situation, and tried to popularise their ideas. This had already been attempted during the Sobor of 1642, as well as during discussions in 1662 between the government commission and the Moscow merchants on the reasons for increases in the cost of living.

Although the merchants maintained political discipline and a respectful approach, avoiding vociferous protestations, none the less they managed forcefully to express their views on administrative shortcomings, on the frequent infringement of the laws by the privileged classes, and on the government's disregard for public opinion, as when, for instance, the Sovereign issued an ukase ordering it to seek the merchants' views on a particular problem; instead of dealing with the matter properly, the government concentrated on trivia. However, it must be realised that the merchants were only expressing a guarded and collective opinion of specific class attitudes. Individual commentators were extremely bold in expressing their opinions of what was wrong with the country. Some examples are necessary to show how expression was given to public criticism at this time.

The first endeavours were made early in the seventeenth century during the Time of Troubles, which undoubtedly provoked them. Prince J. A. Khvorostinin was an eminent young man at the court of the First Pretender. He became very friendly with the Poles, taught himself to read Latin, was influenced by Catholic ideas, and worshipped Catholic images as well as Russian ikons. As a result Tsar Vasili Shuisky sent him to the Monastery of St Joseph to be reindoctrinated in the Orthodox religion. He left the Monastery a bitter man, a free-thinker, renouncing all prayers and belief in the resurrection of the dead, 'and did waver in the faith, blasphemed against the truth of Orthodoxy and spoke impiously of the Holy Saints of God'. However, he maintained an interest in Church-Slavonic literature and was an authority in Church history; Prince Khvorostinin also maintained a lively interest in discussions on books, and in general was distinguished by his opinionated erudition: 'he allowed as how nobody was as wise as he'. He was also a gifted writer, and during Tsar Michael's reign wrote a reasonable account of his own times, on which he tended to philosophise rather than discuss men and events. This medley of opinions and attitudes, which never led to the formulation of a unified, consistent philosophy, was in direct opposition to Orthodox-Byzantine traditions and ideas, and set Prince Khvorostinin at variance with everything native to his own country. He was openly contemptuous of Orthodox ceremonial, 'observed neither fasts nor Christian customs', forbade his servants to attend Church; in 1622 he drank his way 'through Holy Week', and was intoxicated before he broke his fast on Easter Day. He did not go to the palace to congratulate the Tsar,[1] nor did he attend either Matins or Mass. Having isolated himself in this way from his own society, he wanted to migrate, or even flee, to Lithuania or Rome; he sold his residence in Moscow, and his estates. The Tsar's ukase, which enumerates all Prince Khvorostinin's crimes, is especially bitter about his sins of commission against his own compatriots. A search of the Prince's house revealed manuscripts of prose and 'verses' in Polish syllabic verse. These documents illustrate his boredom and despondency at finding himself in an alien land, his contempt for the Muscovite order, and his criticisms of many Muscovite personalities whom he accused of the irrational worship of ikons. He complained that 'there are no men in Moscow, all are stupid and one cannot live among them; they sow the land with rye, and live in falsehood'; he believed that he had nothing in common with these people. Officially it was held that he had disgraced and dishonoured the people of Muscovy, and his parents, held them up to ridicule, and had even refused to address the Sovereign correctly, calling him

[1] As was customary on Easter Day.

'the Russian Despot' instead of Tsar or Autocrat. Prince Khvorostinin was banished again, this time to St Cyril's Monastery, where
he repented; subsequently he returned to Moscow, was reinstated
in the nobility, and readmitted to court. He died in 1625.

Prince Khvorostinin was an early, curious phenomenon in
Russian intellectual life, which later was to become far more
common. He was not, however, a prototype heretic of the
sixteenth century influenced by new Protestant ideas which
questioned dogma, ritual and religious interpretations, simply as
an echo of the Reformation in Western Europe. Khvorostinin
was an original Russian free-thinker with a Catholic flavouring,
who was deeply antipathetic to the formality of Byzantine ritual
and every aspect of Russian life which it influenced.[1] As such, he
was a distant precursor of Chaadaev.[2]

An unexpected critic of domestic policies was the arbiter of
church morality, the Patriarch of all Russia, Patriarch Nikon.
It must be remembered that this supreme ecclesiastical dignitary
had been a peasant, and that as Patriarch he enjoyed a profound
influence over Tsar Alexis, who called him 'his special friend', and
that when they quarrelled, Nikon in 1658 voluntarily renounced
his position as Patriarch hoping that the Tsar would humbly beg
him to return. This did not occur. In a mood of pique and
wounded pride Nikon sent Tsar Alexis a letter criticising the
state of affairs. Not unnaturally the Patriarch was not objective
in his views; however, the arguments he used to illustrate the
gloomy situation were all based on the government's financial

---

[1] Prince Khvorostinin became a convert to Socinianism and wrote elegant
syllabic verse well before anyone else in Muscovy. See James H. Billington,
The Icon and the Axe (Weidenfeld & Nicolson, 1966) p. 124; and Pierre Pascal,
Avvakum et les Débuts du Raskol (1938) pp. 18–20.

[2] Peter Chaadaev (1794–1856) formulated his religious and philosophic
opinions under the influence of Jung-Stilling, Eckerthausen, and French
Catholics like Chateaubriand and Maistre. Chaadaev straddled both the
Westerner and the Slavophile schools of thoughts. See Thornton Anderson,
Russian Political Thought (Cornell U.P., 1967) pp. 196–8; Janko Lavrin,
'Chaadayev and the West', *Russian Review* (Jul 1963), pp. 274–88; Raymond T.
McNally, 'The Significance of Chaadayev's Weltanschauung', *Russian Review*
(Oct 1964) pp. 352–61.

difficulties and the depressed state of the economy. Above all Nikon was incensed by the establishment in 1649 of a Monastery Department which had jurisdiction over the clergy in non-spiritual affairs, and which also managed the vast estates of the Church. This particular department was run by boyars and clerks, and not one representative of the clergy was attached to it.

In 1661 Nikon wrote an aggressively personal letter to Tsar Alexis. Alluding to the hated Department he wrote, playing on words:

> The judges of this world do judge and coerce; wherefore you have gathered against yourself on the Day of Judgement a great Council to arraign you for your injustices. You say that all men must fast, but all men do fast because they lack bread, men are fasting to death because they have nothing to eat. Nobody is shown mercy: beggars, blindmen, widows, monks and nuns are all heavily imposed upon. There is weeping throughout the land, and affliction, and no man rejoices.

Nikon was equally gloomy in a letter written to the Eastern Patriarchs in 1665 describing the financial situation, which was intercepted by some agents of Muscovy. Complaining that the Tsar had sequestered Church property, he wrote: 'Men are taken for service, bread and money are mercilessly extracted. All Christians are burdened by the Tsar with two-fold, three-fold tributes, and all is in vain.'

Another critical work was undertaken in the reign of Tsar Alexis in somewhat unusual circumstances. Gregory Kotoshikhin had been an under-secretary in the Ministry of Foreign Affairs with diplomatic responsibilities of no great importance. He was wrongly accused of some inefficiency or other, and in 1660 was birched for having made a mistake in transcribing the Tsar's titles. During the second Polish war he was attached to the army commanded by Prince Yuri Dolguruky when he refused to obey an order from the commander-in-chief which he considered illegal, and in 1664 Kotoshikhin fled first to Poland, then to Germany, and finally settled in Stockholm. Kotoshikhin was so impressed by the contrasts between foreign institutions and those of Muscovy, that he decided to write a treatise on Muscovy. The Swedish Chancellor, Magnus de la Gardie taken by Selitsky's (as Kotoshikhin called himself abroad) intelligence and experience, encouraged him to continue his work, which was so well done that it has become one of the most important seventeenth-century Russian historical documents.[1] However, Kotoshikhin died in stupid circumstances. He lived in Stockholm for about one-and-a-half years, where he was converted to Protestantism; he became too intimate with his landlord's wife, and was executed for having killed the suspicious husband during a quarrel. Kotoshikhin's Swedish translator said that he was incomparably intelligent. The treatise was discovered in the nineteenth century in Upsala by a Russian professor, and published in 1840.[2] The treatise is divided into thirteen chapters and describes life at Court, the structure of the central government, the army, the urban trading and rural populations, and finally, the domestic life of the upper classes.[3] Kotoshikhin made few personal comments, and described his own country in clear, simple official language. The treatise is critical of Muscovy, and although Kotoshikhin paints a gloomy picture, it is, as far as can be ascertained, an objective description of Russian life. What personal comments there are, are unfavourable, and expose the most important defects in Russian life and morality. For instance, he criticises the people for 'not fearing God', for their arrogance, their fraudulence, and above all, for their ignorance. The Russian people, he wrote, 'are by nature arrogant and lazy, since they are taught nothing except conceit, shamelessness, hate and injustice; they do not send their children abroad to learn of other cultures lest foreign faiths, customs, and their goodly freedom turn them away from their own religion, and make them stay with foreign folk, thereby taking away any desire to return home'. Kotoshikhin caricatured

[1] *O. Rosii v tsarstvovanie Aleksiia Mikhailovicha* [Russia in the Reign of Alexis Mikhailovich] (St Petersburg, 1840).

[2] Professor Soloviev found the Swedish text in Stockholm in 1837, and in 1838 he found the Russian text at the University of Upsala.

[3] Excerpts in English can be found in Marthe Blinoff, *Life and Thought in Old Russia* (Pennsylvania State U.P., 1961) pp. 36–45.

a meeting of the Boyar Duma at which the boyars, 'arranging their beards', made no reply to the Tsar's questions, and were unable to proffer good advice 'since the Tsar made men Boyars not because they were wise, but because they were well-born, and most of them were ignorant and illiterate'. His description of Russian domestic life was also sombre. Whoever believes that ancient Russia with all its political and social defects managed, even with Church regulations, to evolve morally and legally sound families should read Kotoshikhin's last chapter 'On the way of the life of the Boyars, Lords of the Chamber and Duma, and other Ranks'. This chapter dispassionately describes the arbitrary powers of parents over their children, their match-making and matrimonial arrangements, the cynicism of the marriage contract, the vulgar deceptions practised by parents of unfortunate daughters of whom they wished to dispose, the lawsuits that ensued, the beatings, and the way unloved wives were forced to take the veil, the poisoning of wives by husbands and *vice versa*, and the heartless, official interference of the Church in family quarrels. The murky descriptions of family life even worried the author who rounded off his simple and frightening picture of domestic felicity as follows: 'Discerning reader, do not wonder at this! It is the honest truth that nowhere in the world is such deception practised about brides as in the State of Muscovy; for there they do not follow the usage of allowing the betrothed couple to see and talk to each other before marriage.'

It is interesting to compare the opinions of this Russian *émigré* with those of a recent arrival in Russia who hoped to make it his home. Juri Krizhanich,[1] a Croatian Catholic priest, was a cultured

---

[1] Juri Krizhanich (1617–83), first arrived in Russia with a Polish Diplomatic mission in 1647, and returned again in 1659 disguised as a Ukrainian war refugee. He sought to advance both an old and a new idea. The old idea was the conversion of Russia to Catholicism; the new was the development of Russia as the centre of a new united Slavdom. See Billington, *The Icon and the Axe*, pp. 168–71; Pascal, *Avvakum et les Débuts du Raskol*, pp. 279–81; P. J. Pierling, *La Russie et le Saint-Siège* (Paris, 1907) vol. 4, pp. 2–39; Miliukov, Seignobos and Eisenman, *Histoire de Russie* (Paris, 1932) pp. 233–9; M. B. Petrovich, Jurej Krizenic, A Precursor of Panslavism, *American Slavic and East European Review*, VI (Dec 1947) pp. 75–92.

man of many interests. He was something of a philosopher, a theologian, and a political-economist; he was a great philologist, and, above all, was an ardent Pan-Slav. He believed that his real fatherland was not a particular state, but a united Slavdom, a purely political concept which had nothing to do with historical development. Krizhanich was by birth a subject of the Turkish Sultan; as a poor orphan he had been taken to Italy, and was educated in ecclesiastical seminaries in Zagreb, Vienna, and Bologna, and finally entered the College of St Athanasius in Rome, where the Sacred Congregation for the Propagation of the Faith[1] (*de propoganda fide*) trained special missionaries for work among the schismatics of the Orthodox East. As a Slav, Krizhanich was destined to work in Muscovy. He was attracted by the idea of this distant land, began to collect information about it, and submitted a detailed plan for its conversion to the Congregation. However, he also had other ideas which he kept to himself; the zeal he showed for his mission was the only way a poor Slav student could enlist material support from the Congregation. He regarded Muscovites as neither heretics nor schismatics; he was not being a sophist about this, but genuinely believed that they were Christians who had lost their way through ignorance and spiritual simplicity.

He began early to consider and deeply grieve for the wretched condition of downtrodden and enslaved Slavdom, and credit must be given to Krizhanich for the political sagacity he displayed in perceiving how Slavdom could be unified. People must be able to communicate with one another if they are ever to agree, but this was impossible because Slavs all talked different languages. Consequently, during his stay in Rome, Krizhanich tried not to forget his native Slav language which he studied carefully in order to perfect his speech. He went to great lengths to get rid of foreign intonation and words so that he might be understood by

[1] The Sacred Congregation for the Propagation of the Faith was founded in 1622 to open lines of communication with Eastern Christians. It was a useful vehicle for Catholic activities inside Russia because, unlike the Society of Jesus, it was not identified with Polish expansion. See Billington, *The Icon and the Axe*, p. 169.

all Slavs. As a consequence he planned and wrote grammar books, dictionaries and philological treatises.

Another, and even more daring, idea is to his credit. He believed that the unification of the dispersed Slavs could only be brought about through the creation of a political focal point, which at that time simply did not exist. Nothing had happened to make this a historical necessity, and as yet this idea had not become incorporated into a political philosophy which later on was to be so vehemently attacked by some, and defended by others. Krizhanich found the answer to this particular problem. This Croatian Catholic realised that a political centre was to be found not in Vienna, Prague or Warsaw but in Orthodox Moscow, notwithstanding the Western European belief that Muscovites were really Tatars. Certainly in the seventeenth century this seemed like a ridiculous idea, and even during the nineteenth century it seemed unreasonable, but there were times when it made sense. Envisaging Muscovy as the future centre of Slavdom, Krizhanich referred to this country as his second homeland, although he had never really had a homeland at all, given that Turkey was only his country of birth. Whether the idea of a political centre was the product of patriotic enthusiasm or the careful reflection of a politician is difficult to know. Be that as it may, he did not remain in Rome where the Congregation had sent him after his polemic on the Greek Schism. In 1659 he left of his own accord for Moscow, where he was forced to abandon the Roman apostolic plan, and had to conceal his priesthood, otherwise he would never have been allowed to enter the country. He was accepted as 'a Serbian émigré, Uri Ivanovich' on equal terms with other foreigners who had entered the service of the state. In order to ensure himself a permanent position in Moscow he made different suggestions to the Tsar: to become a Muscovite Pan-Slav publicist, or a librarian at the Kremlin and write an honest history of Muscovy and all Slav peoples as the Tsar's 'history-chronicler'. He was paid $1\frac{1}{2}$ roubles, and later 3 roubles a day (nineteenth-century values) for his favourite work of compiling a Slavonic grammar and dictionary. After all, he had gone to Moscow intending to continue his work of literary and linguistic Slavonic consolidation. He admitted that he had nowhere else to go except Moscow with his idea of a common Slav language, and that since childhood he had devoted himself to correcting 'our distorted, or more precisely, our dead language, in order to edify my own and the nation's mind'. In one of his essays he wrote: 'I am called a wanderer, a tramp; this is not true; I came to the Tsar of my own race, I came to my own people, to my own country, the only country, which can benefit and profit from my work, and where my merchandise, by which I mean my dictionaries, grammars and translations might be of value, and find a market.' For some reason, after one year he was sent to Tobolsk where he lived for fifteen years.[1] He was very productive in Tobolsk where he was given a pension and enjoyed a great deal of leisure; Krizhanich even complained that he had too much spare time, and that he was not given any work to do, even though he was fed as well as a beast for the slaughterhouse. He wrote a great deal in Siberia, where he completed his Slavonic grammar over which he had taken so much trouble, and about which he had 'thought and worked for twenty-two years'. Tsar Fedor ordered Krizhanich to return to Moscow, where having admitted his mission and canonical orders, or 'shorn priest' as was explained in Moscow, he asked to be allowed to return to 'his own land'. He left Muscovy in 1677.[2]

The circumstances of Krizhanich's life are interesting, and help to explain his opinions of Russia which are set out in his most extensive work, 'Political Thoughts' or 'Conversations on Power' which was written in Siberia. This is divided into three sections. Part one is a discussion of the economic resources of the country; part two is a discussion of its military resources; and part three is a polemic on wisdom, in which he discusses morality and politics. This work reads like a political and economic treatise

[1] Krizhanich lived in Tobolsk from 1661 to 1677. It is possible that he was sent to Tobolsk because he had refused to collaborate in the formation of the new State Church.

[2] From Russia Krizhanich went to Poland where he took monastic vows. He died in 1683 outside Vienna while with the army of Jan Sobieski which turned back the last great Turkish assault on European Christendom.

in which the author shows his wide erudition in ancient and contemporary literature as well as some familiarity with Russian writings.[1] But its real importance lies in the numerous comparisons made by Krizhanich between Western European countries and Muscovy; indeed, this is the first comparative study ever undertaken.

The treatise consists of rough sketches written in Latin, and a strange mixture of Slavonic languages,[2] together with amendments, additions and short notes. Krizhanich's main arguments can be summarised as follows. He believed that Russia and Pan-Slavism had a great destiny; and that they were to benefit from a scientific and artistic exchange between peoples from whom they would emerge as the dominant power. This idea resembles the cyclical theory of civilisation developed both by Leibnitz and Peter the Great. Having described the cultural achievements of other nations Krizhanich went on to remark that no one could say whether or not divine providence had guided the Slavs along the road of knowledge. He believed, moreover, that it was time for the Slavs to improve themselves: 'God has now raised in Russia a Slavonic Tsardom, which in its power and glory has never existed among Slavs before; such Tsardoms are generally dispensers of enlightenment.' 'The time has come for us to learn, so that, under the honourable rule of Tsar Alexis we may obliterate the image of ancient savagery, and gain wisdom and achieve a praiseworthy and blessed way of life.' This quotation is an admirable example of the Pan-Slav language about which Krizhanich talked so much. Krizhanich meant to say that the Muscovites should study hard so that their ignorance which was held by other people to be universal would, under the authority of the Tsar, be abolished; and that with education the Muscovites could create a better society in which happiness could be attained. Krizhanich recognised, however, that this ideal situation had not

---

[1] Krizhanich's arguments for an absolute monarchy, for instance, are based largely on classical and Renaissance authorities, and he was the first writer in Russia to quote extensively from Machiavelli. See Billington, *The Icon and the Axe*, pp. 169–71.

[2] The mixture was mostly Croatian and Russian.

been achieved for two basic reasons which affected all Slavs: 'Foreign madness', which was a wild passion for anything foreign, and its consequence, 'foreign subjugation', or the foreign influence exerted over all Slavonic peoples. Krizhanich was particularly venomous whenever he referred to these two points, and he was vividly repellant in the images he used to describe foreign oppressors, especially the Germans. 'Not one nation under the sun', he wrote,

from time immemorial has been so wronged and shamed by foreigners as we Slavs have been by the Germans; we have been stifled by foreigners; we have been fooled, led by the nose; we have been sat upon and driven as if we were cattle, and we are called swine and dogs; they consider themselves to be gods while we are simpletons. And all that has been squeezed in weighty taxes and oppression from the tears, sweat and enforced fasting of the Russian peoples is devoured by the foreigners, the Greek merchants, and German merchants and colonels, and the Crimean robbers. All this had come about from our 'foreign madness', and still we marvel at foreign objects, praising and extolling them, and decrying everything that is our own.

Krizhanich devotes a whole chapter to an enumeration of the 'disgraces and wrongs' imposed by foreigners on the Slav peoples. He believed that Russia was destined to deliver the Slavs from those very same misfortunes from which she herself was suffering. Krizhanich addressed himself to Tsar Alexis as follows: 'Upon you, most honourable Tsar, has fallen the responsibility for all Slav peoples; you alone, O Tsar, have been given to us by God in order to help those who live beyond the Danube, the Czechs and the Poles, so that they might become aware of their oppression by foreigners, and their shame, and cast off the German yoke from their shoulders.' Yet, when he considered the state of affairs inside Russia, and the lives of these Pan-Slav saviours, Krizhanich could not but wonder at the chaos and vice which existed. He was incensed by the conceit of the Russians, their excessive partiality for their own customs, and above all by their ignorance, which he maintained was the main reason for their economic instability. Russia, he maintained, was poor compared to western European countries because its citizens were not as well educated. Western Europeans, he wrote, were shrewd and calculating; they possessed many books on agriculture and other industries; they have harbours, and enjoy a flourishing maritime trade, agriculture and commerce. Nothing of this kind existed in Russia, which was surrounded by deserts, savage tribes or difficult seas; there were few trading towns, and the country had no valuable or useful products. Russians were stupid and sluggish, unskilled in trade, agriculture and manufacturing; they were uninventive, lazy and improvident and had to be forced into doing things for their own benefit. There were no books on agriculture or manufactures, and the merchants knew no arithmetic, and were constantly being cheated by foreigners. Russians knew no history and were disinterested in the past; they were unable to participate in political discussions, for which the foreigners despised them. Krizhanich criticised the ugliness of Russian apparel, and external appearances, their homes and the way they lived. Unkempt hair and beards made Russians seem like comical and ridiculous savages. Foreigners despised their slovenliness: they concealed money in their mouths, never washed any dishes, and peasants offered their guests full bowls from which to drink 'in which they had dipped their fingers'. Foreign newspapers wrote: if a Russian merchant enters a shop, nobody else can go in for a whole hour because of the stench. Russian houses were uncomfortable; the windows are low, there is no ventilation, and people are blinded by the smoke.

Krizhanich also criticised the Russians' many moral failings, their drunkenness, their cowardice, their lack of pride, and absence of personal and national dignity. Although Turks and Tatars might flee during battle they did not allow themselves to be killed in vain, and would defend themselves to the end; Russian 'warriors' ran away to no purpose, and were easily cut down. The Russians' greatest national vice was their lack of moderation in the exercise of power. They were unable to discipline themselves or pursue moderate policies, but were forever going to extremes. In one part of Russia the administration would be undisciplined, and permissive, while elsewhere it was firm, strict and oppressive. Nowhere in the world was there such a slovenly and ramshackle government as in Poland, or such a harsh government as in the glorious State of Russia.

Deeply concerned by these shortcomings, Krizhanich was quite prepared to favour the Turks and Tatars over the Russians; indeed, he advised the Russians to emulate their standards of sobriety, justice, courage and modesty. It is obvious that Krizhanich was aware of the evils in Russian society; and he might well, as a Slav, have been exaggerating and unable to make an objective, simple appraisal. None the less, he combines criticism with observations and constructive suggestions. The suggestions contained in his reform programme are far more important to historians than the random observations made by this Slav newcomer visiting Moscow in the seventeenth century.

Krizhanich made four basic suggestions. First, enlightenment and learning through books, which although inanimate, were wise and just counsellors. Second, administrative regulations imposed from above. Krizhanich believed in Autocracy, and said that in Russia there was 'complete absolutism'; the Tsar had the means to order improvements, a circumstance which did not exist elsewhere. 'You, O Tsar,' wrote Krizhanich to Tsar Alexis, 'hold in your hand the miraculous staff of Moses by which you can work miracles in government; in your hands lies complete Autocracy.' Krizhanich believed that the existence of an Autocracy was a hopeful sign, even though the ideas he wished to have implemented were strange. For instance, he suggested that merchants who knew no arithmetic should legally be compelled to close their shops until they became numerate. Third, political freedom. In an Autocratic State there should be no harsh government, and the people should not be burdened with extortionate dues and levies, or as Krizhanich puts it, the 'people should not be placed under duress'. A necessary condition in this situation would be a 'defined freedom' consisting of political rights and the self-determination of the different classes. For instance, Krizhanich proposed that merchants should be allowed to elect their own representatives and class tribunals; that artisans should combine in trade associations; that the commercial classes should be able, as of right, to discuss their requirements with the government, from whom they should also be able to seek protection from provincial administrations; and, that peasants should be guaranteed their freedom of labour. Krizhanich believed that a certain degree of emancipation would curb the greed of officials, and was the only way in which subjects could be shielded from official abuse, and justice could be maintained in the state. 'Neither interdictions nor penalties will restrain those in office, "the men of the Duma", from schemes of oppression if there is no freedom.' Fourth, Krizhanich proposed an expanded programme of technical education. Therefore, the state must play an active part, establish technical schools in every town; and implement legislation to create schools of needlework and domestic science for women; Krizhanich wanted it to be mandatory for intending bridegrooms to ask their future wives to attest precisely what they had learned. He wanted the government to free the bondsmen so that they might learn a craft demanding special technical knowledge. He suggested that foreign books on commerce and craftsmanship should be translated into Russian and that foreign craftsmen and capitalists should be invited to come to impart their skills to the Russians. All these measures should be directed towards an intensive exploitation of the country's natural resources, as well as towards the creation of new industries, particularly mining.

This then was Juri Krizhanich's programme. It was complicated, internally inconsistent, and in some places, ambiguous. It is difficult to understand how he reconciled some of his suggestions for eradicating the faults in Russian society. For instance, what distinctions did he intend between government regulations, strengthened by an Autocracy, and the self-determination of groups within the social structure; how did he intend to get rid of foreigners while translating their books and using them as instructors; how could he reconcile expelling foreigners and doing without foreign master-craftsmen? However, the immediate reaction must be: how this resembles Peter the Great's programme of reforms. Both programmes share the same faults and contradictions, the same idyllic faith in the creative force of an ukase, the same belief that education and commerce can be propagated by translations from foreign works, or by temporarily closing the shop of a merchant who could not count. It is these incongruities and the resemblance to Peter's reforms which make Krizhanich's opinions so interesting. He is, in his own way, a unique observer of Russian life, quite different from most foreigners who came to Moscow by chance, and recorded their impression. After all, most foreigners considered that life in Russia was the curious oddity of an uncultured people, entertaining in its own way, but nothing more. Krizhanich was both an alien and a native: a foreigner by origin and education, and a native in national sympathy and political aspirations. He went to Moscow not only to observe, but to teach and propagate his Pan-Slav ideas and persuade others to join in the struggle.

This aim is clearly stated in the Latin epilogue to his *Discourses*. 'For the protection of the people! I wish to expel all foreigners, and raise the people of the Dnieper, the Poles, Lithuanians, Serbs, and all those who are Slavs and warlike who wish to battle with me.' When two opposing forces are about to do battle it is necessary to calculate their comparative strengths, and supplement the shortcomings on one side by examining the strength on the other side, and learning from, and adapting oneself to it. Indeed, this was Krizhanich's favourite method of exposition. He was continually making comparisons and projections, contrasting characteristics of the Slavs with similar hostile Western European characteristics, and proposing that in some cases the Slavs would do well to copy them, while in others they should stay as they were. This type of reasoning was bound to produce incongruities: the subject of the analysis was full of contradictions, not the analyst. Although he realised that the Russians had to adopt foreign ideas and learn from them he was always prepared to say when he believed something was better in Russia than elsewhere and refute slanderous allegations made by foreigners. However, he was not prepared to deceive himself or others: he expected the Autocracy to produce a miracle. No other foreigner has described as vividly as Krizhanich in his chapter 'On Duress' in *Discourses* the deleterious influence exerted by harsh Muscovite administrations on Russian morals, welfare and foreign relations.

He was no admirer of power for its own sake and said that if he were able to ask all the rulers in the world why they existed, most of them would be unable to reply. He valued power for its cultural benefits, and had a mystical faith in the Muscovite staff of Moses, even though he must have known of Ivan the Terrible's dreadful staff,[1] and the lame Tsar Michael's crutch! Krizhanich's general comparison was by no means favourable to his own people; he recognised the intellectual and moral superiority of foreigners over Russians, and believed that they were better off. He asked: 'What place do we Russians and Slavs have among other nations, and what historical role have we been ordained to play on the stage of the world? Our nation lies between the cultured peoples and the barbarians from the East and as such should become an intermediary between the two.' Krizhanich expounded some broad generalisations which he developed from trifling observations and detailed projects: the Slavonic-Russian East and the foreign West were two worlds apart, two distinctly separate cultural types. He made a fairly shrewd comparison of the qualities which distinguished Slavs in general, and Russians in particular, from Western Europeans.

The latter are handsome, and since comeliness leads to insolence and pride, they are proud and overbearing; whereas we are neither one nor the other, being only moderately attractive. We are not eloquent and cannot explain ourselves clearly, while they are loquacious, bold and abusive, and sarcastic. We are slow witted and simple-hearted; they are full of cunning. We are improvident and extravagant and never estimate our income and expenditure, but throw our money away; they are thrifty and grasping, and day and night think only how to amass more money. We are physically and mentally lazy; they are hardworking and never sleep away one hour that could be profitable. We live in a poor land; they are natives of rich and bounteous lands, and lure us with their attractive products as hunters stalk game. We speak, think and behave simply, we quarrel and become reconciled; they are secretive, and dissemble, and until the day they die they never forget an

[1] Ivan the Terrible is reputed to have killed his own son with his staff.

angry word, and having once quarrelled they never become sincerely reconciled; once they have made peace they continue to seek opportunities for revenge.

Krizhanich is particularly important in Russian historiography, since his observations and opinions remained unique for over a hundred years. Nothing quite like them existed, and his observations provide the student of seventeenth-century Russian life with an invaluable insight.

Neither Nikon's letters nor Kotoshikhin's essays were particularly well known in their own time. Kotoshikhin's writings were not read in Russia until the end of the nineteenth century following upon their re-discovery by a Russian professor in the library of Upsala University. Krizhanich's works were kept 'upstairs' in the palace of Tsars Alexis and Fedor; copies were to be found in the residences of Medvedev and Prince V. Golitsin, who had been adherents of the Tsarevna Sophia; apparently, during the reign of Tsar Fedor there had even been some impetus to publish his works. Krizhanich's ideas and observations may well have contributed to the programme of reforms which were currently being discussed in administrative circles.

The importance of contributions made by these seventeenth-century personalities cannot be underrated, particularly since they are symptomatic of the mood of the times.[1] Discontent with the state of affairs predominated; and here again Krizhanich's observations are valuable, since he would much rather have not described the disturbing features of a country which offered powerful, though distant, support for Pan-Slavism.

This discontent and its expression are an important turning-point in seventeenth-century Russian life. Its consequences were incalculable; of immediate note was the introduction of western influence into Russia whose origins and effects will be discussed in the following chapter.

[1] Another interesting personality was Quirinus Kuhlmann, a Silesian, who sought to realise through 'the unknown people of the north' the fading, messianic expectations of the radical Reformation. See Billington, *The Icon and the Axe*, pp. 171-3.

Chapter Thirteen

★

BEFORE A detailed examination can be made of western influences in Russia it would be as well to define more precisely what is meant by influence. Muscovy was known to Western European countries in the fifteenth and sixteenth centuries with whom diplomatic and trade relations existed; artists, craftsmen, physicians and soldiers were encouraged to settle in Muscovy. This however, was *contact*, and not influence. There is influence when one society becomes aware of the superiority of another's culture and environment, and wishes to emulate its morals, attitudes, ideas, customs and social relations. Indeed, in this sense, Western European influence in Russia only occurred in the seventeenth century, and therefore it is correct to say that Western influence in Russia dates only from the seventeenth century.

How did this develop, and why was there no desire to emulate Western European intellectual and moral achievements during the sixteenth century? This desire to emulate the West sprang from deep Russian dissatisfaction with existing conditions; it was rooted in the problems confronting the administration of the new dynasty which, to a greater or lesser degree, affected all classes and the whole of society; the administration was incapable of balancing income and expenditure. It was recognised that the existing system had fundamentally to be changed so as to provide the state with sufficient revenue. This was not, of course, a new problem, nor the first time that a desire for reform had occurred. But in the seventeenth century reform became a matter of urgency.

Having united Greater Russia, the Muscovite government, from the middle of the fifteenth century, felt itself increasingly incapable of solving the problem arising from unification with existing methods. It tried to create a different system of government relying, not on foreign examples, but on its own experience, and judgement of the past. It believed that a new system could be based on old precepts. However, this approach only created stronger authoritarianism, and a sense of national strength which led to chauvinism.

During the sixteenth century Russians even believed that having unified Greater Russia, Moscow had become the centre and bulwark of the Orthodox East. The situation altered subsequently as the inadequacies of the existing system became apparent, and all attempts at improvement failed. Men began to realise that the nation's creative powers were moribund, and that it was intellectually bankrupt; that the past had no guidance for the present, and that as a result there was no reason to cling to it. A rupture in contemporary thinking took place. Men appeared in government circles, and in society, who doubted whether the past had bequeathed anything of value for the establishment of a satisfactory future existence. They lost their national complacency, and turned for guidance and ideas to Western Europe, and they became increasingly convinced of Western superiority and of their own backwardness. This lack of confidence in their own past, and in their own people, created a mood of despondency, an inferiority complex which opened the doors to foreign influence.

What was the difference between sixteenth and seventeenth-century events? Why had the Russians been unaware of their relative backwardness? Why were they less constructive than their immediate predecessors? Was the seventeenth-century Russian less bold and spiritually weaker than the sixteenth-century Russian? Or had the religious and moral self-confidence of one generation sapped the spiritual energy of the next? The most convincing reason which accounts for the differences between the two centuries was that Russian attitudes towards Western Europe had changed substantially.

In Western Europe during the sixteenth and seventeenth centuries centralised states emerged from the ruins of a feudal system; and a labour force broke out of the confines of a feudal agricultural system. Geographical discoveries and technical innovation created new activities which were eagerly seized on by the new labour force, while new urban and commercial capital vied successfully with the remaining feudal, seignorial capital. Political centralisation and urban, bourgeois industrialisation led to important improvements in administrative, financial, and military techniques, in the organisation of standing armies, and taxation; and national economic and political theories became more sophisticated. Improvements in economic management occurred, mercantile fleets expanded, industrial output increased, commercial markets, and a system of credit were successfully established. Russia did not participate in any of these successful endeavours, but wasted her resources and efforts on defence, and on maintaining a Court, a government, and privileged classes including the clergy, who were incapable of making positive contributions to the country's economic and moral development. Thus, in the seventeenth century the difference between Russia and Western Europe was greater than it had been at the beginning of the sixteenth century.[1] This sense of impotence which existed in Russia created the necessary conditions for the penetration of Western European influence. Russians became increasingly aware of their material and intellectual weaknesses in comparison with Western Europe, as evidenced in particular in Russia's wars, and in her diplomatic and commercial relations. The realisation grew that Russia was indeed backward.

In penetrating Russia, Western influence clashed with the prevailing Eastern Greek or Byzantine influence. The differences between these were striking, and it is interesting to compare them in order to appreciate what remained of one influence in Russia, and what was entailed in the other.

Greek influence was introduced, and propagated throughout Russia by the Church, which was concerned with religion and morality. Western influence was encouraged by a government

[1] The fundamental features differentiating Russia from Western and Central Europe during this period are discussed by Marc Szeftel, 'Some Reflections on the Particular Characteristics of the Russian Historical Process', *Russian Review* (Jul 1964) pp. 223–37.

to satisfy its own material requirements; however, it did confine itself to the activities of state as the Church confined Greek influence to religious matters. Byzantine influence was by no means all-pervading; it concerned itself only with the religious and moral life of the people, and while it upheld and participated in the ceremonial of the indigenous state authority, it was of little assistance in affairs of state. It played a minor role in establishing civic rights, and especially in family relations; it was almost irrelevant as far as daily life was concerned, and completely irrelevant where the national economy was concerned. It regulated behaviour during holidays and peoples' leisure until the end of Mass. Its contribution to the fund of knowledge was minimal and did not leave any noticeable traces in the daily customs and ideas of a nation which had complete freedom either to develop or to continue in its state of primitive ignorance. Although it was not concerned with the individual, and did not deprive him of his own native characteristics and originality, it none the less pervaded the whole of society, thereby imparting a spiritual unity to the whole medieval Russian community.

Western influence, on the other hand, gradually penetrated every sphere of life in both the public and private sectors modifying ideas and attitudes. It was responsible for the formation of new political ideas, new social requirements, new forms of communal life, new areas of knowledge, and quite changed the clothes, manners, customs and beliefs of the people. As a result the Russian was changed externally and inwardly. However, while Western influence affected the individual personality, it never successfully pervaded the whole of society, and was not absorbed by the subtle, ceaselessly mobile and sensitive layers which enveloped this society. Greek influence was ecclesiastical, while Western influence was temporal; Greek influence pervaded the community and ignored the individual; Western influence affected the individual but not the community. From the encounter, and subsequent clash between these opposing influences, there developed two main trends in the intellectual life of Russia, and two opinions concerning its cultural standing. Both influences flowed through the mainstream of Russian thought, becoming more sophisticated and complex, with varying degrees of emphasis, and under different names. Like rivulets in a desert, sometimes underground, sometimes in the open, both influences increasingly enervated a sluggish existence ordered by drab, ignorant and oppressive policies which, except on rare occasions, were pursued until the middle of the nineteenth century.

The first clash occurred in the second half of the seventeenth century over the problem of Transubstantiation and the closely connected problem of the comparative advantages of learning Greek and Latin. The protagonists might well have been called Hellenists and Latinists.

During the second half of the eighteenth century the literature of the Enlightenment in France dealing with the meaning of the Petrine reforms and the question of independent national growth, led to a serious rift in Russian society. The nationalists called themselves Russophiles, and their opponents Russo-Frenchmen, Francophiles, free thinkers, and most commonly, Voltairians. In the 1840s adherents of one school of thought became known as Westerners, while their opponents were called Slavophiles. Their beliefs can be expressed as follows. The Westerners maintained that Russian civilisation was European even though Russia had appeared on the European scene at a late stage, and that Russia should take advantage of the benefits of this civilisation. The Slavophiles contended that although Russians were Europeans, they were Easterners with their own unique historical roots, and should work out their own destiny through their own efforts without any assistance from Western Europe. They maintained that Russia was neither a disciple, a satellite, nor even a rival; Russia was Europe's successor. Russia and Europe represented a universal and contiguous historical development, two successive phases in the growth of civilisation. Parodying the somewhat stilted Slavophile phraseology it could be said that Western Europe was a vast cemetery where, beneath stately marble tombs, sleep the great dead; whereas the Russia of the forest and the steppe is a vast wooden cradle wherein lies the world's future tossing restlessly and crying helplessly. Europe, said the Slavophiles, has had her day; Russia has just started to live, and since

Russia will continue to live after Europe has disappeared, she must learn to do without European help, developing her own intellect and principles, and eventually supplant the basic tenets of European life in order to illuminate the world with a new light. The Slavophiles maintained that because Russia was at an early stage of historical development it was encumbent upon her neither to imitate nor to borrow from other cultures, but to work out her own destiny from principles which were concealed in the depths of her native soil, and were, as yet, pure.

Slavophiles and Westerners were not only diametrically opposed in their understanding of Russia's historical position in Europe, but they both indicated a different historical development. However, this is not the place to evaluate these different viewpoints, nor to analyse Russia's historical destiny in order to ascertain whether she was fated to become a light in the East or a mere shadow of Europe. It is only possible to refer briefly to the more attractive characteristics of both schools of thought.

The Westerners excelled in disciplined thought, love of precision, and respect for knowledge. The Slavophiles were interested in broad generalisations, believing in the strength of the nation, and developing a sort of lyrical dialectic which concealed their errors in logic and the gaps in their erudition.

This brief exposition has shown the final outcome of the Greek and Western influences as they developed through two centuries of accumulated indigenous and foreign arguments.

When did these influences appear, and how were they originally expressed? They certainly did not originate with the Petrine reforms. The ideas they expressed were voiced in the seventeenth century by those who had survived the Time of Troubles. Possibly the clerk, Ivan Timofeev, who wrote his *Vremenik* or Chronicle at the beginning of Tsar Michael's reign, and started with the reign of Ivan the Terrible, was right in his observations. Timofeev was a man of ideas and principles. Politically he was a conservative. He ascribed the misery of his own times to a betrayal of the past, to the disruption of the ancient legal structure, which he said, caused the Russians to rotate like a wheel. He bitterly regretted the lack of manly determination in the Russians, and their inability to resist arbitrary and illegal innovations. Timofeev believed that the Russians lacked confidence in each other; some looked to the East, others to the West; or, as he wrote in his flowery language, 'we are becoming distant from one another in our friendly union, each of us turns his back on the other – some look to the East, others to the West'. It is difficult to know whether this was a well-turned phrase or an accurate observation. However, during the second decade of the seventeenth century, when Timofeev was writing, 'westernism' in Russia was propagated by individual eccentrics like Prince Khvorostinin; it was not a conscious social movement. Every society produces a number of introspective men who, in advance of their contemporaries, expound ideas, and are unconscious of their motivation, in the same way that there are people who can feel a change in the weather before others.

What were the earliest manifestations of Western influences? In as much as they were adopted and propagated by the government, they developed sequentially and over a wide range of activities; this was in accordance with the government's desires that there should be a degree of concordance between its own requirements, the psychology of the people, and its own tendency to inertia, which, of course, exerted a counter influence. The government turned to foreigners first of all, for assistance, which was urgently required, in the field of defence. Somewhat reluctantly it introduced military, and then technical, improvements from abroad, without considering what would be their effects, and without enquiring how Western Europeans had achieved their technical successes or what their motives had been.

Russia needed artillery, muskets, machinery, ships and craftsmen; none of these was considered harmful spiritually; the government even decided that morally no harm could come from studying these cunning devices since, when required, Church statutes permitted deviations from Church ordinances, in so far as daily conduct was concerned. However, it was decided that there should be absolutely no compromise with any foreign influence in matters of conscience affecting the feelings, ideas and beliefs of the Russian people.

The Russian army of the seventeenth century owed many important innovations to this first, cautious, concession, which also led to Russian manufacturing industry's first successes. The Russians had experienced the inefficiency of their mounted militia of noblemen whenever they faced a regular, properly trained Western force armed with muskets. Already towards the end of the sixteenth century the government of Muscovy had started to strengthen its forces with foreign contingents;[1] the government originally intended to utilise Western military techniques by hiring foreign soldiers and buying military equipment abroad. At the beginning of Tsar Michael's reign foreign detachments went into battle alongside Russian troops; one such detachment was commanded by an Englishman, Lord Aston. The government then realised that it might be more profitable to imitate the foreign military structure than to hire foreign troops; as a result, Russian troops were instructed by foreign officers, and properly trained and equipped Russian regiments were created. The difficult transformation from a militia to a regular army was undertaken around 1630, prior to the second war with Poland. With the care of those who had known defeat, lengthy and detailed preparations were made for this war. There was no shortage of volunteers wanting to serve the Muscovites: soldiers of fortune seeking employment abounded in those countries directly or indirectly involved in the Thirty Years War. It was well known that the truce between Muscovy and Poland concluded at Dulino was over, and that war was imminent. In 1631 Colonel Leslie[2] undertook to recruit in Sweden 5,800

[1] Sir Jerome Horsey, agent for the Muscovy Company, and subsequently Ambassador to Muscovy, told Ivan the Terrible that the Scots 'were a venturous and warlike people, ready to serve any Christian Prince for maintenance and pay; as they would appear and prove, if it pleased His Majesty to employ and spare them such maintenance'. Ivan the Terrible accepted this advice, and formed the Scots and other mercenaries into special companies with their own national captains. See Sir Robert Bruce Lockhart, 'The Scots in Russia', *The Penguin Russian Review* (1948) pp. 66–7.

[2] This was Sir Alexander Leslie of Auchintoul, who arrived in Russia with a letter from Charles I. Leslie was appointed Lieutenant-General of the Foreign Forces of the Emperor of Russia and was given full powers to enlist soldiers

volunteer infantrymen, equip them, and engage German artificers for the new cannon works recently built in Moscow by the Dutchman, Koet. Another recruiting officer, Van Dam,[1] undertook to hire in other countries a *regiment* of 1,760 capable and well-trained soldiers; he also promised to find German gunners and experienced instructors to train the Russian men of service in the art of war. The importation of foreign military skills into Russia was not cheap: the raising, equipping, and maintenance of Van Dam's regiment cost $1\frac{1}{4}$ million roubles (nineteenth-century values); the commander of Colonel Leslie's infantry regiment was guaranteed under contract an annual salary of no less than 27,000 roubles (nineteenth-century values).

Finally, in 1632, an army of 32,000 men with 158 guns moved against Smolensk. This army contained 6 foreign infantry regiments commanded by foreign colonels, in which there were more than 1,500 German mercenaries and 13,000 foreign-trained Russian soldiers. A contemporary Russian chronicler observed with astonishment that never before had a Russian army consisted of so many infantrymen armed with weapons, and never before had they been so well drilled and trained. The failure of the campaign against Smolensk did not prevent the complete reorganisation of the Russian army, with the consequences mentioned above. Under Tsar Michael a statute was drawn up authorising the training of Russian soldiers in foreign methods which was published in 1647 under Tsar Alexis and entitled *A study and stratagem of military infantry formations.*

The creation of a semi-regular army created armament problems. Small arms and artillery were invariably imported.[2] Before the 1632 war Colonel Leslie was ordered to buy 10,000 muskets,

---

from abroad including Scotland. He was, however, explicitly instructed not to hire Catholics. A brief biography and details of his conditions of service can be found in, I. Lubimenko, *La Russie et l'Angleterre avant Pierre le Grand* (Paris, 1933) pp. 167–72.

[1] Colonel Heinrich Van Dam was advised to recruit Lutherans, but unlike the order given to Leslie, he was not specifically barred from hiring Catholics.

[2] On 18 June 1632 the Tsar authorised the purchase in England of 5,000 *épées,* and two years later a request was made for 2,000 muskets.

powder, and 5,000 swords in Sweden; and during the war tens of thousands of poods[1] of powder and iron shot, all subject to a high tariff, were ordered from Holland. Importing their requirements was both expensive and tiresome, and the Russians began to consider manufacturing their own arms. The requirement for arsenals forced the government to survey the country's mineral wealth. Hitherto iron-ore had come from mines around Tula and Usytug where it was smelted in local furnaces and turned into nails and other items for domestic use. Some weapons and matchlocks were made in Tula, but they were quite insufficient to satisfy the country's military requirements. Therefore, thousands of poods of iron were ordered from Sweden. Foreign skills and capital were required to expand the Russian metallurgical industry. Intensive ore surveys were undertaken, and men 'skilled in metal', mining engineers and master-craftsmen were invited to come to Russia from abroad. As early as 1626 an English engineer called Bulmer[2] was given free passage to Russia, so that 'by his skill and wisdom he can find deposits of gold, silver, copper and rare stones, and he will know where to look'. Prospecting expeditions assisted by foreign technicians were sent out to locate and exploit silver and other mines at Solikamsk, on the Northern Dvina, at Mezen, on the Kanin Nos, at Yugorsky Shar, at Pechora, on the River Kosva, and even at Eniseisk. In 1634 a mission was sent to Saxony and Brunswick to hire copper-smelting experts, and an undertaking was given that 'in the State of Muscovy they would be able to work much copper'; clearly, abundant copper had been found. Foreign manufacturers and capitalists were also found. Just before the war with Poland in 1632, a Dutch merchant, Andrew Vinius[3] together with some

[1] 1 pood equals 36·113 lb.

[2] This was John Bulmer. He was followed by Cartwright in 1640, who arrived with ten artisans. See I. Lubimenko, *Les Marchands Anglais au XVIIe siècle* (Paris, 1921) p. 28.

[3] Andrew Vinius organised the processing of iron ore, and built the first ironworks in Russia. He was given a monopoly and a subvention of 3,000 roubles on condition that he developed the iron deposits at Tula, and instructed the Russians. See B. Gille, *Histoire Économique et Sociale de la Russie* (Paris, 1949) pp. 68–9. To help finance the enterprise Vinius took Peter Marselis and F.

associates was granted a concession to build a number of works near Tula to manufacture iron and cast iron; in exchange Vinius had to undertake that he would make cannon, cannon balls, musket barrels and other items at specially reduced prices for the Treasury. A complete territorial circumscription belonging to the Crown was allotted to these works to provide them with a labour force; and this was the foundation of a class of factory peasants. In 1644 another association of foreigners, headed by Marselis,[1] a Hamburg merchant, was given a twenty-year concession to build ironworks along the rivers Vaja, Kostroma, Sheksna and elsewhere on identical conditions. In Moscow itself as early as Tsar Michael's reign a factory had been set up on the river Neglinnaya where foreign master-craftsmen cast many bells and cannon, and where Russians were taught to become fairly competent foundrymen.

Foreign manufacturers were obliged to teach the Russians apprenticed to them all their manufacturing processes and other skills. Potash, glass and other industries were established at the same time as the iron works. Foreign metallurgists were followed by master-gunners, velvet weavers, wire spinners, clockmakers, water-diviners, masons, smelters and artists, who came to Muscovy at the government's invitation. Indeed it would be difficult to name a specialist craftsman who was not invited. All were obliged 'to teach the people of our State their skills'. Even the services of Western European scholars were required. Adam Olearius, a graduate of Leipzig University, who had visited Moscow on several occasions as secretary of the Holstein Embassy, and written a remarkable account about the State of Muscovy, received the following invitation in 1639 to enter the Tsar's service: 'You are very learned and skilled in astronomy and

---

Akema into the company. Later Vinius was ousted, and the others took charge, expanding their operations, and initiating new ones in other areas.

[1] Peter Marselis tried to persuade the Russians to abandon their restrictive attitudes to trade. See *A History of Russian Economic Thought*, ed. John M. Letiche (University of California Press, 1964) pp. 207–8. For a history of the remarkable Marselis family, see E. Amburger, *Die Familie Marselis: Studien zur russischen Wirtschafsgeschichte* (Giessen, 1957).

geography, and the movement of the heavens, and the measurement of the earth, and other useful skills and knowledge; and such skilled men are wanted by us, the great Sovereign.' It was rumoured that a magician was coming who could read the future in the stars, and Olearius declined the invitation.[1]

In Western Europe men and countries grew rich from an extensive overseas trade which was carried by large mercantile fleets. In the second half of the seventeenth century the government of Muscovy began seriously to concern itself with ideas of a fleet, harbours, and maritime commerce. The government intended to hire shipwrights and sailors from Holland, and Vinius, who has been mentioned earlier, offered to build a fleet of barges for the Caspian Sea. In 1669 on the river Oka in the village of Dyedinovo (in the district of Kolomna), a vessel called the *Orel* – the *Eagle* – was built by hired Dutch shipwrights for use in the Caspian Sea. The *Orel* together with some other small vessels cost 9,000 roubles (125,000 in nineteenth-century values) and was launched at Astrakhan. In 1670 this 'father of the Russian fleet' was burnt by Stenka Razin.

Muscovy's ports were on the White Sea at Archangel, and on the mouth of the River Kola at Murman. Both were too far from Moscow and Western European markets; access to the Baltic was denied to Russia by the Swedes. In Moscow they had the original idea of hiring foreign ports for their future fleet. In 1662 a Muscovite emissary on his way to England discussed the possibility with the Chancellor of Courland of Russian ships being maintained in the ports of Courland. The Chancellor replied that it would be better for the Great Tsar to maintain the ships in his own port of Archangel.

Throughout this mining and manufacturing activity a new idea emerged which was understood only with great difficulty. The Muscovite financial system was built on a narrow fiscal base; the government was interested only in revenue, and not in

[1] The Tsar renewed his invitation again in 1643, but again Olearius declined, probably because he received assurances of a distinguished and satisfactory career in Holstein. See *Travels of Olearius in Seventeenth-century Russia*, trans. and ed. Samuel H. Baron (Stanford U.P., 1967) pp. 12–13.

the national economy. Whenever expenditure outran income, the government would resort to its customary 'financial arithmetics', calculate the number of registered taxpayers, and divide the sum required among them. Collection of these moneys was enforced with the threat that if arrears occurred the government would impose a mandatory surcharge payable once and for all, or by way of a permanent tax. The taxpayers could apportion among themselves the amounts due as they wished and were free to get the money in whatever way they could.

Arrears and tiresome complaints were the only answers to this irresponsible financial policy. Although the government raised the level of taxes it did nothing to increase the taxpaying capacity of the people. Never the less, observation of the commercial-industrial skills and technical competence of foreigners, combined with insistent representations by Russian merchants gradually induced Muscovite financiers to consider unfamiliar economic ideas and relationships. Against their wills their administrative horizon was enlarged and they were forced to accept ideas which were alien to them; for instance, that increases in taxation should be preceded by an increase in productivity, and that to achieve this labour should be directed to new, income-producing industries, to the discovery and exploitation of the country's natural wealth, which called for new skills, knowledge and organisation.

These ideas produced the first major impact of Western thought on the government of Muscovy; and produced a response in society. The ferment in government; the searches made for minerals, and shipbuilding timber; the locating of sites for saltworks; the building of sawmills; and the interrogation of local inhabitants concerning profitable natural assets known to them, all gave the people hope of new employment, and government rewards for information. For instance, whoever discovered a virgin mineral deposit was promised a reward of 500 or 1,000 roubles and more. As soon as the government heard that a hill of alabaster had been found on the Northern Dvina it despatched an expedition led by Germans to survey and describe it; the expedition was told to find out what price could be obtained for alabaster abroad, and it was authorised to hire quarrymen. It was rumoured that those in high circles were willing to pay for information leading to new discoveries or inventions. The impetus in a society to produce material gain can affect men like a fashion or epidemic; it can evoke wild schemes, unhealthy passions, and speculative undertakings. Following the defeats and humiliations caused by foreigners during the Time of Troubles the problems of defence, and any discoveries and inventions which could strengthen the economy, became lively issues.

In 1629 a priest from Tver called Nestor presented a petition to the Tsar informing him 'of a great work which has hitherto never been revealed by God to any man either in our country or elsewhere, but which He has revealed to me, the priest Nestor, for the glory of the Sovereign and the salvation of our afflicted land, to the confusion and amazement of our enemies'. Nestor undertook to build the Tsar a cheap, mobile, citadel in which soldiers could take refuge, as though it were a real, immovable fortress. The boyars were unsuccessful in their attempts to persuade the inventor to make a sketch or model of his mobile citadel in order to show it to the Tsar. The priest stated that he had not beheld the Tsar's eyes, and would reveal nothing because he did not trust the boyars. He was exiled to Kazan where he was kept in chains in a monastery for three years for having boasted that he could perform a great work while refusing to reveal any details, thereby causing confusion; clearly he was mad.

As has been shown, both the Muscovite government and society became aware of how desperately they needed to adapt Western European military and industrial techniques to their own purposes, until finally they resolved to learn them both. It may well be that originally the requirements of state could have been satisfied through the use of foreign techniques alone; however, as soon as a social movement gathers momentum, it tends to develop new motives, and a new framework within which to act.

Foreign technicians, officers, soldiers, physicians, artisans, merchants and manufacturers were attracted to Muscovy as soon as it was realised that there was a demand for their services.

Already in the sixteenth century, during the reign of Ivan the Terrible, Western European immigrants had settled on the river Yaüza outside Moscow in what was called the German suburb; it was swept away during the Time of Troubles. After Tsar Michael's accession foreigners flocked once more to the capital, settling where they could, buying houses from the Russians, opening taverns, and building churches within the walls of the city. Close contacts between foreigners and Russians created tensions and violence, as well as complaints from the Muscovite clergy that foreign churches were too close to Orthodox churches. The government was embarrassed by the situation, and an ukase was issued under Tsar Michael forbidding foreigners either to buy homes from Muscovites or to build churches inside the city.

Olearius gave an account of one of the incidents which forced the government to keep the two communities apart. Some German officers had married women from the foreign merchant community in Moscow, who despised the wives of ordinary merchants and insisted on sitting in front of them in church; the latter invariably refused to move, and on one occasion a quarrel broke out inside the church which grew into a fight. The noise was heard in the street, and attracted the attention of the Patriarch, who unfortunately happened to be passing by. When the Patriarch learned what the trouble was about he, as guardian of ecclesiastical order, which extended to other faiths, ordered the church to be demolished, and on the same day it was destroyed right down to its foundations. This could have taken place in 1643 when all the old foreign churches inside Moscow were ordered to be destroyed; and another site was allocated beyond the Zemlianyi Rampart for a new church. In 1652 the numerous foreigners who were scattered throughout Moscow were evicted from the capital, and sent to Pokrovka on the river Yaüza, where plots of land previously occupied by foreign houses were distributed according to rank and occupation.[1]

[1] None the less the order that foreigners should live in the new suburb initially caused dismay, among other reasons because those who owned houses, which they were obliged to sell quickly, expected to suffer serious losses. For this reason the ukase was not completely enforced, and sixteen months later the

A new German or Foreign suburb was created in this way which soon grew into an important and well built small town with broad, straight streets and alleys, and attractive wooden houses. During the first years of its existence it contained, according to Olearius, nearly 1,000 inhabitants; another foreigner, Meyerberg,[1] who lived in Moscow in 1660 also stated that a large number of foreigners were living in this suburb. It contained three Lutheran churches, one Reformed church, and one school. The inhabitants of this suburb were a heterogeneous, polyglot group representing many skills; comfortable and contented, they were free to live according to their own customs and habits. This suburb represented a small part of Western Europe which had come to rest at the eastern outskirts of Moscow.

Western European culture flowed through the German suburb to influence even those parts of Muscovite life which were irrelevant to the government's policy of technical change. The technicians, manufacturers and officers whom the government had hired to help organise either the country's defences or its industry, brought with them not only their military and industrial skills, but their Western European comforts, amenities, and amusements; and it is curious to note how eagerly the Muscovite upper classes adopted foreign luxuries, and imported amusements, thereby effecting a break with their own prejudices, tastes and customs. There can be no doubt that foreign political relations helped to encourage a desire for foreign comforts and entertainment. The frequency with which foreign diplomatic missions visited Moscow made the Muscovites want to show themselves in the best possible light, and demonstrate that they too could live well. Furthermore, as was mentioned above, Tsar Alexis had at one time considered himself as a candidate for the Polish throne, and had tried to make Muscovite court life resemble the Polish King's court. Muscovite envoys sent abroad were instructed

---

authorities were still pressing some of the foreigners to move. However, some twenty families, whom the Tsar trusted, were allowed to stay on in the city. Ibid. p. 124 n. 32.

[1] Baron von Meyerberg wrote *Journey to Muscovy by the Ambassador of Emperor Leopold to Tsar Alexis Mikhailovich* (Leyden, 1669).

by their government to observe the setting and entertainments of foreign courts. Indeed, it is interesting to notice the importance attached by these envoys in their diplomatic dispatches to Court balls and entertainments. In 1659 the courtier Likhachev was sent on a diplomatic mission to the Duke of Tuscany;[1] while in Florence he was invited to a Court ball and entertainment. An indication that Moscow was deeply interested in such matters can be seen from the mission's report which contained a detailed description of the 'play' or 'comedy'.[2] The Muscovites tried not to omit a single scene, or any detail of the décor.

> Rooms appear, one room appears and then vanished below, and there were six such changes in all. A sea appears disturbed by waves, and in the sea, fish with men riding upon them. Above is the sky complete with clouds with people sitting upon them. A man descends from a cloud in a coach and opposite him, in another coach, is a most beautiful maiden. The horses harnessed to the coaches seem to be alive, and move their limbs. The Prince explains that the man represents the sun, and the woman, the moon. In another scene, a man enters accompanied by 50 others, all clad in armour who begin to fight with swords and sabres, and to fire muskets upon which it seems that three men are killed. Then a number of handsome young men and maidens emerge from behind the curtain all dressed in gold, and dance. And many other marvels were performed.

Describing the life of the Muscovite upper classes Kotoshikhin remarked that they lived in 'badly conceived houses' 'without much order', by which he meant that the houses were inconvenient and uncomfortable. Meyerberg's sketches contain descriptions of the Metropolitan of the Krutitsky Monastery travelling in a clumsy sledge, and a tightly covered cart which was used by the Tsaritsa. In imitation of foreign customs, however, the Tsar and boyars of Moscow now started to travel in smart,

[1] Tsar Alexis sent Alexis Likhachev to thank the Grand Duke Ferdinand of Tuscany for the welcome he had given Muscovite envoys in Venice. Likhachev was also told to negotiate customs exemptions for Russian traders, offering Tuscan merchants a caviare concession in return.
[2] This was the first profane play ever seen by Likhachev.

German coaches, upholstered in velvet, fitted with crystal windows and decorated with painted panels. Boyars and wealthy merchants began to build stone mansions in the place of wretched wooden dwellings, and even furnishings were copied from abroad. Walls were hung with 'gold leather' of Flemish manufacture; and the rooms were decorated with paintings and clocks. Indeed, Tsar Michael, who was lame, and perforce had to remain in one place, was so often bored, that he developed a passion for clocks and filled his chamber with them.[1] Music was played at banquets, and during Tsar Alexis' evening meal at the palace 'a German played upon the organ, trumpets were blown, and kettle-drums beaten'. In this way foreign arts were used to improve upon native Muscovite coarseness. Tsar Alexis gave the boyar Boris Morozov, a favourite of his who had once been his tutor and was to become his brother-in-law, a wedding coach upholstered in gold brocade, lined with costly sable, and hooped with silver instead of iron; even the thick wheel-rims were made of silver. During the riots of 1648, pillagers entered Boris Morozov's house and smashed this treasure. It is worth noting that while Tsar Alexis was being entertained with music during his evening meal he would toast his guests, including his confessor, until they were all intoxicated; the guests would leave these banquets long past midnight. Muscovite ambassadors were ordered to hire on the Tsar's behalf the best and most gifted trumpeters who could be guaranteed to play dance tunes on this instrument. The Court and upper classes developed a passion for 'comedy acts', i.e. theatrical performances. However, these 'devil's plays, these spiritual aberrations' were not introduced in Moscow without some religious qualms. Tsar Alexis discussed the matter with his confessor, who agreed to allow them to be staged: his justification was that Byzantine Emperors had allowed theatrical performances. These 'comedies' were acted on the Court stage

[1] The collection of watches and clocks owned by the royal family was most bizarre. The Russian watches told the time by dividing the day into two parts: day from sunrise to sunset, and night from sunset to dawn. The foreign timepieces showed the time in the manner of its land of origin. See Zinaïda Schakovskoy, *Precursors of Peter the Great* (Cape, 1964) p. 27.

by a troupe of actors hurriedly chosen from the children of
foreigners who were engaged in commerce or state service, and
were trained somehow by the pastor of the Lutheran Church in
the German suburb. This pastor was Master Johan Gottfried
Gregory[1] whom Tsar Alexis ordered in 1672 to 'create a comedy'
to celebrate the birth of Tsarevich Peter. For this purpose a
theatre, or 'hall of comedy' was built in the village of Preobrazhensky near Moscow, which was to become the favourite
place for Peter's games.[2] Towards the end of 1672 the Tsar saw
Esther staged by Pastor Gregory at Preobrazhensky. Tsar Alexis
was so pleased that he rewarded the régisseur with 1500 roubles
worth of sables (in nineteenth-century values).[3] Apart from
Esther Pastor Gregory also staged at Preobrazhensky a 'light
comedy' called *Judith*, and a 'pitiful' comedy about *Adam and Eve;*
the plays were a mixture of comedy or farce, with an obligatory
character of a Jester who made coarse and unseemly jokes. Russian
actors were hurriedly trained. In 1673 twenty-six young people
from the Novomeshchansky suburb in Moscow were chosen to
study dramatic art under Pastor Gregory. Elementary schools
might not exist to teach people to read and write, yet all haste
was made to establish drama schools! Plays with biblical contents
were soon succeeded by ballets. A few days before Lent in 1674,
the Tsar and Tsaritsa, together with their children and boyars
watched a play at Preobrazhensky in which Artaxerxes ordered

[1] Johan Gottfried Gregory had formerly been a Polish cavalryman. His first
two plays were followed by four others and two ballets. His original troupe of
sixty, recruited from the German suburb, was soon augmented by recruits from
the Baltic regions. *Esther* was performed in German.

[2] The theatre was a vast hall with walls swathed in emerald green and
raspberry red cloth; the floors were covered with thick carpets. The seats consisted of benches, arranged in a semi-circle with the 'Tsar's seat' upholstered in
red in the foreground. The stage was enclosed by curtains and illuminated by a
multitude of tallow candles marshalled in rows flush with the floor of the
proscenium. See Schakovskoy, *The Precursors of Peter the Great,* p. 131.

[3] Ringubern, one of Gregory's assistants, was right when he forecast at the
time of the first performance of *Esther* that it would prove 'the making of our
fortune'. Foreigners received handsome salaries and theatres multiplied. Ibid.
pp. 132-3.

Haiman to be hung. This play was performed to an orchestral accompaniment of 'viols, organs and other instruments', and dances by foreigners and officials from Matveev's Ministry of Foreign Affairs, who had also studied dramatic art under Pastor Gregory. These novelties and amusements were luxuries to be indulged in only by the upper classes;[1] and, as a result, they acquired new and more refined tastes and desires which were alien to Russians of previous generations. But was Muscovite society not going to look beyond the amenities and recreations it had so impatiently adopted?

The amenities and refinements of life in Western Europe were not solely due to the fortunate economic position of the wealthy and leisured classes, nor were they the creation of some idle fancy: they owed their existence to prolonged spiritual efforts of individuals and entire communities.

Visual refinements developed concurrently with intellectual achievements, and an increased sense of dignity. Man strives to create an environment which corresponds to his tastes and outlook; in order to achieve a proper balance man must reflect deeply on his own tastes, and on life itself. The transposition of one environment to another setting involves the unconscious and involuntary assimilation of those tastes and attitudes which created that environment, otherwise in its new setting it would seem to be senseless and meaningless.

Seventeenth-century Russians thought otherwise. They believed at the beginning that it did not necessarily follow that because they had adopted Western European amenities they would have to accept foreign knowledge and ideas, and dispense with their own. This was a simple-minded error which is shared by all suspicious and belated imitators. Consequently, as seventeenth-century Muscovites adopted foreign customs so they gradually became aware of the underlying spiritual interests and efforts which had created them. Increased awareness led to respect for these interests and efforts even before there was any proper understanding of their relationship to Russian ideas and

[1] However, a popular theatre, the Peoples' Theatre, was built not far from the Novodevichi Monastery.

tastes. Moreover, the Russians were interested in this subject as though it were an abstraction, an intellectual exercise in a hitherto unexplored area of endeavour.

At the same time as the upper classes were copying foreign 'tricks' and entertaining 'devices', they were becoming intellectually curious, and interested in scientific subjects; they even showed a desire to think about subjects which had nothing whatever to do with the actualities and problems of medieval Russian life. A small circle of influential admirers of Western European amenities and culture was formed at Court. Tsar Alexis' uncle, the kindhearted and cheerful Nikita Ivanovich Romanov, who was the wealthiest man in the country after the Tsar, and certainly the most popular of all the boyars, was a member of this circle.[1] He not only protected and admired foreigners, but was a great lover of their music and dress; he was also a free thinker. Another member of this circle was the Tsar's tutor and brother-in-law, Boris Morozov, who used to complain bitterly that he had never been given a proper education, and dressed his foster child and playmates in German clothes. Then there was Fedor Rtishchev,[2] a zealot for knowledge and the establishment of an elementary school system. The fourth member of this group was the head of the Department of Foreign Affairs, an educated diplomat called Athanasius Ordin-Nashchokin.[3] Finally there was his successor, boyar Artamon Matveev, the son of a clerk, and another of the Tsar's favourites, who was the first Muscovite to hold a sort of debating society in his Europeanised home, with the

[1] Nikita Romanov owned 7,012 peasant homesteads, and was reputed to be as rich as Croesus.

[2] Fedor Rtishchev was an influential member of the Zealots of Faith, a society founded at Court. Rtishchev's reputation was so great that an anonymous contemporary wrote his biography during his lifetime. See Pierre Pascal, *Avvakum et les Débuts de Raskol* (1938) pp. 125–6; Serge A. Zenkovsky, 'The Russian Church Schism: Its Background and Repercussions', *Russian Review* (Oct 1957) pp. 37–49.

[3] Athanasius Ordin-Nashchokin, was a statesman of unique ability. There is unfortunately, very little about him in English. But see *A History of Russian Economic Thought*, pp. 210–28; Schakovskoy, *The Precursors of Peter the Great* pp. 47–50.

object of exchanging and discussing ideas, news and opinions not only in the presence of his wife, but without serving alcohol. Matveev was also responsible for organising the Court theatre.

Almost imperceptibly the attitudes of Russian society towards Western Europe were changing. Previously, Western Europe was looked on as the place where military and domestic articles might be purchased, and no thought was given as to how they were made. Now, Western Europe was considered to be a school in which it might be possible not only to learn handicrafts, but also how to live and think.

Yet even now Muscovy did not abandon customary caution. It was decided that Western European education was not to be imported direct from the countries of origin. Muscovy decided to look for an intermediary through whom that education could be transmitted in an innocuous form. Who could that intermediary be? Between ancient Muscovite Russia and Western Europe lay a country, Poland, which was Slavonic and Catholic. Poland was closely connected with Romano-German Europe through religious and geographic ties, while the early and un-restrained development of serfdom, and its connection with the political freedom of the Polish upper classes, made Polish noble-men susceptible to the influence of Western culture. However, the peculiarities of the country and its national characteristics modified and polarised Western culture. Restricted to a single class which was pre-eminent in the state, Polish culture fostered a lively and animated, albeit narrow-minded and undisciplined, outlook on the world. Never the less, it was through Poland that Western European influence was first transmitted to Muscovy. Seventeenth-century Western European civilisation came to Muscovy with a Polish gloss on it, having first been adapted by the Polish gentry. And yet, in fact, the original transmitting agents were not real Poles at all. There were strong political links between large segments of Orthodox Rus and the Polish Retch *Porpolita*. The national and religious struggles between the Orthodox communities of Western Rus and the Polish govern-ment and Roman Catholicism forced the Russian participants to investigate their opponents' strength, which lay in their schools, their literature, and in the Latin language. By the middle of the seventeenth century, Western Rus was much further advanced than the rest of the country. In this way it was the Western Russian Orthodox monks educated in Latin or Russian schools modelled on European establishments, who were, in fact, the first exponents of Western learning to be summoned to Moscow.

The summons came from the Muscovite government itself. However, Western influence clashed with a movement emanating from a totally different quarter. In Chapter xv the origins of the schism in the Russian Church will be discussed, and it will be shown that this counter-movement owed its existence to the needs of the Church, and was partly directed against Western influences. However, both sides agreed that enlightenment was necessary to Russia, and for a while they joined forces. No complete or precise text of the Bible was available in medieval Russian literature. The Orthodox Russian hierarchy, who had raised an oecumenical and dogmatic storm over the question of *allelulias* and the secularisation of monastic lands, had managed quite contentedly for centuries without a complete or reliable version of the words of God.

In the middle of the seventeenth century (1649–50) Moscow summoned three learned Kievan monks, Epiphanius Slavinetsky, Arseny Satanovsky and Damaskin Ptitsky, from the Bratsky and Pechersky Monasteries, and instructed them to translate the Bible from Greek into Slavonic. These Kievan scholars received lower salaries than the hired foreign mercenaries: Slavinetsky and Satanovsky received a maintenance allowance of 4 altins a day (about 600 roubles a year in nineteenth-century values), and free lodgings in the Chudovo Monastery together with food and drink, amounting to two mugs of wine and four tankards of beer and mead supplied by the palace. However, after a while, their daily salary was doubled. Apart from their main task, these scholars from Kiev had also to fulfil other requirements of government and society. On instructions from the Tsar or Patriarch they compiled and translated educational textbooks, encyclopedias, geographies, cosmographies, and dictionaries. These types of books were in great demand by the literate members of

Moscow society, and especially by the courtiers and the officials attached to the Department of Foreign Affairs. Books on similar subjects were obtained through the good offices of Russian ambassadors in Poland and elsewhere. Slavinetsky translated a geography book, a *Book of Medicine and Anatomy*, and some essays on politics and education called *Citizenship and the Instruction of Children's Morals*. Satanovsky translated a book entitled *On the Position of a Tsar*, and compiled and translated articles from Greek, Latin, heathen and Christian authors dealing with every known scientific subject, from theology and philosophy to zoology, minerology and medicine. Anybody who had any literary skill was called on to assist the Kievan and foreign scholars. A von Delden, who was an interpreter in the service of Muscovy, translated several books from Latin and French into Russian; and a former Austrian ambassador to Muscovy, translated a short work on cosmography.[1] Olearius stated that books dealing with similar subjects were read by many intellectually curious noblemen. Writings on these subjects were stimulated not only by an intense academic curiosity, but also by enquiries of a more practical nature. Translations of books of remedies started to circulate about this time; and a curious occurrence is mentioned in the proceedings of the Department of Foreign Affairs. In 1623 a Dutchman in the service of the state of Muscovy, called van der Hin, submitted an article to this Department on 'The Wisdom of Alchemy, and other matters'; in 1626 he submitted a further article 'On the Higher Philosophy of Alchemy'. Any information on this mysterious and seductive science was apparently of great interest in Moscow, since it was hoped that it would reveal a method of making gold. The subject matter, however, of the works translated by Slavinetsky and Satanovsky demonstrates an increasing interest in science in so far as it was accessible to the Muscovites of that period.

The acquisition of knowledge from books, and the desire for a scientific education became necessities which Moscow society wanted to satisfy; and this laid the basis for a systematic

[1] This must have been Adam Dorn, who is reputed to have translated Mercator's *Cosmography*.

educational system. As Muscovy's relations with Western European countries developed, so it became necessary to enquire into their situation and mutual relationships. Both government and private individuals tried to establish schools in Moscow. The Eastern Greek Orthodox hierarchy had told the Muscovite Tsars on numerous occasions that it was necessary to establish a Greek school and printing-press in Moscow. Although the government tried to find teachers, and some did come to Moscow from the East, the school never came into existence. This school, which had been required for such a long time, was barely finished in the reign of Tsar Michael.

In 1632 the Patriarch of Alexandria sent a monk called Joseph to Moscow. He was persuaded to stay, and entrusted with the translation into Slavonic of some Greek polemics against Latin heresies. He was also expected 'to teach young children the Greek language and letters in the hall of learning'. However, Joseph died soon after, and his work was discontinued, although neither in Moscow nor in the East was the idea abandoned that an educational establishment should be founded to serve as a study centre for the Orthodox East. Near the Patriarch's Palace, in the Chudovo Monastery, a Greek and Latin school was established under the direction of Arsenius the Greek who had arrived in Moscow in 1649. However, he was suspected of not being pure Orthodox, and banished to Solovky. In passing it should be mentioned that Slavinetsky and Satanovsky had been summoned to Moscow originally to 'teach rhetoric', but there is no evidence that they ever had any pupils. In 1665 three secretaries from the Department of Secret and Palace Affairs were ordered to learn Latin from the West Russian scholar, Simeon Polotsky.[1] A special building was constructed within the confines of the Spassky Monastery in Moscow, which was referred to in documents as 'the school for grammatical instruction'. Not one of these establishments could be called, in the modern sense of the word, a school with a set curriculum or a permanent teaching staff. They

[1] For Simeon Polotsky's role in the development and propagation of Western European influence see James H. Billington, *The Icon and the Axe* (Weidenfeld & Nicolson, 1966) pp. 146–7.

are better described as providing the odd, visiting scholar to Moscow with a temporary brief to teach Greek and Latin to young people who came of their own volition, or were sent by the government. These establishments formed the basis of the seventeenth-century Russian government schools which continued to teach reading and writing by traditional methods. Members of the clergy or special teachers accepted children as pupils in return for an agreed fee. In some parts of the country special buildings were erected by individuals or even communities, and a type of permanent public school was created. In 1658 in the town of Borovsk a 'school for the teaching of children' was built beside the municipal almshouse near the market square by the local priests. It is probable that a number of textbooks were published around the middle of the seventeenth century to meet the requirements of private and school instruction. Thus in 1648 a Slavonic grammar by a West Russian scholar, Meletius Smotritsky[1] was published in Moscow, and in 1649 Peter Mogila,[2] Rector of the Kievan Academy and later Patriarch of Kiev, had reprinted a short *Catechism*, which had been originally published in Kiev.

Individuals vied with the government in propagating enlightenment. Most of these progressives belonged to the governing class, and certainly their most enthusiastic representative was Fedor Rtishchev, Tsar Alexis' confidential adviser. He built the Andreevsky Monastery outside Moscow and in 1649, at his own expense, engaged nearly thirty learned monks from the Kiev Pechersky and other monasteries in Little Russia to translate books into Russian, and teach those who wished to read and write,

[1] The first Slavonic grammar appeared in 1596 and was written by Steven Zizanios, a White Russian. Meletius Smotritsky was the author of the second Slavonic grammar; he also wrote in 1610 a famous *Lament of the Eastern Church Against Rome*. He became Bishop of Polotsk, and finally accepted union.

[2] Peter Mogila was the most influential ecclesiastical leader in Orthodox Slavdom between 1633 and his death in 1647. His career illustrates the way in which non-Muscovite elements were beginning to control the development of the Russian Church. See Hugh F. Graham, 'Peter Mogila – Metropolitan of Kiev', *The Russian Review* (Oct 1955) pp. 345–56; and Billington, *The Icon and the Axe*, pp. 127–9.

and learn Greek, Latin, Slavonic, rhetoric, philosophy and philology. Rtishchev himself became a student at this free school, and spent whole nights in the monastery talking to the scholars from whom he learnt Greek. He asked Slavinetsky to compile a Greek–Slavonic lexicon specially for the school. Some scholarly monks and priests from Moscow joined the visiting scholars from Southern Russia. A brotherhood of learning was created in Moscow, which represented a sort of free academy. Rtishchev took advantage of his position at Court to compel a few young men in state service to go to the Andreevsky Monastery to study Greek and Latin under the Kievan scholars.

In 1667 the parishioners of the Moscow Church of St John the Divine in Kitaigorod decided to build a school next to their church. This was not to be a simple parish school, but a general educational establishment offering 'grammatical skill and Slavonic Greek, Latin, other languages, and other free studies'. A suitable petition was presented to the Tsar, as well as a request 'for an honest and virtuous man' to plead for them at Court. They asked the blessing of the Patriarch of Moscow and some Eastern Patriarchs who happened to be in Moscow to discuss the Nikon affair. Finally the Patriarch of Moscow, probably out of respect for 'the importunate prayers' of the devout Rtishchev, who had suggested this idea, agreed to give his blessing. 'May the work-loving students rejoice in their freedom to seek the free study of wisdom, and may they assemble together in a common school for the sake of the refinement of their minds through well-skilled teachers.' No evidence exists as to whether this school was ever opened.

Upper-class Muscovites tried to educate their children at home, and engaged West Russian monks, and even Poles as teachers. Tsar Alexis himself set the example. He became dissatisfied with the elementary education his eldest sons, Alexis and Fedor, were receiving from their Moscow tutor, who was an official. He gave instructions that the boys were to learn Latin and Polish, and summoned a monk, Simeon Polotsky, a West Russian scholar and teacher at the Kievan Academy who was familiar with Polish schools, to instruct them. Polotsky was a good teacher who made his subjects interesting. He set out his curriculum in verse form. Dealing with politics, he tried to impart a political sense to his royal pupils.

> It becomes the ruler of citizens to know
> How excellent a thing is citizenship.

He drew a politically ideal picture for his pupils, of the relations that should exist between a Tsar and his subjects, using the analogy of the good shepherd and his flock:

> Thus must the master
> Right sturdily his subjects' burden bear,
> Not scorning them nor treating them like dogs
> But loving them like children.

With the assistance of private tutors, interest in the Polish language, in translation from the Polish, or in original works was disseminated in the homes of Moscow boyars, and in the Palace of the Tsar of Muscovy. Tsar Alexis' eldest sons were taught Latin and Polish; and the Tsarevich Fedor even learnt the art of versification, helping Polotsky to write the Psalter in verse, and transposing two psalms. It was said that he became extremely interested in science, particularly in mathematics. Sophia, one of Tsar Alexis' daughters, also studied Polish, read Polish books, and could even write the letter u in Roman script. Lazarus Baranovich, Archbishop of Chernigorsk, stated that in his time 'the Tsar's privy Council did not scorn the Polish language but read their books and histories with delight'.

Other Muscovites tried to acquire a Western European education from primary sources, and studied so hard that it was considered a prerequisite for a successful service career. The boyar Artamon Matveev taught his son Latin and Greek, while his predecessor as head of the Department of Foreign Affairs, Ordin-Nashchokin, surrounded his son with Polish prisoners of war who inspired him with such a veneration of Western Europe that he was tempted to flee abroad. Tiapkin, the first Russian Resident in Poland, sent his son to a Polish school, and in 1675 he presented his son to the Polish king, Jan Sobieski, in Lvov, before setting off on a diplomatic mission to Moscow. The young man made a speech thanking the King 'for his bread, his salt, and his schooling'. It was delivered in the contemporary school jargon of a mixture of Polish and Latin, yet according to the father's report 'my son made his speech so clearly and figuratively that he did not hesitate over one word'. The King rewarded the young orator with a hundred pieces of gold and 15 arshin[1] of red velvet.

These then were the reasons why Muscovy first felt a need for European skills and comforts, and later for a scientific education. It began with a foreign officer, a foreign artilleryman, and ended with foreign ballet and a Latin grammar. Evoked by the urgent material requirements of state, Western European influence certainly consisted of what was needed, but there was also much which was superfluous which the Russians could have managed without, and which was premature.

[1] 1 arshin equals 28 inches.

Chapter Fourteen

★

TRADITIONAL SUSPICION and resentment towards anything emanating from the Catholic and Protestant West conflicted with the stated desire to take advantage of Western European learning. No sooner had the Muscovites started to benefit from this accretion of knowledge than they began to question the wisdom of this policy, and worry about the effect it would have on the purity of their faith and morals. Another movement developed in the seventeenth century among those who shared this attitude reflecting dissatisfaction with the state of affairs. The consequences were extremely important.

Part of a document referring to an incident in 1650 has been preserved, illustrating the origins of this anti-Western movement. There existed a group of like-minded and prominent young men in Moscow: Lucian Golosov, a future member of the State Council, Steven Alyabev, Ivan Zasetsky, and Constantine Ivanov, a lay-reader at the Cathedral of the Annunciation. They complained 'that Fedor Rtishchev was learning Greek from his Kievan scholars even though this is a subject fraught with heresy'. Steven Alyabev testified that he had wished to learn Latin from Arsenius the Greek who was then living in Moscow. When, however, Arsenius was sent to Solovky, Alyabev gave up his studies and destroyed the alphabet because Lucian Golosov, Ivan Zasetsky and his relatives urged him 'to stop learning Latin; it is stupid and that which is stupid is not worth studying'. Golosov had been invited by Rtishchev to study Latin with the Kievan scholars at the Andreevsky Monastery; but he was opposed to this subject which he believed presented a threat to the Orthodox religion, and said to Ivanov, the lay-reader: 'Tell your arch-priest (Steven Vonifatiev, the Tsar's confessor serving in the Cathedral of the Annunciation) that I do not wish to study with the Kievan scholars since they are not good men, and there is nothing good in their teaching; hitherto, I have done what Fedor Rtishchev has asked me to do from fear, but henceforth I wish to have nothing more to do with his scholars.' Lucian Golosov added 'that whosoever has studied Latin has strayed from the true path'.

At about the same time two other young men, Ozerov and Zverkalnikov, encouraged by Rtishchev, left Moscow for Kiev to complete their education. Ivanov and his friends disapproved of this endeavour, and believed that when the two young men returned to Moscow having completed their studies they would cause trouble. Ivanov and his group decided, therefore, that it would be best if the two young men were intercepted *en route* to Kiev, and brought back to Moscow. 'As it is they criticise everybody, and scoff at the pious Moscow arch-priests saying that they are idle chatterers from whom there is nothing to be learned, since they know not what, or how, to teach.' This group of religious fanatics even gossiped about Boris Morozov saying that he only kept a confessor 'for public decency', and that if he contributed to the upkeep of the Kievan scholars it was clear that he also was inclined to share their heretical beliefs.

That one section of the rising Moscow generation should accuse those of their peers who were protagonists of Western European learning of arrogance, and of being presumptuous in criticising established beliefs is revealing, in that this was no display of conservative intolerance for innovation, but an attitude deeply rooted in the ethos of the medieval Muscovite religious conscience. In Medieval Rus knowledge and art were only valued within the context of the Church, as a means towards an understanding of the word of God, and of assuring man's spiritual salvation. Knowledge, and embellishments of life outside the religious context were deemed to be superficial, and unnecessary frivolities. Story-tellers, fairy tales and buffoons all came within this category, and were tolerated in silence by the Church which looked on them as children's games or recreations. Strict Orthodox priests condemned these activities as dangerous distractions which all too easily could become the playthings of the Devil. At any rate, the Church did not consider that this type of knowledge or art had an educational value, nor did it form part of the educational system. Indeed, they were considered as belonging to a lower form of life, and if they were not actual vices, they were certainly symptomatic of man's tendency to sin.

Western European knowledge introduced into Russia was considered at a different level; not as a concession to the frailty of human nature, but as the lawful requirements of the human heart and intellect, conditions precedent for the proper realisation of a well-ordered and comfortable society. Moreover, as the arguments developed Western European knowledge was justified for itself, and not as a way of satisfying the requirements of the Church.

A Western European artist or scholar living in Russia was not regarded as a buffoon or a purveyor of heretical works but as a respected theatrical producer or geographer whom the government recognised 'as very learned in many useful skills and talents'. Western European knowledge, or in more general terms, Western European culture, came to Russia as a somewhat recalcitrant servant of the Church, to be tolerated and not condemned. The Church considered that at worst it had a rival, and at best a collaborator, in its mission to establish happiness on earth. It was inevitable that medieval Russian thinkers, circumscribed by tradition, would react through fear, and denounce this collaborator, and likely rival. And it is easy to appreciate why increasing familiarity with Western European culture should cause deep anxiety in Muscovite society which began to wonder whether their faith and morality and age-old customs were being threatened. These doubts were made explicit at the same time as the protagonists of Western European culture in Russia were Orthodox West Russian scholars. When, however, the teachers were Protestant and Catholic foreigners, the problem became far more acute, and suspicions that Western European culture and influence lacked a sound moral or religious foundation led to a serious division within the Russian Church. This division was known as the *raskol* or schism.[1] The close connection between the schism, and the moral and intellectual movement in seventeenth-century Muscovy requires an explanation of the origins of this schism within the Russian Church.

The schism in the Russian Orthodox Church occurred when a significant group of Orthodox believers broke away from the established Russian Orthodox Church. This trend developed following upon the ecclesiastical innovations introduced by the Patriarch Nikon in the reign of Tsar Alexis, and exists to this day. The *raskolniki*, the dissenters, considered themselves as much Orthodox Christians as their co-religionists. There was no difference between the Old Believers and the rest of the Orthodox community in either dogma or its teaching. The Old Believers broke away from the established Church, and ceased to recognise its authority in the name of 'the old beliefs' which they maintained had been discarded by the established Church. It is for this reason that the Old Believers were considered to be dissenters and not heretics. The Old Believers called all other Orthodox 'church-goers' or 'Nikonians', and called themselves Old Believers, or believers in the old faith following the medieval pre-Nikonian rites and devotions. But if then there was no difference in dogma or in religious teaching why did a schism develop within the Church, and why did so many god-fearing people place themselves beyond the authority of the established Orthodox Church?

Until Nikon became Patriarch, the Russian Church was a united body under one leader. Through time, and from a variety of sources, local ecclesiastical opinions, customs and rites had developed and become established, differing from those accepted by the Greek Church, from whom Russia had derived its form of Christianity. There are many examples of these deviations: making the sign of the cross with two, instead of three, fingers; writing *Isus*, instead of Jesus; serving communion with seven

[1] See Paul Miliukov, *Outlines of Russian Culture: Religion and the Church* (A. S. Barnes & Co. Inc., 1942) pp. 27–39; also Serge A. Zenkovsky, 'The Russian Church Schism: Its Background and Repercussions', *Russian Review* (Oct 1957) pp. 37–58; Frederick C. Conybeare, *Russian Dissenters* (Harvard U.P., 1921) pp. 13–77.

instead of five, wafers; or moving in procession from left to right while facing the altar according to the movement of the sun (*posolon*), which occurred during baptisms when processions moved around the font, or during weddings when it moved around the lectern. Sometimes even special emphasis was placed on words symbolic of the faith: 'there is *no* end to His rule', or 'in the Holy Ghost, *true*, and giver of life', and *Alleluias* were repeated twice. The Church Council of 1551 had formally approved some of these rites and rituals, which thereby received the legal approbation of the supreme ecclesiastical authorities.

With the introduction of printing presses in Moscow during the second half of the sixteenth century these rites and textual variations were incorporated into printed editions of the divine service adapted from manuscripts, and subsequently distributed throughout Russia. In this way the printing press changed the significance of local ceremonial and textual variations, and extended their use. Further textual amendments were introduced by the revisionists of liturgical works which were printed while Joseph was Patriarch between 1642 and 1652.[1] Since, in fact, most Russian liturgical works remained unamended, Joseph's successor, Nikon attempted, from the very beginning of his ecclesiastical rule, to remove existing inaccuracies. At the Church Council of 1654 Nikon ordained that all Church books were to be reprinted in accordance with the true texts which were to be found in old Slavonic parchments and medieval Greek books. Piles of old Greek and Church Slavonic manuscripts were brought to Moscow from the Orthodox East, and from different parts of Russia. New and corrected editions were sent throughout the country to the churches with instructions that all old, uncorrected printed or manuscript versions were to be removed and destroyed.

Orthodox Russians were appalled by the revised editions which contained no reference to the sign of the cross being made with two fingers, misspelled *Isus*, and ignored age-old hallowed rites and texts. They believed that the new writings had created

[1] During the last seven years of Joseph's patriarchate nearly eight printings of the Book of Hours and nine of the Psalter were turned out by the patriarchal printing press, which was the only one in Moscow.

a new faith which the Holy Fathers had never blessed, and which were, therefore, heretical; as a result, they continued to conduct their services and perform their rites according to the older manuals. The Church Council of 1666–7, which was attended by two Eastern Patriarchs, anathematised and excommunicated all who opposed the authority of the Church. The excommunicated for their part refused to recognise the authority of the established Church, and henceforward there was to be a schism within the Russian religious community.

Why did the schism occur? The Old Believers explained that in correcting the service books, Nikon had of his own volition abolished the two-fingered sign of the cross and other rites embodied in the ancient Orthodox traditions, and that redemption was therefore impossible; and that when the fundamentalists defended the old traditions the Church hierarchy excommunicated them from their tainted Church. This explanation, however, is not satisfactory. How was it that the two-fingered sign of the cross or processionals moving in the same direction as the sun had become sanctified traditions for the Old Believers without whose observance there could be no redemption? How could a simple Church custom, a religious rite or text acquire such importance as to become inviolable? The explanations offered by the Orthodox were more profound. They believed that the schism occurred as a result of the ignorance of the dissenters, from their narrow concepts of Christianity and from their inability to distinguish between what was fundamental and what was trivial in their religion, or between content and ritual. Nor is this explanation entirely satisfactory. Assume that certain rites hallowed by tradition or antiquity could acquire the inappropriate characteristics and importance of dogma; yet the authority of the Church hierarchy was sanctified by antiquity which was universal; the recognition of which was necessary if men were to be saved. There could be no salvation for the Holy Fathers unless they recognised the authority of the Church Hierarchy, but whether the sign of the cross was made with two or three fingers was irrelevant, so far as salvation was concerned. How then could the Old Believers sacrifice one ecclesiastical establishment for another, and seek salvation without the guidance of the established, legal hierarchy whom they had rejected?

Explanations of the origin of the schism usually emphasise and criticise the Old Believers' blind attachment to ritual and texts, and to the literal meaning of the Holy Scriptures as if they were without religious significance. The author does not share this contempt for religious rites and texts, and recognises that not being a theologian it is not his place to attempt a theological explanation. However, the daily observance of ritual and use of texts have both a theological and a general historical significance: it is the historical significance of the origin of schism which must now be discussed.

Religious rites and texts express the essence or the substance of religious doctrine. Doctrine consists of two elements. First, there are *truths* which establish a believer's outlook on life and solve for him the problem of creation. Second, there are *exigencies* which govern the moral behaviour of a believer and point out the problems of daily life. *Truths* and *exigencies* in this context have nothing to do with logic, and are not susceptible to rational understanding; and both involve an act of faith. Religious truths which are susceptible of being understood are called dogmas; while religious exigencies governing behaviour are called commandments. How then can either be assimilated by men when neither logic nor free will are involved?

They can only be assimilated through religious perception, religious thinking and religious education. There is no need to be bewildered by these words: religious thinking or religious perception go through the same intuitive processes as artistic creations which have nothing to do either with logic or reason, but both are concerned with metaphysics. Not everything can be explained by logic, and it may well be that man is only capable of understanding a small part of that which is comprehensible. In assimilating dogma and commandments a believer adopts certain religious ideas and morals which have as little to do with logic as artistic ideas. It is these religious ideas and moral attitudes which are the basis of religious belief.

Religious education was provided through certain activities

of the Church which culminated in the divine service. Dogma and commandments found their expression in Holy Writ, while the activities of the Church were emphasised through the performance of ritual. However, ritual is only the external expression of a religious doctrine and does not form the philosophic basis of that doctrine. Both artistic and religious appreciation differ from logic and mathematics in that the inner meaning is inseparably linked to the external form which gives it expression; whereas a logically developed idea or a mathematically proven theorem can be understood whether expressed in narrative form or symbolically.

Religious and aesthetic feelings function otherwise: by definition, there exists a psychological empathy with a text, a ritual, a form, a rhythm or a sound. An individual who cannot recall the painting or tune which evoked a certain mood, will be unable to recall that mood. A poem transposed into prose loses its charm. Holy writ and ritual evolved historically, and are neither invariable nor inviolable. Although it is possible to envisage more effective sacred writings and ritual than those which give a believer his religious fervour, none the less they would not serve to deflect man from his wrongdoing. When an Orthodox Russian priest intones before the altar 'Lift up your hearts' the Orthodox congregation experience their customary spiritual uplift which helps them to put aside their daily cares. If, however, the same priest were to intone the words of a Catholic priest 'Sursum corda' an Orthodox congregation would derive no spiritual uplift simply because they were unfamiliar with the words, even though they knew that it had the same meaning in Latin, albeit expressed differently. *Thus, the religious attitudes and dispositions of every society are inextricably involved with the religious writings and ritual in which it has been educated.*

Possibly, however, the interrelationship between doctrine, ritual and form arises from a mistaken approach to religious education. Is it therefore conceivable that a believer could dispense with cumbersome ritual, and that he should be encouraged to so do? Indeed, in time ritual may become superfluous, and man will free himself from external influences and the need for them, and be able to pray 'in spirit and in truth'. At such a time religious psychology will have completely altered and all semblance to the practices hitherto taught by all known religions will have disappeared. But from time immemorial man has not found it possible to dispense with ritual, whether in religion or in morality. It is important to distinguish between the unconscious and the conscious striving for virtue. An individual engages his whole intellect in his attempt to achieve virtue. Yet this calculated effort is not enough to make virtue the arbiter of either human affairs or the lives of entire communities. It becomes necessary to envelop virtue in forms, in rituals, and in complete systems which are all-pervading, and which introduce order into man's thoughts, direct his senses, and act as a counterbalance to his crude desires. In this way a desire for virtue would become a constant moral necessity. Much that has served to inspire the spirit of man and could have enriched the lives of whole communities has left no trace, and has therefore been unavailable to historical investigation! As with religion so with everything else.

Appreciation of a beautiful melody differs completely from the appreciation that would be evoked by the schematic form called forth from the artistic imagination of the composer. He has to work on it, transpose it for an instrument or orchestra, repeat it in harmonies and variations, and perform it before an audience. A listener's slightest pleasure is shared by his neighbours; these small, personal delights create one general impression which is carried away by each member of the audience, and helps the individual to withstand the adversities and drudgeries of daily life.

Those who heard Christ's Sermon on the Mount died a long time ago taking with them the impressions experienced by them. However, this impression can in some measure be shared today because the text of the Sermon has been embodied in the framework of the divine service. A rite or text is like a gramophone record which captures a moment of moral ecstasy, inducing good deeds and feelings in people. These people died a long time ago, and the identical moment has never been repeated; but it has been preserved for eternity in the rite or text, and with their assistance it can be reproduced, and, depending upon one's moral sensibilities, its effect can be experienced.

Through a progression of shocks, quarrels, wars and bloodshed the social life of mankind has taken shape formed by rites, habits, conventions and relationships, moulding thoughts and feelings, which improved the quality of life, and gave the people their ideals. It is impossible to know what man will be like in a thousand years; but strip contemporary man of his inherited rites, customs and conventions, and he will forget everything, and have to start again from the beginning.

If the religious outlook of every Church is such that it cannot dispense with ritual and texts why then has no other country experienced such clamour and schism as occurred in seventeenth-century Russia? An exposé of certain events which occurred within the Russian Church during the seventeenth century will help to provide some of the answers.

Until the fifteenth century, the Russian Church had been subservient to Byzantium, her Metropolitan See.[1] From Byzantium came Russia's metropolitans, bishops, canon law and ceremonial. For many centuries the authority of the Greek Orthodox Church had been undisputed, but from the fifteenth century the situation changed. The Grand Princes of Moscow, increasingly aware of their own national importance, were not slow to question their relationship to the Church and did not wish to be dependent upon a foreign power, whether represented by an Emperor or by a Patriarch in Constantinople. Restricting their choice to the Russian clergy, they began to appoint and ordain Metropolitans of all Russia from Moscow. This change in procedure was effected quite easily because the Greek hierarchy was not held in high esteem in Russia. Whereas medieval Russia had a high regard for the authority of the Greek Church and the

[1] Until the Council of Florence in 1439 the Metropolitan of Moscow was nominated by the Patriarch of Constantinople. In 1449 Russian Bishops elected Metropolitan Jonas. Constantinople was informed of the election but was not requested to confirm it. Byzantium accepted the *fait accompli* without protest. For recent studies of the Council of Florence, and in particular its consequences for the Slavic East, see Joseph Gill, *The Council of Florence* (Cambridge, 1959); Oscar Haleck, *From Florence to Brest* (1439-1596) (Rome, 1958); Gustave Alef, 'Muscovy and the Council of Florence', *Slavic Review*, (Oct 1961) pp. 389-401.

sanctity of Byzantium, a Greek and a cheat had always been considered to be synonymous. A twelfth-century Russian chronicler commenting on a Greek Bishop said: 'He was smooth-tongued because he was a Greek.'

This opinion had been formed early, and for a simple reason. The dissemination of Christianity throughout a distant and barbarian metropolitan see of the Constantinople patriarchate was carried out by inferior members of the Greek hierarchy. Estranged from their flock by differences in language, ideas, and official ceremonial, they are unable to exercise any pastoral influence and contented themselves with creating visual splendour, cultivating the fervour of devout princes, and assiduously sending Russian money to their homeland. The latter practice was referred to by a notable eighteenth-century Russian archbishop of Novgorod in his pastoral address to the clergy in his diocese. Moreover, ordinary Greeks followed closely behind the Greek Orthodox hierarchs hoping to profit from the newly converted Russians. The acceptance of union between the Catholic and Orthodox Churches agreed at the Council of Florence in 1439 did the Greek hierarchy irreparable damage in Russia.

Russia had had utmost faith in the Byzantine struggle against the Latins; but the Byzantine hierarchs had given in to the Pope in Rome, betrayed Eastern Orthodoxy which had been propagated by the Apostles and confirmed by the Holy Fathers and seven oecumenical councils. Had the Grand Prince of Moscow Vasili not exposed the crafty enemy, the Devil's son, the Greek metropolitan Isidore, who had committed Russia to Union, then this prelate would have Latinised the Russian Church and destroyed the pure faith brought to Russia by the Holy Prince Vladimir.[1]

In 1453 Constantinople fell to the Turks; even before this the Russians had despised the Greeks, and been suspicious of them.

[1] It has been suggested that the consecration of a native Metropolitan in Moscow was a consequence of severe secular pressures resulting from a local crisis. Ibid. pp. 394–9; Michael Cherniavsky, 'The Reception of the Council of Florence in Moscow', *Church History*, XXIV (1955) pp. 347–59; A. M. Ammann, *Abriss der ostslawischen Kirchengeschichte* (Vienna, 1950) pp. 145–6.

Russia believed that the capture of Constantinople by the pagan Turks meant the inevitable collapse of Greek Orthodoxy. There is a remarkable self-assurance in the way the Russian metropolitan Philip I explains the connection between different contemporary events. In 1471 Philip wrote to Novgorod, which was about to rebel against Moscow:[1] 'And think on this, my children, Constantinople stood firm so long as faith shone upon it like the sun; but as soon as it forsook the truth and united with the Latins, it fell into pagan hands.' He goes on to say that for the Russians the light of the Orthodox East had been extinguished; and as the first Rome had fallen from heresy and pride, so now the second Rome, Constantinople, had fallen through inconsistency and the attacks of the pagan eaters of raw meat.

These events exerted a serious, though not disastrous, impression on Russia; the ancient light of the Church had been extinguished, and the Greek faith was under a dark cloud. Orthodox Russia felt that she was all alone in the world. Events in the world had forced her into opposition to Byzantium. Moscow threw off the Agar Yoke[2] almost at the same time as Byzantium was harnessing it around her neck.

If other empires had fallen as a result of their betrayal of the Orthodox faith, Moscow would stand firm, and remain constant. Moscow was the third and last Rome, the final and only refuge of the true faith in the world. These thoughts enlarged the historical horizon of medieval sixteenth-century Russian thinkers, and caused them to worry about Russia's fate. It seemed to them that their country had acquired a new and great significance.

A Russian monk called Philotheus wrote the following in a

[1] The Novgorodians were, in fact, considering recognising the suzerainty of the King of Poland and Grand Duke of Lithuania. Metropolitan Philip, in this epistle to the Novgorodians, was advancing the argument that people should recognise as a power established by God that which had been so recognised by their ancestors, in this case the dynasty of Rurik which was now ruling Moscow. See S. V. Utechin, *Russian Political Thought* (Praeger, New York, 1963) p. 19.

[2] This is a biblical term meaning the Turks; it was the expression used by Philotheus of the Eleazer Monastery in Pskov in a letter to Vasili III.

letter to Vasili III, father of Ivan the Terrible:[1] 'Hear me, pious Tsar. Two Romes have fallen, a third – Moscow – stands, a fourth there shall not be. The Universal Church stands alone in your powerful State, and shines under the heavens more brightly than the sun; all Christian Kingdoms have come together into your Kingdom; in all the universe only you are a Christian Tsar.'[2] Sixteenth-century Russian writers wrote: 'The Orthodox faith in Byzantium fell victim to the Mahommedan charm of the pagan Turks, while in Russia it was illuminated by the teachings of the Holy Fathers.' Ideas like these were believed by educated medieval society, and even penetrated the masses, giving rise to a series of legends dealing with the escapes of saints with holy relics from both fallen Romes to the new, third Rome in the state of Muscovy. This was how stories originated during the fifteenth and sixteenth

[1] Philotheus probably first propounded this famous image to Ivan III, although the earliest surviving statement is contained in his letter to Vasili III, of 1511. For the dating of Philotheus' letter see N. Andreyev, 'Filofey and his Epistle to Ivan Vasilyevich', *Slavonic and East European Review*, xxviii (Dec 1959) pp. 1–31; also Dimitri Stremooukhoff, 'Moscow, the Third Rome: Sources of the Doctrine', *Speculum*, vol. 28, no. 1 (Jan 1953) pp. 84–101.

[2] The relevant part of this letter reads:

As it is from the supreme and the all-powerful, the all-supporting right hand of God, that tsars reign, and that the great are glorified and the mighty administer justice – so to thee, most serene and supreme sovereign and grand prince, Orthodox Christian tsar and lord of all, ruler of God's holy thrones, is the holy, oecumenical and apostolic church . . . which has shone through in the place of those of Rome and Constantinople. For the church of ancient Rome was destroyed through the apostasy of the Apollindrian heresy; and the doors of the church of the second Rome, the city of Constantinople, were cut asunder by the battle axes of Hagar's posterity. But the holy, apostolic church of the oecumenical councils, of this third new Rome of thy sovereign power, which extends to the ends of the earth in the Orthodox Christian faith, shines everywhere under the heavens more brightly than the sun. And may thy dominion realise O pious tsar, that all the empires of the Orthodox Christian faith have come together into thy sole empire: thou alone in all the earth art tsar to the Christians . . . Observe and take heed, O pious tsar, that all Christian empires came together into thine alone, that two Romes fell, but the third stands, and there will be no fourth for thy Christian empire 'shall not be left to other people' (quoting Daniel, 2: 44).

See Thornton Anderson, *Russian Political Thought* (Cornell U.P., 1967) pp. 72–3.

centuries about St Anthony the Roman who was purported to have sailed across the sea to Novgorod in a stone bringing with him sacred objects, or about the miraculous transmigration from the Byzantine East to Russia of the miracle-working ikon of Tikhvin of the Blessed Mother. National Russian self-confidence was bolstered even further by the number of people who fled from the shattered Orthodox East seeking mercy and asylum in Russia. Jeremiah, Patriarch of Constantinople, came to Russia in the reign of Tsar Fedor for this reason.[1]

In 1589 Jeremiah had consecrated the Metropolitan of Moscow, Job, in the rank of Patriarch of all Russia which finally confirmed the *de facto* separation between the Russian Church and the Constantinople Patriarchy.[2] The similarity between Jeremiah's statement on the establishment of a Patriarchate in Moscow and Philotheus' ideas is so striking that it seemed as if Jeremiah knew what was closest to the hearts of the Russian people of the sixteenth century. Addressing the Muscovite Tsar he said: 'In truth, the Holy Spirit reigns in you, and this idea has been inspired in you by God, ancient Rome fell through heresy; the second Rome, Constantinople, was overrun by the descendants of Agar, the pagan Turks; your mighty Russian kingdom, the third Rome, has surpassed all in piety; you alone in all the world carry the name of Christian Tsar.'

These events and impressions affected the Russian religious community in a variety of ways. At the beginning of the seventeenth century the religious community was permeated with religious self-assurance, which was, however, nourished not by the religious successes of Orthodox Russia, but by its political successes, and the political reverses of the Orthodox East. The basis for this self-confidence was the idea that Orthodox Russia

[1] Boris Godunov, ever suspicious, would not allow Jeremiah to remain permanently in Moscow, and offered him Vladimir, the old capital. When Jeremiah refused this provincial exile, he was asked, or perhaps demanded that he create a new patriarchate. See Thornton Anderson, *Russian Politica Thought*, p. 97.

[2] During the ceremony, the crozier was handed to Job by Tsar Fedor and not by Jeremiah, an action symbolic of the secular supremacy prevalent in Moscow.

alone enjoyed and retained the Christian truth which was purely Orthodox. This idea, together with certain re-arrangements in their own concepts of nationalism, led the Russians to conclude that the Christianity practised in their own country was the only true Christianity in the world, regional variations not withstanding; and that no other pure Orthodoxy existed nor could exist. However, Russian dogma states that Christian truth is not the prerogative of any local church, but of the universal Church which transcends time and space, and is shared by all Orthodox at any time and in any place. No sooner had the Russian Church recognised that it alone was the guardian of the true faith than it began to measure Christian truth from its own religious standpoint. In other words, the Russian Church propagated the idea that a universal Church could be contained within the geographical delineation of a local Church, and also that a universal Christian belief could be enclosed within the narrow horizon of a people of a given place and at a particular time.

Christian dogma is vested in certain forms, and is expressed through ritual for easier comprehension; it is formulated in texts so that it can be studied, and is given effect through canonical rules. Textual understanding, and obedience to canonical rules are extended and perfected following an increase in religious awareness and its dynamic, which is reason reinforced by faith. Ritual, texts, and rules help to penetrate the mysteries of dogma, elucidating and guiding. But none of them form the essence of dogma. However, by the very nature of religious understanding and education, there is close connection between them and the dogma of every religious community so that they become part of the religious *Weltanschauung* and feeling which is not easily separable from the content which they express.

Members of a religious community who diverge or deviate from accepted religious dogma can be corrected because of the existence of the religious concept of a universal Church which has the authority to rectify any purely local digressions. However, this authority Orthodox Russia negated as soon as it arrogated to itself the belief that it was the sole repository of Christian truth. Having asserted the view that it was the universal Church,

Orthodox Russia could no longer permit any external control of its dogma and ritual. Having argued the case thus far Russian Orthodox believers drew certain conclusions in which they believed implicitly. First, that the local Russian Church was the recognised master of the entire Christian universe. Second, that the Russian Church had consecrated within it all that was necessary for the redemption of the faithful and that there was nothing more to be learned or adopted from anywhere else in matters of faith. Third, its only obligation was carefully to preserve the treasure it had inherited.

In this way ancient Russian Church customs replaced the concepts of the universal Church as the standard of Christian truth. It was the Russian Church which stated that the right way to pray and to believe was the way their fathers and forefathers had prayed and believed; that grandsons had to preserve ancestral traditions without questioning them. But these traditions, themselves a progression in understanding, were now fixed immutably; acceptance of these traditions meant rejecting any further developments in religious understanding, and any possible way of correcting mistakes and shortcomings. From this moment in time it was inevitable that instead of continuing to elucidate the mysteries of Christian dogma, and creating a truer, fuller and more vital universal religious feeling, the Russian Church would try to preserve the fund of existing local religious knowledge and local ritual and preserve them from impure external change or contact.

Important consequences followed from this religious attitude and mentality, and both were interwoven into the origin of the schism. First, Church ritual, developed from ancient local traditions, acquired the characteristic of inviolable and unalterable sanctity. Second, Russian society became suspicious and supercilious in dealing with any intellectual and scientific approach to religion. The Russians maintained that this knowledge, which had flourished in other Christian societies, had not saved them from heresy; reason had not prevented the extinction of belief. Moreover, they vaguely remembered that the seeds of knowledge had originally been sown in Graeco-Roman countries, and the

Russians reasoned, with distaste, that this knowledge was still being nourished by the impure springs of contaminated ground. The medieval Russian was filled with fear and disgust when he considered the rhetoric and philosophy of Greece: the result of a sinful mind left to its own devices.

A medieval Russian sermon has it that 'any man who likes geometry is impious in the eyes of God; it is a spiritual sin to study astronomy and Greek books; a believer is easily led astray by his reasoning; love simplicity more than wisdom, do not seek that which is above you, do not attempt what is deeper than you; cherish knowledge which is given to you by God'.

Another text states: 'Brothers, do not be high-minded. If you are asked whether you know philosophy, reply: I have not run with the swiftness of the Greeks, I have not read the rhetoric of astronomers, I do not frequent with wise philosophers, but have averted my eyes from philosophy. I study the books of the heavenly law, so that I may purify my sinful soul.' This attitude was nourished by pride in their ignorance. 'I am not learned in words or in reason,' wrote a medieval scribe about himself, 'nor am I learned in dialectic, rhetoric or philosophy but I have the reason of Christ within me.' In this way the medieval Russian Church lost the means, and even the incentive, for self-correction.

The seventeenth-century Russian religious community held firmly to the opinions and outlook mentioned above, and however naïve they might have been, these opinions were shared by both the masses and most of the clergy, whether black or white. The leading members of the church hierarchy were not quite so unsophisticated, although even they held similar opinions. Visiting Greek archbishops, and even patriarchs, were carefully watched during services at which they officiated, and Russian 'dignitaries' would, with magnanimous condescension, draw attention to any variations from the accepted ceremony performed in Moscow: 'this ritual is not practised here', or 'our true Christian Orthodox Church has not accepted this order of service'. Convinced of the superiority of Russian ritual over Greek ritual, and content withal, the Russian prelates were quite disinterested in the effect that interruptions of the service might have on the congregation.

There was nothing unusual in the Russians being attached to the ritual in which they had been brought up, which was after all natural and historically inevitable; in no circumstances could this attachment be considered a chronic or organic defect in the Russian religion. It was merely indicative of the maturity of the people.

The chronic ailment of the medieval religious Russian community was the certainty with which it believed that the Russian Orthodox was the only true religion in the world, that its conception of God was the only right one, that the creator of the universe was identified with their own Russian God who belonged only to them, and was unknown elsewhere, and that the Russian Church had replaced the Universal Church. Complacent and content with their tenets, the Russians regarded their own purely national ceremonies as sacrosanct and inviolable, and their own religious view as the norm, and their knowledge of God as the true knowledge. Moreover, fanaticism increased as their attitudes came into direct conflict with stated government policies.

Mention has already been made of the political and economic measures which the new dynasty introduced, as for instance, those affecting the national economy and defence. Realising the extent to which technical innovation was needed inside the country, the government invited foreigners, who were either Calvinists or Lutherans to come to Russia. They were invited to train soldiers, cast cannon, and build factories; these skills had little connection with morality, and even less with popular religious opinions. However, the medieval Russian with his rigid and literal mentality was unable to distinguish between the essential and the peripheral aspects of practical situations. If a German commanded and instructed Russian soldiers the medieval Russian believed it followed inevitably that the soldiers would have to dress and shave their beards in the German style, adopt the German faith, smoke tobacco, drink milk on Wednesdays and Fridays, and abandon their own religion. The Russian conscience began to waver between native traditions and those of the German suburb!

These considerations caused the seventeenth-century Russians exceptional anxiety, and their suspicions were revealed on all occasions. In 1648, for instance, when the young Tsar Alexis was about to marry, there were rumours in Moscow that old customs were going to be abolished, and new, foreign customs introduced. Given such a mentality any attempt to alter Church ritual and the texts of sacred books might well have appeared to a confused and frightened believer as an attack upon his religion. As it happened, the dignitary who undertook these emendations was the one man, who by his very nature, was capable of bringing these issues to a climax.

Nikon, who became Patriarch in 1652, played an important part in the origin of the schism. He was born in 1605 of peasant stock, and because he could read and write, he became a village priest. However, shortly after, he became a monk and submitted himself to an ascetic hermit-like existence in Northern Monasteries. He had a powerful personality and won Tsar Alexis' complete confidence. In 1649 he was appointed Metropolitan of Novgorod. In 1652, when he was forty-seven, Nikon became Patriarch of All Russia. He was by far and away the most powerful and remarkable Russian of the seventeenth century. Difficult and complex, he had a volatile temper, and was normally awkward, temperamental, quick-tempered and ambitious; above all he was proud. However, these were not his fundamental characteristics. He was capable of exerting a strong moral influence, not generally the attribute of a proud man. His opponents considered him to be cruel and callous, although, in fact, disagreements upset him, and he was always prepared to forgive his enemies if he thought they would come half way to meet him. It is true that he was brutal to those who consistently opposed him; however, human suffering and tears invariably affected him deeply so that he became magnanimous with his erstwhile enemies. Nikon believed that charity, helping the weak and the sick were not so much attributes of his pastoral duties but the instinctive inclinations of a good nature. His intellect and moral strength made him a great man of action, a man who wanted, and was capable of doing, great things – but only great things.

What was ordinary and commonplace he did atrociously; on the other hand, he wanted and was prepared to undertake what nobody else would do. Nikon displayed rare courage and self-possession when he risked his life to argue with the Novgorod rebels in 1650, as well as during the Moscow plague of 1654 when, in the Tsar's absence, he helped the imperial family to escape from the infection.[1] However, he would lose his temper and all sense of proportion when dealing with trivia. When difficulties arose, often self-created, demanding his undivided attention, he would concentrate on unimportant side-issues, and make a big issue of them.

Sentenced and exiled to the Ferapontov Monastery, Nikon still received gifts from the Tsar. On one occasion Tsar Alexis sent him some excellent fish; Nikon however was offended, and reproached the Tsar for not having sent fruit, grapes in syrup and apples. When he was in a good mood, Nikon was resourceful and ingenious; but when he was offended or irritable he became tactless and would mistake figments of his embittered imagination for reality. In exile he cured the sick, and unable to resist taunting the Tsar with his powers of healing would send Alexis a list of those he had cured.[2] On one occasion he informed the Tsar's envoy that he should tell the Tsar that 'in exchange for having taken away my Patriarch I send him a medicine glass with the words "Heal the sick" '.

Stoically able to bear terrible pain, Nikon was quite unnerved by the trivial effect of a pin-prick. In common with many powerful personalities, and unlike ordinary people, he was bored by peace and quiet, and was incapable of biding his time. Nikon required the stimulus of a grandiose scheme or idea, or even a quarrel with a protagonist. He was like a sail which comes into its own in a high wind, but which in a calm hangs limply against the mast.

[1] Plague outbreaks during the reign of Tsar Alexis produced the first generalised quarantine regulations and the means to enforce them. See Roderick E. McGrew, *Russia and the Cholera 1823–32* (Wisconsin U.P., 1965) p. 26.

[2] During the last years of his life Nikon is said to have cured one hundred and thirty-two people in one three-year period. See James H. Billington, *The Icon and the Axe* (Weidenfeld & Nicolson, 1966) p. 158.

Chapter Fifteen

★

NIKON BECAME Patriarch of the Russian Church while he was in the prime of life, and with his energies unimpaired.[1] He became involved in a maelstrom of conflicting aspirations, political projects, ecclesiastical misunderstandings, and court intrigues. The country was ready to go to war with Poland to settle accounts which had been outstanding since the Time of Troubles, and to protect Western Russia from the Catholic onslaught which was about to be launched under the Polish banner. In order to win the war the Russians needed the military skills and industrial expertise which had been developed by the Protestants. As a result, the Russian Church was faced with two problems. On the one hand it had to encourage the Tsar's government in its struggle against Catholics, and on the other it had to prevent Protestants from exerting too great an influence over the government. The Church emerged from a period of stagnation and forced itself to act. In its preparation for war the Church took its own precautions, hurriedly putting its affairs in order, purifying itself, rallying its forces, and examining its own defects. It issued strict injunctions against superstition, heathen customs, unseemly behaviour during religious festivals, fist-fights, gaming, drunkenness, ignorance, and liturgical irregularities by the clergy. Furthermore the Church hastily attempted to suppress the arguments which had raged round the wealth it had accumulated over six-and-a-

[1] A detailed account of Nikon's career can be found in W. K. Medlin, *Moscow and East Rome* (Geneva, 1952) pp. 152–210.

half centuries.[1] Moreover, it began to look for allies. If the state need foreign craftsmen, so the Church felt a need for Greek or Kievan scholars. Indeed, its relations with the Greeks were improving; whereas previously the Greeks had been mistrusted, and their beliefs had been suspect, Moscow now recognised that they were strictly Orthodox. Contacts with the Eastern Hierarchy increased, and Eastern prelates began to visit Moscow with petitions and suggestions; and the Muscovite prelates began increasingly to turn to the Eastern dignitaries to resolve their own religious doubts. The Russian autocephalous Church began to treat the Church in Constantinople with the respect due to its former metropolitan see. The opinions of the Eastern Patriarchate were accepted as the dicta of the Universal Church, and no important ecclesiastical problem was resolved without their agreement. The Greeks met the Russians half-way. While Moscow sought enlightenment from the Greek East, the Eastern Orthodox Church suggested that this enlightenment should emanate from Moscow which would become the spiritual centre of the Orthodox world; they also suggested that the Russians should establish a superior seminary for the clergy in Moscow, as well as a Greek printing press. Confidence in the Kievan scholars and their work was increasing, although it was easier to assemble their ecclesiastics together than to make them work in unity and harmony. The Kievan academicians and Greek scholars were arrogant guests who despised their host's ignorance. Protagonists of Western European culture, such as Morozov and Rtishchev who valued foreigners as master-craftsmen, looked on the Kievans and Greeks as religious teachers. Together with Steven Vonifatiev, the Tsar's confessor, they had helped Nikon's predecessor, Patriarch Joseph, also a reformer, to agitate for schools and the translation and publication of educational books. In an attempt to raise the intellectual and moral standards of the people, Steven Vonifatiev had summoned a number of popular preachers from all over Russia: Ivan Neronov from Nizhni-Novgorod, Daniel from Kostroma, Loggin from the Murom, Avvakum

[1] For an analysis of the wealth of the church see Jerome Blum, *Lord and Peasant in Russia* (Princeton U.P., 1961) pp. 188–98.

from Yurievets on the Volga, and Lazarus from Romanov-Borisoglebsk. Nikon was also one of this group, although as yet he was silent, content to observe his colleagues, who were to be his future enemies.

Because of his scientific interests, Rtishchev was eventually suspected of heresy; and Steven Vonifatiev, to all appearances a benign and pacific adviser to the Tsar, during the first clashes of interest berated the Patriarch and the entire Holy Council in the Tsar's presence, calling them wolves and destroyers; and he went on to declare that there was nothing holy in Muscovy or in her Church. Whereupon the Patriarch demanded that, in accordance with an article in the *Ulozhenie* the Tsar should sentence Vonifatiev to death for having maligned the Holy Council and the Apostolic Church. Finally, even Vonifatiev's followers ceased to obey him, spoke to him 'harshly and rudely', cursing him to his face, and with fanatical abandon, in the name of their common Russian God, turned on the Patriarch and all the reformers with their new books, new ideas, new systems and teachers; and in so doing they did not distinguish between Germans, Greeks or Kievans!

Steven Vonifatiev was quite correct in saying that no Holy Church existed in Muscovy if by Church he meant a disciplined hierarchy and liturgy. For within the Church there was total disorder and licence. The pious, churchgoing Russian congregation became bored with standing for so long in church; in order to accommodate them, the clergy voluntarily introduced an accelerated order of service during which there was a simultaneous reading and singing in two or three parts. A cantor intoned the canticles, a deacon recited the *ektenia*[1] and a priest uttered the responses, so that everything became quite incomprehensible. The only concession made was that the songs and the readings had to come from the Liturgy.

The Stoglav Council had forbidden polyphonic singing, but its strictures were ignored even though the disobedient clergy could

[1] The *ektenia* resembles the Litany in the number of petitions which are given out by the deacon, while the congregation make short responses after each, crossing themselves and bowing towards the sanctuary in token of concurrence.

have been disciplined and punished. In 1649 the Tsar ordered the Patriarch to convene a Church Council to consider this matter; but because both clergy and laity protested, the Council sanctioned these irregularities. In 1651 dissatisfaction among those who believed in the orderly conduct of church services forced a new Council to reverse the previous decision. The senior clergy were afraid of their own congregations and their own subordinates; the congregations had no respect for their pastors who were inconsistent and easily influenced and were quite unable to divorce themselves from government action.

Nikon's spiritual determination to evolve and retain a clear picture of his idea of a Universal Church, and the relationship between it and the Russian local Church, until he reached the Patriarch's throne might have merited admiration. Unfortunately, his ideas were unrealistic. He became head of the Russian Church firmly resolved to restore complete harmony between it and the Greek Church, and to abolish the existing ritualistic distinctions. Numerous suggestions were made to convince him that complete harmony was necessary. Eastern prelates, who increasingly visited Moscow during the seventeenth century, pointed out to the Russian clerics that the ritualistic differences were local innovations which must end by destroying any harmony between the two Orthodox Churches.

Immediately before Nikon's elevation to the Patriarchal throne an event took place which proved this point. Monks representing all Greek monasteries met in Council at Mount Athos and decided that the sign of the cross made with two fingers was heretical; they burned the Muscovite service books which promulgated this rite and even wanted to burn the brother in whose possession these books were found. It is not difficult to imagine the personal motives which led Nikon actively to pursue a policy of consolidation between the Russian and the Eastern Churches, between the Russian Patriarchate and the Patriarchate of the Universal Church. He realised that the weak, reforming efforts initiated by Patriarch Joseph and his colleagues would not be able to alter the desolate situation of the Russian Church. He had seen for himself what a pitiful cipher the Patriarch of all Rus could become at Court, and he knew from his own experience how easily a persistent man could influence a young Tsar. Excessively conceited, he could not bear to think of himself, Patriarch Nikon, as a toy in the hands of a clever Royal confessor, as his Patriarchal predecessor had been, who, towards the end of his tenure, had daily awaited his dismissal.

Nikon no doubt felt somewhat isolated on his high apostolic throne in Moscow, and he turned towards the Universal Church in the East for support, and to his fellow Patriarchs in the East for a closer union. The authority of the Universal Church still frightened the piously timid but arrogant Muscovites. Evincing an excess of zeal, as was his custom, he was determined to take his ideas to their logical conclusion. Ignoring his birthplace near Nizhni-Novgorod, he wanted to force himself to become a Greek. At the Church Council of 1655, he explained that although he was a Russian and the son of a Russian, his *faith* and convictions were those of a Greek. In the same year after a solemn service in the Usspensky Cathedral he publicly divested himself of his Russian cassock, and put on a Greek one.[1] Nobody smiled; the congregation muttered loudly at this challenge to their faith, since they believed that in the Russian Church everything had been bequeathed by the Apostles and inspired by the Holy Ghost. Nikon even wished to eat Greek dishes, and in 1658 the Archimandrite of a Greek Monastery in Nikovskaya Street together with his cellarer, 'prepared a banquet for my lord Patriarch in the Greek fashion'; for this they received a *poltina* (seven roubles in nineteenth-century currency).

Supported by authorities which were beyond Muscovy, Nikon was not satisfied with being simply the Patriarch of Moscow and all Rus. He wanted to be one of the Universal Patriarchs and act independently. He wanted to give real meaning to the title of 'Great Lord', which he carried in common with the Tsar. Whether this title had been condescendingly usurped, or whether it had been bestowed imprudently by the Tsar upon his 'very dear friend' is immaterial. Nikon placed the priesthood, not on a

[1] This particular incident is described in detail in William Palmer, *The Patriarch and the Tsar* (London, 1873) II 271-2.

par with, but above the Sovereign.[1] On being accused of Popery, Nikon replied nonchalantly: 'Why do you not respect the Pope for the good he does? There were two great Apostles in Rome, St Peter and St Paul, and he serves where they served.'

Nikon challenged the Russian Church's past as well as its contemporary situation. He did not, however, consider himself part of all this; in the presence of the bearer of the idea of an Eternal and Universal Church everything local and temporal had to disappear. The problem was to re-establish complete agreement and union between the Russian Church and the other Orthodox Churches, in which Nikon, Patriarch of all Rus, could take his rightful place among the hierarchy of the Universal Church.

Nikon set about restoring this unanimity with his usual zeal and enthusiasm. As soon as he became Patriarch he forced the boyars and the people to swear to give him full powers to re-organise the affairs of the Church; in his own way he had acquired dictatorship over the Church. Next, he shut himself up in a library to examine and study old books and controversial texts. Among them he discovered a charter dated 1593 dealing with the establishment of a Patriarchate in Muscovy, signed by the Eastern Patriarchs. This document stated that, as brother to all neighbouring Orthodox Patriarchs, the Patriarch of Moscow should agree everything with them, and root out all innovations within his Church, because innovations were invariably the cause of religious dissent. Greatly troubled by the suspicion that

[1] Nikon asserted that 'Royalty, it is true, was given from God to the world; but it was given in his wrath ... But to us even he himself who wears the diadem is under the duty of offering gifts and obedience in all things, as the Lord has commanded ... But thou ... wouldst bring us down to submit ourselves to kings.' Ibid. (1871) 1 234. Nikon also said 'that the highest authority of the priesthood is not received from Tsars, but contrariwise, it is by the priesthood that rulers are anointed to the empire. Therefore it is abundantly plain that priesthood is a very much greater thing than royalty.' Ibid. pp. 189–90. Finally Nikon asserted that he had the power to excommunicate the Tsar if he 'does not what is proper for him to do in obedience to the laws of God'. Ibid. p. 252. See also Mathew Spinka, 'Patriarch Nikon and the Subjection of the Russian Church to the State', *Church History*, vol. 10 (Dec 1941) pp. 347–66.

the Russian Church had allowed departures from Orthodox Greek Law to take place, he proceeded to examine and compare the Slavonic and Greek basic texts: he found many changes and discrepancies.[1] Recognising that it was his duty to keep faith with the Greek Church, he decided to undertake the correction of Russian service books and ritual.[2] In 1653, on his own initiative and without consulting the Church Council, he sent an ordinance to all the churches just before Lent, stating how many full obeisances were to be made during the reading of the well-known prayer of St Ephraim Sirin, with an injunction that the sign of the cross was to be made with three fingers.

Nikon then began to criticise contemporary Russian ikon painters who had digressed from the Greek model, and had copied Catholic artists.[3] Furthermore, with the help of monks from South-

[1] In fact correction of texts and changes in ritual began in the fourteenth century when Hesychast influence transmitted the Neoplatonic concern with words and meanings; Russia was probably flooded with corrected texts from the South slavic lands; in the fifteenth century Grand Prince Ivan III and Metropolitan Gerontii clashed on points of ritual; and in 1551 Ivan the Terrible called together the Stoglav Council to legislate reforms of morals and ritual. See Michael Cherniavsky, 'The Old Believers and the New Religion', *Slavic Review*, vol. xxv, no. 1 (Mar 1966) p. 6.

[2] Nikon suggested that Tsar Alexis convene a Council to consider the correction of books. 'Whereas in the new books printed at Moscow there are found many discrepancies from the ancient Greek and Slavonian copies, and these errors have come down from the ignorance of transcribers and printers, ought we therefore to prefer the new books to the old ones which the great divines and teachers of the East and of the whole Church followed and following them pleased God, which were used by Athanasius and Basil, Gregory Chrysostom, and Damascene, and by the Russian Saints and workers of miracles, Peter, Alexis, Jonah and Philip?' Tsar and Council unanimously replied: 'It is meet and right to correct the new books by the old Slavonic and Greek manuscripts, that we may in all things follow the primitive rule of the Church.' See A. N. Mouravieff, *A History of the Russian Church* (Oxford, 1842) pp. 203–5; and Palmer, *The Patriarch and the Tsar* (1876) IV 31–40.

[3] In the seventeenth century there were two schools of ikon painters, the Moscow school and the Stroganov school. The Stroganov school, so called because they were trained in the workshops the Stroganovs had established at Solvychegodsk, their Perm estate, began to copy Western techniques and break away from the iconogaphic convention. See Tamara Talbot Rice, *A Concise*

West Russia, he replaced the medieval Russian plainsong with Kievan part-singing; and he also established the hitherto unprecedented habit of preaching sermons written by the priest. In medieval Russia this practice was regarded with suspicion because men believed that this was a sign of arrogance by the preacher.[1] They preferred to hear the teachings of the Holy Fathers read, although, in fact, readings were generally avoided in order to speed up the service. Nikon himself excelled in composition and enjoyed delivering his own sermons. Following upon his suggestion and example, a number of recently-arrived Kievans started to deliver their own sermons in the churches of Moscow, sometimes even dealing with topical issues.

It is not difficult to imagine the confusion these innovations created among Orthodox Russians, who were already sufficiently concerned with other matters. Nikon's ordinances inferred that the Russian Orthodox community had hitherto not known how to pray or paint ikons, and that the clergy did not know how to conduct a service. One of the first leaders of the Old Believers, the Archpriest Avvakum, vividly described the ensuing confusion. When the ordinances concerning the Lenten obeisances had been issued, 'we gathered together and reflected; it was as though winter were approaching; out hearts grew cold and our legs began to tremble'. Confusion undoubtedly increased when Nikon began to correct the service books, although in this he was assisted by the Church Council of 1654, over which the Tsar himself presided, and in the presence of the Boyar Duma. The Council decreed that all Church books which were to be printed were to be corrected according to Old Slavonic and Greek texts. Medieval Russian

---

History of Russian Art (Thames & Hudson, 1963) pp. 139–43. Nikon also obtained an edict banning the steeple church and ordering a return to the domed one, five domes being recommended as the ideal number. During the Time of Troubles tent-shaped churches began to outnumber domed churches, a deviation from Byzantine precedent which particularly roused Nikon's anger.

[1] Since the instruction of Metropolitan Photius (1410–32) no single instance of oral preaching in the churches can be found in Russia. Gradually a belief had been formed that oral preaching was the preaching of heresy.

church manuals differed considerably from the Holy Scriptures. Nikon's reforms made people wonder whether Holy Writ was wrong and whether in consequence anything at all was right with the Russian Church. The violence and vigour with which Nikon introduced his reforms created deep anxiety in a society, which was not ready for them, and which were stringently enforced. His usual methods were to snub, abuse, curse or destroy his opponents. Paul, Bishop of Kolomna, who had opposed Nikon at the Council of 1654 was deprived of his See without trial, 'cruelly beaten', and exiled; subsequently he went mad, and died from unknown causes.

A contemporary description exists of the measures taken by Nikon against the new school of ikon painters. While the Tsar was on campaign in 1654, the Patriarch ordered a search to be made of all houses in Moscow, not excluding those belonging to influential individuals, and new-style ikons seized. The confiscated ikons were then paraded through the city with their eyes gouged out, in order to advertise the ukase which threatened to punish the painters severely. Immediately following this incident the plague broke out in Moscow, and there was an eclipse of the sun. The inhabitants of Moscow became thoroughly agitated, and blamed the Patriarch, saying that these occurrences had been visited upon them by God as a punishment for Nikon's profanity in defaming the ikons and threatening their creators with death. On Quadragesima Sunday in 1655 the Patriarch held a solemn service in the Usspensky Cathedral in the presence of two Eastern Patriarchs from Antioch and Serbia. After the Litany Nikon read a homily on genuflecting before ikons, criticised the new school of ikon painters, and threatened to excommunicate both the painters and those who owned their works. He had the confiscated ikons brought to him, and, in front of the congregation, threw them down upon the iron floor with such violence that they broke. He ordered the rest of the offending ikons to be burnt. Tsar Alexis, who had been listening to the Patriarch, went up to him, and said quietly: 'No Father, do not order them to be burnt; it would be better to bury them.'

What was even worse, however, was that Nikon's hostility

towards traditional Church rites and ceremonies was not merited, since he was not convinced that they were spiritually harmful; nor did he believe that his reforms offered exclusive spiritual salvation. Before textual emendations became an issue Nikon had always crossed himself with two fingers; as Patriarch he sanctioned the use of both the double and treble alleluia in the Usspensky Cathedral. Towards the end of his Patriarchate, in a conversation with Ivan Neronov, an erstwhile antagonist now reconciled with the Church, Nikon said, referring to the old and new texts: 'Both are good; it does not matter which is used.' It is clear that Nikon was concerned not with any ritualistic problem, but with the question of opposition to ecclesiastical authority. Ivan Neronov and his supporters were not anathematised by the Council of 1556 because they made the sign of the cross with two fingers, or because they used unamended texts, but because they failed to submit to the authority of the Council. It was not a question of ritual, but one of *principle*, which entailed complete submission to the authority of the Church. Indeed, it was for this reason that the Old Believers were anathematised by the Council of 1666–7. A situation had developed in which the Church prescribed a strange ritual; disobedience led to excommunication, not because of any observance of traditional rites, but as a result of the refusal to obey a Church edict.[1] Repentance led to readmittance to the Church and permission to observe the traditional rites. This approach is analogous to a system of alarms designed to keep men on constant alert.

These never-ending tests of obedience to the Church were nothing more than a game indulged in by the clergy with the consciences of their congregations. The Archpriest Avvakum, and others, lacked a sufficiently flexible conscience, and became the leaders of the schism. Had Nikon from inception told the Church at large what he had said to Neronov after he had recanted there would never have been a schism. Nikon himself contributed to

[1] For a development of the argument that one of the Old Believers' chief concerns was with authority, government, or, symbolically, the Tsar, see Cherniavsky, 'The Old Believers and the New Religion', *Slavic Review*, vol. xxv, no. 1 (Mar 1966) pp. 1–39.

the schism in so far as he failed to understand the very people with whom he had to reckon, and grossly underestimated his first opponents, principally Neronov, Avvakum, and other former friends, who were not only popular preachers but also agitators. They showed their pedagogic talents in their sermons on the Holy Fathers, and in their comments on John Chrysostom's *Margarit*[1] (the name given to his collection of teachings). Neronov, ministering in Nizhni-Novgorod, was never parted from this book, which he would read and explain from the pulpit, in the squares and in the streets to large crowds. Whether these explanations had much theological content is not known; certainly their delivery was fiery! Neronov declaimed against worldly vice, the drunkenness of the clergy, chicanery, and even the abuse of governors, with such vehemence that he was frequently beaten. When he became Father Superior at Kazan Cathedral in Moscow everybody flocked to hear him; the Cathedral overflowed, people stood in the porch, and listened at the windows; even the Tsar and his family came to listen to him. There were others of Neronov's persuasion whose popularity and favour at Court made them extremely audacious. They had treated Nikon without any formality before he became Patriarch; now, however, they became rude, insulted him at Council meetings, and even complained about him to the Tsar. Nikon retaliated with brutality. When Loggin, who was Archpriest of Murom, blessed the wife of a local governor in her own home, he asked her whether she had whitened her face; her husband and their guests indignantly shouted: 'You, priest, you condemn the paint, yet without it ikons cannot be painted.' To which Loggin retorted: 'If the stuff with which ikons are painted were put on your ugly faces you would not like it. The Saviour himself, the Holy Mother of God, and the Holy Fathers are more honourable than their images.' Loggin was denounced in Moscow by the local governor, who stated that the ikons of the Saviour, the Holy Mother and the Holy Fathers had been denigrated. Without an investigation, Nikon

[1] John Chrysostom's sermons were known in Russia under the title of *Margarit*. See G. P. Fedotov, *The Russian Religious Mind* (Harvard U.P., 1966) II 30 and 36–7.

arrested Loggin, thereby revenging himself for an occasion when the archpriest had attacked him for being proud and high-minded.

While on one hand Nikon was making enemies within the Church, on the other he was weakening his own pastoral authority. His opponents became martyrs, and were dispersed throughout Russia, thereby providing the remotest areas with experienced proponents of the Old Belief.[1] Nikon's policies did not justify his dictatorial powers; nor did he improve the situation within the Church. On the contrary, he confused the situation even further. His lust for power, and his relationship with the Court, finally extinguished those spiritual powers with which he had been so generously endowed by nature. His religious innovations contained little that was new, and were not reforms. In so far as textual emendations and ritualistic corrections were concerned, it must be remembered that emendations cannot be equated with reforms. If one section of society and the clergy confused textual emendations with dogma, and caused a rebellion within the Church, then Nikon and the entire Russian hierarchy were equally at fault. Why did Nikon pursue a policy, knowing as he did, what its outcome would be? What had the Russian clergy been doing during the past centuries if they had not been teaching their congregations to distinguish between dogma, and say, a double Alleluia?

Nikon did not reorganise the Church, nor did he inspire it with a new sense of purpose: he merely replaced one type of structure with another. His own understanding of the meaning of a Universal Church, in whose name his work was undertaken, was too narrowly and tendentiously based. Both he, and the dissenters, were primarily concerned with the external aspects of ritual. As a result, Nikon was incapable of imbuing the Russian religious community with any understanding of the true meaning of a Universal Church. Furthermore, any appeal to universality was completely absent from decisions taken by the Church Council. Towards the end of his rule as Patriarch he turned against the Eastern Patriarchs who had condemned him, calling them

---

[1] For details of the dispersion throughout Russia of proponents of the Old Belief see F. Conybeare, *Russian Dissenters* (Harvard U.P., 1921) pp. 59–89.

sultans, slaves, rogues and thieves. Nikon's concern with a Universal Church caused a schism in his own Church. The reactions of a hitherto inert religious community were galvanised by Nikon's policies, and violently affected both Nikon and the Russian Church hierarchy who had approved of, and encouraged, his work.

Nikon employed two methods in particular, over and above his own peculiarly personal mode of action, in his struggle against the stubborn Old Believers which, in fact, contributed to their success. His immediate collaborators and sympathisers were South Russian scholars who were in close contact with the Polish, Catholic world as well as Greeks; and this was well known in Moscow. One of these Greeks, Arsenius, has been mentioned above. He was known as the wandering convert from Catholicism, and rumour had it that he was even a Mahommedan. More important, however, was the fact that Nikon recalled Arsenius, that 'banished monk of wicked Roman digressions', from the Solovetsky Monastery where he had been under corrective discipline, to act as literary adviser. The introduction of the Nikonian innovations was simultaneously accompanied by criticisms of the Great Russians by the Little Russians and Greeks. On every possible occasion the Kievan monks maliciously reminded the Great Russians and their clergy of their ignorance, their illiteracy, and of their unfamiliarity with grammar, rhetoric and other academic subjects. Simeon Polotsky once declared from the pulpit in the Usspensky Cathedral in Moscow that wisdom had no place in Russia, that Russians despised knowledge, and scorned enlightenment which was God-given. With particular reference to the clergy of Moscow, he stated that they were ignorant men who called themselves pedagogues but had never been scholars; 'verily, they are not pedagogues but tormentors'.

Criticisms of this nature provoked the angry Old Believers into asking themselves whether these assertions were justified, and whether imported knowledge was required to preserve the glory of the Russian Church. The influx of foreigners, in any event, made the Russians suspicious and anxious, and there was a further deterioration in the mood of the people who felt that they had been humiliated by their own Orthodox brethren. Finally, although the Stoglav Council of 1551 had given its assent to the practice of making the sign of the cross with two fingers and other rites, the Russian and Eastern dignitaries at the Council of 1666–7 condemned these practices and solemnly announced that 'the fathers of that Council had erred in thought and shown great ignorance'. In this manner the Russian hierarchy of the seventeenth century disposed of the ancient practices of the Russian Church, which were of prime importance for large sections of the community. It is easy to understand the confusion these events had on the hitherto complacent Orthodox Russians; and as soon as a solution to incomprehensible innovations was found, this confusion resulted in the schism.

There were many other reasons why the ordinary Russian suspected that the innovations were the responsibility of secret Latinist propagandists, and that Nikon together with his Greek and Kievan collaborators were instruments of the Pope who was determined to Latinise the Russian Orthodox peoples. First, they were worried about the part played by visiting Greek and Western Russian scholars in church reforms, particularly since they had long been suspected of Latinist proclivities; second, because these groups were associated with the scholasticism which flourished in the Latin West; third, because church reform was started immediately after the introduction into Russia of Western European innovations and last, because of the government's foolish predilection for borrowing what seemed to be unnecessary elements from Western Europe, namely heretics, who were overfed and overpaid.

It is sufficient to glance at the early literary work of the Old Believers to realise that they deliberately fostered the impressions and fears mentioned above. In this context a prominent place must be given to two petitions presented to Tsar Alexis, one in 1662 by a monk called Sabbatius, and another in 1667 by the monks of the Solovetsky Monastery, who had rebelled against Nikon's innovations.[1] The publishers of the new and corrected

[1] A translation of this petition can be found in Palmer, *The Patriarch and the Tsar* (1873) II 449–59. For details of the rebellion of the monks see Conybeare, *Russian Dissenters*, pp. 79–85.

service books had accused the adherents of the old, unamended version of grammatical and rhetorical ignorance. Sabbatius answered the publishers by writing to the Tsar: 'O Sovereign, they are confused and they taint the books; their errors are recent; their ignorance and the Ukrainians have made them mad.'

Nikon justified his reforms by pointing out that they had been approved by the Eastern Prelates. However, the Russians had long suspected that the Greeks practised an impure variety of Orthodoxy; and Nikon's references to Greek authority were answered by the Solovetsky monks who stated in their petition that the Greek teachers did not know how to cross their foreheads 'as was fitting', and walked about without crucifixes; moreover, they would do better to learn piety from the Russians rather than try to teach it. The Church reformers were convinced that the Russian Church's ritual was incorrect. The Solovetsky petition on the other hand, confusing ritual with dogma, defended ancient practices: 'Now the new dogmatists are teaching us a new and unknown faith, as though we were Mordvinians or Cheremisians who know not God. We will have to be baptised anew and cast out from the Church all holy disciples and miracle workers. The foreigners laugh at us and say that we have not known Christianity.' Church reform was obviously a sensitive subject for the Russians, and affected their national-religious self-confidence.

Archpriest Avvakum, one of the schism's first and most ardent protagonists, was also the most reliable interpreter of the dissenters' views and motives.[1] His actions and writings expressed the essence of medieval Russia's religious outlook as it existed at this time. Avvakum believed that the causes of the misfortunes which had overtaken the Church were new Western European customs and new books: 'Alas! poor Russia,' he exclaimed in one of his works, 'why did you want Latin customs and foreign fashions?' He also believed that the Eastern theologians who had come to Russia to teach and clarify religious problems were themselves in need of instruction and a course in reasoning from the Russians.

[1] See in particular *The Life of the Archpriest Avvakum by Himself*, trans. I. Harrison and H. Mirrlees (Hogarth Press, 1924).

In his autobiography he described an unparalleled scene that took place during a meeting of the Holy Synod of 1667, and his own behaviour in the presence of the Eastern Patriarchs. These prelates said to him: 'Why art thou stubborn? The folk of Palestine, Serbia, Albania, the Wallachians, they of Rome and Poland, all these do cross themselves with three fingers, only thou standest out in thine obstinacy and dost cross thyself with two fingers; it is not seemly.' Avvakum replied: 'O you Teachers of Christendom. Rome fell away long ago and lies prostrate, and the Poles fell in the like ruin with her, being to the end the enemies of the Christian. And among you Orthodoxy is of mongrel creed; and no wonder – if by the violence of the Turkish Mahound you have become impotent, and henceforth it is you who should come to us to learn. By the gift of God among us there is autocracy, till the time of Nikon, the apostate, in our Russia under our pious princes and Tsars the Orthodox faith was pure and undefiled, and in the Church was no sedition.' Avvakum then went to the door and lay down on his side. 'Ye sit down,' he continued, 'but I lie down.' At that the prelates laughed and said: 'The archpriest is a silly fellow and does not show honour to the Patriarchs.' To which Avvakum replied: 'We are fools for Christ's sake. Ye are great and are without honour; ye are strong and we are weak.'

Avvakum expressed the basic ideas which guided the early leaders of the schismatics as follows: 'Although I am a man of little sense, and am uneducated, I know that everything emanating from the Holy Fathers is pure and sacred; I shall keep this faith until I die, as I received it, and shall not set bounds to the eternal. What has been laid down before our times, let it remain so for eternity.'

These characteristics of medieval Russian religious views, upon which the events of the seventeenth century had such extraordinarily harmful effects, rendering them so very one-sided, were adopted by the dissenters and became the basis of their religious philosophy.

Reasons have been given for the origin of the schism, and a recapitulation of the observations offered above may help to give a clearer and more fundamental appreciation of the importance of this event.

The external disasters which overtook Russia and Byzantium isolated the Russian Church and weakened its communion with the Churches of the Orthodox East. As a result the Russian religious community decided to try to establish a Universal Church, which in turn gave rise to the idea that their Church was the Orthodox Church on which the Universal Church could be based. In this way the authority of a universal Christian consciousness was subordinated to the ancient traditions of a local, national Church. Furthermore the isolation of Russia resulted in the development of local ritualistic peculiarities, while the exaggerated significance given to ancient and local traditions made these appear to be sanctified and inviolate.

The Russians were becoming increasingly aware of the daily temptations and religious perils brought about by Western European influences, which alerted the prelates to the necessity of consolidating their forces for the forthcoming struggle. They also realised that this entailed defining their attitudes, resolving internal Church problems, and strengthening their own Church through a closer communion with other Orthodox Churches. It was for these reasons that, in the middle of the seventeenth century, the more intelligent Russians revived the idea of a Universal Church. The same idea was manifested in Patriarch Nikon's intolerant and violent efforts to establish uniform rites in both the Russian and the Eastern Churches. Both the idea and the circumstances which evoked it, as well as the methods used to enforce it, caused considerable anxiety among the Russian Orthodox community. Indeed, the very idea of a Universal Church forced this community to abandon its complacent religious attitudes and its nationalist religious conceit. The violent and irritating attempts that were made to suppress traditional rites offended their national pride and allowed insufficient time for consideration to be given to a change in custom. That it was the Latin influence which stimulated reform filled the Russians with panic and horror; they were convinced that a break with their past was being caused by the hidden, insidious hand of Rome.

In this way, the schism, as manifested by religious protest and opposition to Western European influence was evoked as soon as the reform movement within Church and State clashed both with the popular approach to ecclesiastical ritual and the nationalist attitude to the standing of the Russian Church in the Christian world. In this respect, the schism did no more than reflect public opinion. Furthermore, there were basically three elements which determined popular attitudes towards traditional beliefs. First, there was the complacency of the Church, which converted Orthodoxy into a national monopoly (*the nationalisation of the Universal Church*). Second, the stagnation and diffidence of Russian theology which was incapable of appreciating any aspect of Western European knowledge, and which was feared as an unclean Latin emanation (Latinophobia). Finally, third, the inertia of a religious approach which was incapable of abandoning custom and traditional stimuli (ritualistic xenophobia).

Unfortunately, the antagonism against the ecclesiastical establishment was transformed into a revolt within the Church from the moment that the Old Believers refused to obey their spiritual leaders in the matter of a *rapprochement* with Latinism. Indeed, the Russian secular hierarchy and two Eastern Patriarchs during a Council meeting in 1667 excommunicated the recalcitrant Old Believers from the Orthodox Church for having opposed the canonical authority of their ecclesiastical superiors. Henceforth, the schismatics adopted not only separate religious beliefs, but a separate religious existence apart from the established church.

It was not long before the schism influenced the development of both Russian enlightenment and Western European ideas. The schismatics reacted with increasing intensity against their influence, which in turn was stimulated by the continuing opposition. Greek and Western European scholars consistently asserted that the schism was due to Russian ignorance, which was why the Russians started to give some thought to the establishment of a permanent, regular school. But what kind of school was this to be? How was it to be organised? Whereas previously, through misunderstanding, one opinion had existed, now the schism was responsible for there being two disparate opinions. So long as Russians were concerned with foreign heretics, whether Papist or Lutheran, they had always cordially welcomed Greeks and

Kievans to join in the struggle. Hence, at this time, Epiphanius Slavinetsky who introduced the Greek language, and Simeon Polotsky, who introduced Latin, were welcome. Now, however, Russian heretics were beginning to appear, like the Old Believers, who had seceded from the established Church because of its Latin innovations, and the bread-worshippers who preached the Latin doctrine of Transubstantiation, whose leader was purported to be Simeon Polotsky. A heated debate was started as to which should be the official language in the Orthodox school. It was not merely a question of a different grammar and vocabulary; in those days it was held that, since they represented hostile cultures and incompatible philosophies, the issue was over different systems of education.

Latin connoted 'freedom of study', 'freedom of research', that freedom of enquiry referred to in a theological tract distributed among the parishioners of St John the Divine; Latin connoted knowledge which satisfied men's intellectual and mundane requirements. Greek, however, was considered the language of philosophy, grammar, rhetoric, and dialectic, which led to a greater understanding of the word of God. It hardly need be said that in this dispute the Hellenists prevailed.

During the reign of Tsar Fedor a treatise was written in defence of Greek. 'Is it more expedient for us to study grammar, rhetoric, philosophy and theology, and the art of versification, and thence discover the holy writings, or to ignore these cunning arts, act in all simplicity to please God, and through much reading get to know the wisdom of the Holy Scriptures? Verily, it is better for the Russian people to study Greek and not Latin.' The treatise explicitly stated that the study of Latin was undeniably harmful and destructive, and threatened the Russians with two great dangers: 'Having heard that Latin is to be studied in Moscow, the crafty Jesuits would sneak in with their unintelligible syllogisms and soul-corrupting arguments', thereby repeating the experiences of Little Russia in Great Russia 'where almost all men became Uniates, and few remained Orthodox'. 'If the nation, and particularly the simple people, heard about the teaching of Latin I do not know what good we may look for therein, save that God delivers us from all calamities.'

In 1681 a school with two classes, one for the study of Greek, and the other for Slavonic languages, was opened in the Moscow Printing Works in Nikolskaya Street. The school was run by a priest called Timothy, who had lived for a long time in the East, and two Greek teachers. At the beginning there were thirty pupils from different social backgrounds; by 1686 there were two hundred and thirty-three. In the same year an institution for higher education, a Slavonic–Graeco–Latin Academy was opened in the Zaikonospassky Monastery, which was also in Nikolskaya Street. Two Greeks, the brothers Likhudy, were invited to run this establishment which admitted the older pupils from the Printing Works school, the latter being considered the lower division of the Academy.

In 1685 Sylvester Medvedev, one of Simeon Polotsky's pupils, had petitioned the regent Sophia for permission to convert his school into a semi-official academy; its regulations had been drafted in the reign of Tsar Fedor, and its structure and aims had been clearly defined. It was to be open to all, irrespective of background, and official rank was to be conferred on all teachers. The rector and the teachers had to be either Russians or Greeks, and Western Russians could only be appointed on recommendations from worthy and devout men. The Academy was strictly forbidden to employ foreign language teachers or use Latin, Polish, German and other heretical books. The propagation of other religions was strictly forbidden, and whoever blasphemed against Orthodoxy was to be tried, and if found guilty, burned. What had started as a demand for the establishment of a liberal educational centre in Moscow for the whole of the Orthodox East finished with a repressive ecclesiastical educational institution which became the prototype for Church schools. Created to safeguard Orthodoxy from all European heretics, but lacking preparatory schools, the Academy was unable to exert its influence over the masses, and presented no threat to the schismatics.

The schism, however, was a positive benefit to the cause of the West, whose influence had first evoked it. The religious storm raised by Nikon did not affect all Russian churchgoers. The schism was started among the Russian clergy, and originally the struggle was between the ruling hierarchs in the Church and that section of the religious community which supported the opponents of Nikon's ritualistic innovations led by agitations from the lower ranks of black and white clergy. At first even certain members of the ruling hierarchy opposed Nikon: Paul, Bishop of Kolomna, pointed out while he was in exile that there were three other prelates who had retained the old belief. Unanimity was imposed only when the dispute ceased to be over ritual and became one concerned with canonical authority in which the congregations opposed their lawful pastoral leaders. The leading prelates realised that it was no longer a problem confined to the merits of a new, as against an older, form of belief. They had to decide between remaining in office without a congregation, or joining their flock in exile, as had done Paul of Kolomna. The common people and the Tsar produced an interesting reaction. They accepted the innovations because it was their duty to obey the Church, but they disliked the innovator himself because of his repellent character and his methods. They sympathised with the victims of his intolerance, but could not approve of the frenzy displayed by his opponents in their struggle against the Church establishment and its authority, which was considered by most people to be the mainstay of ecclesiastical discipline and morality. The scene in the Cathedral involving the archpriest Loggin must surely have disturbed the more serious members of the congregation: having been unfrocked, Loggin cursed and spat in Nikon's face across the Sanctuary and then, tearing off his shirt, hurled it into the Patriarch's face. Thoughtful people tried to interpret the significance of this event themselves for the sake of their own consciences, since no pastoral guidance was available to them. Fedor Rtishchev's father said to Princess Urussov, one of the earliest martyrs: 'One thing troubles me; I do not know whether it is for truth that you suffer.' He might well have asked whether it was for truth that they were tortured. Even deacon Fedor, another of the schism's first protagonists, fasted of his own volition while in prison in an attempt to discover what was wrong in the old faith, and what was right in the new. Those with similar doubts joined the schismatics. Many of them found peace of mind by remaining within the established Church, but distinguished between it and its secular hierarchy, thereby concealing their complete indifference to the latter beneath seeming respectful attitudes.

Ruling government circles took a more positive approach. It was not forgotten that the head of the Church had tried to raise himself above the Tsar, and that during the Council of 1666 Nikon had shamed the Sovereign. Realising that only trouble could emanate from this body of prelates, it was tacitly agreed to ignore them, and prevent them from participating actively in government. This decision ended the political role of the medieval Russian clergy, which in any event had always been badly defined, and even worse fulfilled. Moreover this removed one of the biggest obstacles to the progress of Western European influence in Russia.

The dispute between the Tsar and the Patriarch in this ecclesiastical–political crisis became increasingly entangled with internal dissensions within the Church, which Nikon himself had created. The consequences of this dispute upon the political importance of the clergy was therefore an indirect benefit conferred upon the progress of Western European influence by the schism. More directly, the schism weakened the opposition to the Western style reforms subsequently introduced and completed by Peter the Great. Suspicion of Western Europe permeated the whole of Russian society; even the ruling classes, who were susceptible to Western European influences, were still enamoured with Russia's ancient traditions. This attitude hampered progress and dissipated the energies of the reformers.

The revolt against the Church, and in so far as they were connected, against the state, harmed the ancient traditions in whose very name the schism had originally been invoked. A significant section of the Russian religious community began to appreciate the wicked sentiments and misguided tendencies which could be evoked by an appeal to the past, and the dangers inherent in an unreasoning attachment to it.

As a result, the leaders of the reform movement, wavering between their own past traditions and the traditions of Western

Europe, were able to pursue a policy of reform with a clearer conscience, and with greater determination and courage. Peter the Great was personally greatly influenced by the schism. The Old Believers staged another revolt in the name of their ancient traditions soon after Peter was proclaimed Tsar in 1682. On 5 July there was a disorderly demonstration in the Hall of Angels. This event together with other childhood impressions he remembered for the rest of his life. Peter believed that the past, the schism, and the revolt were inextricably connected. He concluded that the past meant the schism, the schism meant revolt, and that therefore the past meant revolt. With these impressions it is not difficult to understand why the past would have little appeal to Peter the Great.

GLOSSARY

Asaul An adjutant in a Cossack army.

Barshchina Labour obligation of peasants.

Bobili An old term for landless peasants or cotters.

Denga, pl. *dengi* A silver coin equal to one-half of one kopek. In modern Russian *dengi* means 'money'.

Desyatin Literally, a 'tenth'. A land measure equal to 2·7 acres, or 1·092 hectares.

Dvoryanin A nobleman.

Dvoryanstvo The nobility.

Efimok, pl. *efimki* A Joachimsthaler; a monetary unit used in seventeenth-century Russia.

Gubnaya izba Offices used by police and judicial officials.

Gubnoe starosta A police and judicial officer.

Hetman Name given to the commander-in-chief and his deputy in the Polish and Lithuanian armies, and among the Zaporozhie Cossacks.

Kabala A form of servitude secured by contract.

Kantsler West Russian term for Keeper of the Seal.

Kashtelyani West Russian term for town prefects.

Kholops Bondsmen.

Kholopy Kabalnye Serfs bonded by contract.

Kolo A circle; an assembly of the Zaporozhie Cossacks.

Kosh A camp; the military brotherhood of the Zaporozhie Cossacks.

Krepostnye lyudi Bonded people.

Kuren Detachments in a company of the Zaporozhie Cossacks.

Mestnichestvo A system of precedence.

Nadvorni   A court chamberlain.

Namestnik   A prefect, a lieutenant, an administrator of a large administrative unit of medieval Russia.

Obrok   Quitrents paid by peasants in cash or in kind.

Okolnichi   A courtier attached to the person of the Tsar; in importance he came immediately below the rank of boyar.

Oprichnina   An entailed domain created by Ivan IV. A special household, whose members were called *oprichniks*, was created to administer this domain, which was exempt from the jurisdiction of the general administration.

Perepisnaya Kniga   A special type of tax schedule.

Polonyanichny   Ransom tax.

Poltina   A monetary unit equal to one-half of one rouble.

Polushka   A monetary unit equal to one-quarter of one kopek.

Pomeshchik   The possessor of a *pomestie*.

Pomestie   An estate held in service tenure. The enjoyment of an estate of this kind was conditional on the tenant and his heirs performing military service and other duties. After the eighteenth century the general name for estates owned by the nobility.

Prikaz, pl. *prikazy*   A government department.

Privileyi   Charters of Lithuanian Grand Dukes.

Rab   A bondswoman; a term used in ecclesiastical records.

Rada   A council.

Razryady   Military districts.

Sejm   A diet.

Sobor   A council or assembly.

Sokha   A unit of taxation; an old measure of tillable land.

Soshnoye pismo   Cadastral survey.

Starosta   An elder; a prefect.

Starosti povetov   A district warden.

Stolniks   Courtiers who served food and drink at the Tsar's ceremonial banquets.

Stryapchie   Courtiers who carried the Tsar's sceptre, head-dress and mantle in processions or at church, and who in wartime looked after the Tsar's armour and sword.

Sudebnik   A code of laws.

Tiaglo A system of taxation which allocated special compulsory obligations to the state among different classes of society; also the capacity of the peasant to meet these obligations; also the total fiscal obligations owed by the peasant.

Ulozhenie Law code of 1649.

Veche Popular assemblies; city or village assemblies in medieval Russia.

Voevoda A military and administrative leader in medieval Russia; a governor.

Votchina An hereditary estate originally unencumbered by service obligations.

Yamy Posting-stations.

Zadvornye lyudi Backyard people.

Zakup Indentured peasants.

Zemianin A boyar from Volynia.

Zhiltsy Courtiers who slept at Court.

INDEX

Daniel, priest, 342
Decision of 30 June 1611: and the 'troika', 61-2
Diet of Grodno (1413): confirms unification of Poland and Lithuania, 118-20
Dimitri, the False, the first Pretender, 39-40; background and policies, 44-8
Dimitri, the False, the second Pretender, 54
Dimitri, Tsarevich (son of Ivan the Terrible): and rumours of his death, 34; and Boris Godunov, 38-9
Dorn, Adam: and Mercator's *Cosmography*, 315 n. 1
Dvoryanstvo, 15, 17-22, 24. *See also* nobility

education: monopoly of ruling class, 19; and a secret commission, 19-20; desire for, 313-20
ektenia, 343 and n. 1

Fedor, Tsar (1584-98): and Time of Troubles, 28; description, 29-33; death, 35, 82, 83, 188; and enserfment, 198, 242, 270, 273, 334, 359
Fletcher, Giles, 194-5, 206 n. 1
'fools for Christ's sake': significance, 30

Godunov, Boris: background, 31-5; description, 35-6; criticisms of, 37-38; and Time of Troubles, 39-44, 46, 69; and social confusion, 73-5, 81-2; and enserfment, 198
Golitsin, Prince Vasili, 61; and Zemsky Sobor, 78-9
Golosov, Lucian (anti-westerner), 321-322
governors: and local government, 177-82
Greek influence, 294-7, 316-17, 324-326, 330-5, 342-5, 346-7
Gregory, Johan Gottfried, pastor: as régisseur, 310-11

Horsey, Sir Jerome: on mercenaries, 299

ikon painters criticised, 347-9
Ivan III, Grand Prince: political outlook, 26; and political unification, 112; and Law Code of 1497, 194 n. 1

Ivan IV (1533-85): size of realm, 15; and Time of Troubles, 28-30, 33, 34, 37, 72-3; and territorial expansion, 112-13, 150, 178; and *kabala* contracts, 194 n. 1, 273
Ivan, Tsarevich: killed by his father, 29
Ivanov, Constantine (anti-westerner), 321-2

Jagiello, Grand Prince of Lithuania, 115
Jeremiah, Patriarch of Constantinople, 334
Joachimsthalers, 256, 257, 259
Job, Patriarch: Boris Godunov's friend, 34-5, 42, 334
Joseph, Patriarch, 344

Kalita, Ivan, 14; his descendants, 29, 35, 69
Karamzin, Nicholas (1766-1826): his *History of the Russian State*, 31 n. 1
Katyrev-Rostovsky, Prince Ivan, 30-1, 33
Khmelnitsky, Bogdan: and the Cossacks, 114-15; his uprising, 142-8
Khvorostinin, Prince J. A.: early freethinker, 275-7, 298
Kissel, Adam: on Cossacks and religion, 137
Kochubey, Count Victor (1768-1834): and educational reforms, 19-20
Kosinski, Christopher: and the Cossacks, 137-8
Kotoshikhin, Gregory, 27; on hereditary succession, 95-6, 159; on the military, 247-8; on taxes, 252; on copper coins, 259; homestead figures, 267; on Treasury receipts, 270-1, 273; critique of Alexian Muscovy, 278-80; on upper classes, 308
Krizhanich, Juri: his Pan-Slav views, 280-91
Kuhlmann, Quirinus, 291 n. 1
Kurbsky, Prince Andrew, 89

Lambert, Count: his views on education, 20 n. 1
Lappo-Danilevsky, A. S.: his analysis of direct taxation, 260
Lazarus, priest, 343
Leslie, Colonel Sir Alexander, 299-301
Liapunov, Prokofy, 60-3
Liapunov, Zachary: deposes Tsar Vasili Shuisky, 59, 61